Church of England Record Society
Volume 17

THE DIARY OF THOMAS LARKHAM
1647–1669

D1429492

THE DIARY OF THOMAS LARKHAM
1647–1669

EDITED BY

Susan Hardman Moore

THE BOYDELL PRESS

CHURCH OF ENGLAND RECORD SOCIETY

First published 2011

A Church of England Record Society publication
Published by The Boydell Press
an imprint of Boydell & Brewer Ltd
PO Box 9, Woodbridge, Suffolk IP12 3DF, UK
and of Boydell & Brewer Inc.
668 Mt Hope Avenue, Rochester, NY 14620, USA
website: www.boydellandbrewer.com

ISBN 978–1–84383–705–3

ISSN 1351–3087

Series information is printed at the back of this volume

A CIP catalogue record for this book is available
from the British Library

The publisher has no responsibility for the continued existence or accuracy
of URLs for external or third-party internet websites referred to in this book,
and does not guarantee that any content on such websites is,
or will remain, accurate or appropriate.

Papers used by Boydell & Brewer Ltd are natural, recyclable products
made from wood grown in sustainable forests

Printed in Great Britain by
CPI Group (UK) Ltd, Croydon, CR0 4YY

For Rannoch and Helena
and in memory of Rachel

Contents

Illustrations

1   Portrait of Thomas Larkham, prefixed to his tract *The wedding-supper* (London, 1652). Antiq. F.E. 1652. Reproduced by permission of the Bodleian Library, University of Oxford.

2–7   Folios 'W'r, 9r, 10v, 16r, 39r, 40r, the Diary of Thomas Larkham, British Library, London, MS Loan 9. Reproduced by permission of Mr Neil Redwood and Mrs Jo Rutter.

8   The title-page of *Naboth, in a narrative and complaint of the church of God ... at Tavistock in Devon* (London, 1657). Courtesy of Special Collections, The College of Wooster Libraries, Wooster, Ohio.

9   The title-page of F.G. D.P. W.G. N.W. W.H. &c, *The Tavistocke Naboth proved Nabal: in an answer unto a scandalous narrative published by Mr Tho: Larkham in the name (but without the consent) of the church of Tavistocke in Devon* (London, 1658). Pamph. C 106 (1). Reproduced by permission of the Bodleian Library, University of Oxford.

10   The title-page of *Judas hanging himselfe: or Naboths false accuser intangled in his own testimony. Set forth in a rejoinder of the church of Christ in Tavistock, to a scurrillous pamphlet published lately by N. W. &c* ([London?], 1658). Courtesy of Special Collections, The College of Wooster Libraries, Wooster, Ohio.

11   The title-page of *A strange metamorphosis in Tavistock, or the Nabal-Naboth improved a Judas. Set forth in reply to a scurrilous pamphlet called Judas, &c* (London, [1658]). © The British Library Board. All Rights Reserved. Thomason E. 940 (2).

12   Detail from 'The South East Prospect of yᵉ Town of Tavistock in yᵉ County of Devon' (London: C. Dicey & Co., 1741), drawn by Charles Delafontaine and engraved by R. Parr. Taken from a reproduction printed by the Trustees of the Tavistock Museum Charitable Trust, with permission.

Acknowledgements

I would like to thank Mr Neil Redwood and Mrs Jo Rutter for giving me permission to publish an edition of the manuscript of their ancestor, Thomas Larkham. The two rare tracts which are also included in this volume, *Naboth* and *Judas*, appear by courtesy of Special Collections, the College of Wooster Libraries, Ohio.

The Church of England Record Society, in agreeing to publish the Larkham diary, has made accessible a manuscript which sheds light on parish life in the days of Cromwell's Commonweath and on the early experience of nonconformists after the Restoration of Charles II. I am grateful to the Society for publishing this volume on the eve of the 350th anniversary of the Act of Uniformity, 1662. Professor Stephen Taylor, Honorary General Editor, has been generous with his wisdom and patience as the project took shape, as has Michael Middeke of Boydell and Brewer. Linda Randall has been an exemplary copy-editor.

I am indebted to other scholars who have shared the fruits of their research. Dr Arnold Hunt, Curator of Manuscripts at the British Library and one of my fellow convenors at the 'Religious History of Britain 1500–1800' seminar at the Institute of Historical Research, unlocked the mystery of the first writer in the manuscript, George Lane. Dr Adam Smyth of Birkbeck College, London, not only alerted me to the survival of the tracts *Naboth* and *Judas*, but also shared with me his digital images of these works. Robert Wordsworth, whose edition of the Cockermouth Church Book is soon to be published by the Cumberland and Westmorland Antiquarian and Archaeological Society, enlightened me on Larkham's contacts in Cumbria.

In the process of bringing this edition to press, I have had support from many quarters. The Arts and Humanities Research Council financed research leave to extend a sabbatical kindly granted by my colleagues at Edinburgh. The pleasure of the work has been enhanced by the friendly professionalism of staff at the British Library, at the Devon Record Office and at Dr Williams's Library. I would also like to thank Christina Napier, and Celia, Clare and Emma Hardman. I enjoyed visiting Tavistock, where I had a warm welcome at the parish church of St Eustachius and from Rev. Roger Cornish and the congregation of Tavistock United Reformed Church. Last but not least, I must thank my family, who have allowed me to keep company with 'Mr Larkham'.

Susan Hardman Moore
University of Edinburgh
May 2011

Abbreviations

CR	A. G. Matthews (ed.), *Calamy revised* (Oxford, 1934, reissued 1988).
Diary	British Library, London, MS Loan 9, the Diary of Thomas Larkham.
DTGC	*Dictionary of traded goods and commodities, 1550–1820*, ed. Nancy Cox and Karin Dannehl (2007), *British history online*. [www.british-history.ac.uk/source.aspx?pubid=739. Part of a larger dataset produced by the Dictionary Project at the University of Wolverhampton.]
ESTC	English Short Title Catalogue. [Online at http://estc.bl.uk.]
Judas	*Judas hanging himselfe: or Naboths false accuser intangled in his own testimony. Set forth in a rejoinder of the church of Christ in Tavistock, to a scurrillous pamphlet published lately by N. W. &c* ([London?], 1658). ESTC Citation No. R469334. [Thomas Larkham is likely to have been the principal or sole author.]
KJV	King James Bible (Authorized Version), 1611. [Online at http://quod.lib.umich.edu/k/kjv/.]
Naboth	*Naboth, in a narrative and complaint of the church of God ... at Tavistock in Devon* (London, 1657). ESTC Citation No. R469333. [Thomas Larkham is likely to have been the principal or sole author.]
ODNB	*Oxford dictionary of national biography*, 61 vols. (Oxford, 2004). [*Oxford DNB online* at www.oxforddnb.com, 2004– .]
OED	*Oxford English dictionary online*. [www.oed.com.]
Strange metamorphosis	*A strange metamorphosis in Tavistock, or the Nabal-Naboth improved a Judas. Set forth in reply to a scurrilous pamphlet called Judas, &c* (London, [1658]). ESTC Citation No. R207552. [Thomas Larkham attributed this to Nicholas Watts.]
Tavistock Naboth	F.G. D.P. W.G. N.W. W.H. &c, *The Tavistocke Naboth proved Nabal: in an answer unto a scandalous narrative published by Mr Tho: Larkham in the name (but without the consent) of the church of Tavistocke in Devon* (London, 1658). ESTC Citation No. R184887. [The title-page of the Bodleian Library copy has been annotated in a seventeenth-century hand and fills out the initials with the names Francis Glanville, Digory Polwhele, Walter Godbeare, Nicholas Watts and William Hore.]
Tavistock PR	Devon Record Office, Exeter, 482A add 2/PR1, Tavistock Parish Register, 1614–1793.

Editorial Method

Larkham reckoned time in a particular fashion: he made the start of the year his birthday, 18 August. This edition follows the logic of the manuscript by presenting the text in 'Larkham years', August–August. The header carries the year in modern style. Starting from 18 August, Larkham's personal 'quarter days' for the rest of the year fell on 18 November, 18 February and 18 May. For some stretches of the diary, he carried the system to its logical end: if 18 August fell on a Wednesday, all his weeks that first quarter began on Wednesday. He adjusted the start of the week thereafter depending on which weekday the quarter days came up. Of course, despite this personal calendar, Larkham could not fall out of step with the conventional quarter days that ordered life in Tavistock: 25 March (Lady Day), 24 June (Midsummer), 29 September (Michaelmas) and 25 December (Christmas). He worked to these when it came to calling in rents or paying out wages, and also used used the old style or Julian calendar which started the new year from 25 March. (For clarity, this edition annotates dates 1 January – 24 March in the style 1650/1.) To add another layer of complexity, he was also conscious of 31 December as 'the end of the yeare … according to the Almanack computation' (fo. 27r). On more than one occasion he bought a new almanac as the end of December came, although his entries usually ran straight on into January without comment.

The intricate early history of the manuscript 'paper-book' itself – first used by a scrivener, George Lane, in 1597, and then by Thomas Larkham and his son George from 1647 – is discussed in the Introduction. At this point it is necessary to note that the foliation of the manuscript is idiosyncratic and partial. It starts with folios that carry (most of) the letters of the alphabet: tabbed index pages made by George Lane. After this comes fo. 1. Because Larkham was the second owner of the notebook, and wrote over and around Lane's entries wherever he could find space, his regular entries start at fo. 2v. The folio numbers in the edition follow the manuscript: for the section of the paper-book Larkham used, there is often a folio mark on the recto side, made by Lane or Larkham. Where these marks are missing or worn away, I have supplied numbers in sequence. At the close of the manuscript Larkham made additional entries working backwards from the last folio: this material (presented in Appendices 1–3) is unfoliated.

An important feature of this edition is its layout on left/right facing pages. As a rule Larkham made entries mostly in parallel columns, with occasional headings and comments written across the folio. He used the columns to separate income from expenses (but by no means consistently). He also included observations and poems within the columns. To accommodate the sheer amount of text he entered on each folio – usually around 750 words, but on one folio 1,300 – this edition sets out his parallel columns on facing pages. Where material runs across the whole folio this has been set on the left page, and noted. The pattern of left/right facing pages holds good for almost the whole diary text, and for Appendix 3. However, in some parts of this volume the text is laid out continuously: in the diary, 17 April–20 June 1661, when his intermittent entries ran across whole folios; also the tracts *Naboth* (1657) and *Judas* (1658), and Appendices 1 and 2.

Larkham crammed words onto his pages. To separate items he often drew lines across the columns or bracketed material together. To save this edition from being as hard on the eye as the original, these lines and brackets have been omitted and space has been inserted to break up the material – not only where Larkham placed a line but also in many other places. Sometimes he underlined or boxed off text: where this is important to show special emphasis, it has been reproduced.

The manuscript presents special challenges because Larkham overwrote earlier entries by George Lane. Conjectured readings are given in italics. He had a habit of adopting Lane's letters or figures to help him form his own words, either letting them stand 'as is' or changing them from, for example, zero to 'a' with a stroke of the pen. Sometimes Larkham's ink has faded but Lane's has lasted and shows through.

The edition retains most of Larkham's spelling, punctuation and capitalization. Certain letters are rendered in modern style ('j' for 'i', 'u' for 'v' and vice versa, 'th' for the thorn which is similar to a modern 'y'). Standard contractions which occur often – 'yᵗ' for 'that', 'dd' for 'delivered', 'pᵈ' for 'paid', 'wᶜʰ' for 'which' – have been changed into their modern equivalent. Other contractions he used habitually (such as 'D' or 'Da:' for daughter) have also been silently expanded. Where he used what to modern readers is an idiosyncratic abbreviation for a month ('Ap' for 'April') or common name ('Rich:' for 'Richard'), this has also been silently emended. He often failed to cross right through a double 't': this has also been silently corrected. A further list of silent emendments appears below. Other additions within the text are enclosed in square brackets. Where Larkham later inserted a word or phrase above or below the line, this is marked by ˆ or ˇ at the start and finish. Material he deleted so completely that it cannot now be read has been omitted but is mentioned in a footnote. Entries in the margin are also identified in the footnotes.

Larkham's addition of '£ s d' was usually accurate, although he sometimes made mistakes (which have not been corrected). Often, the financial trail is hard to follow because he did not fill out all the detail or because the figures are illegible. He used 'ld' for £, 'ss' or 's' for shillings, and 'd' for pence, sometimes superscript, sometimes not. He also used a variety of methods to separate figures – dots, dashes, space. This edition uses plain '£' 's' and 'd', separates figures with dashes, and (for readability) has aligned the numbers in columns. Sometimes Larkham left out lines beneath totals, or inserted more lines than the modern eye is used to: these have been silently added or removed, for clarity.

Silent emendments

aco	account	Memʳᵈum	memorandum
agᵗ	against	Mⁿʳ	minister
Co.	cousin	p	for par, per, pro, as in dep[ar]ture,
Ct / X	Christ		p[ar]liament, p[ro]vision, p[er],
bro	brother		P[ro]vidence
D: / da:	daughter	plunderd	plundered
Doi	Domini	pt	part (but if perhaps 'payment', noted)
ff	F/f	porton	portion
It	Item	qʳ /qᵗʳ /quart	quarter
	(but if perhaps	Rec or Recd:	received
	'iterato', noted)	remd:	remained
Maᵗⁱᵉ	majesty	S / So:/ Su:	Son

| w^t: | white (wine) | 1^{d}½ | 1½d |
| wid: | widow | 59^{ld} | 59 pounds (of butter) |

Where a line over a letter indicates an 'm' or 'n', this has been added silently: as in Willia [William], Larka [Larkham], comunion [communion], fro [from], annoru [anorum], Christu [Christum], Kirto [Kirton] comunio [communion].

The text has been silently expanded when he left out letters on a regular basis e.g. 'bring[ing] e', 'chill[d]ren', 'spe[n]t', 'spend[in]g', 'th[i]ngs'.

I have benefited from the wisdom of Michael Hunter, *Editing early modern texts: an introduction to principles and practice* (New York, 2007), P. D. A. Harvey, *Editing historical records* (London, 2001), and R. F. Hunnisett, *Editing records for publication* (London, 1977).

Introduction

This is the Day on which I did begin
Heere in this vale of teares to live & breath
On this day 'twas my Saviour for me died
Men did His blessed forhead with thornes wreath
And should I thinke it much to be abus'd
Sith he for my sake was by men thus us'd?

Let me not feare fury of men or devil's
Although I compas'd am with many evill[s]
Rage wrath & pride of men shall do no harm
Keepe me Will God in his fatherly arme[s]
As thou O God hast said I shall not Dy[e]
Make me on thy promise still to rely.

Larkham's birthday poem, 18 August 1654[1]

So Thomas Larkham (1602–69) wrote in his diary, at the start of 'the three and fiftieth year of myne age', in a poem that more than hints at battle-scars. Larkham's career – as a Church of England cleric, New England colonist, chaplain in Cromwell's New Model Army, preacher in the wilds of Cumberland and Ireland – came to a peak of controversy in his days as vicar of Tavistock, Devon, in the Cromwellian 1650s, and plunged to the depths in his time as a fugitive nonconformist in the 1660s. His history captures most of the dramatic twists and turns the career of a zealous Protestant could take in the mid-seventeenth century.

Thomas Larkham's diary, long neglected – even thought lost, although safely tucked up in the British Library since 1929 – is a resource for understanding religious life at the parish level in the 1650s and the early experience of nonconformity.[2] Between 1647 and 1669, Larkham brought ledger-keeping and soul-keeping together in a manuscript of around 65,000 words, all (but a dozen or so) penned in Tavistock. His 'diary' is neither a journal of spiritual experience, nor a narrative of everyday events – although it contains a good dash of both, in passing. For over twenty years, Larkham noted down income and expenditure in a Micawberish spirit, and made this the starting point for prayer and reflection. When in the red, he threw a plea to heaven: 'I have no money.' In the black, his refrain was always 'Thus far the Lord hath holpen me.' He moved between financial and spiritual reckoning, determined to make pious profit from everything, however mundane: 'Jan 5: Mrs Eliz Edgcumb a pecke of wheate. Jan 6th Mrs Brownsdon a very good loyne of veale. Put all these to thine account o my God'; 'all accounts cleared betweene My God & me'.[3] For his own scrutiny and for the eyes of God, he 'accounted' for his

---

1 Diary, fo. 15v.

2 British Library, MS Loan 9, the Diary of Thomas Larkham. The manuscript was offered to the Library on indefinite loan by Larkham's descendants, and is still owned by the family: I am grateful to Mr Neil Redwood and Mrs Jo Rutter for permission to publish. Its unusual place in the Library's collections (as a loan) meant for a long time it was little known. Anne Laurence, *Parliamentary army chaplains, 1642–1651* (Woodbridge, 1990), p. 146, declared it lost. Many authors cited from the limited extracts published by William Lewis (ed.), *The diary of the Revd Thomas Larkham, MA, vicar of Tavistock 1647–1660* (Cockermouth, 1871; 2nd (rev.) edn, Bristol, 1888).

3 Diary, fos. 13v, 26v. I am indebted to Adam Smyth for his fresh discussion of Larkham's diary and its context: *Autobiography in early modern England* (Cambridge, 2010), especially pp. 7–14, 104–22. Smyth shows how early modern culture 'did not prioritise development, coherence and pattern in life-writing' (p. 7), and suggests that systems of financial accounting migrated into spiritual

life. This is reflected in a fundamental decision he took which shapes the structure and logic of his record. He reckoned time from his birthday – the anniversary of the day God gave him life. This was always his 'new year' and he usually wrote a poem to mark the occasion.[4]

Larkham is an intriguing character, always leaving a trace in the records but never especially prominent.[5] He started out as a minister in Devon, left for New England in 1639 and after three turbulent years returned home with relief. He became a preacher in Kent, then enlisted as a chaplain in the parliamentary army and served a short spell in Ireland. In April 1648 he came with his regiment to Tavistock: stannary town and parliamentary borough, fiefdom of the earl of Bedford (with a Court Leet where the earl's steward presided over the 'Portreeve', 'Eight Men' and other Tavistock worthies); famous for its Friday market, its fairs, its woollen cloth. During the First Civil War Tavistock had been occupied in turn by royalists and parliamentarians eager to seize Plymouth. The previous minister, George Hughes, fled to escape battle in 1643.[6] By the time parliament won the day and Larkham came on the scene, the townspeople were eager to find a new vicar, after 'so long and sad a vacancy of the mysteries of salvation, to this poor ignorant place, wherein are so many hundred souls that know not the right hand from the left in matters of Religion'. The earl of Bedford, patron of the living, agreed to appoint the parishioners' choice. Larkham later claimed he was 'chosen by the inhabitants of Tavistock … under many score hands'.[7] During the 1650s, he steered a controversial course,

---

reckoning. The Larkham diary is one of a series of case-studies he presents to argue for an expanded understanding of what early modern 'autobiography' or 'life-writing' can be. Other recent work on life-writing includes: David Booy (ed.), *Personal disclosures: an anthology of self-writings from the seventeenth century* (Aldershot, 2002); Effie Botonaki, 'Seventeenth-century Englishwomen's spiritual diaries: self-examination, covenanting, and account-keeping', *Sixteenth Century Journal*, 30 (1999), 3–21; Andrew Cambers, 'Reading, the godly, and self-writing in England, circa 1580–1720', *Journal of British Studies*, 46 (2007), 796–825; D. Bruce Hindmarsh, *The evangelical conversion narrative: spiritual autobiography in early modern England* (Oxford, 2005); David George Mullan, *Narratives of the religious self in early-modern Scotland* (Aldershot, 2010), pp. 1–37; Tom Webster, 'Writing to redundancy: approaches to spiritual journals and early modern spirituality', *Historical Journal*, 39 (1996), 33–56.

4   This edition follows the logic of the manuscript by presenting the diary in 'Larkham years', starting on 18 August: see the discussion of editorial method, p. xi.

5   Susan Hardman Moore, 'Larkham, Thomas (1602–1669)', *ODNB*; Susan Hardman Moore, '"Pure folkes" and the parish: Thomas Larkham in Cockermouth and Tavistock', in *Life and thought in the northern church, c. 1100–1700*, ed. D. Wood (Woodbridge, 1999), pp. 489–509; Susan Hardman Moore, *Pilgrims: New World settlers and the call of home* (New Haven and London, 2007), pp. 61–2, 130–3.

6   The most detailed study of Tavistock in the period is Harold J. Hopkins, 'Thomas Larkham's Tavistock: change and continuity in an English town, 1600–1670', Ph.D. dissertation, University of Austin at Texas, 1981; see also Eugene A. Andriette, *Devon and Exeter in the Civil War* (Newton Abbot, 1971), pp. 74–5; for George Hughes, *ODNB*, *CR*. Gerry Woodcock, president of the Tavistock Local History Society, has done much to promote interest in the town's past, as in his recent *Tavistock: a history* (Chichester, 2008).

7   Thomas Larkham, *The parable of the wedding-supper explained* (London, 1656), 'To the saints and people of England' (a second edition of his *Wedding-supper* with new prefatory material). The earl of Bedford, William Russell, served in the Short and Long Parliament for Tavistock with John Pym and had presbyterian sympathies. In the 1650s, out of favour with Cromwell, he occupied himself with his father's fen drainage project, the 'Bedford Level'. Victor Stater, 'Russell, William, first duke of Bedford (1616–1700)', *ODNB*. Larkham had dealings with Gilbert Eveleigh, the earl's steward in Tavistock and elsewhere. 'Mr Eveleigh's Account Ano 1654' survives in the Devon Record Office, Exeter: W1258/LP/9/14.

pursuing reformation in a kind of 'parish congregationalism'. He identified himself as both 'public preacher' to the parish at large and pastor to a gathered church within it. He restricted the sacraments to an ever smaller circle, to which only those who signed a covenant were admitted. This was not what even some of Tavistock's more ardent godly citizens had in mind – particularly as they knew their former minister George Hughes, down the road in Plymouth, adopted a softer line. Local resentment erupted in a no-holds-barred pamphlet war. The disputes that wracked Tavistock appear elliptically and intermittently in Larkham's diary, amid notes of 6d for a trim at the barber's and spending money for grandchildren at the fair. In October 1660, he drew a thick black line under an entry that marked a watershed: 'I left mine imployment of preaching in feare & upon demand of the Patron.'[8] The entries that follow show how his fortunes changed as a result: prisoner, fugitive nonconformist preacher, apothecary.

The manuscript, as well as its maker, has an interesting tale to tell. Strictly speaking, it is not Thomas Larkham's manuscript at all. It is a palimpsest, with a history before and after he wrote in its pages. The story begins in 1597 in London and East Greenwich, with a scrivener who later turned cleric, George Lane.[9] Larkham's first entry dates from 1647, half a century later. He took the notebook from Kent to Tavistock and used it regularly from February 1651 until a month before his death in December 1669. After Larkham died, his son George – another vicar turned nonconformist preacher – carried the manuscript north from Devon to Cumberland, where he used it from 1670 to 1676 for farm accounts, letter-drafts, sermon notes and occasional poems.[10] So this single 'paper-book' was well travelled and heavily used: a possession kept close at hand by three clerical writers, in different parts of England, over a period of eighty years. George Lane began with empty pages. By the time Thomas and George Larkham had finished, the paper had been written on – and written on again, over and around Lane's entries – with virtually every folio crammed full of material. The manuscript is 8½ in by 6 in (21.5 x 15.5 cm), with around 120 folios, partially numbered. It now has a nineteenth-century leather binding and endpapers but probably started life as a blank pre-bound notebook.[11]

Deciphering this 'dizzingly complicated manuscript'[12] has been like exploring a vast dark attic with a torch: seeing only small patches at a time, disturbing forgotten heaps, grappling with the task of simply discovering what is there. To complement the diary, this edition also includes two tracts from Larkham's side in the Tavistock controversies, *Naboth* (1657) and *Judas hanging himselfe* (1658). Until now, Larkham has usually been seen through the highly coloured filter of his oppo-

---

8 Diary, fo. 39r.

9 I am indebted to Arnold Hunt, Curator of Manuscripts at the British Library and Senior Research Fellow at King's College London, for identifying Lane for me and for sharing his research on Lane's part in making the manuscript.

10 After this Larkham's descendants passed the manuscript down within the family. Larkham Bowes practised his signature enthusiastically in the early 1700s but otherwise the book stayed untouched. The only other hand may be Larkham's grandson, Thomas Larkham, who perhaps practised his signature and a few other words in schoolboy italic (fo. 1r): for a parallel, see Mark Bland, *A guide to early printed books and manuscripts* (Oxford, 2010), fig. 4.2.

11 Bland discusses the availability of such notebooks and the uses to which they were put: *Guide to early printed books and manuscripts*, pp. 68, 97.

12 Smyth, *Autobiography in early modern England*, p. 104.

nents' polemic: copies of long-lost books from Larkham's camp have only recently surfaced and because of their fragile condition are made accessible here.[13]

To set Larkham and his diary in context, this Introduction will give a perspective from three different angles: first, a look at how the manuscript and the man came to Tavistock; then an 'aerial view' – the diary and its hinterland, Larkham's world; finally, a drive through the territory, chronologically, to give a sense of the events behind the entries on paper.

I

The story of the manuscript begins in London, with its original owner, George Lane. Lane's entries show how a humble 'beer clerk' could advance to be a minister, and also suggest how the manuscript fell into Thomas Larkham's hands.[14] Lane originally acquired the paper-book to keep track of accounts for his work as a scrivener in 1597–8. He cut the edges of early folios to make a tabbed index of clients: 'Mr Bensome fustian dyer at moregate'; 'Mr Clarke at the sign of the Angell in cheap side'; 'Mr Conyers in coleman street lawyer'; Mrs heathe gentlewoman in gracious street'. Scriveners had a dubious reputation in early modern London for being in cahoots with rascal lawyers and moneylenders. Lane wrote papers for all sorts, from prisoners to gentlemen.[15] Something more of his history is revealed in a draft copy he made of a petition as 'George Lane, a very poore man', to the King's Court of Requests: he protested against an unjust case brought against him for work he had done as a brewer's clerk.[16] In addition to clerking and scrivening, Lane worked as a schoolmaster. He recorded money due to him for 'pens inke & pay 2 quarters' (2s-6d), 'a bound writing booke' (2s), a 'siphering booke' (1s), and for 'wine suger

---

13 *Naboth, in a narrative and complaint of the church of God ... at Tavistock in Devon* (London, 1657); *Judas hanging himselfe: or Naboths false accuser intangled in his own testimony. Set forth in a rejoinder of the church of Christ in Tavistock, to a scurrillous pamphlet published lately by N. W. &c* ([London?], 1658). The two counterpart tracts from Larkham's opponents are: F[rancis]. G[lanville]. D[igory]. P[olwhele]. W[alter]. G[odbeare]. N[icholas]. W[atts].W[illiam]. H[ore]. &c, *The Tavistocke Naboth proved Nabal: in an answer unto a scandalous narrative published by Mr Tho: Larkham in the name (but without the consent) of the church of Tavistocke in Devon* (London, 1658), and *A Strange Metamorphosis in Tavistock, or the Nabal-Naboth improved a Judas. Set forth in reply to a scurrilous pamphlet called Judas, &c* (London, [1658]), a tract Larkham attributed to Nicholas Watts. All are in the English Short Title Catalogue http://estc.bl.uk , ESTC numbers *Naboth* R469333, *Judas* R469334, *Tavistock Naboth* R184887 (the spelling of the title is modernized from here on), *Strange metamorphosis* R207552. In 1999, I wrote that *Tavistock Naboth* (which I had tracked down in the Bodleian) seemed to be the only tract from these exchanges to survive: Hardman Moore, '"Pure folkes" and the parish', p. 499 n. 36. I am grateful to Adam Smyth for unearthing the others and putting me right, and for generously sharing digital images of *Naboth* and *Judas*. The text in this edition is printed from the copies in the Wallace Notestein Collection, by courtesy of Special Collections, the College of Wooster Libraries, Ohio.

14 For what follows I am indebted to Arnold Hunt's detective work on Lane.

15 Diary, fos. 'B'r, 'C'r, 'H'r, 'Y'v. On scriveners' reputations: P. Beal, *In praise of scribes: manuscripts and their makers in seventeenth century England* (Oxford, 1998), pp. 5–11; Bland, *Guide to early printed books and manuscripts*, pp. 99–101.

16 On the reverse of the first blank folio. Lane's petition addressed Sir Julius Caesar, a Master in the King's Court of Requests (a court intended to provide the poor with access to royal justice): Alain Wijffels, 'Caesar , Sir Julius (*bap.* 1558, *d.* 1636)', *ODNB*.

& spice' (2s-6d) when his pupil was sick; he copied mathematical puzzles.[17] Lane also filled up many folios towards the end of the manuscript with extracts copied from printed books. Some relate to his work as a scrivener – drawing techniques, recipes for cheap ink – but he took an interest in remedies for common ailments like stinking breath, sunburn and pimples. He wrote out page after page of useful 'secrets': how 'To make heare yellow as gold', how 'To make a Candell that can not be put out', and – a commercial aspiration then as now – 'A verie good water to make the face appere of the age of XXV yeares.'[18] The first trace of Lane's interest in religion shows in 1606 when he copied out 'A true and parfect rekoning of the yeres and time' from Adam to his own day. In 1611, he corrected and elaborated all the details, and calculated in the margin how long it would be until the millennium dawned – following the customary belief that this would happen 6,000 years after Creation, he reckoned this up as 415 years away (2026 for the curious).[19]

Scattered through Lane's book are entries about christenings and burials, receipts and payments, from the parish of East Greenwich in Kent, 'by me G: L: elected Clarke this 25th daie of december 1615'.[20] These entries run to November 1616, then stop. Lane, by now a parish clerk, seems to have abandoned the paper-book in favour of a formal register. Twenty-five years later he seems still to have been in the parish: in all likelihood, the self-same man who signed his will on 13 December 1641 as 'George Lane of East Greenwich in the Countie of Kent minister'.[21]

So how did Larkham acquire Lane's notebook? A plausible – if entirely specu-lative – answer is that he found it in the vestry of East Greenwich parish church. Perhaps Lane left it there, bundled with other records because of its notes on parish business. Seeing empty space and useful medical remedies, Larkham perhaps adopted the paper-book as his own. What is certain is that he made his first entry in the manuscript in June 1647, on the 'W' page of Lane's client index: 'Mr Obed Wills Schoolmaster at Collonell Blounts oweth me for the bookes he bought', £2.[22] This locates Larkham close to East Greenwich, within the orbit of Colonel Thomas Blount, a colourful Parliamentarian with an estate at Wricklemarsh, a couple of miles away. Blount, who led a Kentish regiment, on one occasion deployed troops to stage a mock battle between Cavaliers and Roundheads at Blackheath, to compen-sate locals for the loss of May Day games. In 1652, when Larkham published his first book (Tavistock sermons), he had a copy specially bound as a gift for Blount.[23]

---

17 Diary, fos. 'O'v (money due), 'C'v (rhymes).
18 Arnold Hunt has identified the sources as Girolamo Ruscelli's *The secretes of ... Maister Alexis of Piemont* (published in various English editions from 1558) and *A very proper treatise wherein is briefly set forth the arte of limming* (first published 1573).
19 Diary, fo. 'F'v. In 1663, Thomas Larkham brought the calculation up to date. For the common notion that there would be 6,000 years between Adam and the end of time, see Crawford Gribben, *The puritan millennium* (Milton Keynes, 2008), p. 22.
20 These fragmentary parish records crop up as rough notes on odd folios near the start of the manuscript ('G'v, 'W'v) and on several systematic but unfoliated pages towards the end.
21 Lane's will, originally written 18 July 1640, was proved at the Prerogative Court of Canterbury on 14 January 1641/2. National Archives, London, PROB/11/188.
22 Diary, fo. 'W'v. 'Obed Wills' could have been a young Obadiah Wills (*CR*) who, like Larkham, came from Dorset. In June 1647, Wills had recently left Exeter College, Oxford, where Larkham's son George matriculated on 9 April 1647.
23 Appendix 1; Anita McConnell and Tim Wales, 'Blount, Thomas (1605/6–1678), *ODNB*. The general context is well portrayed by J. Eales, 'So many sects and schisms: religious diversity in revolutionary

By the time Larkham arrived in Greenwich and acquired Lane's manuscript, he had already travelled thousands of miles from his native Dorset, to New England and back. He was born in Lyme Regis, the son of a linen draper, and graduated BA from Trinity Hall, Cambridge, in 1622. He married Patience Wilton of Crediton that year and by this marriage came into property which kept him afloat financially and would be an important part of his story. Larkham became vicar of Northam, Devon, in 1626. He later claimed that he had endured 'suffering (in the time of the prelacy) in almost all the courts in England', including High Commission and Star Chamber, but no evidence exists to substantiate this. Northam stood between the ports of Appledore and Bideford, on the River Torridge. Larkham would have seen ships setting sail to fish for cod off Newfoundland and to carry passengers across the Atlantic. Late in 1639, Larkham and his family joined the 'Great Migration' to New England.[24] His adventures in New England are interesting as a foil for the later Tavistock controversies. He settled with his family at Dover, a small fishing community on the Piscataqua River, seventy miles north of Boston. He soon fell into a spectacular dispute with Hanserd Knollys (who became well known as a Baptist in Civil War England). Knollys had already formed a church 'of such as he could get, men very raw for the most part'. When Larkham arrived, the church favoured Larkham over Knollys because, as Governor John Winthrop of Massachusetts put it, he was 'a man not savouring the right way of church discipline, but of good parts and wealthy'. Winthrop reported that Larkham admitted to the church 'all who offered themselves, though men notoriously scandalous and ignorant', as long as they promised to repent. This is surprising, given Larkham's later reputation in Tavistock as a stickler for making the church less inclusive. The tension was perhaps as much over Knollys' antinomian preaching (or so Larkham alleged). Knollys excommunicated Larkham, who then 'laid violent hands on Mr. Knollys'. Not for the last time in Larkham's life – history repeated itself in Tavistock – a riot broke out. Knollys' party took to the streets with a Bible strapped to a pikestaff, and the reverend Mr Knollys brandishing a pistol. Arbitrators from the Massachusetts Bay Colony waded in. Larkham was vindicated and Knollys left for England. Within a year or so, Larkham also sailed home. John Winthrop, jaundiced by this desertion, set down the local scandal: 'it was time for him to be gone, for not long after a widow which kept in his house, being a very handsome woman … proved to be with child, and being examined, at first refused to confess the father, but in the end she laid it to Mr Larkham'. Larkham (perhaps conveniently for the widow, who found an absent scapegoat) was no longer in New England, but the tale followed him across the Atlantic to be retold in Tavistock.[25] Larkham's time in America held

---

Kent, 1640–1660', in C. Durston and J. Maltby (eds.), *Religion in revolutionary England* (Manchester, 2006), pp. 226–48.

[24] Thomas Larkham, *The wedding-supper* (London, 1652), 'The epistle dedicatory' (to parliament). The authorities deprived him as vicar of Northam in August 1640, for neglect by absence: Devon Record Office, Exeter, CC7/21. His father's will: Thomas Larkham, linen draper, Wiltshire and Swindon Archives, Chippenham, P5/13Reg/221B, P5/1640/40.

[25] Hardman Moore, *Pilgrims*, pp. 61–2; Richard S. Dunn, James Savage and Laetitia Yeandle (eds.), *The journal of John Winthrop* (Cambridge, MA, and London, 1996), pp. 348–50, 421. The arbitrators from Massachusetts included Larkham's fellow West Countryman Hugh Peter, to whom he looked for support in the 1650s: *Naboth*, p. 31. Kenneth G. C. Newport, 'Knollys, Hanserd (1598–1691)', and Carla Gardina Pestana, 'Peter, Hugh (*bap.*1598, *d.* 1660)', *ODNB*. For the circulation of the tale in Tavistock: *Tavistock Naboth*, p. 15.

no charm, looking back. He often gave thanks on the anniversary of the day he set sail for home: 'I call to mind with a humble and thankful hearte that upon the 12th day of November 1642 I left my house in the morninge and came down to the Mouth of the River Paskataquacke in New England to come for England.'[26]

For the years between Larkham's return to England and his arrival in Tavistock there are only fragments to go on. For the first four years he was at Greenwich and 'elsewhere in Kent'.[27] In June 1645, a 'Mr Larkham of Greenwich' appeared in the papers of the Committee for Plundered Ministers, in a dispute with 'Mr Sprat'. In 1646, the presbyterian propagandist Thomas Edwards – keen to make much of Larkham's scandalous conduct in New England and since – reported to his readers that 'In Kent, not farre from Greenwich, there is a feirce Independent, one Master Larkin.'[28] Not long after, Larkham signed up as chaplain to Sir Hardress Waller's regiment of foot in the New Model Army. He went to Ireland with Waller early in 1647, in an expedition which sailed over and came back by April.[29] Perhaps for the rest of that year, while Waller was occupied in London and the regiment was not on active service, Larkham gravitated back to old haunts in Kent. Judging from the dates of his first entries – June and October 1647 – this may have been when he commandeered Lane's notebook.

Was George Lane's notebook in Larkham's baggage when he set off once again with Waller? The regiment marched into Devon in January 1648, during the Second Civil War, and first came to Tavistock in April.[30] Perhaps for a while Larkham left the notebook with other goods and chattels at his house in Crediton, where some of his family stayed while he was on active service.[31] At any rate, around a year after he settled in the parish as vicar (or 'public preacher' as he preferred to call himself) Larkham started to make entries in earnest. From February 1651 until his death in December 1669, he kept the paper-book beside him in Tavistock.

II

Larkham's home in Tavistock stood close to the River Tavy with a large garden that ran down to the riverbank.[32] From Larkham's diary, a piecemeal picture of it

---

26 Diary, fo. 16r; see also fos. 21r, 24r, 27r, 32r, 35v, 43v.

27 This is from a poorly printed marginal note which misprints Greenwich as 'Breer-wich': Larkham, *Wedding-supper*, 'Epistle dedicatory' (to parliament).

28 British Library, London, Add. MS 15669, fo. 90; Thomas Edwards, *The third part of Gangraena, or a new and higher discovery of the errors ... of the sectaries* (London, 1646), p. 97. Larkham's opponents later referred to him as a 'sower of discord and hatred', a 'proud and turbulent spirit' in Northam in Devon, Greenwich in Kent, and New England (*Tavistock Naboth*, p. 24).

29 Larkham, *Wedding-supper*, 'Epistle dedicatory' (to parliament); C. H. Firth and G. Davies, *The regimental history of Cromwell's army* (Oxford, 1940), pp. 443–4; Patrick Little, 'Waller, Sir Hardress (c.1604–1666)', *ODNB*. Larkham's attachment to Waller may have come about because in 1645 the regiment had been stationed at Crediton, where Larkham had connexions and property.

30 Firth and Davies, *Regimental history*, p. 444. Larkham recalled the arrival of the regiment in Devon (January 1648) and Tavistock (April 1648): Diary, fo. 9r.

31 Larkham's daughter Patience Miller (whose husband, like Larkham, served in the parliamentary army) gave birth to her first son, Thomas, at 'my house in Crediton', 9 June 1648: Diary, fo. 30v. Larkham's will, written in 1668, still mentioned a mansion house there: A. G. Matthews's Notes of Nonconformist Ministers' Wills, Dr Williams's Library, London, MS 38.59, fos. 607–11 (the original in the Devon Record Office perished during the Blitz).

32 It is likely Larkham occupied the dwelling on the south side of (St) Matthew Street which was still

emerges. He made many entries about the garden, usually when he paid others to tend it – prosaic entries which show the rhythm of the year: 'for setting of cabbidg plants' (3d) and 'settinge of leekes for seede' (3d) in March; for 'carrying and casting' dung in April (2s-6d if bought in, but at least once 'the Dung was made in my stable & court '); 'Paringe hedges' (2d) in May; 'for gathering in of apples & trimminge orchard' (1s-4d) in September. The apples he sold (100 for 4d), or stored (in an apple loft he built), or had 'powned & prest' into gallons of cider (by his neighbour and church deacon William Webb).[33] Larkham also committed special moments to paper: 'June the third I pluckt in my Garden at Tavistocke the first Rose &c'; 'As I was walking in my garden groaninge under many evills & [in] particular my deadnes in prayer [a]n answeare of comfort came to me refreshinge me.'[34] As for the house, his manuscript mentions a hall and forehall, a parlour, various chambers and even the proverbial kitchen sink – 'for mending the sinke of the kitchen 10d'. In the late 1650s, when his finances were most robust, he had the builders in. He paid 'heliars' (slaters), masons, carpenters, plasterers and glaziers. He paid for a forehall window with 6½ feet of glass, for 'New laying of the New plancking over the Hall', for 'stones for the stairs'.[35] Larkham made alterations to a room which he started to rent out for private meetings of the church at 10s a quarter: 'Received of the Deacons for the use of My chamber for the church.'[36] Although Larkham never mentioned a study, one chilly November he paid the tailor Daniel Sowton to make him a 'study coat', a 'shagg coat' of warm long-piled fabric. Occasionally he referred to a place he retreated to for private devotion: 'I went into my chamber & on my knees praised God.'[37] Whether Larkham worked where he prayed is unclear (it would not have been unusual to have a 'closet' set aside for prayer), but no doubt the room he used for paperwork also held his books. He bought and sold through the Exeter bookseller John Mungwell; he had extra shelves built; he paid 4d 'for mending and dressing my bookes'. After he left the vicarage and took lodgings in the 1660s, one of his first payments was 'for making shelves for my bookes'. Larkham still had £20 worth of books when he died in 1669, though earlier that year he sold a good part of his library to 'Mr Quicke a Minister living at Plimouth'.[38]

Looking over Larkham's shoulder as he sat in his study coat and sharpened his

---

the vicarage in 1741: see Plate 12. The first detailed and accurate map of Tavistock dates from 1752, commissioned by the duke of Bedford and surveyed by his agent John Wynne. The map is available online: 'Tavistock 1752. The Tavistock Wynne Map Heritage Project', www.tavistock1752.co.uk/. Nowadays, a 'new' vicarage, dating from 1818, stands on Plymouth Road close to the parish church. Matthew Street disappeared in the 1860s when the earl of Bedford cleared slums in a redevelopment which created the Town Hall, Pannier Market and Market Road.

33 Diary, fos. 28v, 25r, 37r, 34r, 26v, 13r, 31v, 38v.
34 Diary, fos. 12r, 20v.
35 Diary, fos. 27v, 28r, 28v, 29v, 31v, 33r.
36 Diary, fo. 30v, June 1658. He made similar entries quarterly thereafter in September and December 1658, March, June, September and December 1659. In March 1659, the church made a larger payment of £1–5s-0d, 'for the meeting chamber and towards the staires and fitting of' (fo. 33r). In September 1660 Larkham noted 'at last had £5 of the Churches stocke, something is due for the Chamber & if they give it wholy to me it will be fitt enough' (fo. 38r). The character of the gathered church will be discussed below.
37 Diary, fo. 20v; also 23r.
38 Diary, fos. 10r, 13v, 15v, 14v, 44r, 48r; for the value of books in Larkham's estate, see CR. John Quick (CR, ODNB) was close to Dr Daniel Williams (who preached his funeral sermon). Quick's manuscripts are now in Dr Williams's Library, London; unfortunately it is impossible to know whether some of the books Larkham sold to Quick reached the Library too.

quill, what concerns did he have in mind? The diary shows him to be a relentless multi-tasker. His paper-book acted as a hub for keeping track of activities on many fronts, with every entry a potential opportunity for slipping into prayer, to reckon up before God. He vigilantly recorded his income as vicar of Tavistock, a particular anxiety in the early 1650s when a dispute over the non-payment of an augmentation to his stipend left him seriously out of pocket. When controversy threatened his reputation, he monitored the progress of his cause – appearances before courts and commissioners, and publications to defend his corner.[39] Firing off in a different direction, a vital arrow in his quiver – through financial difficulties in the early 1650s, and even more so as a nonconformist in the 1660s – was his activity as a landlord. Larkham had assets not only at Kirton (Crediton), where he had come into substantial property through his wife, but also in Tavistock. He had leases to issue, and bought writing paper and sealing wax for the purpose; he kept track of rents, chased up late payments.[40] As well as his business as pastor and property-owner, Larkham chose to mastermind the household expenses. A contemporary writer, enumerating different kinds of record-keeping, remarked wryly that 'Some wary husbands have kept a Diary of dayly disbursements'.[41] Larkham was that man. More will be said shortly about his relations with (the perhaps aptly-named) Mrs Patience Larkham; enough for now to note that Larkham kept track of everything he handed over – usually to the maid – for housekeeping. As well as weekly expenses at Tavistock's Friday market, Larkham noted a vast array of other items: sugar and herrings from Plymouth; 'seames' (horse-loads) of 'turffes' (peat); small gifts from his flock – 'pork and puddings', a 'limon & an orange'.[42] The household had a brewing day once a month. The diary mentions table beer, 'wormwood beer', and beer made from 'furses' (gorse-flowers).[43] As a linen-draper's son, Larkham knew about cloth, and displayed this in notes of the fabrics he paid out for: dowlas, calamanco, 'alamode', ducape.[44] Larkham often spent money on making and mending clothes – and even more on mending shoes – not least because his household included grandchildren. He also incurred expenses because of relatives further afield, in Ireland, London and Cumberland, which required carriage of letters and papers, sometimes of goods and people. The names of two carriers crop up: 'old Clogg', who plied the route north to the port of Bideford, and 'Drake', who worked the route to Exeter. Now and again Larkham paid horse-hire, for example to go to Exeter in sessions week. In May 1651, with a major journey to Cumberland in prospect, he bought a horse for £9-19s: with an extra 2s-6d paid to 'smith & sadler', this was more than a quarter's stipend as vicar.[45]

His entries in the diary, at first sight, are chaotic. It is tempting to conclude that the piles of paper on his desk must have looked the same. To bring some order to the chaos, it is important to realize, first, that Larkham crammed entries onto pages

---

39 Larkham's financial and spiritual disputes are discussed in the next section.
40 Diary, fo. 12v and *passim*.
41 Thomas Fuller, 'Epistle to the reader', John Beadle, *The journal or diary of a thankful Christian* (London, 1656).
42 Diary, fos. 25v, 32v, 10r, 13v, 3v and *passim*. On household accounting, see Beverly Lemire, *The business of everyday life: gender, practice and social politics in England, c. 1600–1900* (Manchester 2005), pp. 190–1, 195–7.
43 Diary, fos. 45r, 37r and *passim*.
44 Diary, fos. 13v, 30v, 24v, 26v and *passim*.
45 Diary, fos. 38r, 46v, 41r, 11r, 4r.

in an important cause: veracity. A full folio is hard to tamper with: later additions, squeezed in, are easy to spot.[46] Second, Larkham had a method. He worked in quarters from his birthday. Within each quarter most of the entries fell into two columns: receipts on the left, together with debts he owed; expenses on the right. This layout was not always consistent, not least because Larkham sometimes filled up the receipts column (where entries might, regrettably, be thin) with expenses (where, alas, the density of entries was always thick). Also, some of his reckonings happened at interim mileposts, the conventional quarter days, when he received rents and paid wages. Quite often, Larkham abandoned the parallel-column structure, briefly, to enter an important item across the whole folio. It is striking that his system broke down for the most extended period between 17 April and 20 June 1661, when he was newly out of office as vicar of Tavistock and had just spent four months in jail. The shape of his life had been shaken up, and it showed on paper.[47]

To make sense of Larkham's diary, it has to be seen as part of a mass of material that crossed his desk on loose sheets and in other notebooks.[48] A vast hinterland of paperwork lies behind his manuscript. When he began to make regular entries in February 1651, he started in the midst and picked up the thread from records made earlier, with a confident summary of income (£40-10s-8d) and expenses (£39-18s-4d) over the previous two quarters.[49] He could set down 'an accompt of what God hath allowed me yeerely since I came from N. England', starting in 1643.[50] Often, he made entries with a sheaf of papers before him: expenses itemized as 'laid out ... upon ticket' (in rough notes or bills);[51] paperwork sent by tenants or jottings made on visits (Larkham often called in at Crediton on his way to Exeter, to collect rents).[52] Other documents in the background include the 'shop books' of various Tavistock traders. Larkham bought goods on credit and settled up later: 'I cleared the shop booke of my Son Condy and now I owe him nothing but ut supra'.[53] The diary was not the only personal notebook he ever kept: at one point, he noted, he was moved to prayer by finding and 'reading ... of the wonderfull goodnesses and providences of God as I found I had written in a paper booke which by providence I mett withall'.[54] In the forest of papers behind the diary, the changing character of church life in the 1650s also needs to be reckoned with. By act of parliament, from 29 September 1653 parish registers detailed births not baptisms, and marriage became a civil ceremony. 'Parish' and 'church' records moved apart. A defining document for Larkham's community of saints – a manuscript he wrote in tandem with the diary – was a 'book of Church Acts and Censures', to record admissions and dismissions, debates and discipline. This has not survived, but his opponents

---

[46] Smyth, *Autobiography in early modern England*, p. 110: Larkham's diary 'has a spectacular fullness which enacts text-book prescriptions that "one parcell without intermission must follow another, otherwise the books are of no credit in Law, or before any Magistrat"'.

[47] The discussion of editorial method (p. xi) contains more on the layout of the manuscript.

[48] Smyth, *Autobiography in early modern England*, pp. 63–72, illuminates the use of multiple interconnected notebooks.

[49] Diary, fo. 2v.

[50] Diary, fo. 9v.

[51] Diary, fo. 17r; *OED*, 'ticket'.

[52] Diary, fo. 4r and *passim*.

[53] Diary, fo. 43v. 'Tradesmen keep their shop books': one of various types of record listed in Thomas Fuller's preface to Beadle's *Journal or diary of a thankful Christian* (cited by Smyth, *Autobiography in early modern England*, p. 118). On credit: Lemire, *The business of everyday life*, pp. 18–26.

[54] Diary, fo. 23r.

alleged it was full of slander and lies, and objected to his relentless 'booking down of things'.[55] Why and how Tavistock's controversy exploded will be considered later. At this point it is useful to observe how the paper-trail in and out of Larkham's study shows the symbiotic relationships between pen and print and between local controversy and the London press.[56] First, Larkham wrote off for official copies of articles presented against him and gathered letters that showed how much support he enjoyed; then he wove this material into sermon-prefaces and tracts, well glossed to defend his reputation; next he delivered his manuscript to London. When the printer sent the books to Tavistock, Larkham sat down with his diary to record the costs and plot distribution. Soon he noted with dismay that his opponents had responded in kind – disputing his account in print – and this set off a fresh round of exchanges.[57] Larkham's opponents recognized and ridiculed his strategy to secure 'truth' by gathering paperwork: 'the first thing this Judas plucks out of his bag is a bundle of old antiquated letters, certificates and attestations'.[58] In all kinds of ways, Larkham's paper-book was the tip of a documentary iceberg.

When he wrote in his manuscript, Larkham had not only papers on the desk but also people at the door. A proper preface to the diary requires some introductions, although of necessity brief. Dozens of people are named – neighbours and friends, tenants, traders and labourers: Augustine Bond and Henry Greene, schoolmasters; Ellis (Elizeus) Bray, barber and parish clerk, one of Larkham's companions on the bowling-green; Dinah Woodman, the maid, who married Nathaniel Knight, one of the Larkhams' gardeners; Richard Hitchins, shopkeeper; widow Mary Gibb, who gave Larkham dishes of fresh butter; John Sheere, church deacon, joiner, witness of Larkham's will; William Webb, church deacon, cider-maker and supplier of wood; Bevill Wivell, maltster. A good few of those who appear in the diary's pages would also have figured in Larkham's long-lost church book. Some can be found in fragments of local records. Many carry common Tavistock names, familiar long before and long after Larkham's time.[59]

What is clear from the diary is that Larkham's world centred on family and church but was not narrowly confined. Beyond everyday business, he enjoyed 'Wine at a dinner of friends' (1s-6d), 'a quart of clarett wine on my birthday' (8d). Once – at a low point in his early days as a nonconformist – he over-indulged, and admitted (in large untidy writing) 'I dranke much Wine this day I am apt to be vaine when

---

55 *Judas*, p. 35, referring back to *Tavistock Naboth*, p. 60.

56 A theme richly explored for the 1640s by Ann Hughes, *Gangraena and the struggle for the English Revolution* (Oxford, 2004).

57 In January 1656/7, Larkham paid 2s-6d for an attested copy of the commissioners' order in his case, and 2s-6d again in October 1657 for a copy of 'new Articles' against him (Diary, fos. 24v, 26v). He printed this material in *Naboth*. For his distribution lists of books, see Appendices 1 and 2. His reaction to his opponents' riposte, *Tavistock Naboth*, will be discussed shortly. Arnold Hunt, *The art of hearing: English preachers and their audiences, 1590–1640* (Cambridge, 2010), pp. 164–5, uses Larkham to illustrate how preachers funded publication of their sermons with the expectation of strong local sales.

58 *Strange metamorphosis*, p. 4. To avoid confusion amid the mud-slinging: Larkham had called Nicholas Watts a 'Judas' but here Watts and his supporters turned the tables and called Larkham 'Judas'.

59 The index to this volume gives a comprehensive list of the people who appear in the manuscript and provides a brief identification where possible. Individuals are not identified in the notes that accompany the text, unless there is a special reason for doing so.

occasion is given, Lord remitt & helpe[.] I spent in Wine £00-03s-02d.'[60] His opponents made much of his fondness for 'pots and tobacco pipes', and for playing for
'ale and cakes' on Tavistock's new bowling-green. Larkham usually played for 4d
or 6d, but on one occasion spent 1s 'about a goose for which I went to Bowles, &
at night was sicke & vomited up al, God was gratious'.[61] Scores of entries concern
his children. Larkham had two sons: Thomas, who died in 1649 (Larkham later paid
8d for an iron rod and six rings, to hang a 'felt Picture of my eldest son'); George,
a student at Exeter College in Oxford when Larkham's record began, but soon a
preacher in Cockermouth, Cumberland (Larkham often noted when letters came
from the north).[62] He had two daughters: Patience, who married a Cromwellian
army officer, Joseph Miller, and lived for some years in Ireland; Jane, who married
a shopkeeper, Daniel Condy, and settled in Tavistock for good. In 1656, Larkham
returned to Ireland to help the newly widowed Patience Miller sort out her affairs.[63]
In the 1660s, her son Tom became Larkham's aide in his Tavistock apothecary
shop, and Larkham sent her daughter Jane to Lyme Regis, to learn how to make
bone-lace, the up-and-coming speciality of his home town.[64] Jane Condy and her
husband Daniel – 'My Daughter Condy', 'My Son Condy' – had a special place
in Larkham's affection and supported him through thick and thin in the 1660s.
Daniel and his brother David became stalwarts of the church as it went forward
into nonconformity.[65] Larkham paid a lavish £10-2s-1d for Jane's wedding clothes
from London in 1652, and wondered how he would ever pay 'the London Bill'.[66]
Jane's first-born, a daughter, was baptized 'Azarel', in a play on the Hebrew behind
Larkham's favourite phrase, 'the Lord hath holpen'.[67] The Condys gave Larkham six
grandchildren. In 1664, he recorded that when his Son Condy was away at Exeter
fair, 'I invited his wife my daughter to supper & I beheld her & her 6 children
according to Psal: 128.6. [Yea, thou shalt see thy children's children].'[68] Larkham's
attention to 'children's children' included raising the orphaned Tom Larkham, 'son
of my eldest son'. Larkham spent good money on Tom, as many diary entries testify.
In 1654, Tom came before the Tavistock Court Leet for 'driving and beating a
sow'. Larkham lost his temper and a fair amount of cash trying to sort this out.
Nothing much changed over the decades. In his will (1668), Larkham referred to his

---

[60] Diary, fos. 13r, 35r, 42r.

[61] *Tavistock Naboth*, p. 74; *Strange metamorphosis*, p. 21; Diary, fo. 26r. Bowls was the sport of Sir
      Francis Drake, Tavistock's most famous son.

[62] Diary, fos. 14r, 21v and *passim*. George Larkham (*CR*).

[63] For this visit to Ireland, see Diary fo. 23r. Larkham 'Called by the world a Minister, at Wexford he
      was then' featured in a tract by a Quaker missionary he opposed there: Humphrey Norton, *To all
      people that speakes of an outward baptisme* (London, 1659), title-page.

[64] Diary, fo. 43v.

[65] In 1672, David Condy's house was licensed for worship under the Declaration of Indulgence: G.
      Lyon Turner, *Original records of early nonconformity under persecution and indulgence* (London,
      1911), I, pp. 540, 566.

[66] Diary, fo. 10v.

[67] Diary, fos. 12v, 13r. He recorded the perilous arrival of another child: 'about 3 of the Clocke in
      the morninge after a sore Travell & danger … the Lord was pleased gratiously to deliver my poore
      daughter Condy of a sore bruised child which came in an unusual manner in to the world. Blessed
      be the name of my God for ever' (fo. 28r).

[68] Diary, fo. 45r.

grandson as 'very chargeable to me from the time of his birth' and by-passed Tom as his heir because of 'his miscarriage which I hope he do begin to see'.[69]

Closest to home, Larkham's silence about his wife is eloquent. In twenty years he made two comments about Patience. In December 1658 he wrote, without any elaboration, 'My poore Rocky Untoward Wife! O my unsuitablenes to her! Lord helpe'.[70] In 1661, on his 39th wedding anniversary – after he had brought all his children and grandchildren before God – he finally came to his spouse: 'For my unworthy selfe & poore wife, My father thou knowest how it is with me and her, O thy spirit is all I crave for us both, And then all will be well enough.'[71] Apart from these telling moments, he stuck to the facts. Every quarter he noted 10s given 'to my Wife' out of the Crediton rents which had come to him by their marriage. He paid 'for surgery Wives foote 00-03-00', for spectacles (4d), and splashed out 11s to buy her a Bible. He bought 'a pair of Pantofles' (slippers) and spent 1s on a 'red jumpe' (underbodice).[72] Occasionally, he allowed her something á la mode: 'sarge & lace for a Gowne for my wife 01-13-10 this was bought at Mr foxwells shop in Exeter … for making my wives gowne 00-14-00½ and things about it sacke bows shoes &c All au french'.[73] But in comparison with his generosity to both his daughters, Patience Larkham came off poorly: 'paid Dan: Sowton for fitting an old gowne for my wife which was a Gowne of Mine 00-06-0'.[74] Larkham's opponents called him 'a bird that loves not his own nest', 'an abuser of his wife', making capital out of talk that he had a bastard child in New England.[75] They also dropped broad hints: he conducted himself in a way unbefitting a pastor 'towards his relations at home, *especially the nearest*: more we shall not say'.[76]

Before leaving these impressions from the diary for the morass of Tavistock controversy, Larkham's private comments about his critics deserve attention. In print, they painted him as a vile-mouthed braggard. The diary gives a different picture. When he referred to his opponents it was almost always in verse, not prose. The rhythm and language of metrical Psalms came readily to mind. He often concluded his poems with 'thus sang Larkham, servant of the Lord', echoing the Song of Moses (Exodus 15). This added an eschatological edge: as the Book of Revelation told it, the saints in heaven, finally victorious over Antichrist, would 'sing the song of Moses the servant of God, and the song of the Lamb, saying, Great and marvellous are thy works, Lord God Almighty; just and true are thy ways'.[77] A small example of what Larkham 'sang' illustrates the tenor: 'Glanvile, Watts, Polewheele, Godbeare, Gove, & Hore / Bole, and all others that me vexe full sore, / O Lord forgive if they belong to thee, / Or else on them let me thy justice

---

69 Diary, fo. 15v (the court case) and *passim*. Larkham's will, in A. G. Matthews's Notes of Nonconformist Ministers' Wills, Dr Williams's Library, London, MS 38.59, fos. 607–11. The younger Thomas Larkham made his will as a 'Merchant of Saint Martin Orgar, City of London', 20 June 1685 (National Archives, London, PROB11/382): he bequeathed his grandfather's gold ring, probably the one Larkham bought in February 1652/3 for £1–3s (Diary, fo. 11r).

70 Diary, fo. 32v.

71 Diary, fo. 41v.

72 Diary, fos. 11v, 47r, 15v, 12r, 23v and *passim*.

73 Diary, fo. 11v.

74 Diary, fo. 16v.

75 Larkham reported this invective: *Judas*, p. 27.

76 *Tavistock Naboth*, p. 76 ['74'].

77 Revelation 15:3 (KJV).

see.' He could not resist a note of triumph when his birthday – always a red-letter day – coincided with the funeral of his arch-critic Francis Glanville, and marked the occasion with a poem that celebrated 'Glanvill this day laid at the Churches feete / though Pompously by men brought through the streete.'[78] On one occasion only he let fly in prose. This was when copies of *The Tavistocke Naboth* arrived in town:

> on this day God (which ordereth everythinge in the World) suffered yea ordered the comeinge to this Towne of a booke, written as it seemes principally by Nicholas Watts[.] The Authors names that owne it being written in Capitall letters shew them Capitall offenders yet ashamed to write thier names at large. O my God before thee doth thy old poore servant spread this heape of trash. thou knowest it is full fraught with lies, slanders, calumnies, false accusations: and was written in extreame malice & revenge & wrath of pride[.] Therefore O Righteous God take it on the account of thy Son Jesus whose I am by ˆunion inˆ the covenant ˆof graceˆ & worke for thy names sake, that thy greate & holy name be not prophaned.[79]

Even here, he wrestled anger into prayer.

The diary reveals a world behind the controversies in print – a hinterland of papers and people. In this panoramic sketch of the landscape, it has only been possible to hint at the material the diary offers for exploring social and cultural themes. Always, controversy leaps out from between the lines and demands attention. So now it is time to abandon the lofty overview and beat a path through the thicket of controversy.

III

The thicket of controversy grew out of a quagmire of charge and counter-charge. The story has to be pieced together from Larkham's diary and polemical pamphlets and – reader beware – all may not quite be as it seems.

Larkham started to write in the diary in February 1651, when he had already been Tavistock's 'public preacher' for more than a year. By this time the honeymoon was over. Conflict had broken out over Larkham's drive to bring reformation to Tavistock. In Larkham's words,

> I continued as Preaching Minister quietly some time, and might still, had not my judgement concerning Discipline made me liable to dislike and Obloquy. But now, they that were other wise judgemented, and profane ones, gnash their teeth to see Christ's Ordinances on foot in public, and themselves laid by as Reprobate Silver; and begin to quarrel at my preaching, and to joyne shoulder to shoulder against the new Church (as they were pleased to call us that laboured to serve God in the spirit, according to his Word) ... The ringleader of this ... adverse Party ... stands up like a Champion and with big words thinks to trample down Gods People whom he called ... the Rigid Faction.

[78] Diary, fos. 23r, 31r. Francis Glanville was buried on 18 August 1658: Tavistock PR. Larkham's clashes with his opponents will be the substance of the next section.
[79] Diary, fo. 30r. *Tavistock Naboth* was the riposte to Larkham's *Naboth*: this pamphlet exchange will be considered shortly.

Larkham later attributed his early troubles to the 'implacable malice' of three people – one the unnamed ringleader here – Francis Glanville (a member of Tavistock's most prominent family and a justice of the peace), John Jacob (who had been an officer in the king's army) and Walter Godbeare ('an excise man by commission from Sir Richard Grenvile').[80] The bitterness of Civil War divisions, vented on a parliamentary army chaplain turned vicar, forms the backdrop. Francis Glanville was always one of Larkham's fiercest opponents. In 1662, a 'Thomas Glanvill' became vicar of Tavistock while Larkham lived out his days as a nonconformist.

Larkham's zeal for purity, and the character of his preaching, set Tavistock teeth on edge. His eagerness to distinguish 'God's People' from 'Reprobate Silver'suggests he had already begun to limit access to the sacraments. The hurdle for admission was not yet a written covenant – that came later – but as early as 1649, it seems, members vowed 'at their first admittance to submit to the discipline of the Church so far as it was transacted according to the Word of God'.[81] Above and beyond this, Larkham's pulpit utterances were declared by some 'to be such unsufferable Sermons as the like have not been Preached'.[82] They made much of his abusive manner. Articles presented against him complained

> He is a common rayler, calling in the Pulpit the inhabitants of the Parish of *Tavistock* by several scandalous and opprobrious names, as dogs, snarling curs, swine, grunting swine, serpents, vipers, devils, rogues, ragged rogues, rascals, scabs, ninnihammers, purquinions, fools, squint-eyed fools, sons of witches, knaves, a pack of knaves, the devils dishclouts, with frequent and horrid curses and imprecations, saying to one as he was going out of the church, Goe and the curse of God go with thee; and to the Congregation, God pour on you and yours the vials of his wrath.[83]

This sounds dramatic, but the reality may not have been quite as it seems. Larkham certainly adopted the old-fashioned godly practice of 'particular preaching', where public reproof and pointed comment, couched in heady biblical language, pressed home the gospel message. The result of such tactics was that, as a recent study has put it, 'one of the commonest grievances against godly ministers, and obviously one of the most deeply felt, was that they abused their parishioners in their sermons'.[84] Among his Tavistock hearers there was perhaps also a spot of wilful misunderstanding, as illustrated by the spin they put on a story Larkham told (somewhat unwisely) from the pulpit. As Larkham relayed it, 'Walking alone in a close near the Town of Tavistock', he met 'a late Captain in the Kings Army', who accosted him with the words 'Thou didst preach last Sunday a base rascally scandalous seditious Sermon.' When Larkham replied that many people approved of his preaching,

---

80 Larkham, *Wedding-supper*, 'Epistle dedicatory' (to parliament); *Naboth*, p. 14. Francis Glanville was a nephew of Sir John Glanville, Speaker of the House of Commons, impeached in 1644 for his loyalty to the king: Stuart Handley, 'Glanville, Sir John, the younger (1585/6–1661)' and J. A. Hamilton (rev. David Ibbetson) 'Glanville, John (1542–1600)', *ODNB*; Hopkins, 'Thomas Larkham's Tavistock', pp. 130–2, 232. For Grenville, who defected from parliament's cause to the king and led royalist forces in the south-west, see Ian Roy, 'Grenville, Sir Richard, baronet (*bap.* 1600, *d.* 1659)', *ODNB*.

81 *Tavistock Naboth*, p. 67.

82 Larkham, *Wedding-supper*, 'To the reader'.

83 From articles exhibited to the Committee for Plundered Ministers, printed by Larkham, *Naboth*, p. 6. The 'one cursed' was John Pointer, ejected from the church for drunkenness.

84 Hunt, *The art of hearing*, pp. 251–4, quotation from p. 253.

the captain responded that 'none heard him but the scum of the Town'. To which Larkham said, '(smiling), that sometimes the scum was the best and uppermost as in a milk Pan'. In the hands of his opponents, this turned into an offensive pulpit pronouncement that 'there were none but scums that came to hear me'.[85]

By 1650, efforts started to oust Larkham from his post. His critics cut the cloth of their complaints to suit the times. Protests against a 'scandalous' minister might succeed; objections to an over-zealous drive for purity would not. Larkham's opponents sent a letter detailing their grievances to Colonel John Disbrowe, the most powerful figure in the south-west. Larkham's supporters feared the intent was 'to quench the Gospel light among us'.[86] Another strategy was to turn off the tap of finance. If accusations of scandalous preaching did not shift him, pressure on his pocket might. From the start, resistance to Larkham's ministry was intertwined with a refusal to pay him an extra £50 a year, from Lamerton parish. Lamerton stood adjacent to Tavistock, to the north-west. As part of the fallout of Civil War, the parliamentary authorities levied a fine for delinquency on the patron of Lamerton, Sir John Glanville, of which £50 a year was allocated to augment the income of the vicar of Tavistock. But the trustees of the Lamerton money – John Pointer, William Grills and Walter Godbeare – refused to pay up, judging Larkham 'unworthy to be continued in the employment of Gospel-preaching'.[87] According to Larkham, Pointer – ejected from the church for drunkenness – insisted on bringing 'libels of contention and strife to be read on Lords dayes', especially when the church intended to celebrate communion.[88] For Larkham, the loss of income mattered: his Tavistock stipend, paid by the earl of Bedford's steward, was a steady £9-15s a quarter; he stood to gain an extra £12–10s each quarter from Lamerton. He made the first detailed entries in his diary in early 1651, when money was tight. He recorded how his income had plummeted. In the year to August 1650, he received £151-3s-8d (from all sources, including Crediton rents). In August 1651, the total fell to £66-18s-2d, 'by reason that the wicked Trustees paid nothing out of Lamerton'.[89]

The financial strategy had an effect. In the summer of 1651, Larkham decided to abandon Tavistock and go north to join his son George in Cumberland: 'receiving (as I apprehended it) a Call from God, to be employed in my Function elsewhere, I obeyed it; and departed from the ... Towne of Tavistock with a purpose to return thither no more to dwell among them'. Soon he was preaching in Cumberland near

---

[85] *Naboth*, p. 17; *Tavistock Naboth*, p. 64. Joel Halcomb, 'A social history of congregational religious practice during the Puritan Revolution', Ph.D. dissertation, University of Cambridge, 2009, pp. 90–3, shows that congregational churches drew members from 'all layers of society'. Hopkins, 'Thomas Larkham's Tavistock', pp. 236–41, has analysed the economic status of Larkham's 'supporters' (defining these as the people who gave him small gifts), using hearth tax returns from 1662. Hopkins suggests that Larkham's followers were mostly from lower status groups: artisans, husbandmen and women (particularly widows). However, the evidence is not conclusive. It is clear that Larkham had also support from wealthier citizens (like the mercer Nicholas Watts, who although he turned into a strident critic of Larkham for a time, seems to have been reconciled with him in the 1660s.)

[86] *Judas*, pp. 4–5; Stephen K. Roberts, 'Disbrowe , John (*bap.* 1608, *d.* 1680)', *ODNB*.

[87] Sir John Glanville the younger, *ODNB*. Larkham, *Wedding-supper*, 'Epistle dedicatory' (to parliament). Committee for Advance of Money, papers relating to the Lamerton dispute (which dragged on through the 1650s): National Archives, London, SP19/11, fos. 364–5, SP19/12, fos. 29, 76, 241, 341, 387, SP19/25, fo. 11, SP19/95, nos. 68, 89, 108–13, 115–33, 387.

[88] *Naboth*, p. 12.

[89] Diary, fo. 9v; see also the calculations on fos. 4v, 9r.

Cockermouth, at Cross Canonby, Dearham and Flimby.[90] That autumn, Larkham gathered a church by covenant at Cockermouth: 'October 2nd 1651 The Foundation of this particular church was laid in the Towne of Cockermouth ... through the instigation of Mr Thomas Larkham Pastor of the church of Christ at Tavistock in Devon: A blessed instrument in promoting and Furthering so good a worke.'[91] George Larkham was by this time curate of Cockermouth, and he and George Benson, vicar of Bridekirk, were among the 'foundation stones' of the new church, and became its pastor and teaching elder. But Thomas Larkham led the way. When the church 'did solemnly dedicate herselfe to God by fasting and praier', 'the worke of the day was carried on by Mr Thomas Larkham'. When the congregation celebrated communion for the first time, 'they gave a call to the aforementioned Mr. Tho. Larkham Pastor of the church of Christ at Tavistock in Devon, to administer that ordinance'. An unusual co-existence of the old and the new evolved, personified in the activity of George Larkham and Benson: they 'went on in the worke of their places, from time to time Baptizing children and administering the Lords Supper'. The 'worke of their places' included, besides ministry to the gathered church, public preaching in their own parishes. Members of the gathered church attended preaching services on Sundays with their neighbours, but also met in private. Thus Larkham and Son pressed forward in Cumberland with the aspirations for preaching and purity that had caused a row in Tavistock.[92]

Larkham found it far easier to carry the day in the 'dark corners of the North' than in Tavistock. The model established at Cockermouth proved popular in other parishes in Cumberland and Westmorland, because (in a rural setting with scattered parishes and population) it provided support for godly fellowship and effective public preaching. In Tavistock the dynamic was altogether different. Larkham contended with long-established parish interests. However, his success in gathering the godly at Cockermouth must have raised his expectations of what could be achieved, and sharpened his frustration with resistance. His Tavistock enemies later complained "'tis very common with him to vaunt what seals he hath to his Ministry in other places as well as here'.[93]

Larkham's association with Tavistock might have ended when he left for Cumberland in 1651, but he was persuaded to return. 'Above 60 of the most considerable persons for Religion in the Town and Parish' sent a letter: 'We humbly desire you ... speedily come among us ... let not the work of God amongst us come to nought ... We shall wait at the throne of grace with teares for a comfortable answer: in the meantime subscribe ourselves your sheep in the Lord.'[94] Nicholas Watts headed the signatories – Watts, who later turned against Larkham and so became the 'Judas' of Larkham's *Judas hanging himselfe*. Larkham left Cumberland but first went to

---

90 Larkham, *Wedding-supper*, 'Epistle dedicatory' (to parliament).

91 The register of Cockermouth congregational church, 1651–1771, Cumbria Record Office and Local Studies Library, Whitehaven, MS YDFCCL 3/1, fo. 1. An edition of the early part of the record has been completed: Robert Wordsworth, 'The church book of Cockermouth congregational church, 1651–1700', M.Phil. dissertation, Lancaster University, 2008. An expanded and revised edition by Mr Wordsworth will soon be published by the Cumberland and Westmorland Antiquarian and Archaeological Society.

92 Register of Cockermouth congregational church, fos. 3–4. The contrasts between the context in the north and in Tavistock are explored in Hardman Moore, '"Pure folkes" and the parish'.

93 *Tavistock Naboth*, p. 62.

94 Larkham, *Parable of the Wedding-supper*, 'To the reader'.

London to petition the Committee for Advance of Money about the missing £50 a year from Lamerton. He also wanted to wrongfoot his Tavistock critics by putting his supposedly 'unsufferable' sermons into print. The result, *The wedding-supper*, was a book designed to impress, with a dedication to parliament and a portrait of Larkham by a rising star, the engraver Thomas Cross.[95]

Larkham's return to Tavistock in May 1652 provoked a combustion. Although he managed to preach on the first Lord's Day, morning and afternoon, trouble came on Wednesday: 'when Mr *L.* thought to have preached his usual Lecture, the doors of the Parish Meeting-house were shut against him'. He rushed back to London to complain to the Committee for Plundered Ministers, who confirmed his rights as vicar.[96] Brandishing the Committee's order, he returned to Tavistock. He arrived on a Sunday morning, to discover 'the doores of the parish Church Shutt up against me by Hawksworthe a late trooper in the Kings army Chosen A litle before to be church warden and confirmed by Glanvile and others.' Larkham's flock took action. A witness testified – before Larkham's implacable opponent, Francis Glanville JP – that 'hee saw Augustine Bond Thomas Thorne & John Sheares ... with others that weare spectators in a Riotouse manor use violence to the Church dore ... with a Barr of Iron hamer & other thinges with which they broke open the said Church dore'.[97] Larkham and his associates were hauled before the Quarter Sessions and Assizes, accused of riot, but secured an acquittal.[98] Determined to press their case, his opponents submitted articles to the Committee for Plundered Ministers, which yet again made loud complaint.[99] Reviewing events some months later, from a safe distance, Larkham noted: 'I have beene this yeere exceedingly persecuted; by arrests, in the Comitee for Plundered Ministers, by enditement for a Supposed Riott with divers of my brethren to the expence of at least £50 in charges. Yet out of all the Lord hath delivered me blessed be his name.'[100] The church helped to pay Larkham's legal expenses. These payments – recorded in the diary – mark the start of separate payments by the church to Larkham as pastor, separate from his income as public preacher.

Hostility against Larkham raged for the rest of the 1650s, and expressed itself in repeated attempts to persuade the Interregnum authorities to remove him from office. From 1654, Cromwell's Protectorate established new structures. Oversight for the national church came from the Commissioners for the Approbation of Public

---

[95] See Plate 1 and Appendix 1.

[96] *Judas*, pp. 7–8; Diary, fo. 12r. The Committee for Plundered Ministers had been established by the Long Parliament in 1642–3 to provide for 'poor plundered' ministers forced out by royalist forces. It gathered other functions to it, including the approval of presentations to vacant livings and examination of 'scandalous' clergy. W. A. Shaw, *A history of the English church during the Civil Wars and under the Commonwealth, 1640–1660*, 2 vols. (London, 1900), II, pp. 193, 197–8.

[97] Diary, fo. 12r; Devon Record Office, Exeter, QS/B 1652, Easter – Michaelmas, deposition taken on 8 July 1652 before Francis Glanville and John Elford, JPs, from Jonathan Tilham of Tavistock, weaver, about events on 27 June 1652; see also, on the same paper, similar depositions on 29 June from Richard Parkin, William North, Walter Harris.

[98] *Tavistock Naboth*, p. 11; Diary, fo. 10r, 10v, 11v. Larkham often called it 'Row's Riot': in a poem, he named those who stirred it up as Nicholas Row, William Pointer, Glanville and Godbeare: Diary, fo. 12v. Row came from Lamerton (Devon Record Office, Exeter, QS1/9, Quarter Sessions Order Book 1652–61, 9 January 1654/5); the others from Tavistock.

[99] Larkham recorded that justices came to Tavistock to examine witnesses, and later put the articles into print: Diary, fo. 10r; *Naboth*, p. 6.

[100] Diary, fo. 12r.

Preachers (the 'Triers' in London), and from Commissioners for the Ejection of Scandalous Ministers (the county-based 'Ejectors', lay commissioners assisted by ministers). The disputes in Larkham's Tavistock provide a good case-study of the way all parties in local spats could lobby relentlessly, in efforts to bend the ears of 'Triers' and 'Ejectors'.[101]

Opposition to Larkham came principally from two quarters. At first, people with a stake in the hoary Lamerton dispute were well to the fore: John Pointer, William Grills and Walter Godbeare, backed by Francis Glanville. On the way back from Cumberland, Larkham had accused Pointer, Grills and Godbeare of fraudulently pocketing sums that should have been paid to the vicar of Tavistock. For a brief time, he won the day. The Committee for Advance of Money endorsed his right to the money. In his diary, Larkham exclaimed 'in this nicke of time I had good newes from haberdashers hall. The Lord is worthy to be praised' (at that moment he was was desperate for money to pay for his daughter's wedding). When £100 of arrears arrived, he gave £5 to 'the chosen men of the Church' as a thank-offering. The delight did not last. The Lamerton money stopped again and the wrangling dragged on.[102] Larkham's critics thought it took the biscuit, given the fuss about Lamerton, when he published a pamphlet to argue against compulsory tithes.[103] Underlying this was a theological debate, aired not only in Tavistock but elsewhere, that a voluntary church – where people opted in by a commitment of faith before they received sacraments – should be supported by voluntary means. This was actually welcome news to mere 'parishioners' who (under Cromwell) were no longer compelled to attend church, and resented paying tithes to a minister who turned them away from the Lord's Supper and denied their children baptism. Around this time, 1656, Larkham went to great pains to put his principles into practice: to calculate a tenth of every scrap of income he received, and set it apart 'for piety and charity', 'in a purse by it selfe'.[104] But his declarations from the pulpit against tithes – 'he can live if he never received any Parish maintenance more' – infuriated the Lamerton trustees, and kept the dispute on the boil.[105]

The campaign to oust Larkham gained new bite when disenchanted supporters started to speak against him. For a time, all seemed sweetness and light within 'the church' – the inner circle who agreed to submit to a discipline 'transacted according to the Word of God' – but peace did not last.

Before the noise of contention is heard, it is wise to take stock of what Larkham had afoot. He wanted a reformation in Tavistock, with a strong commitment to public preaching, but which also allowed the church to pursue purity in a biblically sanctioned form. With hindsight, his 'gathered church' looks like the germs of Dissent – as it would come to be, with the events of 1662. But in the 1650s,

101 For discussion of the Commissioners' work, see Ann Hughes, '"The public profession of these nations": the national church in Interregnum England', in *Religion in Revolutionary England*, ed. Christopher Durston and Judith Maltby (Manchester and New York, 2006), pp. 97–102.

102 Diary, fos. 10v, 11r, 26r. The Committee for Advance of Money met at Haberdashers Hall, London. For papers presented to the committee about the Lamerton case, see n. 87. In August 1657, Larkham noted that nothing had been paid for three and a half years. Glanville and Godbeare have been introduced earlier; Pointer was a merchant; Grills, another merchant, served many times on the Tavistock Court Leet. See Hopkins, 'Thomas Larkham's Tavistock', pp. 130–2, 232.

103 Thomas Larkham, *A discourse of paying tithes* (London, 1656); *Tavistock Naboth*, p. 13.

104 His entries on fo. 26r are particularly detailed; see also fos. 24v, 25v, 27r, 28v.

105 *Tavistock Naboth*, p. 62.

Larkham and his like pressed the cause of reformation for the populace at large, not only for an inner circle. Up and down the land, varieties of 'parish congregation-alism' (a phrase that fits well with Larkham's commitment to public preaching and gathered church) were reasonably common.[106] Cromwell's national church allowed great freedom for parish-based initiatives, with broad oversight from the 'Ejectors' and 'Triers'.[107] In his diary, Larkham recorded his duties to parish and gathered church: for the parish, preaching at 'publike meeting' on the Lord's Day, at his Wednesday lecture, and at funerals; for the church, weekday house meetings and (at least from 1654 onwards) communions on the first Sunday of the month, after the public preaching service.[108] The diary shows not only how Larkham distinguished his work as public preacher and pastor, but also his grasp of the overlap: 'a day of humiliation for Parish and Church, both'.[109] The inner life of the gathered church is largely hidden because Larkham's book of 'Church Acts and Censures' does not survive. His opponents alleged a dizzying variety of schemes for church govern-ment, adopted one day and abandoned the next.[110] It was not unusual in the 'parish congregationalism' of the 1650s to find that churches had multiple small *rôles* for members to fill, and shifting patterns of organization. Looking at other church books gives a sense of what may need to be read between the lines of hostile polemic.[111] Larkham's diary gives occasional glimpses of what went on. By 1653, the church had 'chosen men' (later re-named deacons) who handled money and cared for the poor.[112] Early in 1654, when peace still reigned among the Tavistock godly, Larkham came home from London laden with books. He brought '6 doz: of perkins Cate-chisme', probably for use in the parish: for these, Nicholas Watts paid Larkham 8s (Watts was soon to turn against Larkham, but at this point was still a leading light in the church and perhaps paid the money in its name).[113] Larkham also brought

---

[106] See Halcomb, 'Social history of congregational religious practice'.

[107] Hughes, '"The public profession of these nations"'. There was nothing like a Presbytery to set the rules. The movement for 'voluntary association' among ministers in the later 1650s (led in Devon by Tavistock's former minister, George Hughes of Plymouth) was just that: voluntary. On the Associa-tion Movement see Halcomb, 'Social history of congregational religious practice', pp. 216–27.

[108] Diary, *passim*. Larkham set high hurdles for admission to the sacraments, but once within the fold the 'covenanted saints' could expect monthly communion. It was different in Ralph Josselin's Essex parish – Josselin was so unsure about whom to admit to communion that he did not celebrate the sacrament for nine years: Patrick Collinson, 'The English Conventicle', in *Voluntary religion*, ed. W. J. Sheils and D. Wood, Studies in Church History, 23 (Oxford, 1986), p. 257. The practices of Tavistock's gathered church had close parallels elsewhere, vis-á-vis frequency of communion and the character of public and private worship: Halcomb, 'Social History of Congregational Religious Practice', pp. 71–2, 107–113.

[109] Diary, fo. 36r.

[110] *Tavistock Naboth*, pp. 66–7.

[111] Halcomb points to the 'fluid and ad hoc' character of everyday practice, and how church duties could be spread across many people with 'messengers', 'helpers' and the like – sixty of the ninety-one members in the Bedford church minutes had some special *rôle*: 'Social history of congrega-tional religious practice', p. 80.

[112] Diary, fos. 11r, 11v ('chosen men'). Larkham's diary never mentions elders, but there are references in print: *Tavistock Naboth*, p. 75; *Judas*, p. 15. Many churches instituted deacons first and only later elected elders: Halcomb, 'Social history of congregational religious practice', pp. 66–8.

[113] Diary, fo. 14v. This could well have been the new edition, hot from the press: William Perkins, *The foundation of Christian religion, gathered into six principles ... to be learned of ignorant people, that they may be fit to hear sermons with profit, and to receive the Lords Supper with comfort* (London, 1654). If so, the title suggests Larkham's catechizing campaign may have been intended to increase the circle of people admitted to communion.

back from London a box of psalm books, which he sold on at 1s-6d apiece, to some if not all to members of the church.[114] The church held private weekday meetings. On 17 November 1657, a Tuesday, the gathered saints celebrated a golden day for the godly, the anniversary of Elizabeth I's accession: 'this 17th day the Church kept solemnly & praised the Lord for all gratious providences. Such as were able invited to eate at their tables the rest of the members O Lord accept this sacrifice in X.'[115] By 1658, the gathered church paid 10s a quarter to rent a 'meeting chamber' in Larkham's house, and had talks with Larkham's ally, the Exeter congregationalist Lewis Stucley, about 'Mutuall Communion between the Churches'.[116] How large was Larkham's flock? He began his godly experiment, at least, with a good measure of support. A letter of September 1650, which urged him 'not to be disheartened, in your labour of love, in this work of the Lord among us', was 'publickly read and assented to by at least two hundred persons, and above sixty hands subscribed in the name of all the rest'.[117]

Towards the end of 1654, a 'plague of divisions' broke out in the church. Several founding members, including Nicholas Watts, were excommunicated. In the streets of Tavistock, Larkham's enemies rejoiced. Watts joined forces with Francis Glanville and others to bring fresh vigour to the lobbying campaign against Larkham. In the late 1650s they orchestrated complaints to the county Ejectors in Exeter (more than once), to the Triers in London, and finally to the Council of State. The catalyst for the alienation of Watts and others was Larkham's decision to produce a written church covenant. He insisted everyone must sign. The penalty? No signature, no sacraments. Larkham's action was not necessarily unusual: gathered churches could take time to settle themselves with a covenant (months or even years), and a shift from verbal consent to written agreement was sometimes part of this; also, the common practice of 'covenant renewal' might well involve a freshly drafted vow.[118] But whatever Larkham had put on paper was a step too far for some of the Tavistock godly. They objected 'the Church had been five years without any other Covenant then the Members made at their first admittance to submit to the discipline of the Church so far as it was transacted according to the Word of God'.[119] Larkham was drawing the bounds of the church too tight. John Edgcombe, like Watts a founding member who turned against Larkham, made an eloquent protest against the requirement to sign the covenant:

---

114 Diary, fos. 14r, 14v, 15r. This may have been the verse translation by William Barton, which also came out that year in a fresh edition: *The Book of Psalms in metre. Close and proper to the Hebrew: smooth and pleasant for the metre* (London, 1654). A. B. Grosart, 'Barton, William (1597/8–1678)', rev. D. K. Money, *ODNB*. Barton and Larkham had been exact contemporaries at Trinity and Trinity Hall, Cambridge, and (although there is no record of continuing contact in the 1650s) seem to have had similar interests in the poetry of the Hebrew Bible and in congregationalism. Barton was minister of St John Zachary in London, 1646–56. His psalter was sold by (among others) Francis Eglesfield, who had close links with the West Country and in 1656 published several tracts by Larkham. Barton's commitments in matters of church order are suggested by Halcomb, 'Social history of congregational religious practice', p. 226.

115 Diary, fo. 27v.

116 For the rental of the chamber, see n. 36; on the talks with Stucley (*CR*), Diary, fo. 32v.

117 Larkham, *Parable of the Wedding-supper*, 'To the reader'; *Judas*, p. 4.

118 David A. Weir, *Early New England: a covenanted society* (Grand Rapids, MI, 2005), pp. 136–46; Halcomb, 'Social history of congregational religious practice', pp. 55–8.

119 *Tavistock Naboth*, p. 67.

I cannot find any such precept … in the word of our God in Gospel times … You know to put on the Surplice is a thing lawful in it self, but when men did enjoyn it as necessary, it became sinful in the thoughts of many of God's dearest children; and though it may be lawful to subscribe that paper as to the matter, yet as you impose it, it seems to me altogether sinful; we have no such custome [in] the Churches of Christ. Had you left it to every one at their will as a thing indifferent, I suppose none would have refused it, but you lay it on us as absolutely necessary to communion, and therefore I do not subscribe it.[120]

When Edgcombe and others tried to remonstrate with Larkham before the assembled church, 'whilst they waited for a fit time, Mr. L. fell out into a bitter passion, and so to prayer, and immediately (having gathered up his gloves and papers on the table while he was praying) got away into his house'.[121] From the furore that followed, it is clear Larkham was as good as his word and restricted the sacraments to those who signed. In his diary, he recorded more celebrations of communion for the church – once a month – after the defining moment of covenant-signing. He had already nailed his colours to the mast about the evils of indiscriminate baptism: 'how … are they deceived, that think it enough to be born in Christian lands, and to perform outward actions of religion; and to buy for their babies 12 penniworth of water to sprinkle in their faces … I tremble to think how this sealing ordinance is abused, prophaned, even every week almost'.[122] In 1656, he declared 'I teach all in the publike meeting-house, but do only baptize the children of such as are received and allowed members of the Church, and admitted to the Lords Table.'[123] Entries in the Tavistock parish register for this period suggest that many children went unbaptized or were baptized by neighbour ministers when Larkham would not.[124]

The Tavistock developments cannot be isolated from events elsewhere in the county. Initiatives were underway to form a voluntary association of ministers: the Devon Association met for the first time in October 1655, led by George Hughes of Plymouth, Larkham's predecessor at Tavistock. Hughes, a moderate presbyterian, was on good terms with episcopalian sympathizers in Devon and managed to bring many into the fold.[125] Larkham took an interest in the Association movement – in August 1654, he bought a copy of *Christian concord, or the agreement of the associated pastors and churches of Worcester-shire* (London, 1653) – but stayed out of it.[126] On all sides of Tavistock, his neighbours in ministry joined up: Richard Ham

---

[120] *Ibid.*, pp. 53–4.
[121] *Ibid.*, p. 59.
[122] Larkham, *Wedding-supper*, p. 250.
[123] Larkham, *Discourse of paying tithes*, p. 25.
[124] Devon Record Office, Exeter, 482A add 2/PR1, Tavistock Parish Register, 1614–1793. Parliament ordered that from 29 September 1653, parish registers should record births not baptisms. The Tavistock register switched to recording births but sometimes added a date of baptism. If the record reflects the proportion of births to baptisms accurately (and it is impossible to be sure of this, so the evidence cannot be quantified precisely) a large cohort of children went unbaptized, perhaps half those born between 1653 and 1660. The register also notes when the baptism of Tavistock infants took place in the neighbouring parishes of Whitchurch, Peter Tavy and Mary Tavy.
[125] Halcomb, 'Social history of congregational religious practice', p. 224; for similar developments elsewhere, John Spurr, *The Restoration Church of England, 1646–1689* (New Haven and London, 1991), pp. 25–6.
[126] Diary, fo. 15v. Halcomb, 'Social history of congregational religious practice', p. 225, states that Lewis Stucley and Thomas Mall of Exeter were the only Devon congregationalists to join the Association; Nathaniel Mather (*CR*), who had returned from New England, has been overlooked.

of Lamerton (some travelled to hear 'godly Mr Ham' preach instead of Larkham); Andrew Gove of Peter Tavy (nephew to Alexander Gove of Tavistock who had fallen out with Larkham); Digory Polewhele of Whitchurch (who joined forces with Watts and Glanville against Larkham).[127] Larkham was said to have snubbed two of Hughes' proteges, John Howe and Ralph Venning, and to have refused to allow Hughes to come back to preach.[128] Larkham's uneasy relations with his peers showed in a clash with Howe, George Hughes' son-in-law, in January 1656:

> Mr John Howe Minister of Greate Torrington had leave to preach heere at Tavis-tocke who most fiercely lashed at me in his sermon about the improper obedience of such as are truly gratious. I wrote to him that I would make good what I had preached the next lecture day &c against which time there was great riding and sending to gather the Ministers of the Contry together, in hope that I should have been swallowed up ... [the next week] I preached upon the same text Mr Howe preached on the week before, and after sermon a conference in the parish Church and in the afternoone among the ministers in private. I acknowledge thankfully Gods hand over me[.] We all parted lovingly at the last.[129]

Those who left the church over Larkham's covenant-making saw the written covenant as his way to shut out people who wanted George Hughes' moderate style of ministry,

> for by the way ... he hath often said there were two parties in the Church, the Hugonites and the Larkamites (as he was pleased to name them) the Hugonites such as were professours in Mr Hughes his time, the Larkamites such as were so for the most part since his coming.[130]

Fired up by tense exchanges, strident letters and complaints to Commonwealth Committees, Tavistock's arguments exploded into print. Larkham lit the touchpaper between two bouts with the Devon Commissioners for the Ejection of Scandalous Ministers. During the autumn of 1656, Pointer, Glanville, Watts and Hore had used their position as parish officers – setting parish firmly against church – to present articles against Larkham.[131] In January 1657, Larkham emerged from a hearing in Exeter with a ruling broadly in his favour: he had made an offer to resign in favour of someone nominated by his allies Lewis Stucley of Exeter and William Bartlet of Bideford, and this was accepted. But the inaction of Stucley and Bartlet – Who could possibly serve the cause of the gospel in Tavistock better than Larkham?

---

127 For their membership of the Association: Shaw, *A history of the English church*, II, p. 449. On the popularity of Ham's sermons, *Tavistock Naboth*, p. 28. (Ham had been appointed vicar of Lamerton in 1650 by the parliamentary commissioners: A. G. Matthews, *Walker revised* (Oxford, 1988), s.v. John Cooper.) Larkham's dispute with the Goves began over a child's funeral: *Tavistock Naboth*, p. 71. Polewhele's initials were on the title-page of *Tavistock Naboth*.

128 *Tavistock Naboth*, pp. 49–50.

129 Diary, fo. 21v. *Tavistock Naboth*, p. 8, reported 'a grave and solemn admonition given him by fourteen Ministers at one time in Tavistock, to preach the truth as it is in Jesus'.

130 *Tavistock Naboth*, p. 67.

131 Larkham later printed the articles against him: *Naboth*, pp. 6–10. Glanville served as a feofee of Tavistock parish lands with Pointer and Godbeare, and was churchwarden (1657). Pointer served as an overseer of the poor (1656). Watts served as overseer (1655), and as churchwarden (1656). Hore was a collector for the poor (1655), an overseer (1656) and churchwarden (1657). Devon Record Office, Exeter, 482A/PF135, 'Feofees of lands belonging to the parish of Tavistock', 482A/PV1, 'Tavistock vestry minutes 9 July 1660–1740' (with a backlist of parish officers to 1655), fos. 1v–2r.

– meant that for his opponents nothing was settled.[132] They launched a fresh prosecution. In anticipation of further appearances before the commissioners (all now
rumoured to be presbyterians and so against him) Larkham went into print with
Naboth, to show how well his case had stood up in the previous round. He identified
himself with Naboth the faithful Jezreelite, who refused to surrender his vineyard to
the evil ruler Ahab (1 Kings 21). Ahab's wife rigged Naboth's death by arranging for
two 'base fellows' to accuse him of cursing God and the king, so that he was carried
away and stoned. Naboth's story was a quarrel which pivoted on false accusations.
In Larkham's mind, it was a small step from Naboth's vineyard to Tavistock. In
December 1657 he secured yet another vindication from the Commissioners and
celebrated in private with a verse:

> Men they mustt Doe what God above Commands,
> He guids their tongues their judgement & their hands.
> Unworthy Dust deserves nothing at all
> but Wrath. for praise this mercy now doeth Call.
> I am this farre from all my troubles freed
> God grant some Comfort now may come insteede.[133]

In response to *Naboth*, Larkham's opponents hit the streets with an attack on him as
The Tavistocke Naboth turned Nabal: belligerent drunken Nabal, 'Nabal is his name,
and folly is with him' (1 Samuel 25). The tract carried the initials of allies-in-contro-
versy: Francis Glanville and Walter Godbeare (implicated in locking the church
door against Larkham, and the riot), Digory Polewhele (minister of Whitchurch),
William Hore and Nicholas Watts (former church members). Larkham's riposte
singled out Watts as his target, and called him a Judas – *Judas hanging himselfe*.
In a final effort, Watts and company slugged away at Larkham once again with *A
strange metamorphosis in Tavistock, or the Naboth-Nabal improved a Judas*.[134] By
this time it was November 1658. Oliver Cromwell had died in September, and times
were changing.

The end of Larkham's ministry in Tavistock came with the disintegration of the
Protectorate and the Restoration of Charles II. The year 1659 saw political upheaval
after the resignation of Richard Cromwell. With the political clout of Independency
dissipated at a national and local level, Nicholas Watts and his allies made progress.
Watts recruited his step-brother, John Tickel of Exeter – a presbyterian who had
grown up in Tavistock under George Hughes' ministry – to come and preach:

> October 9th [1659] Mr John Tikle brother by the Mother to Watts the Grand
> Rebell had leave to preach in Tavistocke Pulpit & partly upon his principles partly
> upon prejudice & partly upon his brothers interest did not preach Candidly the
> syncere sound word, he flew out into some gnashing expressions &c Lord before
> thy mercifull Majestie I spread it Remember thy greate name & thy poor trampled
> Church.[135]

---

[132] *Naboth*, pp. 22–3, 28. Lewis Stucley, William Bartlet: *CR*.
[133] Diary, fo. 27v.
[134] Larkham's diary entries show how the chronology of the print controversy ran: *Naboth* (September
       1657), fo. 26v; *Tavistock Naboth* (April 1658), fo. 30r; *Judas* (August 1658?), fo. 31v; *Strange
       metamorphosis* (November 1658), fo. 32v.
[135] Diary, fo. 35r. John Tickel (*CR*).

A week later, Larkham found his Wednesday lecture under challenge:

> Watts and his Confederates have sett up a lecture in opposition to me & the Church (as I conceive) and in prosecution of this proud Rebellion, in the Hall of Mrs Glanviles house on Thursdayes; it was begun October. 20 by Mr Gove, & the weeke following Seconded by Mr Polewheele. So let it prosper as it is of God, & may be for the Salvation of poore Soules.[136]

Notwithstanding his pious hope that it might turn out well 'for the Salvation of poore Soules', Larkham tried to stop this fresh initiative. He had no success: in March 1660 the Council of State ordered that the new lecture should continue.[137] On 21 October 1660, 'the Lord's day', Larkham wrote 'I left mine imployment of preaching in feare & upon demand of the Patron.' Then he drew a thick line across the page.[138] In the months leading up to this watershed, and the years beyond, the only documentary evidence about Larkham is the diary. His entries open a window onto a personal experience of defeat and nonconformity, even though he wrote sporadically and left much unsaid.

From parsonage to prison: this was Larkham's fate. In February 1659/60, he noted with disapproval 'bonfires & ringing all day' to celebrate General Monck's restoration of the Long Parliament: 'greate joy amonge all the Rascall crue in the Towne … Polewheele Watts & that crue call it the [most] blessed of newes that ever came to Tavistocke. O Horrible Blasphemy against the Gospel!'[139] Charles II's triumphant return to London in May went unmentioned, but Larkham's knowledge of politics gave import to his note in July1660, 'Newes of A New attempt to remoove me out of Tavistocke … Only God guide me & deliver me.'[140] On 19 October, he appeared before five justices 'about my being outed of the place of preach-[er]'. Nothing was decided but he was bound over to the Assizes. Two days later, 'in feare & upon demand of the Patron', he left his 'imployment of preaching'. As was his habit at significant moments, he turned to verse:

In Patience (Soule) be content, X shall raigne
His Rod & staffe shall me & mine sustaine.
Is living gone? do friends begin to hid[e]?
Do not distrust (take heed) God will provide.
No power or hate can hurt those that are his
to such as trust in God nought comes amisse.

my stumbling reason let faith help me over.
and eke my doubting shaking soule recover
Sathan hath cast many a fie'ry dart.
Which but for faith would surely kill my heart
Concerning ordinances guide me now,
Lest I be found a breaker of my vow.[141]

So much is left out of the record. What conversations and correspondence lay behind 'in feare & upon demand of the Patron'? What financial arrangements were made, what orders given about moving out of the vicarage? In November and December 1660, Larkham's entries continued almost as normal: a gift of chickens, purchases

---

136 Diary, fo. 35v.
137 National Archives, London, SP25/99, fos. 226–225. Larkham Diary, fo. 37r: 'at the meeting of Justices to examine complaints all is husht & the lecture on Wedn[e]sdaies as formerly & I desired to admitt others to preach which I have many yeeres offered & desired'.
138 Diary, fo. 39r.
139 Diary, fo. 36v.
140 Diary, fo. 37r; on the background, Spurr, *The Restoration Church of England*, pp. 29–42.
141 Diary, fo. 39r.

of tobacco and soap, a visit to the barber. He noted Wednesday lecture days (but surely now as auditor not preacher). He gave his usual 6d on 'Communion day', the first Sunday of the month – presumably he felt he could still celebrate the Lord's Supper for the gathered church, since what he had been compelled to resign was his employment as public preacher? However, the changed times show in a couple of entries. On 3 December, 'Mr Robert Bennet Came of purpose to visit me & Comfort me.'[142] A few days later, Larkham had news from Cumberland:

> My son's displac'd, with faith let's feete be shod,
> With Noah & Enoch to walke with God. [143]

Then, dramatically, on 18 January 1660/1 'I was made a prisoner by C. Howard & had a guard of 6 souldiers put into my house & the Munday following was conveyed by six troopers to the Provost Marshall at Exon [*returned not*] untill Aprill 11th 84 Daies in all.'[144] Later, he said he had been 'under imprisonment in both Goales viz at the Castle & Southgate & under the Marshalls power at an Inne in Exeter'.[145]

After Larkham came out of prison, for a few weeks – the only time in twenty years – he abandoned the two-column structure of his diary and wrote across the whole page. He composed a poem to mark his return home and signed it as 'a partiall prisoner & kept out by violence & oppress[ion] of the place of publiq[ue] preaching'.[146] In the entries that followed, Larkham tried to sort out his finances. He was desperate to record his thanks to those who had helped him in prison, but (for once) lost track of the detail:

> Diverse men & Women sent tokens of their love to me the particulars I wrote out
> & cannot now find, the Lord grant that it may be for the furtherance of their profit
> & abound to their account respectively. Thou Lord knowest them by name & what
> they did in way of Communicating with mine affliction And I do humbly beg thy
> Majestie in X Jesus to accept of the worke of faith & labour of love of all those
> thy poore ones that had care of me in that my distress Amen Amen. [147]

He had an attack of the 'most sharpe paines of the chollicke the like paine (I do not remember) I ever felt'. When he revived – 'at 4 of the clocke in the morning arose, read, sang, prayed & praised God with my famely' – he turned to prayer, seeking a similar revival for the godly cause: 'Even so o Lord let it be with thy (seemingly) Dying Church & Cause Revive thy worke &c Amen.' Around this time – perhaps vacating the vicarage at the last moment before the new incumbent arrived – Larkham sent his sister and grandson away and 'May 27th Resolved upon giving over houskeeping'. On 31 May 1661, 'Mr Browne ... with his wife & 3 chilldren came to Tavistocke, great joy ... manifestations of it by ridinge runninge ringing among superstitious ignorant prophane people.' When Browne did not preach on his first Sunday, Larkham did: 'I went with Some scores in the afternoone to Sanford

---

142   Diary, fo. 39v.
143   Diary, fo. 39v.
144   Diary, fo. 39v.
145   Diary, fo. 42v.
146   Diary, fo. 40r.
147   Diary, fo. 40r.

Spiny & there preached the word of God.'[148] In the diary he recorded prayers and hopes: 'O that God would once againe once againe restore the glory to England. Amen Amen Amen'; 'What is the signe that I shall goe againe to the house of the Lord?'; 'July 19[th] in letters from London ... hope was manifested of some indulgence to be granted to the people of God'. In August, he appeared at Exeter Assizes but his case was put off until the following Lent. 'Hearing of Waite laid for me I Rode toward Cumberland where the Lord preserved me in health & saf[e]ty.' The decision to go North was informed by rumours of greater freedom up there: 'my sone Condy writes from London that my son George had written to him out of Cumberland that he hath not missed to preach not so much as one Lords day since he was ejected'.[149]

Larkham always left the diary in Tavistock for safe-keeping as a record of his life there – he never penned a word out of town – so a long gap ensued before his next entry: 'I Returned to Tavistocke March the first 166½ And am now living in the house of my Son Condy together with My Wife.'[150] Here, on 18 August 1662, he composed a verse for his 61st birthday. This happened to fall on a Monday, one day after a significant moment – the last 'Lord's Day' on which nonconformists could preach freely. The axe of the Act of Uniformity was raised high, ready to fall on Sunday 24 August. Larkham looked to the week ahead:

> The saddest weeke that ever England saw
> Witnesses slaine by vertue of a Law.
> Many fall off in this sad day of triall,
> God's cause meetes now with many a deniall.
> All proves not gold that glister'd and was specious,
> All are not found to have that faith that's pretious.
> Yesterday ended godly men's preaching
> that do refuse traditions of men's teaching.[151]

Larkham's life from then on was constrained by the conflict between his principles and what the authorities would allow. He lived in the household of Daniel and Jane Condy and their swarms of children until July 1664, when he moved out to make space. But in truth he was hardly there. An evocative entry in September 1662 recorded that Miriam Brownsdon gave him 10s, 'in acknowledgment of her duty though I could not do the office of a Pastor'. This was his first income since the previous March. Then in February 1662/3 he had news of a warrant out against him and fled. Apart from a handful of days in April 1663, he was away from Tavistock until April 1664. His whereabouts are unknown. The diary is a blank, except that he gave thanks later for 'the Lords preserving me now a whole yeare since my last returne (after a long absence) for feare of enimies'.[152]

---

148   Diary, fos. 41r, 41v. Sampford Spiney is a parish four miles south-east of Tavistock. Browne was succeeded as vicar in 1662 by Thomas Glanvill: Woodcock, *Tavistock*, p. 24. Glanvill (never mentioned by Larkham) was no doubt from the same prominent Tavistock family as Larkham's arch-critic Francis Glanville, who had died in August 1658 (Tavistock PR, Diary, fo. 31r).

149   Diary, fos. 42r, 42v.

150   Diary, fo. 42v.

151   Diary, fo. 43v.

152   Diary, fo. 43v, 46r. For the wider context, see Spurr, *The Restoration Church of England*, pp. 42–61.

A fleeting peace came between July 1664 and January 1666. Larkham furnished new lodgings with bookshelves and household stuff. He embarked on a fresh venture, an apothecary shop. Nothing is known of what Tavistock people made of their fiery preacher turned pharmacist. Larkham signed up at first for a half-share (and paid 9d for a glass of sack 'at the conclusion' to seal the deal). Later, he took over the shop completely and ran the business with his grandson Tom Miller. At this point the diary is full of notes about apothecary utensils and ingredients.[153]

The peace was transient. In May 1665, Larkham heard he had been excommunicated: 'yong Preston of Maritavy officiating at Tavestocke pronounced me Excom: by authoritie from yong Fulwood now Ar[ch]Deacon of Totnes. Consider O Lord these fooles and pitty them for they know not what they doe. Suffer not thy greate name to be (SO) taken in vaine.'[154] When the Five Mile Act came into force that autumn, nonconformists like Larkham risked a fine of £40 if they strayed within five miles of a former parish. So the apothecary shop in Tavistock had to be handed over to others. In January 1666 Larkham put some of his utensils into store. He bought a horse – a clear sign of plans to travel – and disappeared. He left the notebook in Tavistock and made entries on brief visits home in May and July 1666, then nothing until April 1667, and nothing again until that autumn.[155]

'Having wandred under the hand of providence many yeares I came Sept. 30th 1667 to Take a Chamber to live in Tavistocke': so Larkham marked his return to the town.[156] His entries became more fulsome again after December 1667, when the earl of Clarendon's fall eased pressure on nonconformists. In January 1667/8, Larkham noted 6d given 'at the ordinance of the Lord's Supper', the first time he mentioned communion in many a year. In March, he conducted a baptism. In July, he mentioned 'three church meetings'. On several occasions, he recorded that the deacons brought him money.[157] By this point, his entries were irregular and incomplete, but even so the fragments tell a story.

For the final time, in August 1669, Larkham 'gave over housekeepinge & went to live with my Son Condy'. The Tavistock parish register records his burial on 23 December 1669. A story survives (though no evidence exists to prove it one way or the other) that the earl of Bedford, as patron, gave permission for Larkham to be buried in the chancel, a customary resting-place for vicars of the parish. Larkham's last entry in the manuscript was 6d 'laid out to the barber'.

A final twist of the tale suggests that the wounds of Tavistock strife healed up somewhat after 1660, at least among the godly who had fallen out so spectacularly in the 1650s. In the 1670s, Nicholas Watts – Larkham's ferocious opponent in Tavistock's battle of books – set up a trust to distribute religious literature to the poor of the town, 'that by bestowing of … good books, I may testify true repentance and make some amends for those wretched idle pamphlets wrote in my youthful years for my own Vindication wherein I stuck not to cast Dirt on others for the Clearing

153   Diary, fo. 44r, 44v; Appendix 3.
154   Diary, fo. 46v. The Diocese of Exeter's Episcopal Return, 1665, reported that in 'Tavistock … Tho: Larkeham thence ejected … stands Excommunicate'. Lyon Turner, *Original records*, I, p. 179.
155   Diary, fo. 47v; Appendix 3.
156   Diary, fo. 47v.
157   Diary, fos. 48r, 48v.

of myself'. Not long before this, Watts (Watts the 'Judas', Watts the 'Grand Rebel') helped to make an inventory of Larkham's estate – the final reckoning, diary and all.[158]

IV

Thomas Larkham is long dead, but lives on in Tavistock folklore with a divided reputation. For some, he is a rascal vicar who turned religious life upside down in Cromwell's time. For others he is something of a hero, founder of the Christian community which today is Tavistock United Reformed Church. The historical notes provided in St Eustachius, Tavistock Parish Church, tell a different story from the display about Larkham in the URC church hall. Up in Cumbria, too, Cockermouth URC church remembers Larkham and takes pride in its history: a banner over the church gate is emblazoned with the date of its foundation, '1651'. The Tavistock and Cockermouth URC congregations are two of only a handful in England which have a continuous history from the 'parish congregationalism' of the 1650s. Thomas Larkham pioneered both these local reformations. This volume has taken shape on the eve of 2012, the 350th anniversary of the 1662 Act of Uniformity. It has been interesting to see how, in Tavistock now, the 'winners' of 1662 still have their names etched on the street-map (Glanville Road, Watts Road). The Glanville family influence continued, and Nicholas Watts left bequests which benefit Tavistock people and Tavistock churches to this day. It has also been interesting to see how the apparent 'losers' of 1662, Larkham's gathered church, have survived and flourished. In various places of worship over 350 years, this congregation has moved in a small circle around the parish church – only ever a few steps away from the place where their separate history began in Larkham's time.

---

[158] Diary, fos. 48v, 49r; Devon Record Office, Exeter, W1258M/LP/9/3, 'A copy of the will of Mr Nicholas Watts of Tavistock dated Feb 17th 1674'; A. G. Matthews's Notes of Nonconformist Ministers' Wills, Dr Williams's Library, London, MS 38.59, fo. 611. Watts also named several Larkham supporters (Daniel and David Condy, Stephen Rundle, Richard Hitchens, John Sheere. George Oxenham) as trustees of funds for godly ministers and 'honest and poor' Tavistock people. Nowadays, the Brownsdon & Tremayne Estate Charity administers 'Nicholas Watts' Gift'.

Ætatis Suæ 50=1652
May 4°

The true Effigies of Thomas Larkham,
Minister of the Gospell at Tavistock
in Devon .
T. Cross sculpsit

1 The frontispiece of Larkham's first publication, *The wedding-supper* (London, 1652), by a leading engraver, Thomas Cross. Larkham's book of sermons – with its fine portrait and a dedication to parliament – was intended to impress. Larkham wanted to show the injustice of claims that he delivered 'such unsufferable sermons as the like have not been preached', and to gain support from Commonwealth committees and local allies for his work as 'Minister of the Gospell at Tavistock'. In his diary, he recorded how he distributed 300 bound copies of the book and dozens more 'in the quire' (unbound).

2 Diary, fo. 'W'r. Halfway down this folio, Larkham made his first entry in the manuscript, in June 1647, about money owed by 'Mr Obed Wills, Schoolmaster at Colonell Blounts'. This places Larkham in the orbit of the Kentish parliamentarian Thomas Blount, near Greenwich. This particular folio also illustrates the document's layered history, because it contains the work of two other writers. At the top, c. 1597, the original owner George Lane – a London scrivener who later became minister of East Greenwich – wrote a list of clients whose surnames started with 'W' (which is why Larkham chose this page to record Wills's debt). At the foot, after 1670, Larkham's son George used the remaining space: a nonconformist like his father, he inherited the notebook, took it to Cumberland, and kept it for farm records, letter drafts and sermon notes. So the manuscript usually called 'the diary of Thomas Larkham' was actually filled up by three clerics, in diverse parts of England, at different points in the seventeenth century.

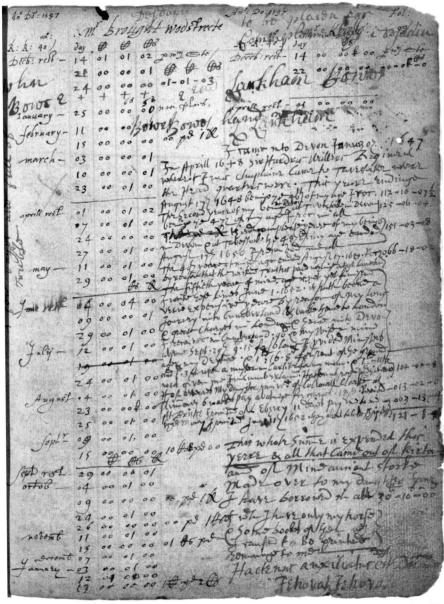

3 Diary, fo. 9r. Here, in June 1652, Larkham recalled his first arrival in Tavistock with
Sir Hardress Waller's regiment in April 1648, and took stock of his finances after a
spell away from the town. He had just returned from Cumberland (where he had gone
to preach in 1651 after his parish opponents restricted his pay). He had come back to
outface his critics, having secured endorsements for his ministry from the Common-
wealth authorities in London. On this particular folio he wrote around Lane's earlier
notes – as a rule he simply wrote over the top of them. Near the foot he summed up
with one of his favourite phrases, 'Hactenus auxiliatus est Dominus', echoing 1 Samuel
7:12 'Hitherto hath the Lord helped us' (KJV).

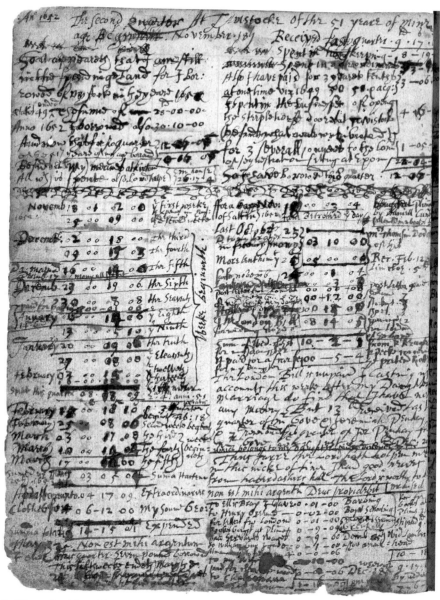

4 Diary, fo. 10v. This folio illustrates Larkham's peculiar method of marking time: the heading of the page proclaims the start of the 'second quarter' of 1652 on 18 November. He reckoned the year in quarters from his birthday on 18 August – that was when the new year began for him. His idiosyncratic calendar shaped the diary from start to finish. This folio also shows how Larkham wrote over Lane's earlier text and amended it to suit his purpose: for example, at the top he changed '1597' to 1652, and lower down he re-used some of the figures. In the entries here, Larkham fretted about his extravagance: 'Daughter married … mony all spent' (on wedding clothes from London). His despair evaporated when the Committee for Advance of Money awarded him £100 held back by his enemies – 'in this nicke of time I had good newes … The Lord is worthy to be praised.' His diary often mentioned his children but rarely his wife: 'O My poore Rocky Untoward Wife! O my unsuitablenes to her! Lord helpe' (fo. 32v).

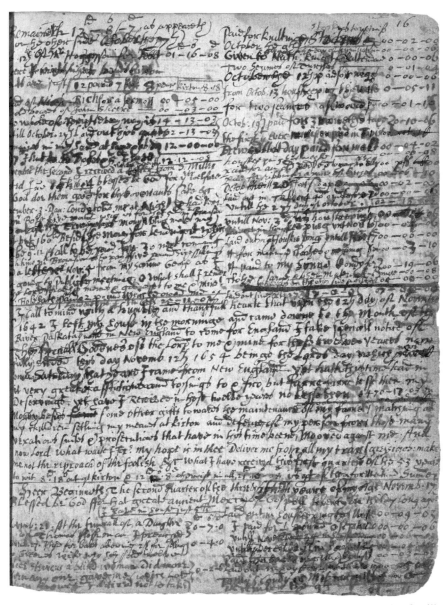

5 Diary, fo. 16r. Here, in the autumn of 1654, Larkham's entries followed a familiar pattern. He wrote mostly in two columns, with (broadly) income on the left and expenses on the right. As was his habit, he interrupted the columns to make a significant entry across the folio. He recalled the day he set sail from America, an anniversary he often marked with pleasure: 'I call to mind with a humble and thankful hearte that upon the 12th day of November 1642 I left my house in the morninge and came downe to the Mouth of the River Paskataquacke in New England to come for England.'

6 Diary, fo. 39r. Larkham was evicted from office as vicar of Tavistock in October 1660, and this folio covers that period. Near the top he recorded 'newes of a Warrant out against me'. Halfway down, he wrote: 'The Lords day Oct. 21. I left mine imployment of preaching in feare & upon demand of the Patron' and underneath drew a line. Before and after this watershed, as was often his practice, he expressed hopes and fears in verse. An entry on 7 November shows how the structures of the gathered church, which had strengthened within the parish in the late 1650s, provided support once his income as public preacher was cut off: 'the Deacons brought to me 01–00–00'.

7 Diary, fo. 40r. In April 1661, coming back to Tavistock after several months in prison, Larkham took up his pen afresh and wrote a poem which began 'Farewell accounts about worldly affaires / Hell hath deflow'rd the earth farwell those cares.' Alongside it, he put 'Written by Thomas Larkham (a partiall prisoner & kept out by violence and oppress[ion] of the place of publiq[ue] preaching).' The shake-up in his circumstances affected the character of his entries: less financial detail, more agonized musing. For a while he abandoned his custom of making entries in two columns and wrote across the page.

NABOTH,

In a

Narrative and Complaint

Of the

Church of God which is in Chrift Jefus,

AT

Taviftock in *Devon*; and efpecially of and concerning Mr. *Thomas Larkham*, Publick Teacher and
Paftor of a defpifed oppreffed handful of- the fheep
of Chrift there;

Humbly prefented to the Churches of Chrift, and to
the Magiftracy and Miniftry of the Nation
in this Common-wealth.

---

*So I returned and confidered all the oppreffions that are done under
the Sun, and behold the tears of fuch as were oppreffed, and they
had no comforter : and on the fide of their oppreffors there was
power, but they had no comforter,* Ecclef. 4. 1.

And the men of Belial *witneffed againft him, even againft* Naboth
in the prefence of his people, faying, Naboth *did blafpheme God
and the.King,* 1 King. 21. 13.

LONDON,

Printed for the ufe of the Author, 1 6 5 7.

8 *Naboth* started the acrimonious pamphlet exchange between
Larkham and his Tavistock opponents in the late 1650s. The title-
page implies authorship by the church, but Larkham's hand in it is
clear. The only copy known to survive is in the Wallace Notestein
Collection at the Library of the College of Wooster, Ohio.

THE
Taviſtocke Naboth
PROVED
NABAL:
IN AN
A N S VV E R
Unto a
SCANDALOUS NARRATIVE
Publiſhed by
Mr Tho: Larkham in the Name,
(but without the Conſent) of the
Church of *Taviſtocke* in D E V O N.

Humbly preſented to the Churches of Chriſt, the Magi-
ſtracy, and the Miniſtry of the Nation in this
COMMONWEALTH.

Francis Glanvile . Diggory polwheel . Walter godbear . Niccolas watts . William Hore .
By F. G. D. P. W. G. N. W. W. H. &c.
Francis Glanville Diggory Polwheele . Walter Godbear Nicolas watts. w^m Hore .

Prov. 18. 17. *He that is firſt in his own cauſe ſeemeth juſt, but his neighbour cometh and ſearcheth him out.*

Duæ res ſunt conſcientia & fama, conſcientia neceſſaria eſt tibi, fama proximo
tuo, qui confidens conſcientiæ negligit famam crudelis eſt. *Aug.*

LONDON,
Printed for the uſe of the Authors.
1658.

9 *Tavistocke Naboth* provided a sharp riposte to *Naboth*. Larkham
called it 'this heape of trash' (Diary, fo. 30r). On the title-page of the
copy in the Bodleian, pictured above, an unknown person filled out
the initials of the authors as 'Francis Glanvile. Diggory Polwheel.
Walter Godbear. Nicholas Watts. William Hore'.

J U D A S Hanging *Himfelfe* :

O R

N A B O T H s

FALSE ACCUSER

INTANGLED

in his own

TESTIMONY.

Set forth in a Rejoinder of the Church of Chrift in *Taviftock,* *Devon,* to a fcurrillous pamphlet publifhed lately by N. *W*, *&c.* once a Member but fince a perfecutor of the faid Church.

Written chiefly for the undeceiving of fuch as have been or may be too credulous thereof; by giving them a Charaéter of the man in his fundry contradiétions, flanders, lies and untruths (befides opprobrious and uncivil language) which fwarm, for multitude like the frogs of *Ægypt,almoft* in every page of his book.

Thy tongue devifeth mifchiefs, like a fharp rayfor working deceitfully. Thou loveft evil more then good, and lying rather then to fpeak Righteoufneffe. Thou loveft all devouring words, O thou deceitful tongue, Pfal 5 2.2,3,4.
*Out of thine own mouth will I judge thee, thou wicked fervant,*Luke 1 9.2 2.
And *Judas alfo-.. --ftood with them,* John 18. 5.

Amara perfecutio in cruore martyrum, amarior in pugna Hæreticorum, amariffima in malis moribus domefticorum. *Ad :* Omnis malus aut ideo vivit ut corrigatur, aut ideo ut per illum bonus Exerceatur. *Aug,*

Printed for the ufe of the Authors. 1658.

10 *Judas hanging himselfe* initiated the next round of the controversy – a pro-Larkham reply to *Tavistocke Naboth*. The 'Judas' was Nicholas Watts, once a leader in the gathered church but now identified by Larkham as one of his fiercest critics. This tract, like *Naboth*, claimed to be written by the church, not by Larkham. Only two copies are known to survive: one in the Wallace Notestein Collection at the Library of the College of Wooster, Ohio, the other at University College London.

A Strange
METAMORPHOSIS
I N
TAVISTOCK:
O R
THE *NABAL-NABOTH*
IMPROVED
A JUDAS.

Set forth in a Reply to a fcurrilous Pamphlet, called
Judas, &c. whofe Atteftations are invalidated, contradictions
cleared, and lyes put up again into his own Bag To the
acquitting of the innocent, the manifeftation of the guilty,
and the clear fatisfaction of all fuch as would be informed in
thofe Tranfactions.

---

*Behold he travaileth with iniquity, and hath conceived mifchief,
and hath brought forth a falfhood.*
*He made a pit, and digged it, and is fallen into the ditch which
he made.*
*His mifchief fhall return upon his own head, and his violent deal-
ing fhall come down upon his own pate,* Pfal. 7. 14,15,16.
*Anfwer a fool according to his folly, left he be wife in his own con-
ceit.*

---

*Honefta fama alterum patrocinium eft, & fama pari paffu cum vita am-
bulat.* Auguft.

Aprill 27 **LONDON,**

11 *A strange metamorphosis*, the reply to *Judas*, came from the pen of
Watts and his allies. This anti-Larkham tract had the last word in print.
Not long after came the Restoration of Charles II. In a turnabout which
shows how rifts among the godly in the 1650s could heal in the face of
common adversity after 1660, Nicholas Watts repented of his 'wretched'
pamphlets and served as one of the two overseers of Thomas Larkham's
estate – diary and all – after Larkham's death in December 1669.

12 This detail from an engraving of Tavistock in 1741 centres on the parish church. The vicarage Larkham occupied is in the lower right-hand corner (marked '7'), with a riverside garden and steps down to the Tavy. It no longer stands: that part of the town was swept away in the nineteenth century, in a bold redevelopment by the duke of Bedford which created today's Town Hall and Pannier Market.

1

THE DIARY OF THOMAS LARKHAM, 1647–1669

Early entries

Deaths

[fo. 'H'v][1]

Thomas mine Eldest sonne Died Feb 14th 1648 & left [M]ary his wife ˆa widowˆ
 & one sonne & one Daughter viz Thomas & Mary.[2]

Joseph Miller Lieutenant in Ireland Died May the 8th 1656 & left mine eldest
 daughter Patience ˆa widowˆ & one son & 3 daughters living viz Thomas,
 Mary, Jane, and Anne

> The Lord direct me concerning them

Such as remaine alive of these poore ones
Lord pitty and enrole among thy sonnes.[3]

and Debts

[fo. 'W'r]

		£ s d
June. 1647.	Mr Obed Wills Schoolmaster at Collonell Blounts oweth me for the bookes he bought[4]	2-0-0

[fo. 'G'r]

George Gale oweth me October 4th 1647 upon account *Goinge* for Phisicke for Jane[5]	*0-1-0*

---

[1]   When Thomas Larkham acquired George Lane's manuscript notebook, this was the first empty folio.
   He left most of the page blank. In 1670–1 his son George Larkham (*CR*) filled it up.

[2]   It is not clear when Larkham wrote this, but by February 1648/9 he had been in Tavistock almost
   a year. He brought up his grandson Thomas as an orphan. The two Marys are not mentioned again.
   Larkham dealt with Thomas's uncle on his mother's side, a London merchant, Richard Covert (fo.
   43v; also fos. 11v, 14r, 14v, 15r, 16v). In his will, proved 9 March 1669/70, Larkham remarked that
   his grandson 'hath been very chargeable to me from the time of his birth … by the unkindnesses
   & bad dealing of his mothers relations': A.G. Matthews's Notes of Nonconformist Ministers' Wills,
   Dr Williams's Library, London, MS 38.59, fos. 607–11 (the original in the Devon Record Office
   perished during the Blitz).

[3]   Added later in a smaller hand.

[4]   This is Larkham's earliest entry, made before he came to Tavistock, soon after he acquired George
   Lane's manuscript (a story told in the Introduction). Lane had cut the edges of early folios to make
   a tabbed alphabetical index of clients, for his work as a scrivener. Larkham used 'W' to note a debt
   from 'Obed Wills': perhaps Obadiah Wills (*CR*) who, like Larkham, came from Dorset. Wills had
   recently studied at Exeter College, Oxford, where Larkham's son George matriculated on 9 April
   1647. Colonel Thomas Blount (*ODNB*) was a landowner in north Kent and colonel of a Kentish
   regiment. Larkham sent him a copy of his *Wedding-supper* (see Appendix 1).

[5]   Larkham used Lane's 'G' folio. Gale has not been identified. Jane is probably Larkham's younger
   daughter. Besides these two entries about debts, and perhaps the note about the death of his son
   Thomas (fo. 'H'v), Larkham made no use of the manuscript until February 1650/1 (fo. 2v).

18 August 1650 – 17 August 1652

[fo. 2v]

August. 18th 1650 beginneth the 49th yeare of Mine age[1]

Received the two first quarters Ended Feb. 17th	£40-10s-8d
Spent in that time in meate & drink cloathes and maintenance of chilldren & chilldrens chilldren & in gifts to My sisters at Lyme the sume of	39-18- 4
so there remaineth in my hand. Feb. 18. 1650	00-12- 4
which was delivered for houskeeping the first weeke until Feb. 22 12s 4d	

Of Nicholas fudge I had (I take it) halfe a Pistole[2] in Gold	7s-6d

Delivered to my daughter Feb. 28th towards housekeepinge for the second weeke	06-0
and the other 18d of the fornamed 7-6d being changed was spent in smal things	01-6
	All even
Barth: Rundle sent me by Richard Peeke. 2s-6d which I delivered for spending Money to my sonne George who came from Oxford this weeke to visite me[3]	02-6

1651[4] Anthony Knighton gave me March. 28	4s-4d	his daughter buried[5]
March. 30. Mr Saxfen sent me in a letter	5- 0	
Aprill 3rd John Brownsdon gave me. 2 peices of silver one 4-4 & the other 2s-6d	6-10	
Received of Mr Hogeson Aprill 8th for rent	6- 8	
Received of Mrs Edgcombe to be allowed in my stipend whereof 28s was paid to Nich Watts	£5- [0- 0]	
the other 4-15 I had Aprill 18th of Mr Hogeson whereof Ed. Condy had £4	£4-15s-[0]	
Aprill 18 of Thomasin dodge widdow.	5s-[0]	

---

1 Larkham organized entries in quarters, starting from his birthday on 18 August. Here he made a formal heading for a new year but started with a summary of the year to date, the two quarters to 17 February 1650/1. He added some of the material on this folio in retrospect, after notes of income and expenses from the start of the new quarter on 18 February (fo. 3r). The initial entries run across the whole folio, starting below George Lane's entries in 1597.

2 'Pistole': a Spanish gold double-escudo, or a similar coin (*OED*). Tavistock's proximity to the port of Plymouth meant Spanish and French coins sometimes circulated in the local economy.

3 George Larkham, at this point a student at Exeter College, Oxford. He graduated BA in 1650 (*CR*).

4 Larkham marked the start of 1651: the new year, old style, had begun on 25 March. From here the entries are in two columns, rather erratically divided into income and expenses. His system settled down as time went on.

5 Tavistock PR, burials: 28 March 1651, Mary, daughter of Anthony Knighton.

[fo. 2v]

Paid Dinahs wages[1]	09- 0
Spent in provision	07- 2
Paid Wife & Jane[2]	18- 0
April 9th Given to my Wife to bestow about her selfe	05- 0
Spent in houskeepinge untill friday night Aprill 11th whereof for mine	
garden 1-6 carryinge dung into it. 4d & seedes 1s-2d [3]	13- 8
Paid about Jeanes[4] gowne	19- 6
Paid for carriage from Oxford[5]	02-10
Laid out untill April. 18th	12- 8
paid for malte wheate & butter at one time to Mrs Edgcombe	11- 6
	6-01- 8[6]
paid which was borrowed of Watts & Condy	5-08- 0

---

1   Dinah Woodman, the Larkhams' maid.
2   His wife Patience and daughter Jane.
3   This entry, which runs across whole folio, is the first of many references to Larkham's garden.
4   Jane Miller, Larkham's grand-daughter: this tallies with further entries on fo. 3r. She had been staying in Tavistock at this point (her parents were in Ireland where her father was serving with Cromwell's forces).
5   For his son George.
6   Larkham's reckoning is usually unnervingly accurate, but it is hard to make sense of this interim total.

Receipts Hactenus[1] *last past* quarter 13-15-2   rest.[2] April 21. $\boxed{\text{£2- 5s- 6d}}$

[fo. 3r][3]

Feb. 18th. Delivered yesterday to the younger sonne of *Barlett*[4] to
   be delivered to George at Oxford £5[.] for carriage of it & of a
   letter paid 1s-10d   05-01-10
paid for makinge Ja: Mulls[5] gowne to William Baker   00-02-06
Paid John Cudlips Bill for her Gowne & for cloth for coifes[6]   00-15-06
Paid for a paire of bodies and for cast[i]le soape to give away[7] 00-02-02
Given to Edmond Condy & Stephen Bloy going to Oxford   00-02-00
                                                                   06-04-00
                                                        Borrowed of Cash[8]

[fo. 3v]

	£ s d
Laid out last quarter for a brewinge Pan, a salt, a Pestle & Mortar	2- 6-0
& for canvas for 4 Pillowties[9]	0- 5-4
Barber March 1°	0- 0-6[10]
paid March. 4th for cleaving of wood	0- 2-6
Laid out March 7th to Dinah for to provide victualls & pay for Corne	0-13-4
& Malt to Mrs Edgcombe	0- 5-6
Laid out this weeke ended March 14th	0-10-6
Laid out untill March 22nd	0-16-0
Delivered to George March 20th going to Oxford (whereof £4 was	
borrowed of Ed Condy & the other 20s out of my stocke)	5-00-0
Laid out untill March 28. friday	0- 8-0
	10- 7-8
othersid[11]	6- 4-0

whereof £4 was borrowed of Ed Conday
   and 12-11-8 of the stocke money belonging to Jane[12]   16-11-8

---

[1] 'Hactenus': hitherto.
[2] 'Rest': the balance remaining (*OED* 'rest', *n*³).
[3] Larkham started a new quarter, 18 February 1650/1, reckoning from his birthday on 18 August. Most
    of the folio is taken up with George Lane's entries in 1597.
[4] Not identified: perhaps related to Thomas Bartlet (buried 3 May 1647, Tavistock PR). Typically,
    Larkham has not crossed right through the double 't' (the manuscript reads 'Barlelt').
[5] Jane Miller's.
[6] 'Coif': a close-fitting cap worn by women indoors or under a bonnet (*OED*).
[7] 'Paire of bodies'; a corset or bodice; 'Castile soap'; a fine soap made with olive-oil and soda (*OED*).
[8] Written alongside this column of figures, upwards and sideways.
[9] 'Pillowtie': a regional word in South-West England for 'pillowcase' (*OED*).
[10] The first of many sixpences paid to the barber.
[11] 'From the other side': £6-4s-0d added from the calculation of expenses on fo. 3r.
[12] 'Stock': in a general sense, capital; here in the particular sense of an endowment for a son or dowry
    for a daughter (*OED* 'stock' n¹, 48c). Larkham set aside money for each of his children. He paid Jane
    Larkham's 'portion' after her marriage to Daniel Condy.

11- 9 -8[1]

[fo. 3r]

Feb. 18th 1650　　　　　　　　　　　　　　My stocke is £12 11 8d

[fo. 3v]

1650 Gifts From Feb.17[2]

Roger Jakeman shots[3]	0-0- 4
Stephen Bloy[s] Father a Capon	0-1- 0
Feb. 21. Elizabeth Toller dish of butter	0-0- 8
of Richard Keagle a Turky & another fowle both worth	0-2- 0
March. 1. W. Keagle sent Rosting Pig	0-1- 6
5[th] John Trowt 2 seames[4] of wood	0-2- 0
March. 11[th] Thomas Pennington Porke	0-2- 0
20[th] Mr Leere ½ bushell of wheate	0-6- 8
28 Mrs Edgcombe butter	0-0- 4
Aprill. 11 Mrs Eliz: Row a loine of veale	0-1- 4
April 17. Marg. Condy shoulder pork & puds[5]	0-1- 2
April 19 T. Pen[ning]gt[o]ns wife pork	0-1- 0
Judith Liar 10 bunnes	0-0-10
Jeremiah Penny a limon & an orange	0-0- 3
	1-1- 1

received this quarter de Novo 13-2-10d
rest[6] last quarter 12s-4d

So I have borrowed in all of my stocke £28 and 2s

---

[1]　The foot of the folio is now worn. Larkham entered the total of his quarterly expenses to date (£11-9s-8d) opposite income (£13-15s-2s) and the remainder (£2-5s-6d).

[2]　From the start of the new quarter, 18 February 1650/1.

[3]　'Shot': a share of the bill at a tavern, or payment for drinks (*OED*, which cites Oliver Heywood's diary, 1676, for a reference to 'shots' at '2d a peece').

[4]　'Seam', a horse-load (*OED*): Larkham's usual measure for deliveries of wood and 'turfs' (peat) for fuel.

[5]　'Pork and puddings'. 'Hog's pudding' was 'the entrail of a hog variously stuffed, according to locality' (*OED*).

[6]　'Rest': the remainder (this tallies with an entry on fo. 2v).

March. 31. I had a letter from George that he had received cleare

at Kirton[1]	13-12-4
and had borrowed of Mr Tapper at Exeter which I pay to Nich: Watts	1-08-0
which in all maketh the sume of	15- 0-4

So George had £5 ut supra of me & this 15-0-4	the sume of all borrowed of
which mak[e]th in all £20 & 4d	my *stocke* 31-12-0

Besides 2s-2d. I find George hath mistaken & received more
then he writt & 2s he tooke out of his mothers rent[2]

So I have borrowed in al of my sto[c]ke	25-06-0 is my stocke which I
& of Edmond Condy £4 of my Daughter	have borrowed
Jeane 10s & eight for her mother (by	
deduction of 2s George was willed to stopp	
for a gift[3]) and as I said above £4 to	Wife & daughter are paid 18s
Edmond Condy & 28s to Nicholas Watts[.]	N. Watts paid 28s
so I am indebted £6-6s & £25-6s	paid Ed. Condy £4-6-6s paid[4]

Aprill 7th received of Mr *Gove* out of my sto[c]ke £1
April. 19th Sold 9 yards of stuffe[5] to Mr Edgcombe which is part of my stocke
for 36s

and *so* remaines on the forgoing leafe 2-5-6 which is of receipts remaining
unspent April 21[6]

[fo. 4r]

	£ s [d]
Remaines clear unto me May 5th when I was about to depart[7]	3-17-06[8]
received of William Webb for my wood	4-00- 0
Itur versus Londin[i]u[m] dederunt no[n]nullis Maii 6° circa[9]	00-17-06

---

1 'Kirton': Crediton, Devon, where Larkham rented out property and land which had come to him by marriage.
2 Larkham usually gave his wife 10s a quarter from the Kirton rents: her gift of 2s from it to George is noted below. Alongside this are a few illegible words and deleted numbers.
3 This is the 2s Patience Larkham gave to George (brackets added, for clarity).
4 A later note of sums repaid to his wife and daughter, Watts and Condy.
5 'Stuff': woven material (*OED*). Larkham, son of a linen draper, knew the value of cloth.
6 This is a reference to the £2-5s-6d remaining on 21 April, noted on fo. 2v.
7 Soon after this Larkham travelled to Cumberland, where he stayed until June 1652. First he made a journey to settle business in Crediton and Exeter, returning home on 9 May.
8 Larkham jotted at the top of the folio 'I had 3-17-6'.
9 The meaning is not clear. The sense seems to be 'Travelling toward London they gave for several things on May 6th about 00-17-06'.

April 23rd £5-1s-6 in house[1]

Spent unto April 25 (whereof 6s was for Mault)	0-14- 0
bestowed in a suite for Tom Larkam	0-10-10
spent the weeke followinge (whereof 3s 6d for wheate) untill May 3rd	0-12- 8
	1-17- 6
Tho: fleshman gave me	5s
of stock money for Mr Gove paid upon account May 2nd when I	
paid all due to him &c	8s- 6d

	£ s d
Received this ¼ In all[2]	13-7-10
Spent this quarter	38-0-10
whereof £20 was lent to my sonne George at his	
departure to be paid to me [or] mine Executo[r]s againe.	

I borrowed of my stock this quarter £24-13 shillings

[fo. 4r]

---

[1]   'In house': ready money.
[2]   Larkham summed up here to 17 May 1651, the end of the quarter, but his list of expenses for early
      May continued on fo. 4r.

Received at Crediton May 7th 1651 Inprimis of Henry Jussin for one
    quarters rent due 13th of March 1651[1]   01-10- 0
at the same time of Zachery Rogers for 2 quarters end December. 25th   00-10- 0
Also I had of Wid: Heywod   00-06- 0
of H. Jussine for Widdow *Herniman*   0-04- 0
of J Middleton for *Yanacot*[2] rent   0-04- 4
of Mrs Cole for ¼ ended March 25^{th3}   0-10- 0
                    sume of what I had is   11-19- 4

Bestowed in a horse[4]   09-19- 0
Sent to Lyme to my sisters   01-00-00
The smith and sadler had[5]   00-02-06
Gifts to 2 Boyes &c   00-00-08
To be devided among the poore when I was on horsebacke   00-02- 0
brought home from Exeter only   00-03-04
bestowed in a knife at Exeter   00-01-00
Spent in the citty of Exon   00-06-01
spent at Morton[6] [coming] Homw[a]rd   00-01-00
Spent the night & morning at Kirton   00-03-09
                                       11-19-04

My wife received of Mr Gove in mine absence to Exeter & spent   0-10- 0
May the 14th Received of Mr Gove which was for rent the last
    weekes of the ¼ ended Saturday being the 17th day of May[7]   0-10- 0
together with 3s-4 brought from Exon.

Received 18-5-4 by addition

Spent in all 51-00-02 whereof £30 George & horse
[*illegible*] spent otherwis £21-00-02[8]

---

[1] 'Inprimis': first of all, in particular.
[2] Not identified.
[3] In dealings with others (especially about rents and wages) Larkham used conventional quarter days
    rather than dividing the year from his birthday on 18 August.
[4] A major expense, no doubt in preparation for his journey to Cumberland.
[5] This entry, and the one above, tallies with his rough notes opposite.
[6] Moortown, to the west of Tavistock, on the edge of Dartmoor.
[7] Larkham reverted to his personal custom of reckoning quarters from his birthday, 18 August.
[8] He has jotted down other figures but their connexion to the text is unclear.

sent to Lyme 20s May 8th from Exeter[1]
spent in Kirton May 6th & 7th 1651 3s & 5d
And at Exeter 6s paid a knife 1s
at Moorton[2] 1s May 9th
so I came home
I gave Among the poore at Tavistocke when I tooke horse 2s
gifts to Diers boy And also Will Giles boy each 4d in all 8d
sadler & smith 2s 6d

all stocke money except Webb £4

May 9th 1651 remained at my returne   20- 3- 4
                                                             1-16-08
                                                            22- 0- 0[3]

spent of my stocke in all hactenus[4] besids horse 22-14-10

---

[1] Lyme Regis, Dorset. The notes on the rest of this folio are jottings (in a central column) for entries
     on the left.
[2] Moortown, near Tavistock.
[3] In the right margin Larkham added up figures, but their connexion to the text is unclear.

6-4-0	16-11-8		17-10- 0
2-6-0	12-14-4		03-04- 4
8-4	29-06-0		20-14- 4
8-18-4		I havinge of old money	0- 7- 6
13-4			21-01-10
9-11-8			

[4] 'Hactenus': hitherto, thus far.

[fo. 4v][1]

The 49th year of mine age ended August 17. 1651 In which I Received in all
 £66-18s-02d
I had nothinge out of the sheafe of Lamerton this yeare yet was it a chargeable
 yeere by meanes of My sonne George to whom (beside his expences in Oxford
 & charges of degree of Bachelor) I gave £20 at his going to Cumberland[2]

August 1651
Borrowed in all of my stocke 28-00-00
I have no wood as yet this yeare.

August 1652
Borrowed of my stocke £30-10s-00d

[fo. 9r][3]

I came into Devon January: 30th 1647. In Aprill 1648 Sir Hardres Wallers
 Regiment whereof I was chaplaine came to Tavestocke where the Head
 quarters were.[4]

This yeere endinge August 17th 1648 beinge the 46th of my age I
 received   112-10-07½

The second yeare of my being ˆin Devonˆ at Tavistocke in Devon
 beinge the 47th of my age I received in all   125-06-04

The third compleate yeare of my beinge in Devon & at Tavestocke
 the 48th of my age ended August 17th 1650 I received in all   151-03-08

The 49th yeare of mine age ended August 17. 1651. for by reason
 that the wicked Trustees paid nothing out of Lamerton   066-18-02[5]

The fiftieth yeare of mine age is not yet finished

[1]   All the entries on this folio are down the centre, between two columns of figures by George Lane.
     Larkham used this space to jot down a yearly summary of how far his annual income had dropped
     without a payment from Lamerton, and how much he had borrowed from his 'stock' as a result.
[2]   George Larkham (*CR*) graduated BA from Oxford in 1650 and went north to Cumberland soon after.
[3]   The foliation jumps at this point to '9r'. Starting in August 1648 (his first summer in Tavistock)
     Larkham entered an annual record of his income, on the folio that faced his note of what had gone
     unpaid from the Lamerton augmentation (fo. 4v). He wrote at the right, around George Lane's entries.
     At a later date, Larkham's descendant Larkham Bowes practised his signature on this sheet.
[4]   Larkham arrived in Devon in January 1647/8. Sir Hardress Waller's regiment of foot in the New
     Model Army suppressed the royalist rising in Devon and Cornwall during the Second Civil War: C.
     H. Firth and G. Davies, *The regimental history of Cromwell's army* (Oxford, 1940), p. 444.
[5]   Larkham's income dropped abruptly without money from Lamerton: this record relates to notes he
     made in August 1651 on fo. 4v.

[fo. 4v]

[fo. 9r]

I write these lines June 1. 1652.[1] It hath beene a verie expensive yeare by reason of my long Journey into Cumberland & backe thence to London & greate charges in London & thence into Devon[.] I received in Cumberland. £90. & my Wife in mine absence Sept. 29th £9-15s for so long I provided Ministers after my departure. & £1-16-8d for rent of the ground and £1-3s upon a muster in Carlisle for my men & £1-11s was given me In Cumberland.

Hactenus received this yeare   104-05-08

Item of arreares My daughter received of Colonell Clarke at Plimouth
    6 weekes pay abatinge for charges. 18s. Received   013-02- 0

At Bristol I received of Ebthery 11 daies pay due to me this Money
    I received June 11th 1652. they about to take ship &c[2]   003-13- 4
                                                           121- 1- 0

This whole sume is expended this yeere & all that came out of Kirton
and of Mine ancient stocke Made over to my daughter Jane I have borrowed in all
    £30-10s-00d of which I have only my horse & some bookes of them which I
    caused to be printed remain[in]ge to me[3]

Hactenus auxiliatus est Dominus[4]
Jehovah Jehovah

---

[1]   The previous dated entry is 14 May 1651. Whenever Larkham travelled away from Tavistock, he left the manuscript behind. His activities in Cumberland and London, and the riot that broke out on his return to Tavistock, are discussed in the Introduction.

[2]   This entry is linked to the one above. Colonel Clarke and 'Ebthery' (Major Ebsery) were in Sir Hardress Waller's regiment, which reached Waterford, Ireland, June 1652: Firth and Davies, *Regimental history of Cromwell's army*, p. 449. This payment seems to hark back to Larkham's earlier work as a regimental chaplain and amounts to 6s-8d a day.

[3]   The 'ancient stock' for Jane's marriage portion. The books were copies of his first publication *Wedding-supper* (see Appendix 1).

[4]   Larkham frequently used this phrase, which recalled 1 Samuel 7:12: 'Hucusque auxiliatus est nobis Dominus' (Vulgate), 'Hitherto hath the Lord holpen us' (Geneva Bible 1587), 'Hitherto hath the LORD helped us' (KJV 1611). On fo. 9v and elsewhere he also used an English equivalent, 'Thus far the Lord hath holpen me'. For emphasis here, he added 'Jehovah', God's sacred name, rendered as 'LORD' in the KJV.

[fo. 9v]¹

Nov. 12. 1642   Heere followeth an accompt of what God
I came from New England   hath allowed me yeerely since I came from
                                                N. England

In the yeare, end[ed] ^1643^ 1644 & 1645 I received   230-11-01
Ætatis {44}   Anno 1646 I received   112-14-08
Ætatis {45}   The yeare following. 1647   136-12-04
        {46}   The yeare ending. August. 17. 1648   112-10-07½
Ætatis {47}   The yeare ending August 17. 1649   125-06-04
        {48}   The yeare endinge August 17. 1650   151-03-08
Ætatis {49}   The yeare ending August 17. 1651   066-18-02
        {50}   The yeare ending. August 17ᵗʰ. 1652   121-01-00
                                                   suma totalis   1056-17-10½

┌───┐
│ Thus farre the Lord hath holpen me² │
└───┘

---

¹ George Lane made entries down the left column and at the top of the right. Larkham wrote around
   these, mainly on the right and from part-way down the folio.
² This echoes Larkham's Latin refrain, 'Hactenus auxiliatus Dominus'.

[fo. 9v]

This hath beene   Lustra Decem annorum consumpsi, (mi Deus). Oro
A yeere of   Per Jesum Christum; dilige, dona, juva.
great travell   Tu, tu, vidisti lacrymas super ora cadentes,
trouble &   Aflicto servo semper adesto mihi.
expences   Multa quidem vidi manifesti signa favoris,
                     Pectore quæ teneo non abitura meo:
————   Da precor ut tandem possim celebrare triumphos
Ended   promissa ut possim reddere vota tibi.
August 17th   Cras natalis adest (sed non fuit utile nasci)
1652   flebo, etenim iratum sentio habere Deum.
                 Res, tantum restat, quæ me solabitur, una,
————   qui bene me novit, stat sine fine Deus.
The Lord   O quater (et quoties non est numerare) beatum!
is worthy   In Jesu Christo cui Deus est Dominus.
to be   Lædere nec possunt mihi nec prodesse potentes
praised   Tu mihi salus eris, Tu mihi totus eris:

August 17° 1652 Ita cecinit Larkham servus Do[min]i[1]

[1]

Ten times five years I have consumed (O my God). I pray
     Through Jesus Christ; love, forgive, help.
You, you, have seen the tears falling over my face,
     Be present always to me your afflicted servant.
I have seen many signs of your manifest favour,
     Which I hold in my heart, from whence they will not disappear:
Grant, I pray, that I may finally celebrate a triumph
     So that I may perform the vows promised to you.
Tomorrow is my birthday (but it was not useful to be born)
     I will weep, for I feel I have angered God.
One thing remains, which alone will comfort me,
     God, who knows me well, exists without end.
O four times (how many times is not to be counted) blessed!
     In Jesus Christ, whose God is the Lord.
The powerful can neither harm me nor profit me
     You will be my salvation, You will be my all:

August 17th 1652 Thus sang Larkham, servant of the Lord.

'O four times blessed': Larkham seems to have in mind Nehemiah 9:3–6, where worship four times a day is transformed into an exhortation to 'bless the Lord your God for ever and ever'. 'Thus sang Larkham' recalls 'the song of Moses the servant of God' (Revelation 15:3, Exodus 15).

18 August 1652 – 17 August 1653

[fo. 10r]

An° Do: 1652
4° an°.
Li: Angliæ[1]

Helpe me Lord
for the sake of Christ &c

The end of the fiftieth	Thus farre the Lord	1652
yeere of my age	hath holpen mee	Anni ætatis 51[2]
ended not my trouble		August 18th

Thus beginneth the one & fiftieth yeere of mine age

[week] 1	spent 2 weekes *viz*	Laid out Besids what is spent
weeke 2	untill August 31	in houskeeping 2 paire of
In both these weekes spent	£1-15-0	bodies[3] for wife & daughter
		cost 8s-4 [and] about saddle &
		stirrups 1-8

| September the first 3 weeke[4] | spent given and |
| | bestowed just £1 |

| The 4th weeke beginneth | 3 seames of turffes | 4th weeke given in money |
| Septem 8th | iis spent beside 15s | to poore sailors & others 9d |

And so continueth unto		
Anni. 51 ætatis[5] weeke the 5th	spent 16s 9d
begins Septemb: 15th	Item taken out 1s.

| This weeke ends Sept 22nd | In these five weekes |
| | Laid out in all. 4-09-6 |

So I have in house just 9-10-00 whereof part is in spanish & french money[6]

---

[1]   In this and the two lines above, Larkham amended Lane's earlier entry: on the first line he changed the year from '1597'; he left the next line to stand; he changed this line to read in Latin '51: England' (his age and location).

[2]   'In the 51st year of [my] age'.

[3]   'Pair of bodies': a bodice (*OED*). All these items are excluded from the tally of £4-9s-6d for housekeeping, but Larkham includes in the total the 9d he gave to the poor.

[4]   Larkham calculated not only the start of the year but also often the start of the week from quarter days starting on his birthday, 18 August. In 1652, 18 August fell on a Wednesday, so in this first quarter he reckoned the third week from Wednesday 1 September.

[5]   'In the 51st year of [my] age'.

[6]   Below this Larkham drew a thick black line across the folio to mark the start of the Michaelmas quarter.

[fo. 10r]

I have in house	18-0-0
Received for Bookes	00-7-0
£18-7s Whereof £3 10s in outlandish money and 4-2-8 p[ar]t of	
what I spent at the assisses[1]	4-2-8
Sep 15th Mary Gibb brought me a gift the first penny received	
since I came out of Cumberland which was Aprill 5th 1652	2s 6d
	22-12-2

Deo gratias

Laid out 08-02-08 at the assises whereof £4 was borrowed & paid since out of the £18 &c

---

[1] 'Outlandish': foreign (the French and Spanish coins he referred to at the foot of the left column). This entry is an addition squeezed in at the top of the folio, before the heading 'I have in house'. It has been moved here for clarity. Larkham's reference to the Assizes relates to court proceedings which followed the 'riot' in June 1652 when he came back to Tavistock (see Introduction). He noted here that £4-2s-8d of the costs had been reimbursed. In the margin of this folio he recorded a specific contribution from 'the church' towards this, and other contributions may have come from the same quarter: see p. 53 and fos. 11r, 11v, 12r.

This weeke ending the 29th Layd out in Houskeping   00-10-00

In this weeke viz September 28th Justices sate by commission here at Tavistocke
   to examine witnesses upon articles exhibited into the Comittee for plundred
   Ministers[1]

The seventh Weeke[2] of the 51	sacke	0- 1- 4
yeare of my [age] begineth	mutton	0- 1- 2
September 29th being faire	Laid out the friday[3]	
day at Tavistocke an[d]	for beefe	0- 4- 9
endeth October the 6th In	& other things	0- 2- 8
which weeke I laid out in		
houskeping in all		0-10-01

The eight weeke endeth	spent friday october 8th 7-6
October 12th A day of	
humiliation throughout	
England	

9th weeke	October 13[th]	in housekeeping	10s 6d
	beginneth the ninth	& Given	1- 2
	weeke And the		
	9[th] weeke endeth		
	October 19[th] in		
	which there was		
	spent in all	in all	0-11-08

10[th] weeke	Octob 26 ends the	
	10[th] week of the 51	
	yeare of my age	spent this week 17s & 1d[4]

11[th] weeke	Nov[e]mber 03	10s *spent*
	endeth the 11[th]	01[s] Barber & ^06d^ letter
	weeke spent	

12[th] weeke	Novemb 10[th] endeth	
	the 12[th] weeke spent	
	thus	12s 6d

---

[1]   Larkham's opponents had presented complaints against him to the Committee for Plundered Ministers
(printed in *Naboth*, p. 6). After the examination of witnesses in Tavistock, Larkham made two
journeys to appear before local commissioners in Exeter: see fo. 10r, right column (opposite). Until
1653 (when it ceased to exist) the Committee for Plundered Ministers handled cases against 'unfit'
ministers; thereafter, this task fell to the Commissioners for the Ejection of Scandalous Ministers. See
W. A. Shaw, *A history of the English church during the Civil Wars and under the Commonwealth,
1640–1660*, 2 vols. (London, 1900), II, pp. 244–7.

[2]   He omitted to make an entry for the sixth week.

[3]   Friday, market day in Tavistock. Today this 'Charter Market' (a grant from Henry I to the monks of
Tavistock in 1105) is still going strong, more than 900 years after its foundation.

[4]   A calculation alongside is crossed out.

paid for a coate for My Grandchild Thomas   08 shillings
of my bookes Called the Wedding Supper September 29
    for 2 bookes I had 2s 9d of + Ed Condy[1]   2- 9
To my servant it being quarter day September 29 paid   09-00
more given her   01-00
chilldrens shoes mending boots   03-00
To Richard Arnold of Northam[2]   02-06
given in wosteed   06-00[3]
To my daughter Jane   05-00
~~For entering a plaint against Modford~~   ~~00-06~~
~~for his arrest to Exeter &c~~   ~~02-00~~
~~for bayle to Modfords arrest~~   ~~00-04~~[4]
A journey to Exeter in sessions weeke[5]   07-09
to the Barber Octob. 5th   00-06
Horse shoes   01-08
for Firmans Question bought of Mr Mungwell[6]   00-09
another journey to the commissioners[7]   09-10
To my wife I gave.   10-00
at Exeter A[s] sheweth Laid out as in the Margine[8]   03-00
for Diodates Annotation[9]   11-00
another journey to the commissioners   08-02
Given to Goads daughter pretending to be the daughter of Obed Harries   02-00
for a quire of paper   00-04
Gave to the bringer of my stipend   01-00
    Stipend £9 15s
paid for 3 yeares tenths & 3 acquitts[10]   _05-00_

8-19-10 houskeeping ˆp[as]tˆ q[uar]t[e]r   _16-00_-03 extraord[inaries]

---

1   Larkham marked + when he checked and tallied a sum. For sales of *Wedding-supper*, see Appendix 1.

2   Northam was Larkham's parish before he went to New England. Arnold has not been identified.

3   See Larkham's entry on p, 53 about 6s worth of worsted (cloth) given to him at Kirton, in lieu of money. He used the cloth as payment.

4   He crossed through these entries. Nothing more is mentioned of 'Modford'.

5   Probably related to legal proceedings about allegation of a riot in June 1652 (see Introduction).

6   Giles Firmin, *A serious question stated: viz: whether the ministers of England are bound by the word of God to baptize the children of all such parents which say, they beleeve in Jesus Christ; but are grossly ignorant, scandalous in their conversations, scoffers at godlinesse, and refuse to submit to church-discipline?* (London, 1651). Larkham and Firmin had both been in New England; both had served as chaplains in the parliamentary army. Firmin proposed to restrict baptism and Larkham implemented this in Tavistock: see Introduction. John Mungwell was an Exeter bookseller Larkham often dealt with.

7   Larkham made three journeys to Exeter in rapid succession to appear before commissioners acting for the Committee for Plundered Ministers, to answer complaints brought by his opponents.

8   What this refers to is not clear.

9   In the right margin, near the foot of the folio, Larkham elaborated: 'Received for 20 bookes in the quire of Mr Mungwell Diodati his Annotations valued at 11s.' This was payment for unbound copies of *Wedding-supper* (see also Appendix 1). A third edition of Giovanni Diodati's *Pious and learned annotations upon the Holy Bible* had been published in 1651.

10   'Acquittance': settling or satisfying legal demands, clearing off a debt or obligation (*OED*).

13ᵗʰ weeke   *[Novemb 17ᵗʰ] the 13ᵗʰ week*   *spent 10s[1]*

[fo. 10v]

Anᵒ 1652

At Tavistocke

The second Quarter of the 51 yeare of mine age Beginneth November 18ᵗʰ[2]

So it appeareth that I am still in the spendinge hand[3]
 for I borrowed of my stocke in the yeare 1651
 ætatis 49 ˆendedˆ The sume of   £28-00-00
Anno 1652 I borrowed also   30-10-00
And now that first quarter of the 51ˢᵗ yeare of my age borrowed 12-07-07
                  70-17-07

Weeke beginneth[4]

Novemb	18ᵗʰ 1652[5]	01-02-00	the first weeke expences in hous:keepinge
	25	00-09-00	the second weeke
Decemb:	02	00-18-00	The third
	09	00-15-03	The fourth
	16	00-14-00	The fifth
Daughter married			
Decemb.	17	mony all spent[6]	
Decemb	23	00-19-06	the sixth
	30		
paid for baking		00-08-08	
		00-01-06	the seaventh

---

[1] Indistinct: the foot of the folio is worn.
[2] This heading runs across the whole folio.
[3] In debt, 'in the red.'
[4] Written sideways in the right margin against the tabulated entries.
[5] As the start of the second quarter (reckoned from his birthday) fell on a Thursday, Larkham now switched to start the week on Thursdays. He overwrote figures George Lane had entered earlier and amended them to suit.
[6] Larkham's daughter Jane, who married Daniel Condy. 'Mony all spent' is underlined, with emphasis.

Received at Kirton[1]	2-15-4
& 6s in wosteed	
of a debt owed	13-0-0
of the church towardes charges[2]	£3-5s-6d

[fo. 10v]

Received Last quarter	9-17- 6
Spent in houskeeping	8-19-10
Spent in extraordinaries	3-15- 6
Also I have paid for 3 yeares tenths at one time viz 1649 50 51 & acq:[uitts]	3-06- 3
I spent in the businesse of opening the steeple house doore at Tavistocke (beside what was out in brefes[3])	4-16- 9
for 3 severall journies to the Com[missione]rs of Sequestration sitting at Exon[4]	1-05- 9
	22-04-01

So I have borrowed this quarter 12-07-05

Besids al my meanes at Kirton All which is spente also. Lord helpe
in house 26-17-4

for a Capp of Sattin Nov: 18 1652 Jane Betrothed this day	00-03-04	bought at Plimoth by Daniell Cundy allowed in 2 bookes 2-8[5]
Last October 25 D[*elivered*] to my brother[6] in french mony	03-10-00	Mrs Thomsin Dodge *had* of this
More lent him that 25th	05-00-00	Received Feb.12 in lin[en] cloth £5-10s
sacke november 25th	00-01-04	
Laid *out to [illegible]*	00-03-*03*	
post letter from London decemb 07	*00-00+06*	post letter paid
A wed:[ding] smoke for my daughter	00+12 00	
Holland paid stockens shoes	00-15-00	holland 7 stockens 3 shoes 3 carriage from London & the boxe 2

---

1   He noted this and the following two entries about income sideways, in the left margin of fo. 10r. He noted his stipend of £9-15s in the right margin, alongside a gift of 1s to 'the bringer'.
2   Larkham's gathered congregation contributed to his legal expenses.
3   'Briefs': legal paperwork.
4   Larkham visited the commissioners in pursuit of his claim for the arrears due from the Lamerton augmentation.
5   It is not clear whether the 2s-8d in books was a separate transaction or part payment for the cap.
6   Larkham's younger brother Michael, still in Lyme Regis and – to judge from his payment in cloth – following their father's trade (see the will of Thomas Larkham, linen draper of Lyme Regis, 1640, Wiltshire and Swindon Archives, Chippenham, P5/13Reg/221B, P5/1640/40).

January	06	14-6d	00-14-06	the eighth
	13		00-05-10	the Ninth
January	20		00-09-06	the tenth
	27		00-08-00	the eleventh
February	03		00-15-00	the twelveth
	10		00-*12*-00	the thirteenth
spent this quarter			08-*17*-09	2ª 4ª anni 51 ætatis[1]
February	18		£00-18s-10d	3 quarter begineth Feb: 18th
February	25		00-08-06	second weeke begineth
March	03		00-17-08	the third }
March	10		00-14-04	the fourth } weeke
March	17		00-*14*-00	the fifth } beginneth
sumed up March 25th 1653			03-05-04	summa Hactenu[s]
All Heereunto			04-17-09	extraordinaries
clothes for			06-12-00	my sonne Geo:
summa totalis			14-15-01	expended

March 25th Non est mihi argentum[2]

I owe this quarter seven pound borrowed
This fifth weeke endeth March the 24th [*several illegible words*]

So endeth the third quarter.[3]

---

[1] 'Second quarter of the 51st year of [my] age.'
[2] 'I have no money.'
[3] Larkham marked the end of the quarter in conventional terms (24 March), rather than reckoning from his birthday. It was actually the end of the fourth quarter, not the third.

The London Bill for weding clothes	08-14-05	
Sum of Wed[ding] clothes for my daughter	10- 2- 1[1]	
Item paid for a scarfe for my Daughter	00- 5- 4	

from R Keagle by R Peeke
concerning the pretend Riott 4s-*6d*

The London Bill is unpaid[.] I casting up accounts this weeke after my Daughters marriage do find that I have not any Money But £13 received last quarter of Mr Gove & Jeremiah Penhay & £7 received this quarter of Jer[emiah] Penhay for Mr Gove which is just £20 Dec. 20th which belongs to my daughter. paid 13 *borrowed* £7.

Thus farre the Lord hath holpen me[.] in this nicke of time I had good newes from haberdashers hall[.][2] The Lord is worthy to be praised.

non est mihi argentum Deus providebit[3]

To Ellis Bray I gave.	0-01-00	Barbing
to Henry Greene	0-02-00	Boyes schooling
for letters from London	0-01-00	
Bookes bought at Plimouth	0- 9-09	Marshalls sermon Grenhill[4]
paid servants wages	0- 9-00	Decemb 25th
to William Guy I gave	0- 1-00	a short errand
Almanack ii [2d] to fren*ch*men 4d	0- 0-06	
to my wife	0-10-00	
paid for cleav*ing* wood to Cha*p*man & *his* man	0- 0-06	Dec. 28th
	1-*14*-09	

Received for books at Plimoth	21s-3d[5]
Stipend	£9 15s
Widow Lambshead	2- 6
	10-18- 9

whereof	9-17-6
one *yeare* by addition	37- 6-8[6]

---

1 Larkham's sum for wedding clothes is not the total of the items listed above.
2 The Committee for Advance of Money, which met at Haberdashers Hall in London, ruled in Larkham's favour in his complaint about non-payment of the £50 augmentation from the parish of Lamerton. Larkham's delight is evident. In January 1652/3 he received £100 of arrears. His battles on this front are discussed in the Introduction.
3 'I have no money, God will provide.'
4 Almost certainly works by Stephen Marshall and William Greenhill (for both see *CR, ODNB*).
5 The last few entries on fo. 10v are in the right margin, alongside the expenses immediately above.
6 What these figures refer to is unclear. Several illegible words follow.

[fo. 11r]

An° 1652[1]	one hundred pounds paid to	An°1652	partly in money partly in
Jan. 1	to Daniell Condy in payment		goo*ds* & partly borrowed viz
	of My daughter Jane her		*of* £20 paid aquitans out of
	Portion		money[2]

	Monys Received viz of Mr Gove	20-00-00
	of this quarter received	13-00-00
	Will Webb oweth	09-00-00
	Mr Gove oweth	38

	£ s d
for thirteene bookes, wedding	00-13-00
supper [January] 04th[3]	

January 6   All acounts cleared   I have in house <u>2-05-00</u>

All the rest went to the making up of my daughters portion viz £13
Kirton rent Received Jan 15:   04-09-03
for bookes sold Received   00-05-08
for arreares for Lamerton Janu 14   <u>100-00-00</u>
                                £90 of which is my daughters

Hactenus auxiliatas est Domi[nu]s[4]
7-2-5 Cash since last account
3-3-3 spent Hitherto[5]
Remaines in house
      upon account[6] Jan: 15   03-*09-02*[7]

Jan 15   I have in house the above written:

---

1   1652/3. Larkham squeezed in the notes about Jane's 'portion' across the top, above a rough
     two-column layout.
2   'Aquitans': acquittance, a payment to clear off a debt (*OED*).
3   See Appendix 1.
4   'Thus far the Lord hath holpen.'
5   These two lines are squeezed into the left margin.
6   'Upon account': he reckoned up his accounts on Saturday 15 January.
7   The total has been blotted and clumsily corrected, but this is a plausible reading which tallies with
     the figures Larkham entered above it.

[fo. 11r]

Extraordinaries second quarter continued

paid William Gee Goinge to Exeter	Decemb 29	00-06-00	paid William Gee
I gave to George Chester bringinge my stipend	30	00-00-06	6d to Chester
Dec 31 paid to Chester for shewing a warrant		00-00-06	
	suma totalis	00-07-00	the whole extraordinarys Hactenus 2-03-09

Given to my servant January 6th it being faire day		00-00-06	fairday
A journey at Exeter & horse hire 5s in sessions weeke 7th Januar[1]		00-19-09	that jorney in all spente 1-12-5
Bought 8 yards for two shirts		00-16-00	
bought a paire of shoes & ribbon for shoeties	00-04-06		
Item I paid for the Barber Jan 12		00-00-06	
bought 2 bookes for the chilldren the one New testament the other a Primer	00-01-08		04d & 16d

Totalis summa   02-02-11   Besids houskeep[ing]

Delivered to the chosen men of the Church[2]   Jan 15   0-17-03 to be bestowed

Jan. 15th 1652[3]   In token of thankfulnes to God for his mercies I delivered to
the chosen men of the church 17s-3d. & acquitted 4-02-9 which
the church was indebted to me which I had laid out for the
persecuted brethren which £5 they promised to see bestow[ed]
among such poore saints as most needed.

                                            Lord accept thine owne[4]

---

[1]   Probably another journey related to the indictment against Larkham and his supporters, for riot.
[2]   Larkham referred only twice to 'chosen men'. Later, he referred often to 'deacons'. (For the evolution
of church structures within the parish, see the Introduction.)
[3]   He wrote this formally at the foot of the folio when he made the entry above, and drew a line around
it to keep it separate from entries added later in the quarter.
[4]   The church had promised to assist Larkham with court costs over the riot at his return to Tavistock,
but he released them from this obligation. By 'the persecuted brethren' he meant his supporters, also
cited at the Assizes (see Introduction). The last two words are faded and worn.

Received of the [*illegible*] towards the Riott *order*	00-10-00
[A] funerall sermon Jan 31[1]	00-10-00
In all I have this day	04-*10*-08
for one booke sold by Martin	0- 1- 0
Besids arreares out of Lamerton and Kirton Rents and for bookes[2]	
Received in all this quarter ended Feb. 17. by addition	<u>117-09-02</u>

[*H*]ere follow receipts of the 3rd quarter[3]

Money *Q*[*uarter*]*ly* rest[4] feb:19	00- 4-04	I say foure s four d[5]
Received for ½ a stocke of lin[en] being cloth I had from Lyme	02-15-09	of Co[usin] Cundy[6]
Received for another half Peece	02-15-00	of son Condy[7]
Received for one of my Bookes	00-01-00	sold to Richard Peeke
Of Mary Gibb widow	00-03-00	by addition
Of Thomasin Dodge widow	<u>00-05-00</u>	by addition
Sume February 18th	<u>06-04-01</u>	of what I have in house in all
David Facy buried 21[st][8]	00-07-00	
2 sent out of Cumberland tokens	0-02-00	T. Blethwaite & Jennet Bows[9]
of Mr Saxfen a funeral sermon[10]	00-10-00	

---

1   Tavistock PR, burials: 31 January 1652/3: Mary Burgis, wife of Walter.
2   Not enumerated here: Larkham kept records on loose papers and probably had other notebooks. The amount of detail entered in the manuscript varies.
3   From 18 February 1652/3 (with the first quarter starting on 18 August).
4   He headed his list of receipts with the balance in hand from the previous quarter.
5   He added this clarification because he had corrected and blotted the figures.
6   'Lyme': Lyme Regis, Dorset. Earlier, he noted how his brother had repaid a loan in linen cloth (fo. 10v): now he sold it on to David Condy, brother to his son-in-law Daniel Condy.
7   Daniel Condy.
8   Tavistock PR, burials: 20 February 1652/3, David Facy.
9   Thomas Blethwaite and Jennet Bowes, from the Cockermouth church Larkham founded in 1651. He had not long before sent them copies of his book *Wedding-supper* as tokens (see Appendix 1).
10 Tavistock PR, burials: 6 March 1652/3, Jane Saxphen wife of William; 14 March, William son of William Saxphen.

Paid Will Bakers Note in full untill now	00-19-06	for tailours ^work^
Paid for Lathts and nailes	00-00-09	mending stable
paid for Pavinge before my gate & c	00-00-08	
Paid for Workmen and for morter	00-01-06	Malford
paid for 3 pints of sacke Jan: 23rd & Feb 4th	00-02-02	one quart was for
Given on a day of humiliation Jan: 26[1]	00-01-00	Plimouth
In bookes bought ^clothes^ journies		whence *paid* my
other extraordinaries	17-05-*01*[2]	daughter 10-7-5 in
		wed:[ding] apparell[3]
Laid out in houskeeping this quarter ended		
Feb 17	08-07-09	
paid of Janes portion	180-00-00	for my daughter[4]
In all spent *Hitherto*	*21*-03-10	for my daughter paid
		Apparell at London
I paid of my daughters por*tion*	*180*-00-00	

Extraordinaries the 3 quarter from Feb 18th
  are as followeth

Paid for mending glasse Wind:[ow]	00-02-09	to Jo Anstice
To the barber Feb. 19	00-00-06	Ellis Bray
Given to the Comunion 20 [February]	00-00-04	
To the Collection for N: England	00-15-00	for propagation of the
		Gosple
halfe a pound of Tabacco March 1º	0-00-08	
paid for making my double pockett	04-06	To W: Baker
for 8 yards of cloth March 2nd	02-00-00	To my sonne Cundy
for Buttons silke gall[o]on threed & a little		
Canvas	00-06-06	
day of humili:[ation] March. 3. given	0-00-06	to the poore
Paid Ca: Vivians Bill: clothes	4-09-00	for son George
paid the Taylour for his bill	01-00-04	Buttons silke &c

---

[1] A Wednesday, also the day Larkham preached Tavistock's weekly lecture.

[2] This is not a total of the numbers entered above. It includes some of the items listed earlier, but perhaps not all. Larkham kept records on loose papers and perhaps other books. The amount of detail he entered varied.

[3] The total of £10-2s-1d and 5s-4d, listed on fo. 10v.

[4] Written between the lines, later.

Given to the chilldren by George	00-02-00	each of them 1 shilling[1]
A funerall sermon of Mr R. Edgco[m]be	00 10 00	Elizabeth his daughter buried[2]
Borrowed of my sonne Condy to levell this acco[unt]	07-00-00	
	14-15- 1	Received and Borrowed[3]

spent £7 more then received in these 5 weekes of this 3rd quarter

[fo. 11v]

An° 1653[4]

m[isere]re mei Deus[5]

I Received *In al*[*l*]   £   s   d

March rest[6] nothing; I am indebted in the sume of seven pound borrowed of my Sone Condy		
Received my stipend	09-15-00	of Mrs Edgcum[7]
due March 25th of Commisioners	12-10-00	out of Lamerton
Kirton rents ^due March^ 25th	05-04-00	of Cosen Yong £5 of it[8] to receive it of others
of John Hogson Aprill 09th	01-16-08	quarters rent for the ground
of the Comm[issione]rs [April] 22	12-10-00	out of Lamerton
cleare receipts	36-11-08[9]	on the other sid 1-19s-0
on the other side 1-19-0	38-10-08	By Addition
repaid to son Condy[10]	07-00-00	allowed spent Before
Paid for altering my rocket &c[11]	00-02-00	to William Baker
paid servants wages	00-10-00	ended ¼ March 25th

---

1   Gifts from George Larkham in Cumberland, probably for Larkham's grandchildren Thomas Larkham
     and Thomas (or Jane) Miller.
2   Tavistock PR, burials: 12 March 1652/3, Mrs Elizabeth Edgcombe.
3   This is totalled from £6-4s-1d onwards.
4   Larkham started a new folio for the new year 1653 (which started 25 March), as a sub-division within
     his schema for organizing the year by quarters from his birthday on 18 August.
5   'Have mercy on me, O God.'
6   'Rest': balance, remainder.
7   Perhaps Audrey Edgcombe.
8   George Yong (Young), one of Larkham's tenants at Crediton; probably a relation of Larkham's wife
     Patience.
9   The total (minus the 4s still due from Yong) should be £41-11s-08d, so Larkham must have subtracted
     another £5 which was not yet a 'clear receipt'.
10   At this point Larkham switched to recording expenditure, not receipts.
11   At the foot of the previous folio he entered the cost of cloth for this work.

Grogram[1] bought at Plimoth	1-02-09	
paid for a Gold ring for selfe	1-03-00	for my selfe
for cloth to alter my Rocket[2] into	0-04-00	cloake & coate
The Sume of the Extraord[inaries]		
& apparell for selfe & sonne	11-09-09	

[fo. 11v]

An° 1653   Thus farre the Lord hath holpen me
Hactenus Auxiliatus est Do[m]i[n]us[3]

Laid out weekely
A Co[n]tinuation of the third quar[ter]

March	25	00-10-00	The sixth weeke beginneth
Aprill the	01	00-19-03	I *lost* it going to Exeter
			& paid for Malt & wheat
	08	00-08-08	the 8th weeke
Aprill	15	00-10-00	the 9th weeke
	22	00-08-00	the tenth weeke
Aprill	29	00-15-00	the eleventh weeke
May the	06	00-08-00	the twelvth weeke
	13	01-14-00	the thirteenth weeke

Summa totalis of the expences in		
houskeeping the 8 last weekes is	05-12-11	
and in extraordinaries	16-12- 8[4]	on the other side
Hactenus	£14- 5-01[5]	

Thus *farre* the third quarter of the one and
fiftieth yeare of mine age In which I have

Received	38-10-08	by addition
and have laid out	36-10-08	
remains	2-00-00	

---

[1]   'Grogram' (grosgrain): 'coarse fabric of wool, or silk or mohair mixed with wool, sometimes stiffened with gum' (*OED*).
[2]   'Rocket': a clerical cloak.
[3]   Larkham added the same pious heading in English and Latin.
[4]   On 'the other side' (opposite) this was corrected to £16-15s-08d at the end of the quarter, 17 May.
[5]   This line is squeezed in, with the figures in the right margin.

for Tomes schooling	00-02-00	to old greene[1] untill march 25. 1653
Charges at Assizes Exerter	08-13-03	about the Roes Riott besids what is stood some others[2]
Given to J. Heywood & Mr *Williams*	01-00-00	
Paid J. Heywood for the messenger &c	00-05-00	which was sent to the Commisioners when Roe threatened about the orders
To my Wife	00-10-00	out of Kirton rents
Sent to London	05-05-00	to Richard Covert
to the Barber	00-00-06	at Exeter
About my Garden	00-03-05	wages & seeds
for surgery Wives foote	00-03-00	to Peter County
for Dinah[3] for Drawers tape & making	00-05-00	paid April 9th
paid Aprill 11th	00-00-08	for mending garden wall
Aprill the 12th	00-00-06	thanksgivinge day[4]
Mending the	00-00-04	chilldrens shoes
1653 May 17th	16-15-08[5]	Extraordinaries

Also of that which was laid out in extraordinaries I bestowed in apparell upon my sone George, who came out of Cumberland to visite me (besides plate & other things in house), £6 12s I say [I] bestowed in aparrel for him.[6]

3 quarta ˆuntilˆ April 18th		Laid out as followeth	
anni ætatis 51		continuance of the 3rd quarter	
Received for wood	05-00-00	of Mr Eveleigh	
The *arrears* since last yeare	04-15-00	In Mr Westlakes hands	
of Agnes Skirrett	00-10-00		
towards the Riott	00-10-00	Received May 10th	
so received in all this quarter	44-00-08	by addition	

---

1. Henry Greene.
2. 'Row's Riot', when Larkham was locked out of the church and his supporters broke the door down: see Introduction.
3. Dinah Woodman, the Larkhams' maid.
4. A Tuesday, two days after Easter Sunday (which, like Christmas, never appears in Larkham's text).
5. This is not an exact total of the numbers immediately above but includes other out-of-the-ordinary expenses. In the opposite column Larkham noted the total as £16-12s-08d, but corrected it here.
6. This note is in the right column alongside the total of Larkham's extraordinary expenses, so it is added here. Larkham added brackets which confuse the sense, so the punctuation has been modernized.

whereby it appeareth that I have Received ^only^ to add ^to^ my stocke this
quarter ^£2^ By reason of my greate charges about Row's-Riott Last assizes at
Exeter[1]

I ow unto Daniell Cundy of the first £200 I promised with Jane   £20 only[2]

bought bookes	0-07-06	
sarge & lace for a Gowne for my wife	01-13-10	this was bought at Mr foxwells shop in Exeter[3]
Given to my sisters[4]	02-00-00	
paid Mr Westlakes Bills in all	07-01-04	for Comitees plunder[ed] & Haberdashers hall[5]
Given him for his Labour	02-00-00	
paid tenths & an acquitt:[ance]	01-02-01	
to Richard Carter	00-02-00	somtime Agent[6]
to the Ch[osen] men & comunion	00-01-00	
Exeter journey in	00-15-10	Easter sessions
2 pairs of shoes paid	00-02-02	for the chilldren
for making my wives gowne		

---

1   This has been written in a larger hand. At the end of the preceding line several words have been
     crossed out, perhaps because Larkham decided to add a clear explanatory note.
2   For his first payment of £180, see fo. 11r. [Larkham made a brief note at this point 'The sume of
     extraordinaries … ': this now appears above, with the summary made on 17 May 1653, at the foot
     of fo. 11r.]
3   'Sarge': serge, woollen fabric.
4   Larkham's sisters Elizabeth and Jane, in Lyme Regis.
5   Westlake seems to have acted as Larkham's representative in London for business with the Committee
     for Plundered Ministers, and the Committee for Advance of Money at Haberdasher's Hall.
6   Carter's rôle is unclear. He is mentioned here and nowhere else.

Expended in all this quarter   55-09-03   houskeeping Apparell reparacons[1]
                                            workes of charity & law suites

[Overspent[2]] this ¼   11-08- 7

Hactenus auxiliatus est Dominus.
quibus superbiebant, illis superior erat.[3]
Jehova. O continue thy loving kindnesse &c[4]

[fo. 12r]

An° 1653   £8 2s 0d   May the eighteenth

Heere Beginneth the fourth quarter of the one and fiftieth yeare of mine age[5]

Laid out weekely as followeth

from May the 18th	00-08-06+[6]	
the same moneth 25	00-05-06+	
from June the 01	00-17-00+	
June 7 Brewed		no money in house[7]
from June the 08th	00-07-00+	
the same moneth 15	00-06-00+	
of the same June 22	00-03-00+	
		no money in house[8]
Weeke vii June 27th		
Baking last quarter	00-01-06+	
Laid out this weeke [June] 29	00-06-06+	
[8th] Weeke begins July 6th	00-09-07+	
Brewing this weeke: Malt	05-08	
9th week July the 13th	00-08-00+	
10th July the 20th	00-07-00+	
11th weeke July 27	00-09-08+	
for sope paid August 1:	00-02-00+	
12th [weeke] August the 03	00-14-09+	
13 weeke begineth August the 10th	00-06-00+	

---

[1]   'Reparations': probably the 15s-8d spent on 'old walls' (right column), not compensation after the
      riot – 'law suits' probably relates to the wrangling over that.
[2]   The original word is illegible, but the sense is clear from the figures.
[3]   'Thus far the Lord hath holpen. He was superior to those things in which they boasted.'
[4]   Psalm 36:10 (KJV): 'O continue thy loving kindnesse unto them that know thee; and thy righteousnesse
      to the upright in heart.'
[5]   These first two lines run across the top of the whole folio.
[6]   Larkham sometimes added '+' when he worked over his accounts.
[7]   Written between the other entries.
[8]   Written between the other entries.

sacke bows shoes &c All au french[1]	00-14-00½	and things about it
	5-06½	for hookes & twists
for son Cundies note for shoes for Thom:	01-08-01½	boays shoes *paid*
& [?]		
paid for ˆmakingeˆ Jane [a] Wascott	00-06-00	& for lace of Vivian
		& for making Toms cloaths
About old Walles	00-15-08	
	55-09-03	55-9-3[2]

[fo. 12r]

An° 1653   I have in house viii Poun[d]s ii s

Borrowed last quarter £11-08s-07d

		£ s d	
paid for A paire of Pantofles for my			
wife bought of D.C[3] May 18	00-02-00		
A quart of sacke to strangers [May] 20	00-01-04		
May 19th Tabacco	00-00-02		
paid for dressing & furni[shin]g[4] a hatt			
for Tom	00-00-06		
paid for mending clothes for my selfe	00-00-06	To Will Baker	
paid for shoes for my selfe	00-03-06	May 21	
A journey to Exeter & Kirton			
About comission[er]s & sister Conant	01-02-08	May 23. 6 daies	
Left at Exeter for my son Cundy May 28th		With Mr Raddon	
which is to be for payment of his wives			
Portion	14-00-00	I ow him only £6	
Given to a son of Andrew Cane		00-00-04	May 31st
Paid more to Daniell Cundy the last			
money of the first £200 which is his		June 1° 1653	
Wives port[i]on	00-06-00	all received by D.C	
	21-11-00		
and on the other side for 3 weekes of			
this quarter about the house	01-11-00		
so the whole laid out hitherto is	23-02-00	untill June 1st week end &c	
		the just[5] sum of all my Mony	

---

[1] 'Sack', 'sac' or 'sacque': a loose gown. *OED* cites Samuel Pepys's diary, 2 March 1668/9: 'My wife this day put on first her French gown, called a Sac.'

[2] Written in again, for clarity.

[3] 'Pantofles': loose shoes, slippers, indoor shoes (*OED*). 'DC' is probably Daniel Condy, Larkham's son-in-law, who traded in cloth and haberdashery.

[4] 'Furnishing': embellishing, decorating.

[5] 'Just': 'of a calculation: exact or accurate' (*OED*).

The sume of expences this Quarter
   ended August the 17[th]   06-01-00

Received[1] at Exeter of the
   Comission[er]s *August* 27   14-13-00+
More allowed for the *3* [years']
   salary for £147   07-07-00
   this is so much lost as yet
I had towards the Riott June the 6[th]   00-07-00+
June the 9[th] funerall sermon Mary Toller[2] 01-00-00+
My stipend Due June 24   09-15-00+
Due for rent for my ground   01-16-08+
of Mrs Thomasin Doidge   00-05-00+
An: Knighton his wife Buried June 30[3]   00-10-00+
Towards the Riott July 3   00-11-03+
funerall Mrs Delawny July 12[4]   00-10-00+
Rents at Kirton for Midsomer and later
   Received   03-15-06+
Towards the Riott July 30   00-05-00+
All beinge sumed up which I have
   received besids rents & debts
the sum of receipts by Addition   28-09-08

Heere followeth the particular
   Sums received this yeare
   quarterly; sett downe from
   the eighteenth day of August 1652

		spent this yeare in ordinaries & extra ordinaries quarterly	Kirton Rents cleare this yeare
The first quarter	009-17-06	022-04-01	03-01-04
The second quarter	117-19-02	206-03-10	04-09-03
The third quarter	044-00-08	055-09-03	05-04-00
The last quarter	028-09-08	034-13-02	03-15-06
Cleere receipts by addition	200-07-00	318-10-04 of this [01]-13-3 I had towards the riot	16-10-01

---

[1]   Here Larkham switched from a record of expenses to receipts.
[2]   Tavistock PR, burials: 9 June 1653, Mary Toller, daughter of Mr Francis Toller.
[3]   Tavistock PR, burials: 30 June 1653, Annis Knighton, wife of Anthony.
[4]   Tavistock PR, burials: 12 July 1653, Elizabeth Delany.

Thus farre the Lord hath holpen me and hath delivered me from all my feares troubles and dangers, By him I have leaped over many walles & skipped over many Craggy Mountaines. O Remember thy greate name in England & thy poore despised handfull in Tavistocke.

This present first of Junne[1] I wrote these Lines. This Day twelve month I had the doores of the parish Church Shutt up against me by Hawksworthe a late trooper in the Kings army Chosen A litle before to be church warden & confirmed by Glanvil & others. I have beene this yeere exceedingly persecuted; by arrests, in the Comitee for Plundered Ministers, by enditement for a Supposed Riott with divers of my brethren to the expence of at least £50 in charges. Yet out of all the Lord hath delivered me blessed be his name.

I am at this present [time] owner of no money, but 10s destinated to the expenses of this following weeke ut supra.[2]

June the third I pluckt in my Garden at Tavistocke the first Rose &c

From the 7th weeke beg: Jun 28

Delivered to pay for butter 41 ^po[un]d^ to Joan Elford at 4[d] the pound	13-08
Paid for stayes[3] for clothes for my selfe & Jane Miller &c	2-19-00
Laid out for a Francis *Tobrant*	0- 3-00
	3-15- 8

To distressed Frenchman June *12th*[4]	00-03
To H: Greene for Tom's schooling 24th	02-00
paid servants Wages	10-00
Delivered to my wife	10-00
Paid William Baker for work	04-00
A journey to Fowye[5]	13-00

---

[1] 1 June 1653. The events Larkham recalled here are discussed in the Introduction.
[2] The last three paragraphs appear as one long entry in the original.
[3] 'Stays': a laced underbodice, a corset (*OED*).
[4] The entries from here to the foot of the folio are in the right margin, alongside the material immediately above, but continue Larkham's notes of expenses and so (for clarity) follow here.
[5] Fowey, Cornwall.

[fo. 12v]

Anᵒ 1653
The last weeke of this year my   Gloria Deo & laus   Quinquagesimus
Brother Stone and I concluded   et primus
about Kirton[1]   memorato Anno[2]

	£	s	d
So it appeares that all my Cleare Receipts this yeare ended			
August 17 are	200	07	00
More I had out of Kirton Rents cleare	016	10	01
	216	17	01

I have spent	318-10-04	whereof £200 Daughter's portion
And had again	001-13-03	towards the pr:[etended] Riott of my neighbours
spent in all	316-17-01	in all 117-03-01
		in houskeeping, clothes, law suites, gifts & reparacons

so I have spent more	100-00-00	with portion
then I have received		out of my stocke

---

[1] 'Brother Stone' was Larkham's brother-in-law. There had been a dispute about dividing family estate at Crediton.
[2] 'Glory & praise to God. Fiftieth and first, in the aforementioned year.'

paid for Wine from Plimoth	02-06
given to the Communion July third	00-06
for a samplar & for *Pockets*	*00-08*
Item paid for writing Paper	00-06
for making a *stocke pote*	05-0?[1]
Jour[n]ey to Exeter July *the 6th*	[?]
~~Laid out for~~ [*illegible*]	
To a collection for marlborough[2]	02-0
Paid for Roe[s] riot &c	[?]

Thus farre the Lord hath holpen [me][3]

[fo. 12v]

---

[1]   The edge of the manuscript is badly worn at the right margin, down to the foot of the folio.
[2]   Perhaps Marlborough, Berkshire.
[3]   The last word of Larkham's familiar refrain is supplied. Other words cannot be made out because corner has worn away.

O God, let such as turne aside,
and will not let thee be their guide,
be ruin'd and fall in their pride:
But on thy church let peace abide.

Lord freely lend thy church thy helping hand,
and let the building heere in Tavestocke stand.

Amen Amen Hallelujah.

from Glanvile Row &c
the Lord hath delivered me.

Blest be the Lord which hath considered me
And hath not left me yet as you may see
Pride malice and prophanes 'gainst me fo[*ught*]
But yet my God hath brought it all to nought

Glanviles Arrest that led the Daunce,
Wil: Pointer made his horse to Praunce,
Godbeare he swore by no 'Lowance,
But what's all this to Nich: Row's vaunts

Those Plowers plow'd upon my backe
No pitty would they take on me,
To do me mischeife What did Lacke?
But then the Lord did sett me free[1]

---

[1]   Glanville, Row, Pointer, Godbeare: for Larkham, all implicated in 'Row's Riot', June 1652 (see Introduction).

18 August 1653 – 17 August 1654

[fo. 12v] *continued*

Remains [7-]14-07 In house
O My God upon thee do I waite

Receipts for the yeare of my age 52 beginninge August 18th 1653

	£ s d
Rec[eived] at Kirton for arreares of Rent	00-16-04
Sept. 9th of Mrs T. Doidge	00-04-06
Received towards the Rows-Riott[1]	01-30-00
For Marrying Mr John Edgcumbe[2]	00-05-00
Sept. 29. of Wid:[ow] Lambshead: Lord accept it	02-08
Let this poore widdow be	
an object of thy pitty	
And Lord helpe on thy worke	acquited
in this streete of thy city	10s-00 more riott mony[3]
Sold ~~apples~~ onions for onions	00-02-03
for a booke I had	00-01-00
At Kirton received allowinge charges of	
reparacons &c	03-10-08
Received My stipend due Sept 29th	09-15-00
& arreares formerly accounted for for Midsomer	
quarter	<u>10-06-06</u>
to wit in all £19 10s on cleare receipts by addition	
Hact[enus]:	

---

[1] A contribution to defray Larkham's legal expenses, probably once again from the church.

[2] Tavistock PR, marriages: 22 September 1653, Mr John Edgcombe and Mrs Mary Edgcombe. The records show seven marriages that month, an unusually high number, ahead of the introduction of the new (civil) marriage act on 29 September. The Edgcombes were among the last to be married in church, the day after Digory Polewhele (minister at Whitchurch and later one of Larkham's opponents) tied the knot with 'Mrs Ruth Grills' (probably related to another of Larkham's opponents, William Grills).

[3] In an earlier entry (fo. 11r) Larkham acquitted the church of £5 owed to him for riot expenses, but then gave £5 to the church for the poor. Here his acquittance of 10s of 'riot money' is probably paralleled by the 10s he gave for 'church occasions' (listed in the column opposite).

[fo. 12v] *continued*

Heere follow disbursments this following yeare   Psalme 112. verse 5[th][1]

	£ s d	
for linnen for children	00- 3-09	paid sone Condy
		in August
A journey to Kirton	00-02-11	
Given to a distressed Woman	00-00-04	that had a *toothache*[2]
The houskeeping of this weeke	00-09-04	ended August 24*th*
The second week houskeeping	00-10-03	this weeke ended Aug: 31st
Item for 3 pecke of Malt paid Aug. 31	00-04-03	
for mending both childrens shoes	00-00-09	Septemb. 2nd
paid for butter to Mrs Gove	00-08-02	
The Third weeks houskeeping	00-05-06	ended Septemb. 7[th]
Paid of a pecke & half of wheate	00-03-00	
to the barber 6d poore man 1d	00-00-07	Sept. 13[th]
The 4[th] weeke houskeepinge	00-05-11	ended Sept. 14
The 5[th] weeke for the same	00-06-08	Sept. 21
I gave towards church occasions	00-10-00[3]	Sept[embe]r
		Brewed 22 Sept.
The 6[th] weeke houskeepinge	00-11-10	endeth Sept. 28
Given to midwives about Daughter Jane	00-05-00	
for making & mending chill[drens]clothes	00-03-06	
for sacke & fetching it & Newes of my		
daughters safe deliverance in all[4]	02-00	Sept. 21
paid a Note to Sonne Condy for cloth		
buttons &c for my breeches	00-08-00	Sept 27[th]
for 7 pound of corse sugar to David		
Cundy paid	<u>00-04-01</u>	
	<u>05-05-10</u>	Hactenus[5]
Due to my servant for Wife	00+10+00[6]	Sept. 29th
To H. Greene for T. schooling	00-02-00	
spent this weeke ending	00-08-09	Octob. 6th
Give[n] to R. Peek boy. & L. H. maid	0-00-07	this first
Given to a poore kinsman. *S. Pearer*	0-01-00	weeke in October

---

[1]   Psalm 112:5 (KJV): 'A good man sheweth favour, and lendeth: he will guide his affairs with discretion.'

[2]   A conjecture, but not unlikely.

[3]   See the entry in the opposite column, where Larkham acquitted a debt of 10s in 'riot money'.

[4]   Tavistock PR, baptisms: October 1653, 'Azarel The daughter of Mr Daniell Condy and Mrs Jane his wife was borne September the one and twentieth and baptised the 16 of October 1653.'

[5]   'Hitherto': Larkham took stock of expenses up to this point (just before the start of a new quarter on 29 September) before he made routine quarterly payments – to his wife and maid, for baking, for Tom Larkham's schooling.

[6]   Larkham later marked '+' to show he had checked and accounted for this.

[fo. 13r]

An° 1653[1]
Continuation of the first Quarter of the 52th yeare

John Brownsdon and Wil: Web for halfe yeeres pay out of Lamerton	25-00-00
more for arreares which Pointer deducted	01-04-00
Borrowed of Sonne Condy & his father	60-00-00
received and *Borr[owe]d* hitherto in this quarter	
with what I had lyinge by me at the begininge of this quarter	
	110-05-04[2]

So I have at the present not any money at all in my keeping.
And am indebted to my son Condy & his father   60-00-00

---

[1]   As usual, Larkham amended Lane's '1597'. At the top of the folio he wrote a summary in a tiny hand:

At the beginninge of this quarter viz. August 18. 1653 I had in money	7-14-7
Received viis et modis ['for ways and means']	16-06-9
out of Lamerton & borrowed	86-04-0
	110-05-4

[2]   Larkham's total is for the sums noted in the top margin (see previous note) not for the figures immediately above.

Spent in a journey to Kirton & *supplies*	0-16-08	
Bought sealinge Waxe	0-00-06	
for bakinge last quarter	0-01-06	paid October 3rd
for 2 paire of shoes for chilldren	0-02-06	
Delivered to my wife for her rents	0-10-00	
Spent this weeke houskeepinge	0-05-00	ended october 13th
Given to a poore seaman	0-00-02	
	8-04-06	

more laid out as followeth[1]
Spent in a journey to exeter when I sent
   £100 to my brother stone[2]

Oct. 13th 14th 15th	0-08-06	
Given at my departure to Nath Knight	00-00-04	
Given to a poore Woman at Kirton	00-00-01	
Given to poore Brocke going arrant[3]	00-00-03	
for a letter to the Post sent to Sarisbury[4]	00-00-02	
given to the Almshouse at Okhampton[5]	00-00-02	
delivered for houskeepinge untill		
Octob. 20th	00-06-00	
[d]elivered for houskeeping until		
Octob 27th	00-07-00	
Summa hactenus	01-02-*06*	

[fo. 13r]

An° 1653

Continuation of the first quarter

	£ s d	
October 23rd	00-03-06	for mending bootes
for writinge an award	00-01-00	to Mr Grigg
Sent to Brother stone	100-00-00	to Sarisbury
Houskeeping in all Novemb. 3rd	00-10-08	Brewed Octob. 27th
for linnen for the Children 3 yard ½ at		
11d the yard	00-03-02	paid Son Condy in October

The totall of layings out & paiments hitherto 110-05-04[6] unto November the first

---

[1]   The entries down to the next summary are added at the foot of the left column, because he has come to the foot of the right column on this folio. Larkham squeezed this note in above the entries, to make the connexion clear.

[2]   His brother-in-law: they had just reached an agreement about family property in Crediton.

[3]   'Going arrant': down and out, good for nothing.

[4]   Salisbury.

[5]   Okehampton.

[6]   The sum of the figures immediately above (£100-18s-4d) and the previous interim totals of £8-4s-6d and £1-2s-6d.

But to no other. Except Broth. stone about the Land   192-00-00
[and] more *which* I owe also to my daughters
    daughter Azarel which I promised to be paid at
    her birth, but am not able[1]   050-00-00
                                                            302-00-00

Thus farre the Lord hath   God hath holpen[2]
    asisted & streng[t]hned me.   עַד־כֹּה אָזַר־אֵל or עָזַר־אֵל

                                                        £   s   d
There is due to me upon an award made by Cap. Southwood
    from. W. Griles & Gobbeare[3]   21-06-00
Also out of the profitts of the yeare 1652 which is [in] J Pointers
    hand due to me   20-17-00
    Viz: £12-10s my quarter and £1 *is* kept backe for taxes (besids
    24s I had of John Brownsdon and William Webb which is for
    3 moneths taxe from March 25th last to Midsomer) and £7-7s
    I am out in salary. Which the Comissioners had & promised it,
    when they could get in the other Money of which there is [in]
    John Pointers hand to my knowledge £26-11s-10d
And the church owes me which I laid out about Row's Riott   5-10-00
and hogson oweth 1 quarters Rent

                                                  £   s d
Received of John Hoggeson for a ¼s Rent   01-16-08
Received for 100 of apples   00-00-04
Mrs Eliz: Edgcumbe sent me a pecke of wheate
    Novemb. the 12   00-01-11
The same day of Mary Gibb widdow   00-05-00
Sold one of my bookes to Jane Cloak[4]   00-00-06

---

[1] A Biblical name (usually masculine) meaning 'God has helped' – a favourite theme for Larkham.
[2] Neither of the two phrases appear verbatim in the Hebrew Bible. Both phrases are translated in
    context by Larkham, who was playing with two different Hebrew words, both of which would sound
    to in English pronunciation like 'Azarel', his new granddaughter's name.

    'Thus farre the Lord hath assisted & strengthened me'   'God hath holpen'
    'ad-koh 'azar-'el = עַד־כֹּה אָזַר־אֵל   'azar-'el = עָזַר־אֵל

In the longer phrase, the word is spelled with Hebrew *'aleph* (א). It is a rare verb in the Hebrew Bible,
usually reflected in older translations by 'girding up the loins', and normally used of something that
people do, not what God does for them. An exception is in David's song of deliverance, 2 Samuel 22:40
and Psalm 18:32, 39 (English versions), where 'El' (the Lord) is the subject, as here. In the shorter
phrase, the word is spelled with Heb. *'ayin* (ע): it is common in the Hebrew Bible and means 'help'. I
am grateful to Dr David Reimer for decoding the puzzle of Larkham's Hebrew.
[3] Godbeare.
[4] Or 'Gloak'.

At this present I am so much in debt viz. £302

Paid for 6 pound of sope	00-02-00	Novemb. 4th
Houskeepinge this weeke	00-10-02	ended Nov: 10th
paid W. Baker for mending a Gown	00-06	
Item for 3 seames of Turffes	00-02-00	
for a sampler for Jane[1]	00-00-04	
paid for a *posen*[2] of yarne	00-02-00	
spent this weeke houskeeping	00-07-01	
about letters to & from my sonne & to Sarisbury	00-00-10	Novemb 10 & 11
	01-04-11	Remaines in house £1

---

[1] Jane Condy, or Jane Miller (for whom he bought a sampler soon after, fo. 13v).
[2] The meaning is unclear.

I had also for the act for Marriage of Payein & Harris which act I had upon account of J: Mungwell[1]	00-00-06
The sume *of this*	2 -4-11d

Received in all by addition this quarter	<u>38-14-01</u>	from Kirton £4-7s-00d

November the 18th begineth the second quarter of the two & fiftieth yeare of my age. I have in house *in money* 20s only. On thee O Lord do I waite I have said thou art my God.

Nov. 18 Ed: Cole sent by his daughter a Turkey.	Lord accept it.
John Brownsdon a large 6 ribbs of Beefe.	let it not be lost.
Novemb. 19[th] of arreares out of Lamerton	21-06-00
No: 22[th] Sara Trowt a capon.	Lord know her soule.
Nov. 23 Mrs Julian Doigd a Turkey	Rem[em]b[er] her o Lord
No[vember] 24 for one of my sermon book[2]	00-01-00

Novemb the *27* being the Lords day
upon ocasion of the unworthy carridg of Elizabeth the wife of Moses Stoneham
I resolve*d* by the helpe of Christ to avoide such provocations and after groaninge
yesterday & last night *I* [*illegible*] Received some hope of greate good by her
abusive carriage.   Am*en*

[fo. 13v]

An° 1653 Ætatis. 52

Nov[em]ber 30 The wife of William Hodge Brought me a fat Goose
    Lord do them good
Decemb: 2 Sara Trowt a dish of butter   accept Lord

---

1   The new marriage act of 29 September 1653 required civil ceremonies conducted by a Justice of the
    Peace. Tavistock Parish Register records no marriages at all between 28 September and 8 November
    1653. Thomas Harris and Margaret Payne married on 29 May 1654: it looks as if Larkham obtained
    a copy of the act for them on account from John Mungwell, the Exeter bookseller with whom he had
    regular dealings.
2   Larkham's *Wedding–supper*, a collection of his sermons.

Laid out   £11-10s-03d this quarter *paid*
                                                besids *I Ow* £100 to
                                                my B:[rother] Stone

Bought a bushel of wheate	00-06-08	Novemb. 18
a side of mutton	00-02-07	
4 pound of blacke sugar	00-02-04	
a tongue 8d other *sucklings* 1s[1]	00-01-08	
a quart of sacke to Grills & Godbeare[2]	00-01-04	Novemb. 19th
Wine at a dinner of friends	00-01-06	Novemb 21th
given to Mrs Doidge maid	00-00-02	Novemb 23
An Almanack for 1654	00-00-02	Novemb 24th
Laid out the first weeke	00-16-04	
for mending Tom's shoes	00-00-05	Novemb *28*

[fo. 13v]

Anᵒ 1653 Ætatis. 52

The Continuation of the second quarter
of the one & fiftieth yeare of my age Laid out

December the first endeth 2 weeke	00-04-02
More for Malt ˆ decemb 1ˆ it being breewing ˆweekeˆ	00-05-00
December the 02 halfe a mutton	*00-02-00*
Item a pint of sa[c]ke the same day	00-00-02

---

1 'Suckling meats', suitable for infants (*OED*).
2 William Grills, a merchant, and Walter Godbeare, a clothier, had been locked in cold war with
   Tavistock over the Lamerton augmentation. This seems to be a temporary thaw.

Dec. 6 Margaret Sitwell would not be paid for 2lb.½ butter
    is she not a daughter of Abraham? father be pleased to pay her

mistres Edgcumb paid my stipend before hand	09-15-00
due Decemb. 25th next	
Dec. 9th Borrowed of the Trumpeter[1]	50-00-00

Walter Peeke sent me Dec. 14th a Patridge and William Web
    the same day Pork & puddings Lord forget not & c

Mrs Thomasin Doidge (Lord looke on her in much mercy)	
Dec 19th gave me	00-05-00
Received that day of William Webb and Jo: Brownsdon (kept	
backe by Pointer for rates last yeare out of Lamerton)	01-00-00

Decemb. 24th I cleared accounts & have no money at all left.[2]

Hitherto the Lord hath provided for me

I have received this part of the second quarter of the two &	
fiftieth yeare of my age by addition	32-06-00
which (with what I had in house & had for one booke &	
have borrowed) makes just the sume of £83-07-00 as is	
seene to be paid & laid out this quarter hactenus[3]	<u>83-07-00</u>

Received towards the Riott. Dec. 29th	00-05-09
Jan 3. Mrs Agnis Trowt a bottle of [w]hole *watery raisons*	
Jan 5: Mrs Eliz Edgcumb a pecke of wheate	put all these to thine
Jan 6th Mrs Brownsdon a very good loyne of veale	account o my God
Due for rent of my ground from Hogson for paying the	
headrent for me 3s-4d which accordingly is by him paid	<u>01-16-08</u>

Received by addition this quarter Hitherto	<u>34-02-08</u>

Jan: 20th
So Now once more having laid by 13s. 4 to serve untill this quarter shall end,
which is second of the 52 yeare of my age I have not one penny left. it endeth
not untill Feb 17th next coming

January the 20th 1653[4]

H. Greene's Wife sold 2 bookes for me. 00-02-00
    which went the same day for ˆ6 pounds ofˆ soap 0-2-00

---

[1] 'The Trumpeter': a 'Mr Gearing' (see fo. 20v).
[2] This is an interim reckoning on the eve of the conventional quarter day, 25 December. Larkham usually reckoned up his accounts on 18 November, February and May, quarter days counting from his birthday on 18 August.
[3] 'Just': exactly, precisely. 'Hactenus', hitherto.
[4] 1653/4. For the rest of fo. 13v Larkham's entries run across the whole page.

Item for other smale things about house	00-*02-??*
It paid for Taylours worke to Dan. Sowto[n]	00-01-00
The end of the 3rd [weeke]	*00-06-09*
Decemb 9th Bestowed & paid which was owed 4th weeke	00-05-00
Delivered to son Condy to pay debts in p[ar]t[1]	80-00-00
viz the second £100 sent to bro: stone to Sarisbury	
by a bill of exchange of Walter Trowt of Plimout[h]	
paid for dressing an old hatt Dec 12th	00-00-04
5th ^weeke^ houskeepinge begins Dec 16th endeth Dec. 22th	00-04-08
Paid John Sheere about sheelvs for bookes	00-02-00
Paid for Coates cloth for Tom & dowlas[2] for selfe	00-05-00
Dec. 23 for halfe a mutton & fish	00-02-04
Dec. 24 for Turffes & other smal things	00-02-08
paid Mr Greene for Tomes scho[o]linge	00-02-00
for my servants Wages due tomorrow	00-10-00
paid for 10 pound of sugar at 7d [a pound]	00- 5-10
paid for baking untill December 25	00-01-06
Houskeeping untill Janua 6th	00-04-08
for malt brewing day Jan.3	00-04-06
also given to seamen & a poore maid	00-00-06
Jan:4th day of Humiliation given then	00-01-00
Jan: 8th at supper, Bro: son da: quart of sacke[3]	0-01-06
In houskeeping this week ended Jan 12th	00-03-03
Laid out in victualls & small things about house untill January	
the 19th ending this weeke	*0-09-06*
for a sampler for Jane Miller[4] Jan: 19th	00-00-06
Remaines for houskeeping untill febru 17th	00-13-04
Paid ut supra £80 spent Hitherto 5-5-3	85- 5s- 3d
	Hact: Aux: Dom[5]

---

1 Or 'p[aymen]t'.
2 'Dowlas': a coarse kind of linen popular in the seventeenth century (OED).
3 Probably his son Daniel Condy and daughter Jane; the 'Bro' might be Condy's father or Larkham's brother Michael from Lyme Regis.
4 Larkham's granddaughter.
5 'Hactenus Auxiliatus Dominus': in English, Larkham's refrain 'Thus far the Lord hath holpen'.

January 29th Mrs Audry[1] sent a bushell of Barley malt for Houskeeping,
  Lord smell a sweete savour &c
Patricke Harris sent to me a shoulder of Porke, He is a poore ignorant man, Lord
  pitty him

From Munday January the 30th unto Tuesday Feb 28th I was upon [my] way [to]
  London [a] journey occasioned chiefly by my businesse to Salisbury to and
  with Sister Stone

[And] in my Absence my wife spent in housekeeping wood [&c]	01-12-00
I bestowed in clothes for my selfe & wife & chilldren at London	04-??-08
My journey stood me for my selfe and my horse neare about	05-18-06
[I] bought a pair of plate & sent it to my sonne Condys childe[2]	04-01-08
[Illegible words] making of writings from the hand of [illegible]	00-10-00
[Illegible] to me promised & [illegible][3]	00-04-04
	16-17-??

[fo. 14r]

an° 1653
Rents at Crediton

Received the quarter ended Dec. 25 on the other side it was Laid out	£16- 4-10[4]
Inprimis[5] as I was travelling to London	05-03- 4
At my returne February 28th Received	01-04- 6
Also for Bedsteads and *tables* I had	00-19- 0
and for six stooles of Middleton[6]	00-06- 0
I Borrowed of the Little Trumpeter[7] Jan: the 28th to be paid at the yeares end	115-00- 0
Borrowed in London of Rich: Covert[8]	005-00- 0
sume of receipts & money borrowed	127-12-10
remaininge	02-04-00

[1] Probably Audrey Edgcombe.
[2] Azarel, daughter of Daniel and Jane Condy.
[3] The ink Larkham used for this section (entries made after his return to Tavistock at the end of February) has faded badly. Lane's entries underneath from 1597 are clearer. Also, the foot of the folio is worn.
[4] This entry runs across the top of the whole folio. The £16-4s is not included in the total of £127-12s-10d.
[5] 'Inprimis' or 'imprimis': in the first place, first.
[6] Larkham collected rents at Crediton on his journey to and from London, and sold furniture there. John Middleton lived in Crediton.
[7] Elsewhere named as 'Mr Gearing'.
[8] Richard Covert, referred to a few lines later as 'My cosen Richard Covert of London', was brother-in-law to Larkham's (deceased) eldest son, Thomas.

[fo. 14r]

£ s d

Paid Brother Stone last payment	92- 0- 0
Paid for a horse to Will Hore	05- 5- 0[1]
to sone Cundy in p[aymen]t *of pay*	27- 4-10[2]
	124- 9-10
I left with Mr Mungwell of Exeter to pay the carrier for my boxe	000- 5- 0
At Kirton I spent & gave away	000-14- 0
I have remaining in Money	002-04- 0
So this account is ballanced	127-12-10

Laid out in housekeeping untill March 5th after my coming from London	00-10-06
Item paid which was owing for wheate & malt unto mistres Elizabeth Edgcombe	7s 5d
paid for carriage of my Box to Tavistock	2d
for a paire of shoes for Tom Larkham	00-01-02
March 18th paid to Daniell Sowton for wo[r]ke	0-05-06
for turffes & houskeeping untill March [?]th	05-09
paid for an iron rod for a felt Picture of my eldest son & for 6 rings[3]	00-00-08
P[aid] March 14th ˆto brother Cundyˆ for ribbons buttons and other small things first 3s & 4d & 2s & 10d & for silke fetcht by Mary Sheere 6[d]	0- 6- 8

1   Probably the horse he sold to John Trowt in May 1654 for £5-10s (fo. 15r).
2   The original is obscure, with Lane's earlier entries showing through. The figures are completely illegible: the sum entered is inferred from the total.
3   His eldest son, Thomas, who died in 1648.

I received for 3 Psalme bookes at 18[d] each[1]   00-04-06
Sold to Mrs Elizabeth Edgcumbe one Psalme booke   00-01-06
Sold to Ed: Condy one Psalme booke   00-01-06
Sold to Mr Leere one Psalme book   00-01-06
March 11th received out of the sheafe of Lamerton for the 2 last
      quarters of the yeare 1653 of John Brownsdon & Will: Web   25-00-00
With that 2-4-0 which I had remaining at my retorne from London   27-13-00

I have laid out and paid where I owed no lesse then 27-13-00 as appeareth in the other columne so that now I have not one penny in house this day being March 18th towards the end of the yeare 1653[3]	out of which 2 pounds 4s being deducted it is £25-9s which being added to 127-12-10 maketh 152-1-10[2] since my coming from London

My Debts are to the Trumpeter   165-00-00
to my sonne Condy I do owe   044-00-00
to my cosen Richard Covert of London   10-00-00
Hactenus auxiliatus est Dominus[4]   219-00-00

	£	s	d
Sold one Psalme Booke to W. Webb	00-	1-	6
for a sermon preached 23 of March to Collins ^&c^[5]	00-	07-	0
Mrs Julian Doidge sent me a bushell of wheate	00-	06-	8
Sold a book of Psalmes to Ellis Bray	00-	01-	6
Thom: Pennington sent a holland Cheese[6]			
A Psalme booke to Mr Saxfen	00-	01-	6
Received for one of my bookes	00-	01-	0
Received of Phillip Doidge A debt of	01-	00-	0
My stipend March 28 of Mrs Edgcumbe	09-	15-	0
A Bill of August: Bond turned over to son Condy	3-	00-	0
of Mr Martin for a funerall sermon[7]	00-	10-	0

Received since 18th of March   15-04- 2

---

[1] Larkham seems to have brought a box of psalm books back from London, which he sold on at
     1s-6d apiece. This was perhaps the fresh edition of William Barton's verse-translation, *The Book
     of Psalms in Metre* (London, 1654). Barton and Larkham had been exact contemporaries at Trinity
     and Trinity Hall, Cambridge, 1619–22. A. B. Grosart, 'Barton, William (1597/8–1678)', rev. D. K.
     Money, *ODNB*. Barton was a minister in London, 1646–56, and his psalter was sold by (among
     others) Francis Eglesfield, who had close links with the West Country. In 1656, Eglesfield published
     three books for Larkham – *The parable of the wedding-supper*, *A discourse on paying tithes* and *The
     attributes of God*.
[2] The total should be £153-1s-10d.
[3] 1653/4: in the (old style) Julian calendar the year started on 25 March.
[4] A Latin version of one of Larkham's favourite phrases, 'Thus far the Lord hath holpen.'
[5] Tavistock PR, burials: 23 March 1653/4, Robert Collinge.
[6] Holland cheese, from the Netherlands: *DTGC*, *OED*.
[7] It has not been possible to match this up with an entry in the parish register.

Tom had for the *victors drease*[1]	00-00- 6
stockens for Jane Miller 14[d] & shoes 16[d]	0-02- 6
2 seames of Turffes March 15th	00-01-06
Paid Daniel Condy sen[ior] which I Borrowed	
Which money was received out of Lamerton	25- 0- 0
Laid out until March 18th Saturday	6- 5
2 seames of wood of Abbot	0- 2- 4
paid and spent since my returne from London	27-13- 0
aba[ted] 2-4-0 paid spent &c since last quarter	152-12-10
Laid out about the house this weeke	
ended March 25th 1654	0-07- *3*
Malt used March 23 brewing day	0-04-08
more paid for a pecke of wheate	0-01- 9
put unto houskeeping the bushell of wheate which Mrs Julian Doidge	
gave unto mee	0-06- 8
I gave to the woman brought the Holland *chese*[2]	0-00- 6
paid for Thom. Larkhames schooling	0-02- 0
paid for Baking due March 25th	0-01- *4*
paid to my son Condy in p[aymen]t of w[ha]t I ow him	10-00- 0
deliver[e]d in p[aymen]t of sat[i]sfactions *item* of Aug: Bond	03-00- 0
Item which I received of P. Doidge paid ˆson Condysˆ	01-00- 0
so I have made even hitherto non est mihi argent*um*[3]	
paid & spent since March the 18th	15-04- *2*

---

1 This is hard to decipher but is probably similar to 'chusing victors' (fos. 16v, 21v) where Tom Larkham gave a fee to his schoolmaster. (For the 'victor penny' paid to schoolmasters see *OED*, 'victor'.)

2 The cheese sent by Pennington (see opposite).

3 'I have no money'. Larkham abbreviated 'est' to 'ē'. The edge of the page is worn here.

Heere beginneth the yeare 1654 O my God Continue to be gratious &[c][1]

I have Less[e]ned my debt this weeke £14 which I have paid to my son Cond[y]
so now I ow him only £30 to my cosen Covert £10 to the Trumpeter £165 In all I
    ow [£205]

[fo. 14v]

an° 1654[2] Receipts by addition this quarter   All spent and paid
        hitherto have beene in summe 35-18- 8   away hitherto I
        accountinge a bushell of   6- 7-10 from Kirton am 205 pounds
        wheate given to me by Mrs   in debt
        Julian Doidge

An° 1654   £   s   d
Due from John Hogson Rent   01-16-08

---

[1]   The edge of the manuscript is torn at the foot of the folio.
[2]   The material alongside this is squeezed in as a summary across the top of the folio.

[fo. 14v]

The Disbursements paid & spent from the 25 day of March 1654 as followeth

untill Aprill 1. laid out in houskeeping	00-06- 8
More paid servants wages &c	00-10-00
Item for 2 seames of wood	00-02-04
sent by bill of exchange to my Cosen Covert Aprill 5th	10-00-00
To Mr Ben: Hawkines for my sisters living at Lyme	02-00-00
spent in houskeeping untill Apr. 8th	00-05-00
Given to Mr Brownsdons boy	00-00-06
Given to my wife for her occasions	0-10-00[1]
spent in my journey to Kirton and Exeter (J.B. & W. Web paying the rest)[2]	0-01- 0
Edward Condy cominge to me to take his leave[3] I gave 2 bookes &c	0-01- 0
for mending cloathes paid	0-00-06
8 yards of the broad cloth for 2 shirts of Edward Cole bought Aprill 11th	0-13-04
a letter from London Aprill 11th	0-00-03
paid for mending Tome's shoes	0-00-05
Aprill 13th making garden & seeds	0-01-10
Untill Aprill 15th houskeeping	0-08-06
for mending & dressing my bookes	0-00-04
Two seames of wood Aprill 18th	0-02-04
Laid out for a bushell of Malt it being brewing day Aprill 20th	0-04-07
In houskeeping untill Aprill 22th	0-05-11
paid for altering breeches	0-01-00
for Ribbins linings silke, lace, & buttons	0-04-06
Given to John *Laitheroe* writing notes	0-00-06
Paid for mending a buckett	0-00-06
Laid out in houskeeping untill Aprill 29th	0-05-07
Given to a poore sicke man	0-00-03
paid for 2 seames of Wood	0-02-04
paid my sonne Condy in this month of May	10-00-00

---

[1]   Above, two lines have been inked out.
[2]   John Brownsdon and William Webb: Larkham first referred to church 'deacons' in 1657, but even at this point these two seem to be the officers of the gathered church who handled money. For example, they conveyed the Lamerton augmentation (fos. 'C'r, 13r, 13v, 14r) and in May 1655 brought cash to Larkham with a list of donors (fo. 20r).
[3]   Condy was at Oxford (fo. 3r).

Received arreares out of Lamerton which Pointer paid in money last
   allowing sallary for this yeare 50 and 19-02-0 other odd Money in
   all no lesse then 03-04 more besids what they had before which
   was 07-7s Mr Searle & the other commissioners have had in all
   for sallary £10-11s so much lost[1]

I had for a bedstead & chest of John Middleton of Kirton	01-11-0
Received Kirton rents for March quarter	2-18-06
Borrowed of my Cosen Yong to make up £10 to be sent to London which he is to take up in rent at Kirton.	05-[0]-[0]
I had for a Psalme booke of B Condy	0- 1- 6
Sold 2 Psalm Bookes *upon acct*[2]	0- 3- 0
Sold one booke Called Wedding Supper	0- 1- 0
Ap:[ril] 15 A Psalm Booke to Mr Diers Boy	0- 1- 6
A funerall sermon of Mr Sitwell[3]	1- 0- 0

---

[1]   At around this time – between April and August 1654, when he made repeated entries about Lamerton
   – Larkham found a blank space near the start of the diary (fo. 'C'r, three-quarters full of entries by
   the earlier owner, George Lane), to sum up all the money he had received from Lamerton:

	£ s d
April 6th 1654 I have received in all out of the sheafe of Lamerton	
Inprimis of the Trustees I had at severall times for one yeare	50-00-00
Item upon an award made by Captaine Southwood I had of them	21-06-00
Out of this no sallary paid to the Comission[er]s	71-06-00
Received of Mr Searle at severall times £100 £12-10s & £12-10s	125-00-00
More received of the Comissioners May the 27th insteede of £22 for which I gave mine acquittance (abating £7-7s for sallary) demanded for the former 125 & the said 22 which is in all £147	014-13-00
Item received by the hands of J Brownsdon & William Webb	050-00-00
More in lieu of £14-10 paid in by John Pointer (the comissioners keeping backe 3- 4s for sallary of the formentioned £50) & of the said 14-10 I received	011-06-00
	272-05-00

On the preceding facing page (fo. 'B'v), Larkham noted what had been kept back from the £300 owed
from Lamerton – a rough counterpart for his summary of money received:

Out of Lamerton 27-15 is kept from me by the iniquity of some & by reason of the passing of
my money through the hands of the Comissioners

				Pointer paid in £14-10s instead of £14-14s deceivinge me of 4 shillings	
6- 2-10	{6 yeares came to}	£300			
21-11-00	{Pointer kept back		0- 4-0		
3-15- 8	{Abated Salvey		10-11-0	{I had first of W.Web &c	01-04-0
3-10- 6	{Agas had		12-10-0	{Item had from them	01-00-0
5-00- 0	{Godbeare had pretending he laid it out }		04-10-0	{More I had of them	08-10-0
			27-15-0	Item of Mr Clapp at Exeter April the 6th 1654 I had only	00-12-0
			272- 5-0		11-06-0

   Besids mine expenses of above 40 pounds [entered sideways in the left margin]

[2]   He crossed this through when payment was made.
[3]   Tavistock PR, burials: 15 April 1654, William Sidwell.

Bad Mony[1] about Smithes law suites viz 2s to Mr Aurundell & 6d

    for a Plaint: 4d Baile Money ^&^ 2d to drinke   0-03-00

Item for Aresting Thomasin Smith   0-01-00

Houskeeping ^and Barber [*illegible*]^ untill May the sixth   0-07-02

May the fifth paid for soape   0-02-00

2 seames of wood May the 17th   0-02-04

Housekeeping untill May the 18th   0-09-02

spent since March 25th 1654   27-14-02

All is spent & *gone* towards the paiment of debts.

non est mihi argentum[2]

<hr>

[1]   Larkham seems to be referring to money wasted on the case he lost, rather than debased coinage.

[2]   'I have no money.'

Aprill 18ᵗʰ A triall about my sons son pased, greate abuse by Godbeare, many
   passionate sinfull words spoken by me præses:¹ O Lord Consider: Pardon &c²

Aprill 19ᵗʰ A Psalme book sold	0- 1- 6
more sold the same day another	00- 1- 6
Sold the same day one wedding supper	1- 0
Received April 20 in lieu of Wood	4-00- 0
Received for 6 doz: of perkins Catechisme of Mr Watts he payinge	
charges³	00- 8- 0
Received for three Psalm books	00-04- 6
Item sold A Psa[l]me booke for	00-1s-6
of Mrs Thomasin Doidge Aprill 26ᵗʰ & for a Psalme Booke	00-06-00
Sold to Mrs Sitwell a Psalm booke	0-01-06
of Mary Gib (Lord looke upon her)	0-02-00
Received of Micheas Willesford for a funerall serm[on] *Mother*	
[*illegible*]⁴	0-10-00
Sold a Psalme Booke	<u>0-01-06</u>
whereof by addition *Just* I have received this quarter <u>27-14-02</u>	
[Recei]ved before in this quarter	16-15-08
	<u>35-18-08</u>
Received in all this quarter by addition	<u>52-14-04</u>

[fo. 15r]

May 17 anᵒ 1654	<u>No mony in house</u>	May 18ᵗʰ 1654

May The eigtheenth Beginneth the 4ᵗʰ quarter of the two &	
fiftieth yeare of mine age	all even
May 18ᵗʰ Widdow Lambshead	00-02-06
May 24 Bevile Wivile sent me A Bushel and halfe of Malt for a	
gift worth	0-06-09
I had for a Psalme booke	0-01-06
for my horse I had of John Trowt	5-10s
Received for 4: Wed:[ding] Sup:[pers] from H. Greens wife	<u>0-04-00</u>
Received Hitherto untill June 24ᵗʰ	<u>6-04-09</u>

---

¹ The word looks like 'praise' but the context makes this unlikely. Larkham was probably referring to
   himself (shamefully, in reflection on his conduct before the Tavistock Court Leet) as his grandson's
   præses, Latin for guardian, defender, protector .

² Larkham's grandson Thomas was accused of chasing a sow belonging to Thomasine Smith. Larkham
   made a longer entry about this on 18 August 1654. He lost the case but went down fighting.

³ Probably William Perkins, *The foundation of Christian religion, gathered into six principles … to
   be learned of ignorant people, that they may be fit to hear sermons with profit, and to receive the
   Lords Supper with comfort* (London, 1654). Nicholas Watts was at this point a leading member of
   the church, but later fell out with Larkham in spectacular fashion.

⁴ Nothing has been found in the parish register to tally with this.

[fo. 15r]

May 18th brewing Day Malt	00-04-06
May 19th A letter from my sonne George in a letter from Cosen Covert	00-00-06
for bringing it from plimoth and setting backe another the same day	0-00-04
~~bought a pound of *salmon* of S. Condy~~	~~00-01-04~~
paid for fish	00-00-04
At the *welcom[in]g*[1] Dav: Condy paid for wine	0- 1s-6
Given at the day of thanksgiving	6
Given to Nath Knight 4d Martin 2d	00-00-06
paid for bringing a letter May 22th	00-00- 2
Laid out in houskeeping untill May 25th	0-06- 4
allowed the Malt to houskeeping	0-06-09
for 2 seames of fagotts	0-02-00
for the Barber May 30th	0-00-06
Laid out untill June 2 housekeeping	0-08-02
Item laid out in other things	0-05-00
June 2. beginneth the third week in which was spent in houskeeping	0- 7-02
for a curtaine Rod for my Picture[2]	0- 0- 6
June 14. two seames of fagots	0- 2- 0
I gave to my daughters servant	0- 1- 0

---

[1]   A hard word to decipher: he wrote over an earlier entry by Lane. The meaning is unclear.
[2]   The subject of the picture is not clear. The only known portrait of Larkham is the engraving prefixed to his sermon collection, *Wedding-supper* (1652).

Junne 19th *vis* £3 remains in house uppon account

My loving friend Mr Brownsdon sent me June 20th 3 seames   Lord it was to
   of Turffes   thy Ma[jest]ie
I have bestowed in wood wages and other *th[in]gs* the whole
   three pound <u>Non est mihi argent[um]</u>[1]

I now begin upon a new provision by the Lord My God who first sent me by the
   hands of the wife of Rich: Spry a pecke of wheate. And John Russells maide
   brought 3 chickens

June. 26. Mrs Thomasin doidge brought to me (Lord in mercy accept it)		00-05-00
Received by the hands of Mrs Edgcumb stipend		09-15-00
Mrs Cudlip wife of John: sent me a cheese		
Sold the timber tree that lay in the entry a long time to David Cundy for		00-04-06
Received for a fine at Kirton		13-09-00
for a furnace sold to John Middleton[2]		02-10-00
for a tableboard[3] in the chamber		00-03-00
Received in rents (abating reparacons) July 13th ~~which were £3-13s~~)		05-09- 0½
I had of one Mr Morrice which I laid out in London for him he having no money		00-01-04
of Mr Hoggesson Rent for ground		01-16-08
Received by addition this quarter	11-19-2	<u>33-13-06½</u>
A funerall sermon July 31 Peeks son[4]	0-10-0	39-18-03½
	<u>12- 9-2</u>	<u>00-10-00</u>
		40-08-03½

---

[1] 'I have no money.'

[2] 'Furnace': an oven, or a boiler, cauldron, or crucible (*OED*).

[3] A tabletop or the table itself. The church later paid Larkham 10s a quarter to meet in 'the chamber'.

[4] Tavistock PR, burials: 31 July 1654, 'Roger Pike'.

Paid Cockham for clearing Garden	0- 1- 0
paid Nath Knight for making hay	0- 0- 6
Laid out Houskeeping untill June 24th	0- 5- 6
Paid Mr Arundell upon acc[ount] for Lawsuits	0-10- 0
expended & laid out untill June *19*	3- 4- 9[1]
June 23 market day in butter & victualls	0- 5-10
Paid for wood to William Web	01-06- 0
My servants wages June 24	00-10- 0
To my wife towards privat expense	0-10- 0
for Tom's schooling I paid	0-02- 0
paid for baking ended this quarter	0-01- 4
which was owed for 2 pecks of wheat	0-03- 6
And for a pound of Tabacco I owed	0-01- 4
in all laid out this quarter Hitherto. June 24th 6-4-9	3-00- 0

To P. Glubb going to Oxford I gave	0-02- 6
a token to Ed Condy & Ste[phen] Bloy each 1s	0-02- 0
June 28, to the barber	0-00- 6
untill June 30th in houshold provision	0-05- 8
shoes for the chilldren 3 paire	0-03- 9
for Jean[2] mending shoes	0-00- 4
Paid for stuffe & making clothes	0-18- 9
I gave to Mrs Cudlips maid &c	0-00- 6
to the Communion. July 2d I gave	0-00- 6
given to Nath Knight making the hay	0-00- 6
Houskeeping & Malt untill July 14th	0-16- 9½
Tent[h]s due last December paid	1-02- 1
Woosterd wooll paid for sent by Holmes	0-03- *0*[3]
spent in Exeter & Kirton journey	0-05- *0*
Laid out for houskeeping untill August 17th	1-06- *?*
wood & turffs 8-6 Malt July 27 4-6	0-13- [0]
soape iis more *turffs* 3s	0-05- [0]
In all laid out this quarter 33-8-3½ other side *£20 16s 11d*	12-11- [?]½

About a suite of cloathes for Thom: Larkham	00- 7- 3[4]
for altering my wives Gowne things used about it	00-06- 0
I bought for my selfe a paire of shoes & ties	03-08
I paid Daniel Condy what I borrowed	20-00-00
	20-16-11

[1] This matches up with his reckoning of £3 in hand on 19 June (see column opposite).
[2] Jane: his daughter Jane Condy or granddaughter Jane Miller.
[3] The edge is worn here.
[4] This list continues the expenses noted in the left column, but for clarity is placed here.

Of the yeare of mine	1 quarter	8-14-01	04-07-00
age 52 ending	2 Received	34-02- 8	00-00-00
August 17 1654	3 Received	52-14- 4	14-06-04
	4 Received	12-09- 2	5-09- 0½
		138-00- 3	24-02- 4½
		a fine	13-09- 0
			37-11- 4½[1]

The money out of Lamerton was paid the
   yeare ended March 25 1654 [*there was*]
   a deduction of 50s by the Commissioners

---

[1]   The money in this right-hand column is marked 'Kirton rents'.

18 August 1654 – 17 August 1655

[fo. 15v]

1654

1654   August 18th beginneth the three and fiftieth year of myne age[1]

August the 18th 1654

This is the Day on which I did begin
Heere in this vale of teares to live & breath
On this day 'twas my Saviour for me died[2]
Men did His blessed forhead with thornes wreath
And should I thinke it much to be abus'd
Sith he for my sake was by men thus us'd?

Let me not feare fury of men or devil's
Although I compas'd am with many evill[s]
Rage wrath & pride of men shall do no harm
Keepe me Will God in his fatherly arme[s][3]
As thou O God hast said I shall not Dy[e]
Make me on thy promise still to rely.

Remaineth in house of Money Seven Pounds

I had for books of Mungwell in Money & bookes   1-17-06
Elizabeth Penny Welle sent me a Pricke of Tabacco Upon the
   Returne of her husband from sea

This very Day August 18th 1654 There was a triall in the court of Tavistocke
betweene Thomasin Smith and my grandchild Thomas Larkham for driving and
beating her Sow[.] It was God's pleasure for ends best knowne to his Wisdome to
suffer me to be foiled in this action &c[.] With this fatherly Whip beginneth the
three & fiftieth yeare of mine age. But my hope is that His holy Majestie s[h]all
bringe good out of this afliction and all others which mine unworthy walkinge
have caused his fatherhood to lay uppon me. But the deriding of thy Church,
waies and Worship by Everleigh the steward of the court & others O Lord forget
not. Hallowed be thy name.[4]

---

[1] Beneath this he crossed out George Lane's original heading in an elaborate style.
[2] 18 August 1654 fell on a Friday.
[3] Above this, Larkham crossed out the line he originally drafted for 'K'.
[4] Smith brought legal action against Larkham's grandson at Tavistock's ruling body, the Court Leet,
     presided over by the earl of Bedford's steward, Everleigh. No court records survive, but 'driving and
     beating a Sow' is typical of the neighbour disputes that would be heard: Harold J. Hopkins, 'Thomas
     Larkham's Tavistock: change and continuity in an English town, 1600–1670', Ph.D. dissertation,
     University of Austin at Texas, 1981, pp. 158–60. Larkham made a separate note of legal expenses at
     start of the manuscript (fo. 'B'r):

About the action against Smith	
delivered to Pinsent	0-1-0
paid jury	0-8-0
Item other expenses	0-1-4
the keeper of the jury	0-0-4
swearinge 2 witnesses	0-2-0
Mr Arundells fee	0-1-0
wage to wittnes	0-0-6
	14s-2d

[fo. 15v]

Spent in riding to Kirton & Exeter	00-03-2
Bought a bible for my Wife	00-11-0
& the Saints Treasury[1] for my selfe & Daughter each one cost 20d	00-03-4
Bought the Wostershire agreement[2]	0-01-2
Bought 2 seames of turffes	0-01-4

	£ s d
August 24[th] I preacht to the funerall of Mrs Thomasin Doidg and had	0-10-00[3]
I gave the Counsellour that pleaded	00-10-00
Houskeepinge for this weeke now beg[i]n[nin]ge	00-08-10
To a poore souldier wounded in Scotland	00-00-06
Charges about the 2 suites & arres[t] of judgment[4] whereof 10s was for drawing up exce[r]pts besids 14s formerly expended about these businesses	01-08- 8
August 24[th] I paid for malt & wheate	00-07- 8
Houskeeping untill Sept: 1	00-06-10
(06d to Francis badge which brought a Jole[5] of Sa[l]mon from my D Condy)	00-00-06

---

1   Jeremiah Burroughes, *The saints treasury* (London, 1654), with portrait of Burroughes by Thomas Cross (*fl.* 1644–82, *ODNB*), who had engraved Larkham's portrait for *Wedding-supper* (1652). In 1655 Larkham sold one of the copies to 'Mr Leere' for the same price (fo. 20r).

2   *Christian concord, or the agreement of the associated pastors and churches of Worcester-shire* (London, 1653). Thus Larkham took an interest in the Association movement, although he had an uneasy relationship with its local manifestation, the 'Devon Association': see Introduction.

3   Tavistock PR, burials: 23 August 1654, 'Mrs Thomasin Doidge'.

4   'Arrest of judgement' (a legal term): a stay of proceedings, after a verdict for the plaintiff or the crown, on the ground of an error (*OED*).

5   'Jowl, jole': 'The head of a fish; hence (as a cut or dish), the head and shoulders of certain fish, as the salmon, sturgeon, and ling' (*OED*).

Lord how their Number Multiplies
   and they that ˆhateˆ me sore
Rage! they that doe against me rise
   Waxe Daily more and more.
Let Everleigh know he hath done ill,
   Wither up[1] his heart with shame's face fill[2]
For thy names sake with quickning grace
   Alive do thou me make
And out of trouble bringe my soule
   Lord for thy Justice sake.

September 19ᵗʰ I sent to my Daughter Miller in Ireland by one
    1654   Rob[er]t Wood who dwells in Waterford & was
                borne heere in Tavistocke   01-10-00[3]
Sept 24   Mary bur[ied] Charles daughter[4]   00-06-00
Sept rest[5] 28ᵗʰ In house I have   9-13-06
                of this remaining only 1-7-10

A weeke of greate affliction in body Mind & state

Hitherto cleare receipts are only   00-16-00

October 03 Received stipend   9-15-00
Received at Kirton for Rents &c   8-18- 0
With that which I had remaining last qua*rter* which was £1-7-10 the
   sume of £20 & 10d since which I have laid out and spent as on
   the other side so I have in house at my [c]asting up account
   October the *seventh*[6]   12-08-07

[fo. 16r]

Remaineth £12-8s-7d as appeareth on the other side October the 7ᵗʰ
                                  £   s d
Octob 12ᵗʰ of Mr Hoggeson for Rent   01-16-08
W Leere Receipts hitherto besids Kirton rents are just 12 pounds
   7 shill[ings] 8 pence. Kirton. 8-18
I had of Nich[olas] Rich for a sermon[7]   00-05-00
for old boards of John Sheere   00-03-00

---

1   Indistinct: written over something else, and Larkham has also made corrections.
2   'With shame his face fill'.
3   This entry runs across the whole page.
4   Tavistock PR, burials: 25 September 1654, Mary 'Charells', daughter of Roger.
5   'Sept rest': Larkham used Lane's earlier entry here; 'rest' means the balance.
6   Larkham adds £9-15s, £8-18s and £1-7s-10d: £20-00s-10d.
7   Tavistock PR, burials: 26 October 1654, 'Joane, wife of Nicholas Riche, drowned & buried.'

From Sept. 1 untill Sept: 8th in houskeeping	00-05-06
Septemb. 3. At a Communion &c I gave	00-01-00
The 4th weeke beginneth Septemb. 8th laid out	00-07-06
for Sacke & Bunnes this weeke	00-03-*06*
for March beare paid to Barth: Sowton to drinke with the strangers	
of *Endillis*[1]	00-00-06
The fifth weeke brewing weeke endeth Sept. 22th	00-16- 8

the 6th weeke beginneth Sept 22. untill Sept. 29th	00-10-06
Toms schooling iis, accidence[2] & paper 6d	00-02-06
to a distressed Gentleman Sept. 28th I gave	00-01-00
for 4 seames of Turffes	00-02-06
a quart of sacke at my brother Condies	00-01-06
Hitherto spent untill Septemb. 29th	08-05-08
Paid T fleshmens wife for 58 p[ounds] ½ butter at 4d	00-19-06
paid servants wages & to my wife	01-00-00
& for baking the last quarter	00-01-04
& delivered to houskeepinge	00-04-00
spent in a kirton & ex[e]ter journey Oct. 3. 4. 5.	00-12-08
Given to houskeeping this weeke begin. Oct. 6th	00-05-10
It pleased God for ends knowne to his holiness to brook a	
permission of an *exemin[ati]on* by Evill Eve[*leigh to*] which [*I*]	04-08-11
came unto [*?*] *voluntas*[3]	[15-17-11]

[fo. 16r]

Paid for knitting stockens ˆstockens to my wifeˆ October the 9th	00-02-00
Given at the day of humiliation	00-00-06
Given to Nath: Knight for attendance	0-00-06
Two seames of Turffes	0-01-04
October the 12th paid for wiggs[4]	0-00-06
from Octob: 13 houskeeping this weeke	0-05-11
for two seames of wood paid	0-01-10

---

[1] Not located.
[2] 'Accidence': a book of the rudiments of grammar (*OED*).
[3] Eveleigh, the earl of Bedford's steward, presided over the Tavistock Court Leet and also represented
    Bedford as patron of the living. The foot of the folio is worn.
[4] 'Wig': 'A kind of bun or small cake made of fine flour' (*OED*).

The whole of Receipts every way is	14-13-03
untill October 27th laid out this quart[er]	02-13-03
Remaines in my hand at home & as ab[ove]	12-00-00
[M]y £7 I lent to *W Boles* & £5 I have	
cleare receipts	12-12-08

November the second I received a letter from S. Miller[1] dated June 15th 1654 blessed be God for their welfare O God doe them good for thy Covenants sake &c

November. 3. Dan: Condy told me at Night he had Received of Mr Bole five pound which is for that £5 Mr Brownsdon had out of the Trumpeters mony which makes my debt but £160 Besids the money for lending it which will be £9-12s all to be paid Jan 30 next coming at which time Mr Brownsdon is to pay five pound six shillings

I had a letter Nov: 5 from my sonne George as I was going to Publicke meeting.[2] O What shall I render to the Lord for all his mercies & goodnesses to me & Mine!

Mr Bole hath paid 02 pound which he owed me

Laid out this ¼ In all   25-11-02

I call to mind with a humble and thankful hearte that upon the 12th day of November 1642 I left my house in the morninge and came downe to the Mouth of the River Paskataquacke in New England to come for England[.] I take speciall notice of The speciall Goodnes of the Lord to me & mine for these twelve yeares now fully ended this day Novemb 12th 1654 beinge the Lords day which was on a Saturday that yeare I came from New England.[3]

Yet hath this time had in it very greate afflictions and tossings to & fro, but farre farre lesse then my Deservings. Yet have I Received in these twelve yeares no lesse then 1470-17-03 in Money besids some other gifts towards the maintenance of my famely matching all my chilldren setling my meanes at Kirton and defence of my person from those many vexatious suites & prosecutions that have in this time beene Mooved against me.

And now Lord what waite I for? My hope is in thee Deliver me from all my transgressiones: make me not the reproach of the foolish &c[4]

---

[1] 'Son Miller': Joseph Miller, who died in Ireland 8 May 1656 (fo. 'H'v); married to Larkham's eldest daughter Patience.

[2] 5 November 1654 was a Sunday, so this was public worship, the preaching service.

[3] The entries up to the start of the next quarter are entered across the folio as one paragraph.

[4] Psalm 39:7–8 (KJV): 'And now, Lord, what wait I for? My hope is in thee. Deliver me from all my transgressions: make me not the reproach of the foolish.'

Octob: 19th paid for 3 moneths taxe the first that ever minister paid
    in Tavistocke[1]   0-10-06
Brewed that day paid for malt   00-04-02
houskeepinge this weeke   00-06-08
paid for an old Bedsted to *yong* Mrs Ellis   00-10-00
paid for ribbon for a paire of breeches   00-06-10
Octob the 20th for soap   00-02-00
Laid out in Tabacco 4d and before 2d   00-00- 6
Untill the 27[th] day of October   02-13-03

untill Nov: 3[rd] in houskeeping   00-05-06
Laid out in houskeeping unt[il] Nov 10[th]   00-04-06
Laid out in houskeeping unt[il] Nov 17[th]   00-06-00
Item for making clothes & mending sho[e]s   00-03-10
Item paid to my Sonne Condy for clothe & sarge & other materialls   00-19-06
                                          more   00-08
paid as on the other side debt of   05-00-00
                 Laid out since Oct 27[th] 7-0-0 07-00-00

---

[1] Larkham's opponents commented in 1658 'The next out-cry made is the unjust laying of rates and taxes … [yet] he can hardly mention one rate or tax for the raising of money upon this Town and Parish … wherein one at least (sometimes more; nay often the major part of) the assessours, have been members of his society … he hath as small reason to complain as any man in England, having scarce paid twenty shillings to all rates and taxes whatsoever, since first he came to have his residence amongst us.' *Tavistock Naboth*, pp. 11–12. After this first hefty payment Larkham usually noted a quarterly payment of local tax, at variable monthly rates (1s-6d, 1s-3d, 8d, 4d). As his note here suggests, it was the decision to tax the *minister* that chafed. He routinely paid tax at Crediton, out of the rents on his properties.

What I have received this first quarter of the 53 yeare to wit £8-18s out of Kirton & £12-12s-8d otherwise in all £21-10s-08d is p[ar]t of the aforementioned Sume

Heere Beginneth The second quarter of the three & fiftieth yeare of
my Age Novemb. 17[th]
Blessed be God for that greate ancient Mercy of Gospell liberty
on this day long ago[1]
[I have in house just £5]

	£	s	d
Novemb: 21 At the funerall of a Daughter of Thomas fleshman I preached[2]	0-	7-	0
Novemb. 27 I had for bookes allowing 2s for selling to Greenes wife who hath sold twelve	0-	4-	0
Alice Stevens a blind woman did more then any one. gave me (which Lord thou knowest I desired not to take)	0-	2-	6

[fo. 16v]

	£ s d
the 20th of Decemb of Mary Gibb widdow who came to see me	00-02-00
For V Reeds child buried Decemb 23 I preached then & had[3]	00-07-00
Received of Mrs Edgcombe my stipend	09-15-00

12-10s I have in house 12 pounds 10s

Sold 2 of my bookes Jan 5th for	00-02-00

A letter came to my hands from my sonne George Jan: 7 for which I praised God

Received Rent 11th of January of Hoggeson for the ground he holds of me	01-16-08
for bookes of Mr Leere	00-02-00
January 30 A funerall sermon[4]	01-07-06

Received Clereely 12-17-8 by Addition unto February 2nd at which time I wrote this

Received of William Webb for the acre of Wood for this yere	04-00-00
The sume of this quarter receipts	16-17-08

---

1   The accession of Elizabeth I. Larkham entered this text across the folio as a heading for the quarter.
2   Tavistock PR, burials: 21 November 1654, Ann Fleshman, daughter of Thomas.
3   Tavistock PR, burials: 23 December 1654, 'Thomas Reede' (not noted as a child). This line is hard to read because Larkham wrote over earlier entries and the ink is faint.
4   Nothing is recorded for 30 January but Tavistock PR recorded two funerals on 29 January 1654/5: 'Charles Rundell' and '[ ] Heckes, daughter of Mark'. Larkham usually received 10s: £1-7s-6d was a large sum for a sermon.

Laid out in houskeeping this weeke	00-09-03
I paid for ¼ pound of Tabacco	00-00-06
untill November 24 in houskeeping	00-06-03
untill December 9th in houskeeping	00-*05*-00
Paid for *books in* my house	00-03-00
Laid out in housekeeing untill Dec 15th	00-05-06
To my S Condy'es *Mason*[1] paid December the 9th	00-00-??
	01-11-??[2]

[fo. 16v]

	£ s d
more December 15th	
Delivered for Houskeeping & to pay for malt	00-10-00
I paid for A Cheese to Skirret	0-03-02
December 22 laid out houskeeping	6- 0
paid for baking last quarter	1-04
servants wages the quarter now ended	00-10-00
Laid out Decem 29th in houskeeping	00-05-08
At a Communion December 31 I Gave	00-01-00
Jan. 1 I delivered to my sonne Condy towards the paiment of the	
Trumpeter for me	10-00-00
Jan. 2 paid Aug Bond for Tom's schooling	00-02-00
From January 5th to the next friday Houskeeping	00-06-08
from Jan. 12th to Jan. 19th housekeeping	00-09-08
To son Condies Masons Jan. 15th	00-00-04
paid Dan: Sowton for fitting an old gowne for my wife which was	
a Gowne of Mine	00-06- 0
Laid out in houskeeping from Jan. 19th	00-05- 6
for things used about the Gowne	00-02-08
for mendinge of shoes	00-00-10
for Sacke Ale and Cider this weeke	00-01-09

---

[1]   A conjecture based on a similar entry, fo. 16v.
[2]   The corner is worn.

I Have in house Remaininge at the end of this quarter   04-12-00

I am now indebted just   £ 155-00-00
    havinge *put* ap[ar]t this [£]4-12 to the paiment of the rent for
    the leep yeares Money It was [£]9-12. for 160 pound I have
    paid in all [£]14-12 whereof John Brownsdon hath £5 Daniell
    Condy has rest which is the sume of £9-12s-0d

I have not one penny to begin this next quarter the third of this yeare ˆthe three &
fiftieth of mine ageˆ Deus providebit[1]

I Cannot but take notice of the providence & fatherly provision of My God and
father That whereas this time twelve moneth when I had paid my brother Stone
at Salisbury & was returned from my London Journey I was indebted £244 viz
to my brother Condy £25 to my sonne Condy £44 to my Cosen Covert £10 to the
trumpeter 165. I have brought my debts unto £155 & yet have ˆtoˆ satisfie for the
lent[2] of £160 the sume of £9-12s besids so that it appeares this yeare I have paid
ˆ& haveˆ in all £98-12s besides my expences in meate & drink & charges & other
necessary expenses & gifts. the other £5 of the trumpeters Mony is & hath beene
in John Brownsdons hand, who is to pay 6s for it[.] He hath also now £5 more
of the trumpeters money to his owne use. And my sonne Condy hath the £9 12s
ˆnowˆ to be paid for my last yeares enjoyinge £160

    hactenus et hactenus &c auxiliatus est Dominus. Non est mihi argentum[3]

---

[1] 'God will provide'. These summary entries are made across the whole page.
[2] 'Loan': in other words, here he noted £9-12s interest to be paid on £160.
[3] 'Thus far and thus far &c God hath holpen. I have no money.'

Jan. 25. A pound of Tabacco	00-01-03
for *Beames*[1] & Workemens Wages	00-04-03
for Soape January 27th	00-02-00
Laid out in houskeeping untill Feb. 2nd	00-05-03
from thence in houskeeping turfes & *It[erato]*[2] *beams*	00-08-06
At the Lords supper Feb. 4. I gave	00-00-06
sent to Peter Glubb for his Mothers sake	00-05-00
the boy at chusing victors Feb 8 had[3]	00-00-04
Laid out for houskeeping the 13th & last weeke of the 53 yeare of my age untill Feb. 16th	00-07-06
paid Will Webb for wood sithence December	00-14-08

Spent & bestowed & paid of debts this second quarter of the 53 yeare
of my age   17-12-08

                                                It 04-12-00[4]

whereof paid of Debt. 14-12-00 22-04-08

---

[1] Unclear here, and a few lines later: possibly 'beers', but (given the separate entry two lines earlier 'for Sacke Ale and Cider this week') more likely 'beams'.

[2] 'Once again'.

[3] 'The boy': his grandson Tom Larkham. 'Chusing victors' occurs again in February 1655/6 (fo. 21v) and seems to be related to the 'victor penny', a fee paid to schoolmaster (*OED* 'victor').

[4] 'It': 'iterato', once again, likewise – he had also recorded this amount in the opposite column, as what he had 'in house' at the end of the quarter.

[fo. 17r]

Hence forward is the third quarter of the three & fiftieth yeare of mine age
to wit from Friday Feb. 16 which beginneth the first weeke thereof
mony wood butter, all spent[1]

	£	s	d
Received february 16 for bookes	00	03	00

this day towards the evening my sonne George came to my house
to visite me. Blessed be God

February 22 I received letters from my Sonne Miller & daughter
Patience &c The Lord be praised

for bookes sold by me	00	03	04
for bookes sold to Mr Leere	00	03	06

Received at Kirton for Rent (abating rents & taxes & reparations)
I was there February 27 & 28   10-01-03

Heere I was inforced to have backe againe from my sonne Condy the
9 pound 12s which he had last quarter & I borrowed of him £11-8s
besids all which with 9 pound I put to it made the summe of £30
paid to Lieut. col. Barnes of honiton[2] to take bills of exchange to
convey it to my poore Daughter Patience in Ireland, Lord convey
it safe & blesse it.

Borrowed of my wife & sonne Condy of the former 20s & of the
Latter 12s so I ow him £12

Wid:[ow] Rundle March 17 was buried Received[3]   00-10s-00

March 23rd I had a Letter from my sonne George signif[yi]nge his
safe arrivall to his home, God be praised

March 24 endeth this yeare 1655

And now is due to me for my stipend	09+15-00
And from Mr Hogesson for rent of ground	01+16-08

Which is in all £11-11s-8 out of which the expences in the other
Columne being fully paid I have remain: 10-02-06 towards
paiment of my wife and my sonne Condy what I ow them viz £13

March 25th 1655 beginneth the yeare[4] being the Lords day

The first day of the weeke begins this yeare,
On which Christ did to Mary Magdalene appeare:
And first to her from whom had gon seven Devils,
O feare not then thy many sinnes and evills.
The last the first somtimes become 'tis known,

---

1   This heading runs across the whole page.
2   Honiton, Devon. Larkham had sent a copy of *Wedding-supper* to Lieutenant Colonel Barnes in 1652:
     see Appendix 1.
3   Tavistock PR, burials: 17 March 1654/5, Dorothy Rundell.
4   In the old style calendar.

[fo. 17r]

	£ s d
February 16 paid for wood	00+02-08
February 21 to Ellis Bray booles[1]	0-00+06
Houskeeping untill Feb the 23	00+10-*04*
for three Nailes of Cambric which made me 6 bands	00+02-10
Paid Mary Glubb for making them and for stockes for them[2]	00+01-00
Housekeeping untill March. 2.	00+09-01
I Rode to bring my sonne going Feb. 26 & was absent from home 4 daies & spent in my journey	00+11- 3
From March. 2. Housekeeping	00+10- 0
from March 9th houskeeping	00+07- 6
for my da Miller as in the other columne is mentioned	30+00-00
from March 16th houskeeping	00+04-0[?][3]
March 17. 3 Moneths taxe was taken from me at 1-6 per mo:[nth]	00+04-0[6]
March. 20 for mending a frying pan	00+00-0[?]
until the 25th of March houskeeping	00+06-0[?]
for wood and Candles to Will: Web	00+10-0[?]
for malt and wheate to Mrs Edgcumbe	00+07-0[?]
for baking the last quarter ended March 25th	0+01-0[?]
for servants Wages now also due	00+10-[*00*]
for schooling for the boy to August: Bond	00+02-0[*0*]
for Letters from London & Plimouth	00+00-0[?]
Hitherto laid out this third quarter	35- 02-0[?]

1655 Laid out from March 25th upon ticket[4]	
Inprimis for one seame of faggots	00+01-*06*
for Malt March. 28	00+04-0[?]

---

1 Larkham played bowls with Ellis Bray – barber, parish clerk, church member. Larkham's opponents complained that his conduct was inconsistent: he liked 'to play ... for cakes and ale in the new bowling-green', with dubious characters that he had instructed his flock to shun: *Strange metamorphosis*, p. 21. As the birthplace of Sir Francis Drake, Tavistock has a legendary connexion with the sport.
2 'Nail': a measure for cloth, equal to 2¼ inches (a sixteenth of a yard). 'Cambric': fine linen. 'Bands': neck-bands or collars for shirts, to fit to the neck. 'Stockes' were stiff neckcloths or collarbands to attach the bands. Larkham's portrait (Plate 1) illustrates how this would look. Distinct 'clerical bands' only came in from 1700 (*OED*, 'band' *n*², 4 b).
3 The edge of the folio is ragged from here to the foot.
4 Larkham made the entries here by checking through a separate note, or pieces of paper – a hint of the documents that he had on his desk and summed up in his record.

To me poore wretch become a gratious one.
With upright heart then shall I give thee praise
And I will surely walke in thy sweete waies.

I am deeply indebted Lord undertake for me

To the Little trumpeter I owe £174-18s whereˆofˆ John Brownsden
   is to pay £10 & 6s for last years interest so my debt is £155 and
   9-12s for last yeares interest
I have had nothing out of the Lamerton this yeare
Also I am indebted more then my stipend and rent of the ground
   will hold out to pay   02-17- 6[1]
So I am indebted in all the sume of   167-09-06

                                  God shall helpe and that right early[2]

[fo. 17v]

[On] the other side my Debts appeares to be 167-9-6 Besids what
   I borrowed now to spend upon which was was £2-2s-6d more
   in all £169-12s-00d
whereof the sume of 2-2-6 remaines unspent and Also of one &
   twenty shillings received last weeke Remaineth 6-10s in all
   remaines in house
[Also] M[r] Hogsons rent to be paid which is 1-16-08 abating the
   Lords rent[3] aprill 5ᵗʰ Mr Hoggesson paid his rent   02-09-04
April 29ᵗʰ of Mrs Mary Doidge Lord accept this first gift of this
   yeare from thine hand maid & do her good   00-05-00
for a funerall sermon April 24ᵗʰ at the buriall of Charitie Keagle[4]   00-08-00
At the buriall of Richard Peeke Sen[ior][5]   00-10-00
Cleare receipts this third quarter at Tavistocke are only   13-04-08
from Kirton I had cleare (after Monthly taxes poore high waies
   & for repa[ra]tions were deducted)   07-16-00
So all my tenants have paid Untill March 15ᵗʰ 1655 & such as pay
   not that quarter untill May. third
[&] all taxes are discharged for the yeare last past viz. 1654
[I]n my absence at Exeter May. 5ᵗʰ Thomas Pennington delivered
   my wife   01-00-00
which maketh my cleare receipts this quarter 14-4-8 & Kirton 17-17-03

1   Larkham added, to the right of £2-17s-6d, 'which I owe to my sonne Condy and 2-2-06d': this adds
    up to the £5 debt to Condy that Larkham noted in the other column.
2   Psalm 46:5 (KJV): 'God shall help … and that right early.'
3   Perhaps a feu payment to the earl of Bedford?
4   Tavistock PR, burials: 25 April 1655, 'Charity Keagle'.
5   Tavistock PR, burials: 5 April 1655, 'Richard Pike'.

one penny was paid to Mistresse Edgcu[m]b[e] to make up the sum
    that was owed 7s 4d which I thought had beene 7s 3d   00+00-01
Item laid out for fresh fish March 28[th]   00+00-04
Item for a necke of Mutton   00+00-05
Item delivered to bestow in the Market & necessaries about
    houskeeping Untill the sixth of Aprill   00+06-0[?]
Item for a seame of Broomfagots   00+00-*10*
To a poore man 2d At the Communion 6d   00-00-0[8]
     00-14-0[?]

March 28 I paid my sonne Condy £7   upon p[aymen]t of
    & my wife 20s   this I ow him £5
So I ow my son Condy £5

I had for one of my bookes March 28[th1]   00-01-*06*
of Mr Jacob for a funerall sermon[2]   01-00-[??][3]

[fo. 17v]

                                               £ s d
Laid out & spent on the other side which hath already beene
    deducted.   00-14-02
About my Garden Aprill 5th   00-02-03
More the same day for two seames of wood   00-02-04
Item delivered to houskeeping Aprill 6th   00-05-09
for letters going and coming to London   00-00-07
April the ninth 9[th4] A pecke of wheate   00-01-05
The chilldren each of them shoes   00-02-06
It bestowed in fish and victualls Aprill 11 & 12th   00-01-03
Laid out in houskeeping untill Aprill 20th   00-05-10
aprill 19 for 3 seames of Turffes   00-02-06
The same day 2 seames of Wood of Abbot   0-02-04
from April the 20th Houskeeping   0-08-01[5]
for mending & liquoring[6] my bookes April 22th   00-01-00
April 23th I sent for a pinte of sacke   00-00-09
April 26th Brewing day Malt cost   00-04-00
from Aprill the 27th in Houskeeping   00-08-08
A pound of Tabacco   00-01-06
delivered for houskeeping May *4th*   00-08-02
for a letter from my sone & from plimoth   00-00-08

---

[1]   After he wrote out his expenses Larkham changed tack and filled up the remaining space with notes
    about income.
[2]   Tavistock PR, burials: 29 March 1655, Mrs Elizabeth Jacob.
[3]   The folio is worn. The line below this is illegible.
[4]   Larkham wrote 'ninth' over Lane's earlier entry but added '9th' as well, for clarity.
[5]   Below this he deleted a line of text, which is illegible.
[6]   'Liquor': 'to dress (leather …) with oil or grease' (*OED*).

So the Lord hath Continued my Life thus farre & holpen me and regarded me in my low estate

Quid retribuam![1] I am in debt now only to the Trumpetter £155 & £9-12 for last yeares use of money of which John Brownsdon since hath received £5 & had the yeare past another £5 & is to pay 6s for it & for this yeare now current 12s for the whole £10

[Fi]nitus 3rd 4ta. Non est mihi argentum[2]

Received heere at Tavistocke   14-04-08
[A]nd from Kirton at twice In the space of the last quarter   17-17-03
                                                                   32-01-11

Hitherto from Kirton for these three   And Received otherwise cleare receipts
quarters [o]f the three and [fif]tieth   for these three quarters now ended
yeare [of] my age 26-15-3   43-15-00. so in all my receipts have
                                              been 70-10-3

Out of Lamerton nothing for the yeere
ended March 25th 1655

[fo. 20r][3]

Of the three and fiftieth yeare of mine age
1655 The Last Quarter May 18th beginneth it

Received as followeth   £ s d
Rec[eived] for six bookes the Wed: Supper   00-05-00
for a booke sold to Mr Leare which containeth five sermons of
   Mr Burroughes[4]   00-01-08

---

[1] 'What shall I render!' An allusion to Psalm 116:12 (KJV): 'What shall I render unto the Lord for all his benefits toward me?'
[2] 'Third quarter finished. I have no money.'
[3] The foliation jumps at this point to fo. 20r.
[4] Jeremiah Burroughes' *The saints treasury* was a book of five sermons. Larkham had bought two copies the previous summer (fo. 15v).

At a Communion May the 6th I Gave	00-06

At a Communion May the 6th I Gave — 00-06
May 4th I bought bookes at Exeter — 00-02-00
I gave to Mr Westlakes Man — 00-01-00
my journey to Kirton & Exeter stood me — 00-05-08
I gave to my wife to spend for 2 quarters having[1] laid out *the* rest — 00-11-04

May 7th I paid my sone Condy in p[ar]t for £5 — 02-00-00
halfe of My wood paid backe to William Webb[2] — 2-00-00
Sent to Plimouth for tenths & for acquitance — 01-02-01
Delivered for houskeeping untill May 18th — 00-06-03
I have pay[d] sonne Condy which I owed — 03-00-00
                                                   48-04-09

Spent this 3 quarter of the 53 yeare of my age *13*-4-9[,] paid of debts
    five pounds[,] sent to Ireland to my daughter £30[3]

to Ireland 30 pound.   to sonne Condy paid 12 pounds   houskeeping *9-??-??*
tenths & acquittance 22s-1d   *4-10-2 take 4s-6d*
In all laid out last quarter 48-04-09 as appearethe.[4]

Helpe me my God for men would me devour
they me backbite & do abuse each houre

In doubtfull cases father guid[e] thou me
for I have none to advise w*ith* but thee
Am I a sea or whale?[5] Lord pitty me
and from my pinching hould set me free
Let none that waite on thee be sham'd o God
and for the obstinate provide a Rod.

[fo. 20r]

Laid out as followeth	£ s d
For two seames of Turffs	00-01-0[?]
I delivered to my sonne Condy for which he is to be a debtor to the little trumpetter	10-00-00

---

1   Literally 'hoving' because – a good example of Larkham's practice – he let George Lane's earlier entry of a zero stand for an 'a'.
2   'For £5' starts this line but belongs to the line above: Larkham owed his son-in-law £5 and paid first £2 then £3.
3   These are additional notes squeezed in around the formal total.
4   He jotted these notes in the space around his poem.
5   Job 7:12 (KJV): 'Am I a sea, or a whale, that thou settest a watch over me?' Larkham's composition also drew on Proverbs 20: 25, 'the man who devoureth that which is holy'; Romans 1:30, 'backbiters'; Psalm 25:3, 'let none that wait on thee be ashamed' (all quotations from KJV).

Towards the end of this moneth of May John Brownsdon and
William Web brought [*a*] paper of the names of divers that
had delivered to them money to be delivered to me, in all 14-16-00

O my father in Jesus X accept of it in him.[1]

May 19th I said God Be Mercifull to Me &c[2]
Rebuke Sathan that so rageth in Men, keep Up thy Glory
How long Lord wilt THOU forbear to owne the censures of thy Churche[3]
Goe foorth o God with the censures of thy servants.
Let our weapons be mighty to the pulling downe of strongholds[4]
Let not thine enemies say, there, there, so *would* ˆweˆ have it

The first of June A woman gave my Wife 00-02-00
June the second Peternell Chubb Wed:[ding] Sup:[per] 00-00-10
for a funerall sermon at Mrs Juli:[an] Doidg bu:[rial][5] 01-00-00

Receipts hactenus 16-05-06
whereof cleare receipts 15-18-10
whereof disbursed as on the other Col: 14-05-06

June 24 Remaines in house just 40s

Received My Rent for ground of Mr Hogson 01+16-08
Received My stipend due at Midsomer 09+15-00
June 30th Alice Lambshead, Lord accept it 00+02-00
At the Buriall of Mrs Sitwills father[6] 00+12-00
July 19th At the buriall of Walter Pecke[7] 00+06-00
at the Buriall of old Jane Sowton[8] 00- 07-06

above cleare receipts 15-18-10 &c 12-19-02

The totall Summe of this quarter is 28-18-00
My rents at Kirton[,] charges & taxes abated 12-14-07

---

[1] 'X' is a common abbreviation for 'Christ'.
[2] Larkham recalled here Luke 18:13 (KJV), 'God be merciful to me a sinner', the prayer of repentance from the parable of the Pharisee and the Publican.
[3] Larkham championed the right of the Church to carry out 'censures' (spiritual discipline), and looked for divine support to carry this forward in Tavistock despite opposition from erstwhile supporters: see Introduction.
[4] 2 Corinthians 10:4 (KJV): 'For the weapons of our warfare are not carnal, but mighty through God to the pulling down of strong holds.'
[5] Tavistock PR, burials: 9 June 1655, Mrs Julian Doidge.
[6] Tavistock PR, burials: the only possibility is John Browne, merchant, 12 July 1655.
[7] Tavistock PR, burials: 19 July 1655, 'Walter Pike'.
[8] Tavistock PR, burials: 4 August 1655, Jane Sowton.

For three moneths assessment	00-04-06
Given to sonne Condies man when he died my coate &c	00- 6
more laid out in housekeeping this first weeke of the 4th quarter	00-06- 8
Item for two seames of wood paid	00-02-0*4*
May 20th to poore Frenchmen I gave	00-00-02
A Bushell of Malt *23* of May brewing day	00-04-03
for sixe pound of soape to wash	00-02-0[*0*]
from May 25th second weeke houskee[ping]	00-06-01
from June the first the third weeke	00-08-[??]
J[u]ne third shoes for my selfe	00-03-[??][1]
At the communion given	06
June 6th one seame of fagots cost	00-01-0[?]
Given to drink to *odious B G*[2]	*00- 3*
from June 9th for houskeeping fourth weeke	00-06-0[?]
Two seames of Turffes June 12th	0-01-0[?]
for Mending of cloathes paide	0-01-0[?]
from June 15th housekeeping the 5th weeke	00-06-0[?]
To the distressed protestents in Savoy[3] given	00-05-0[*0*]
paid Bevile Wevill for Malt June 18th	0-04-0[?]
for a seame of faggots the same Day	00-01-0[?]
from June 22th houskeeping the 6th weeke	1- 8-0[?]
Putt ap[ar]t ^& paide^ for servants wages due June 24th whereof	
18d John Bur*gess* had in my servants Absen[ce][4]	00-10-[??]
Until Midsomer in this yeare 1655	14-05-0[?]

---

[1] The edge of the folio is badly worn from here downwards.

[2] 'Odious B G' has proved impossible to identify. Larkham drew a thick line after the 'G' to cross through George Lane's earlier entry, but perhaps originally wrote the full surname and then scored it out.

[3] On 24 April 1655 the duke of Savoy's forces massacred Protestants (Waldensians) in Piedmont. Cromwell called a national fast, threatened military intervention and raised funds for aid – to which Larkham contributed 5s. The event inspired Milton's Sonnet XVIII, 'On the late massacre in Piedmont':

> Avenge O Lord, thy slaughter'd Saints, whose bones
>   Lie scatter'd on the Alpine mountains cold,
>   Ev'n them who kept thy truth so pure of old,
>   When all our Fathers worship'd Stocks and Stones
> Forget not: in thy book record their groanes
>   Who were thy Sheep and in their antient Fold
>   Slain by the bloody *Piemontese* that roll'd
>   Mother with Infant down the Rocks. Their moans
> The Vales redoubl'd to the Hills, and they
>   To Heav'n. Their martyr'd blood and ashes sow
>   O're all th'*Italian* fields where still doth sway
> The triple Tyrant: that from these may grow
>   A hunderd-fold, who having learnt thy way
>   Early may fly the *Babylonian* wo.
>
> *Milton's sonnets*, ed. E. A. J. Honigmann (London, 1966).

[4] The Larkhams' maid, Dinah Woodman, whose 'journey' is noted a few lines later.

So Received this 53 year of Mine age in all	72-13-00
Received from Kirton cleare receipts	39-09-10
Thus farre the Lord hath holpen me	112- 2-10[1]
August the fifth to the Barber[2]	00-00-06
about the carrynge of wood paid	00-01-06
August 1 Delivered to Son Condie for the trump[e]ter	10-00-00
July 28 A paire of shoes for Thomas	00-01-06
For mending childrens cloathes & buttons	0-01-00
Upon the Ensigne in Wine & Bunnes *which my* sonne Condy paid[3]	0-00-04
given to one bringing wood from T *Penn*[*ing*]*to*[*n*]	0-00-02
unto the midwife for my daughter Jean[4]	00-02-06
Given to the woman that kept my daughter in childbirth	00-01-06
July the 11th to the Barber	00-00-06
for 3 moneths taxe at 15 per moneth	00-03-09
at the communion August the 5th	00-00-06
for a letter from Georg & one backe July 6th	00-00-07
for anniess seede water[5] of Richard Hitchens serv[ant]	00-00-07

from July the *8th* unto August the 18th my birthday which endeth the 53 yeare & beginneth the 54 if I live *so long* Putt apart for household expences	02-14-09
	13-09-08

---

[1]   Larkham entered this total again at the top of the next folio.

[2]   The next few entries (which continue his note of expenses from the foot of the column opposite) illustrate how Larkham sometimes noted down expenditure as memory served or as he worked through scraps of paper on his desk.

[3]   See the entry opposite about 'Ensygne Winsmore'.

[4]   Jane, wife of Daniel Condy. Tavistock PR, births: 'Thomas, son of Mr Daniel Condy and Jane his wife borne the 8 of July & baptized the 28 of July 1655' (on a Saturday, no doubt at a church meeting).

[5]   Aniseed-water or anise-water: a by-product of distilling oil of aniseed, a medicinal water to combat flatulence. See *OED* 'anise'; *DTGC*.

for Wine & Bunnes for Ensygne Winsmore	00-01-0[?]
Given to Dinah towards her journey	00-00-[??]
to a boy that brought my horse at Mr Elfords[1]	0-00-0[?]
paid for Tom's schooling to Aug Bond	*02-00*
for houskeeping untill July the 6th	00-06-[??]
Paid W. Gee for 2 skines for linnings	00-02-0[?]
2 seames of faggots June 29th	00-02-00
for Baking until Midsomer	00-01-[??]
July the first given to the Communion	00-00-06
for makeing drawers & tape	00-01-[??]
for a shirt & smok for *the children*	*-04-[??]*
7 yards ½ of dowlas[2] at xiid per yard	*00-07-06*

July the 6th Hactenus[3] expended		01-02-[??]
14-10-09	spent 1-2-9	*28-1[?-??]*[4]

---

[1] John Elford, a local and long-serving Justice of the Peace, who regularly took depositions in Tavistock for the Devon Quarter Sessions.

[2] 'Dowlas': a coarse linen.

[3] 'Hactenus': hitherto, thus far.

[4] This last line is hard to read: the manuscript is badly worn.

18 August 1655 – 17 August 1656

[fo. 20v]

Ætatis 54ᵗʰ   Received last year in all 112-2-10

[T]he 18ᵗʰ day of the 6ᵗʰ moneth being the last day of the weeke 1655
beginneth the foure and fiftieth Yeare of myne age.

The suffering day of Jesus Christ my Lord[1]	A Day of rest begins this following yeare
Began and endeth now the bigone yeare.	On it my Lord lay sleeping in the grave:
In which I have (according to the word)	That I may serve him now without all feare
[B]eene made like unto him my Saviour Deare	In trueth of heart is the choise thing I crave.
[Oh] man of Griefes.[2] Oh that also in Spirit	A breathing Lord to mee poore worme afford,
[I] Might be daily like him more & more	Let thy sweet armes me safely now enfold:
And so at last glory with him inherit	Fight let me with the Spiritts ready sword
When I have fled this *sea*-like World all o're	To preach Christs trueths O do then me uphold.

[*Ita*] pipiavit indignissimus Larkhamus[3]

Memorandum that of the 165 pound principall taken up of Mr Gearing Trumpetter
My sonne Condy hath £20 Twenty pound and Mr Brownsdown hath Ten pounds
and I have one hundred thirty and five to be answeareable for and no more
principall[.] But for the Interest of the last yeare for £160 and this yeare which
will be ended January the 30ᵗʰ next comminge for £135 the whole will be £18
because my sonne Condy had not the last paid untill the 1 of August last past
so he is to pay 18s and John Brownsdon 18s also for interest all which maketh
£19-16s for 2 yeares *att* 16 p[er] cent[4]

I came home from the Assises (held at Exeter) August 22. I went thitherward
August 15ᵗʰ [.] I *lie* at Kirton in my way and perfected myne accounts there &
satisfied for all taxes and rates untill Midsomer last & Received from all my
tenants (except Robert Bolefields forty shillings) untill Midsommer[,] and August
the first from Buckingham & Jussin[,] from Broke & Cooper untill Sept 29ᵗʰ that
quarter being paid also beforehand[;] & from Walter White also whom I paid 15s
and 2d unto & allowed 10s for June & September quarters[,] the whole 25s-2d[.]
I had in payment of a fine of Phillip Wreyford £5 and a bond for £5 to be paid
December 25ᵗʰ next cominge[.] I had 1s from Broke in earnest for £3 he is to pay
for his owne life upon his house. So in all my cleare receipts at Kirton were (as is
set downe in the former page) £12-14s-7d. which with 8 shillings remaining of the
last yeare maketh the just summe of <u>thirteen pound two s[hillings] seven pence</u>[5]
                                    & spent in my journey thereof 00-11-03
[*which*] I have to begin this 54ᵗʰ yeare of mine age

---

1   Friday. Larkham's new year began on 18 August 1655, 'the last day of the weeke', Saturday.
2   Under or over 'Griefes', Larkham wrote 'Sorrows'.
3   'So cried most unworthy Larkham.'
4   This entry is written across the whole folio.
5   This is one long entry, written across the whole folio.

[fo. 20v]

I had backe to hansell of my Mare[1]   00-01-06
So I have at my returne in house £4 *want*[*ing*] 9d
all that is paid in the other colum[n] being deducted
I say August the 23 castinge up my accounts and allowinge the said
    sume of £9-4-10[2] Remaineth to me in house just the sume of
    03-19-03 out of which & what heerafter may come

August 25[th] As I was walking in my garden groaninge under many evills & [in]
particular my deadnes in prayer [a]n answeare of comfort came to me refreshinge
me (My grace is sufficient for thee[3]) whereupon I went into my chamber & on
my knees praised God.

Received towards my charges [a]t ex[e]ter of William Web   0- 5-6
[of] Mrs Audry Edgcombe Gold   0- 5-6
[Laid] out as in the other column. 3-2-9   4-10-3
[Re]maines £1-7-6 this I keepe for my [mean]es untill I receive
    more at Kirton[4]

[fo. 21r]

I have left no money with my wife but have promised her what she laieth out of
    her money I will take order in time, that shee be satisfied againe.[5]
Two acquittances I have left, one for £9-15s the other £1-16s-8d both
    due Sept. 29th
for the other side I had   01-07-06
At Kirton I had for rents in all   08-02-09
Given me by friends at departure   01-02-06
by John Trots wife at my returne   00-01-00
My stipend received by sone Condy   09-15-00
also I had of him to be paid by Hoggeson   1-16-08
of my wife I had to bestow in hoods &c[6]   0-12-00

---

[1]   To 'handsel': to give 'earnest-money' or a 'luck-penny' to seal a deal in auspicious fashion (*OED*):
      Larkham received a small back-payment from Mr Gold, to seal his purchase of Gold's grey mare,
      noted in the right column of this folio.
[2]   This relates to the total of £9-4s-10d expenses in the parallel column.
[3]   2 Corinthians 12:9 (KJV): 'And he said unto me "My grace is sufficient for thee: for my strength is
      made perfect in weakness."'
[4]   The line below this is unreadable because the manuscript has worn away.
[5]   Written at the top, across the whole folio.
[6]   Perhaps as gifts for relatives in London: a hood ('French hood') was an item of women's clothing
      (*OED*).

Bought a Gray Mare of Mr Gold cost	08-00-06
Given to my wife at my returne out of Kirton rents	00-10-00
I bought an oiled hood[1] at Exeter cost	00-03-00
I gave Augustines Bonds little daughter at Exeter	00-00-06
I paid for seale waxe to seale leases at Kirton	00-00-01
	09-04-10

paid for Trimminge a suite for my selfe Ribbons buttons & makeinge	
& silke	00-11-09
for linnen for the children & thread & an apron	00-06-00
for provision for the house untill Aug. 25th	00-06-06
Aug: 28. to be ridd of the Wait players[2]	00-01-00
Aug. 30 to the barber	00-00-06
for provision untill September first	00-06-02
Aug. 31 Paid in full to W Webb charges about my wood	0-07-00
Paid D. Sowton for making coate & buttons & silke	0-05-00
for the cloth & Taffetie & u[nder] silke to D Condy	0-18-04
[*at the*] communion Sept. 2 Given	00-00-06
	? - ? - ?[3]

[fo. 21r]

My Journey stood me in all whereof given at lime[4] 9s	08-03-07
Cloathes bought in London & silkes	5-06-00
about printing of bookes	10-09-00[5]
bought a little Bible	00-03-04
bought a hatt 13s & powders[6] 2-6	00-15-06
	24-17-05

	£ s d
While I was absent my wife hath laid out in houskeeping & other	
necessaries which is by me to be satisfied	03-09-00
paid likewise 3 moneths taxe for Tavist[oc]k to witt untill	
December 25th	00-03-09
Novemb. 4 Given at the Communion	00-01-00
paid for letters from London 9d & 9d	00-01-*06*
to my servant for wages due Sept. 29th	00-10-00
spent sithence my retorne from Lond[on] &c	0-06-00

---

1   Made from oiled cloth, used to make hoods and coats to ward off the rain.
2   'Wait players': a wind band.
3   The last line of the folio is badly worn and illegible.
4   Lyme Regis. This entry was squeezed in later.
5   Larkham's *The attributes of God*: see Appendix 2.
6   'Powders': either hair powders (Larkham lists them along with a hat), or medicine.

of Mr Adrian in London I had[1]   02-00-00

    24-17-05

of A. Lambshead upon my returne sent to me by a girle. Lord accept it 00-02-00

of Mary Gibbs widow Novemb. 5th   00-03-06

My horse valued at   06-05-00

of R.D. Desireing prayers beinge with child   00-02-06

The 12th of this Moneth 1642 I left my house & familie in New England. It is now full 13 yeares agone, and the 17th day endeth the first quarter of the 54th yeare of mine age, The day of Queen Elizabeths coming to the crowne &c Greate have thy mercies beene o Lord to this nation and to this poore sinfull worme in particular

I have received this quarter by addition by the good hand of God for my
    livelihood   15-00-08

And from Kirton I received this quarter   08-02-09

In all Received this first quarter by addition   23-03-05

          left last quarter   -16-03

The second quarter beginning. Nov. 18th 1655

    £ s d

Inprimis for a funerall sermon &c[2]   00-10-00

Novemb. 23rd I had a motion to pray about 4 in the afternoone or
    rather before I obeyed it and expect some comfortable issue.

Novemb. 28 of Mrs Mary Doidge   00-10-00

Decemb. 7 I laid out all the money I had and my wife layeth   cleare receipts
    out for necessary expenses about the house and other things   Hactenus this
    untill it shall please God to send mony to me who never   quarter. £1 the
    yet failed me   rest left last ¼

        16s-3d left last ¼ & £1 received this quarter   01-16-03

My stipend Received[3]   9-15-00   Jan 1

cleare receipts at Kirton, & a fine £5   12- 6-03   Jan 16th

Mr Hogesons rent   01-16-08

    24-17-11   second quarter

---

1 Probably John Adrian, a London merchant with connexions to Larkham's old stamping ground of East Greenwich, whose will was proved in 1669: National Archives, London, PROB11/331.

2 Tavistock PR, burials: 22 November 1655, David White.

3 He jotted these notes in a small space left at the foot of the folio. His total included £1 already received that quarter, noted earlier.

Item laid out for oats & *Gall*[1] for horse	00-01-06
paid for six pound of candles	00-02-06
for altering my cloake to a coate & for silke	00-02-00
for provision from Novemb 9th to the end of this first quarter ending November 17th laid out	0- 4s-6
Item due to my wife for September quarter out of the rents at Crediton	00-10-00
for carriage of Box from London & Exeter	0-05-06
	05-16-03
Remaines only	00-16-03

Second quarter beginning of layings out as followeth

	£ s d
Paid for malt Bought last weeke	0- 4-00
more paid for hopps used then also	0- 0-09
for sending a letter to plimouth	0- 0-02
Item paid which was owing to shoppes	0-01-05
for making coate and breeches for Tom	0-02-0[?]
Item for candles & small things	0-02-00
paid for making of cloathes for J Miller	0- 3- 6
for things used about the clothes for both *children*[2]	0- 5- 9
Item laid out about the house *keeping*	0- 1- 0
Item *in diverse expences* untill Nov 28th	0- 5-08
paid for tubs-mending to brew	0- 1s-0
more laid out about houskeeping Dec *18*	*7-06*
	01-15-03

My wife laid out untill January 4th which I paide here[3] againe	02-00-00
more for shoes, 1-6, & hatt for Tom. 3-8	00-05-02
more for mending shoes for Jane	00-00-02
more for baking last quarter now ended	0-01-0[?]
for the rents at Kirton to my wife given	00-10-[*00*]
paid my servants quarters wages	*00-10-[00]*[4]

---

[1] This word is blotted and hard to decipher but he may be referring to treatement for a 'gall', 'a painful swelling, pustule, or blister, especially in a horse' (*OED*).
[2] Probably his grandchildren Thomas Larkham and Jane Miller.
[3] He perhaps meant 'her' rather than 'here'.
[4] The manuscript is indistinct, but 10s shillings was the usual quarterly payment.

[fo. 21v]

Jan: 16 being the day of the Eclipse of the Sunne,[1] Mr John Howe Minister of
Greate Torrington had leave to preach heere at Tavistocke who most fiercely
lashed at me in his sermon about the improper obedience of such as are truly
gratious. I wrote to him that I would make good what I had preached the next
lecture day &c against which time there was great riding and sending to gather
the Ministers of the Contry together, in hope that I should have been swallowed
up.[2]

Jan: 19th 1655 I delivered of the trumpeters money to my son Condy at his
   house £13-00-00

Jan 23. I preached upon the same text Mr Howe preached on the week before,
and after sermon a conference in the parish Church and in the afternoone among
the ministers in private. I acknowledge thankfully Gods hand over me[.] We all
parted lovingly at the last.

Feb. 2 . delivered to son Condy of the money due to the trumpeter   05-00-00
   so this £18 satisfies for interest Hitherto.   non est mihi argentum[3]
I am to pay £135 more with interest August 1st next coming and my
   son Condy £40 & John Brownsdon £10 which they have out of
   the summe we stand bound joyntly to pay.[4]

So the money that was laid out unto the end of this quarter I had of my wife
   Haveinge not one penny of mine owne

So endeth the second quarter of the 54th of mine age

Incipit 3rd quarta ætatis 54 Feb 17[th][5]

In haste we leape from last to first[6]	Unworthy I to thee do cry,
The quarter to begin at	Lord order mine affaires:
O that I might (for Lord I thirst)	Then to thy name all lasting fame,
To thee leap more from sinne.	Shall shine in my repaires.

---

[1] So far no other record of this eclipse has been found.
[2] David P. Field, 'Howe, John (1630–1705)', *ODNB*. The hinterland here is Larkham's relationship with
   the 'Devon Association', promoted by Howe and his father-in-law George Hughes of Plymouth: see
   Introduction. Halcomb gives an excellent appraisal of the situation: Joel Halcomb,'A social history
   of congregational religious practice during the Puritan Revolution', Ph.D. dissertation, University of
   Cambridge, 2009, pp. 224–7.
[3] 'I have no money.'
[4] This entry concerns the money Larkham had borrowed from 'the Trumpeter', Mr Gearing.
[5] 'Here begins the third quarter of the 54th of [my] age.' Usually, he marked the 18th as the first day
   of a new quarter.
[6] The first two words are hard to decipher. He has written over Lane's earlier entry.

[fo. 21v]

Expenses continued[1]	£ s d
Paid for malt Jan. 4th	00-04-00
towards housekeeping that day	00-05-00
for letters from and to London	00-01-10
more housekeepinge January 11th	05-00
put out for this weeke Jan 18th	05-08
A journey to Kirton & Exeter in sessions week	00-09-08
Laid out about my bootes mending ˆshoesˆ	00-00-11
Jan. 15 Paid the Barber. Ellis Bray	00-01-00
Jan. 17, Paid Rich: Hitchins account	00-01-10
Paid William Webb for candles	00-02-04
Sope. iis Jan. 18 french men 2d letters 4d	02-06
for Three Moneth taxe at Tavistocke	00-04-06
Laid out in housekeepinge Janu: 25th	00-05-00
Paid for mending shoes for Tom	00-00-06
for ˆsome things aboutˆ Houskeeping untill February 2nd	01-00
and to french men sailors	00-00-02
Feb 2nd paid for ˙past˙ housekeeping past[2]	02-10-11
Brewing Day January 31st for Malt paid	0-09-04
Paid for half a peck of Beanes to sett[3]	00-01-00
Paid February 1st for digging for Beans	00- 1-10
Given on Communion Day Feb 3rd	00-00-06
to N: Knight for helping in my wood Feb. 7th	00-00-06
Feb. 8th bestowed in the market houskeeping	00-07-06
Feb 15th housekeeping	00-06-04
Tom Had about chusing of victores to carry to his Mr[4]	00-00-06
My wife hath laid out this sume of	01-19-06

So endeth the second quarter of the 54th of mine age

---

[1] Larkham continued here, from fo. 21r, his list of expenses for the quarter which began 18 November 1655.

[2] Written between the lines in ink which is now faint. He inserted 'past' again, beneath, because it was unclear at the end.

[3] A 'peck' measured dry volume, usually two imperial gallons or a quarter of a bushel, although this varied from place to place and by commodity (*OED*).

[4] A similar expression occurs on fo. 16v and seems to be relate to a fee Tom Larkham paid his schoolmaster, like the 'victor penny' (*OED* 'victor').

Received for bookes untill Feb 21st   02-08-00[1]

February 22nd I received a letter from my son George and in it one
enclosed from my son Miller[.][2] The Lord hath not afflicted me in
them with evill tidings but good news I have of their grace & health[.]
Blessed be the name of the Lord in Jesus Christ O Cast all my sinnes
behind thy backe &c[.][3]

More for bookes in the quire & others	00-13- 8
for one booke of the best sort I had	00-04- 6
of Ellis Bray for one booke unbound	00-03- 0
Item for one booke of Mrs Sitwell	00-04- 0
A funerall sermon, Reddiclifes wife[4]	00-08- 0
To William Webb sold one	00-04- 0
for two bookes in the quire	00-06- 8
To Daniell Sowton one	00-04- 0
	04-15-10

[fo. 22r]

The third quarter continued

	£ s d
I have an° 1655/6 day 1° of the first Mon:[th]	00-04-11
Received for a Booke of Ja: Holland	00-04-00
Received for a booke of Thomas Fleshman	00-04-00
for a booke of Edward Bound	00-04-00
for one from Peter *Tricks* by S.[on] Condy	00-04-06
M.[arch] 12th John Sheare for two bookes	00-08-00
Mo[nth] 1. 17th day for a booke to one of Holsworthy[5]	00-04-06
So there hath been Received for bookes and 8s for a funerall sermon[6] the whole sume is	06-04-10

Thus farre the Lord hath holpen me | I have no money |

---

1 On 15 February 1655/6, Larkham received from London '48 bookes bound and 8 unbound' of his new
    publication, *The Attributes of God*. He made some notes here about sales but used the penultimate
    page of the manuscript to draw up a comprehensive list. See Appendix 2.
2 George Larkham in Cumberland; son-in-law Lieutenant Joseph Miller, in Ireland.
3 Isaiah 38:17 (KJV): 'Behold, for peace I had great bitterness: but thou hast in love to my soul
    delivered it from the pit of corruption: for thou hast cast all my sins behind thy back.'
4 Tavistock PR, burials: 17 February 1655/6, 'Mary Raddacliff'.
5 Holsworthy, Devon, twenty-five miles north-west of Tavistock.
6 Perhaps at the funeral of Thomasin Pitts, 17 March 1655/6 (Tavistock PR) but several other burials
    occurred earlier in the month.

I paid to my wife spent last ¼	01+07- 6
Feb. 19th I bought a quire & 5 sheetes of pap[er]	00+00- 6
Paid for dowles[1] for shirts for my selfe	01+01-06
for a double letter to London & one from there	00+ 0-09
for pruines bought of my daughter[2]	00+ 0-09
for carriage of Bookes from London	00+14- 0
About charges for Georgs bookes to Mr *Nortchot*[3]	00+02-04
for a double letter from London to Tavistocke	00+00-08
I paid my wife which I borrowed of her	00+03-06
Laid out besids that Feb. 22 about the house	00+07-06
Paid Sonne Condy for a bottle of str:[ong] water[4]	00+01-06
paid for malt. Feb the last	00+04-08
for Tabacco inke & houskeepinge untill Feb last which my wife laid	
out (to wit) 5s	00+05-03
Moneth. 1. day the first to the barber	00+00-06
Remaines in house 00-04-11	04- 10-11

[fo. 22r]

	£ s d
	£ s d
Paid for making Tomes Dublett[5]	00-01-06
for things used & sarge[6] to son Condy	00-04-10
for mending a place over the stable & materialls	00-01-08
first Mo:[nth] 7[th] delivered for housekeeping this weeke	00-05-09
for shoes for myselfe and Jane Miller[7]	00-04-06
ˆput ap[ar]tˆ for provision for my family untill the 25[th] day of the	
first Mon:[th] 165⁵⁄₆	00-15-08

Expended on the other side 4-10-11 & on this   01-*13*-11

The whole sume is just 06-04-10 which is all *Reckoninge* this quarter

---

1   'Dowlas': coarse linen.
2   Prunes from Jane Condy.
3   Not identified, and unclear: perhaps Northcot or Northcomb.
4   'Strong water': spirits or 'aqua vitae'; sold as a drink and as medicine (*DTGC*).
5   'Doublet': a close-fitting garment with or without sleeves (*DTGC*).
6   'Serge': a popular textile in the seventeenth century, normally woollen, 'a durable twilled cloth of worsted … of a lighter weight than broadcloth and generally of better quality than kersey' (*DTGC*).
7   Larkham's grandchild. Her parents were in Ireland, with the army.

Now O Lord direct me for this yeare cominge 1656,
Continue my gratious God whether *fo[r]be* ord.[1]

Laid out by my wife as in the other colum[n] because I have not one
penny in possesion this 25[th] day. 1. Mens[e].
O my God remember and enable me to discharge my duty in regard
of my manyfold occasions that thy name be not dishonored

The first that this yeare gave any thinge to me, was Bevile Wivell
who gave me a bushell of Malt. O my God Stail smell[s] sweete
in thy nostrells in Christ.[2] O grant unto this poore man
acquaintance with thy Majesty

Mary Gibb. A dish of fresh butter the 27th day of this 1 moneth

Sold two bookes for   00+08-00

April 2nd Joan Peeke widdow 2 pullets given to me

I had for a booke of Mr Brownsdon   00+04-00

April. 5. I called to remembrance that this day anno 1652 I came
from Cumberland on this day was foure year I began my journey
&c. greate and marvellous have thy mercies & providences beene
o Lord to and over me a poore sinner, vile and contemptible.
O Continue &c.[3]

Mrs Audry Edgcombe, desires to praise &c & gave	00+05-00
Received of Mr Leere for a little bible	00+03-04
Item received for one of my bookes. April 10th	00+04-00
Item received for a booke Aprill the 16th	00+04-00
Due to me for my stipend March 25th last	09+15-00
for rent for my ground from Hogson	1+16-08
for & in lieu of an acre of wood due last yere due and not paid untill	
this year 1656	4+00-00
Sold one of my bookes Called the Wedding Supper[4]	0+01-00

Received all waies 17- 1- 0[0]

This quarter ended this 17th of May beinge the third of the 54th yeare
of Mine Age, I have received by addition only   16-04-08
Heere endeth the quarter

---

1 'Whatever may be ordained.' Larkham marked the start of the new year on 25 March (according to the old style calendar).
2 'Staile': as in stale (not fresh), or even urine (*OED* 'stale' *n*[5]). Larkham wanted to make the point that 'in Christ' everything smells sweet to God. He had in mind texts about sweet or foul smells which pleased or displeased the Almighty such as Genesis 8:21, Isaiah 3:24, Philippians 4:18 and particularly 2 Corinthians 2:15. Wivell usually sold malt to Larkham, and appears in a deed of 1658 as 'Bevill Wyvell', maltster (Plymouth and West Devon Record Office, 349/8/6).
3 Probably an allusion to Psalm 36:10: 'O continue thy loving kindness unto them that know thee; and thy righteousness to the upright in heart' (KJV).
4 Larkham's *Wedding-supper* (London, 1652). For earlier sales see Appendix 1.

Paid for 3 Monthes taxe for Tavistocke for the Army to wit, until	
Midsommer	00-04-06[1]
For wages to my servant,[2] for the quarter ended	00-10-00
Paid for the boyes schooling to A: Bond[3]	00-02-00
Paid for Baking the last quarter	00-01-04
Laid out about the house (and what was owing by my wife because	
I had no money)	00-12-02
	01+10-00
To Calcard of N England in distresse[4]	01+00-00
Aprill 2nd Paid Sara Trowt for old *letters* paid which she said she	
had laid out for mee	[?- ? - ?][5]
Paid for Wine & figgs	00-00-11
Hitherto. So laid out	00-01-09
Item for a Handbasket bought at Plimouth	00-01- 0
Item laid out April 4th Houskeeping. ^ & sacke^	00-08- 0
Item for a letter from London paid	00-00-03
Aprill 7th paid for Tenths due last Xber [6] for an acquittance 21s[,] 9d	
and 4d	01+02-01
Item delivered Aprill 11th 6s & paid & spent 2s	
to wit to R Hitchens 10d & for fish & for other things after the	
Markett 1s ^2d^	00-08-00
Item Delivered for the market and expenses for this weeke ended	00-09-04
Aprill the 19th whereof 6d was for preparing my garden	
for making my garden Aprill. 23. the 3 men had	00-02-00
paid for seedes besids what was given to me	00-00-07
for one bushell and half of Lyme	00-01-06
for 400 of healing stones[7]	00-01-10
Item for Malt Brewed Aprill the 24th	00-05-00
Item for provision April 25th, and for Candles	00-08-06
for Lathts Nailes & pinnes	00-02-08
for wages for 2 [men] & one boy to alter	00-03-03
The second day of the 3 Mo:[nth] houskeeping	00-08-08
May. 2. Shoes for the Rude boy Tom[8]	00-01-06
paid. May. 5 for making a bank in the garden	00-00-10

---

1   Larkham regularly noted tax payments but this is the only time he connected his payment with the
    army. The significance is unclear.
2   Dinah Woodman.
3   Augustine Bond.
4   Not identified.
5   This is impossible to decipher because of crossings out and an earlier entry by George Lane
    underneath.
6   December: the tenth month if the year starts on 25 March (old style).
7   'Heling, healing': a covering, of stones or slates. *OED* cites Richard Carew, *The survey of Cornwall*
    (1602), 'For covering of houses there are three sorts of Slate, which from that use take the name of
    Healing-stones.'
8   'Rude' as in 'ignorant, unskilled': perhaps a young labourer – not identified.

I have not been at Kirton this quarter And therefore have nothing to
    adde ˆoutˆ of the meanes there, to the receipts of this quarter
Since this yeare 1656 began I have spent 9-1-0. And received only 5s
    for all the Rest belonging to the last yeare & to that is to be added.
    I say received only this year 1656 hitherto ~~only~~ five shillings.

[fo. 22v]

The 18ᵗʰ Day of the third moneth vulgo May[1] beginneth
The ~~third~~ 4ᵗʰ quarter of the 54ᵗʰ yeare of myne age, anᵒ 1656.
first eight weekes of this yeare of Expectation *are allready past*[2]

of the Money expended sithence[3] March 25ᵗʰ 10s was wages due to my
    servant for the former quarter. *01-2-1.* for *books* & ano[ther] 2s for
    the boyes schooling and.16d for baking *Which is in all waies*   1-15-05
Which being deducted out of £9-01-0 there remaines. 7-5-7 which
    hathe beene already expended since March 25ᵗʰ last past. All that
    I received besids which was due *that was out o[f] purse owed* 05s
    & no more

I say received as on the other side since March 25ᵗʰ last past	00-05-00
Received for bookes which I sold	00-16-04
Kirton rents untill May 3ʳᵈ last	11-14-09
I received May 27 for earnest[4] for one part of my house in Kirton of John Macy	10-00

---

[1] 'Vulgo': commonly, popularly. Larkham still used the common names for months, although often (like other zealous Protestants of his time) he preferred to number months rather than to use 'pagan' names. He almost always referred to days of the week by numbers not names.

[2] This is across the whole folio.

[3] Since.

[4] 'For earnest': as a downpayment.

for mending the rude boyes shoes	00-00-06
May. 3 for sixe pound of soape	00-02-00
Expenses in houskeeping untill May 17th	00-19-05
for making Joan Miller's New Gowne[1]	00-03-06
for 5 yards of *stuffe* at 2[s] 2[d] & silke & *shirts* is in all	00-14-00
May 9th for letters from London and ˆbyˆ Plimouth	00-01-0[?]
Paid to R. Hitchens May.14 for rent for	00-01-[??][2]
Item Quart of wine to Jonathan Condy	00-01-[??]
And in the former part of the ¼ 06-04-10	09-01-[??]
The totall summe of expenses this last ¼	15-0[?-??]

[fo. 22v]

spent since March 25th last.	07-05-*07*
	[£] s d
May 19th I gave to Wid:[ow] *Morcambe* [of] Northam[3] who came to	
see me	00-01-00
The 20th of May I lent my son Condy going to Exeter	05-00-00
and I delivered him a note of rents Due to me at Kirton untill	
May. 3. last Received by him[4]	10-04-09
For a double accidens[5] for the Boy	00-00-10
Also 30 shillings was Allowed to Buckingham which was sent by	
Mr Peake to my sisters	1-10-00
May 24 the barber	00-00-06
Paid Calman rebinding A Booke	0- 9
Laid out about reparations in May	00-08- 8
And in houskeeping the last weeke of May	0-12- *9*
Item for malt brewed May 20th	00-05-00
I gave to W. Harris bringing books from Plimouth	00-00-06
Houskeeping untill Midsommer	1-13-09
Paid Thom: fleshman for 59 pounds of butter	00-19- 0
June 14th Paid D. Sowton for worke	0-03- 0
for Malt Brewed June 12th	00-05- 0

---

1   Larkham's grandchild Jane Miller.
2   The folio is worn at the edge from here down to the foot.
3   Larkham was rector of Northam, Devon, from 1626 until 1640. This widow (possibly 'Morcombe',
    a Devon surname) has not been identified.
4   The last three words were added later.
5   Possibly 'accidence': a book of the rudiments of grammar (*OED*). Larkham paid for the schooling
    of his grandson Tom Larkham and later Tom Miller.

June 13th I received of George Pearce for earnest for the other part of my house	<u>10s-00</u>

June 13th I received of George Pearce for earnest for the other part
    of my house   10s-00
Received of sonne Condy June 16 of the money he had at Kirton
    for me   00- 4-09
Will. burdred[1] June 24th my stipend   9-15-00
& my rent from Mr Hogson   1-16-08
So all that comes by Way of Addition since March 25th last   12-16-08

That which came from Kirton Belongeth to the last quarter of the last
    yeare except 20s which I had in earnest of them that tooke a stake
    in my house at Kirton[2]
Besides what I shall have cleare from Kirton for the quarter Due June 24th.

June 20th I had a darke letter from Mr Woods about Lamerton o my God
    bringe Glory to thy name joy to thy people the despised handfull, and
    refreshing to the parched soule of thy servant.[3]

The expenses of this quarter ended June the 23rd are more than the
    receipts that came by addition, the *sume* of   £01-12s-00
But the layings out since May the 18th which began the 4th quarter
    of the 54th yeare of Mine age are only   07-03-01
So upon that account my receipts have beene more then mine
    expenses the sume of   05-13-07

The above mentioned Hogsons Rent being unpaid untill July the 18th
    I desired my wife to make provision for my famely.

[fo. 23r]

July the 4th 1656 upon reading somewhat of the wonderfull goodnesses and
providences of God (as I found I had written in a paper booke which by
providence I mett withall) I was stirred in spirit to say, Wonderfully hath the
Lord beene gracious to me, though I should never enjoy mercy more, I have
unspeakable cause to be thankfull I wrote these lines and betook myself to fall
upon the floor of the chamber before the Lord And considered that his mercies
are the mercies of GOD, to raise up my broken soule.

---

[1]   Not identified.
[2]   John Macy and George Pearce: see the entry a few lines earlier.
[3]   'Mr Woods' does not appear elsewhere. Larkham referred here to his protracted dispute over payment
    of the Lamerton augmentation: see Introduction.

Paid the score at R. Hitchins	00-04- 8
Paid Sonne Condy about my dublet	00-05-04
Servants wages, Bakeing, Schooling boy	00-13-04

I have spent and laid out in all since March 25th last (besides the
    paiment of what was due at the end of the last quarter) & beside   £ s d
    what I lent to my Sonne Condy this quarter ended June 24th   14- 8- 8

whereof	01-00-00	Calcard had of N. England[1]
my sisters	01-10-00	at Lyme given them
~~for Tenths~~	~~01-02-01~~	~~paid at Plimouth due~~ last year
For [3] Month:[s] taxes	00-04-06	for Tavistock untill June 24th
for reparations.	00-17-11	of the Ministers house
about Apparell	01-07-10	
charity besids sisters	0-01-06	to poore ones
Boyes Schooling	0-02-00	untill June 24th
Servants wages	0-10-00	ended then also
Letters by Post	0- 3-02	from London
About my Garden	0- 4-05	first & last this ¼

Summe	06-01-04	The rest was in housekeeping to wit £8-7s-4d[2]

June, 21, Saturday My Eldest daughter Patience Miller came to my house at
    Tavistock from Ireland a widow, D.G / D, M[3]
June 24 & 25 I rode to Major Hale about Lamerton business[.] spent
    in sacke when I came home   0-05-6

[fo. 23r]

	£ s d
From June 24th unto June 30th Laid out by my wife which I paid	00-09-06
From July the 01 unto the 8th spent	00-10-06
July 5th paid for bootes for my selfe	00-11-00
for 3 paire of shoes for My D.[aughter] Millers children	00-04-06
for making two gownes & a petticoate for my daughter Miller	00-14-00
for making a Wascot	00-01-06
for malt brewed July the 7th	00-05-00
From Julie 8th in houskeeping	00-09-06
for making a gowne for my wife	00-06-00
July 11th I lent to my daughter Miller	00-05-00
July 14th for 3 moneths taxe at Tavistocke	00-02-00

---

1   It has not been possible to identify this colonist 'Calcard'
2   This comment was written in the right margin, running sideways up the page.
3   'Deo Gloria / Deus Miserere': 'Glory to God / O God, have mercy.' Joseph Miller, lieutenant in
    Ireland, died 8 May 1656. Larkham recorded this in a special place at the start of the manuscript (fo.
    'H' v).

	£ s d		£ s d
1 quarter I received	15-00-08	& from Kirton	08-02-09
The second quarter	12-11-08	& from Kirton	12-06-03
The third quarter	16-04-08	& from Kirton	11-14-09
4 quarter Hactenus	<u>11-11-08</u>	from Kirton Hactenus in	
		earnest &c	<u>01-00-00</u>
July 18th	<u>55-08-08</u>	for my dwelling house	<u>33-03-09</u>

of John Macy £75 of George Pearse 40   <u>115-00-00</u>

July the 29th I took a journey to Kirton did much businesse paid all my debts to the little trumpetter. Returned on Thursday, on the Morrow I went with my Daughter Miller and her daughter to Plimouth intending for Ireland.[1] Saturday August the second I returned under the Will of God to Tavistocke the Wind being Contrary, August third Lords day (God giving one day more) I preached at Tavistocke[.] Munday August the 4th I went to Plimouth accompanied with some brethren[.] About midnight we put forth to sea[.] On Friday following, landed at passage[2] in the Haven of Waterford in Ireland with my daughter Miller[.] Many clouds lay over her estate But by the good hand of my God I dispatched many businesses and on Friday Sept 12th came to Bristol & the Thursday following. Sept. 18th came safe to my house at Tavistock. Blessed be &c. I was absent six Lord's Daies & no More.

---

[1] Patience Miller and her daughter Jane.
[2] 'Passage': 'Passage East', a fishing village on the western shore of Waterford Harbour.

Paid for making Jane Millers Gowne	00-04-00
From July 18th being Market day	00-08-07
Item at Tavistocke untill July 24 more spent	00-02-06
Given to Mr Sowtons & Mr Brownsdons servants	00-01-00
Paid to Richard Hitchins &c	00-05-00
Item laid out about house untill Aug[u]st	00-14-00
Non est mihi argentum[1]	05-13-07

---

[1] 'I have no money.'

18 August 1656 – 17 August 1657

[fo. 23r *continued*]

> In this poore Church thy weake ones Lord support,
> Grant that thy servant may teach and exhort.
> O still in Tav'stocke let none but Christ raigne,
> Tho Pride and Malice rage and Much disdaine.
> From Turk's and Tories[1] men of warr & foes,
> Lord thou has kept thy poore one, and from those
> that sought my shame with malice and despight,
> Me and My brethren O Lord guide aright.
>
> Glanvile, Watts, Polewheele, Godbeare, Gove, & Hore
> Bole, and all others that me vexe full sore,[2]
> O Lord forgive if they belong to thee,
> Or else on them let me thy justice see.
> Let neither wolves not beares nor foxes thy flock wa[ste]
> Let us, O God, thy sweet deliv'rance tast[e].
> Lest other Churches view thy slaughter[ed] ˆshee[p]ˆ
> And Come & With us sweete company keepe
>
>   Ita *pipiavit* Larkham servus Domini[3]

---

[1] 'Turk' was in Larkham's day a synonym for ignorance but, because of his time in New England, he would have known the threat to Atlantic travellers from Muslim corsairs off North Africa: Linda Colley, *Captives: Britain, empire and the world 1600–1850* (London, 2003), pp. 43–72. He would also have had experience of 'Tories', 'one of the dispossessed Irish, who became outlaws, subsisting by plundering and killing the English settlers and soldiers' (*OED*).

[2] Larkham's foremost opponents in Tavistock at this point: see Introduction.

[3] 'So cried Larkham, servant of the Lord.'

[fo. 23r *continued*]

Thus hath the Lord beene pleased to carry me through the 54th yeare of my life I was Ine Ireland[1] and preached at Lieut Coll Scots castell called Langrage about one Mile from Rossgarland castle in which My daughter Miller lived the 17th day of August being the Lords day and the last of the 54th of mine age[.][2] And on[3] Munday August the 18th being the first day of the 55th yeare of mine age I began my journey to Waxford in order to the finishing of My daughters businesses and so to the returne of us for England

Greate & Manifold are thy Providences. o Lord God of Saints.

---

[1] Larkham, away in Ireland on his birthday, marked the occasion on his return to Tavistock with a customary flourish and poem. In the manuscript, the material on this page precedes the poem. He started the first quarter of his new year on the next folio. 'Ine': in.

[2] Rossgarland (Rosegarland), County Wexford. This entry helps to explain why Thomas Larkham 'Called by the world a Minister, at Wexford he was then' featured in tract by a Quaker: Humphrey Norton, *To all people that speakes of an outward baptisme* (London, 1659), title-page. Larkham's visit coincided with Norton's missionary activity in the area. Norton, seized at Wexford while he conducted a meeting, later went into print to refute Larkham's objections to Quakerism. *ODNB*, Steven C. Harper and I. Gadd, 'Norton, Humphrey (*fl.* 1655–1660)'.

[3] The manuscript reads 'one'.

[fo. 23v]

Augusti. 18 beginneth   Ætatis. 55.   Quarta prima[1]
The Lord brought me safe to Tavistocke Septemb. 18. 1656

	£ s d
September 26 of Richawrd Dun*rish*[2]	2-00
Lord smell a sweet savor in it and accept it, & in those who at my	
departure hence Gave me somewhat John Trowt Bevile Wivell	about
Roger Row and Miria[m] Dun*rish*[3]	01-04-06
as I remember Lord remember poor R.R.[4]	
Received for 4 bookes of the attributes which I sold in Ireland[5]	0-16-06
For books sold yong Ed Condy	6-13-06
The Totall summe of Receipts	08-16-06
All this is expended as in the other Columne	

And nowe Righteous Father I come unto thee in my greate distresse and troubles.
I have A famely to care for consistinge of six persons with My Daughter Patience
and her sonne 2 poore Sisters of Mine expect helpe whom I have often holpen
heeretofore & would now againe[6]

I Borrowed of my Sonne Condy £10 to carry for Mine expenses unto Ireland of
which the last twenty shillings is delivered to the carrier towards the defrayinge of
the carriage of my daughters goods from Bristol to Exeter. Besids I am indebted
to my sonne Condy for my wives Gowne & other things about one pound eight
shillings & two pence and I have nothinge to pay or to expend in My famely O my
father consider me and answer me My meanes is detained from me A charge laid
in ˆbookeˆ against me &c.[7]

I will not faile thee nor forsake thee. Heb. 11.5[8]

October. 3rd Elsabeth Knight came to service in my famely, And Dinah Woodman
departed after 8 yeares & ¼ service. she desired my prayers. Lord, bless her

---

1   'August 18th beginneth [of my] age 55 first quarter.'
2   Or perhaps 'Dunrich'.
3   Some, if not all, members of the church.
4   Probably Roger Row.
5   Larkham's *Attributes of God* (1656).
6   The household now consisted of Larkham and his wife Patience, his grandson Tom Larkham and
    his newly widowed daughter Patience Miller with her children Tom and Jane. Larkham's sisters,
    Elizabeth and Jane, lived at Lyme Regis.
7   Larkham referred to charges against him presented to the Devon Commissioners for the Ejection
    of Scandalous Ministers (see *Naboth*, pp. 6–11). The word 'booke', between the lines, could be an
    earlier entry by Lane.
8   Joshua 1:5 (KJV): 'I will not fail thee, nor forsake thee.' Hebrews 11:5 (KJV): 'By faith Enoch …
    pleased God.' Larkham cited Scripture to express his conviction that God would support the stand
    he had taken, in faith..

[fo. 23v]

Sept. 26 paid Tho:[mas] flesh[man] had for butter	00-09-06
To the Barber at My Returne	00-00-06
Paid my wife laid out by her ^whereof for T Larkhams shoes 18d^	02-02-04
Delivered Sept 26 for the Market	00-06-00
Sept 27th paid to sonne Condy for my Daughter Miller for Wares	05-03-00
Remains in house Sept. 27th 00-13-02	08-01-04

Sept. 29 paid for T.L.[1] schooling	00-02-00
Given yesterday at the Communion	00-00-04
Lent to my daughter Miller of which 4d was for the Communion	
and 2d for her sonnes schooling[2]	00-00-06
paid for mending my saddle iid & 2 for somthinge else	00-00-04
My servants Wages due now Sept. 29th	00-10-00
	00-13-02

I have not one penny of Money this day Sept. 30th.

Now whither shall I goe but to my God   the totall summe
& father in Christ whose name is Jehovah   Hactenus[3]   08-14-06

Yet October. 3rd Collectors came to demand for monthly taxe
Whereas not only mine Augmentation ^is detained^ (this beinge
the third year of detaining £50 per annum from me) but also (I
am informed) the Commissioners have commanded Mr Eveleigh
to detaine my stipend yet I borrowed to pay them[4]   00-02-00
which I paide againe Oct. 16th following[5]

Paid my son Condy which I borrowed when I went to Ireland & spent	
in following my daughters businesse & coming home and for	
carriage of her goods	12-05-00
Lent my daughter Patience Oct: 16th	00-02-00
Laid out about the house by my wife & by me paid this Oct: 16th in all	
with 16d for [the] baking part of it	00-14-00
and for a pecke of wheate to my daughter	00-02-00

---

1   Thomas Larkham, his grandson.
2   Patience Miller and her son Tom.
3   'To this point'.
4   Larkham's Lamerton augmentation had gone unpaid. Also, the Devon Commissioners for the Ejection
    of Scandalous Ministers had ordered his stipend to be withheld, pending a resolution on articles
    presented against him. Eveleigh was steward to the earl of Bedford, patron of the living at Tavistock.
    Larkham's stipend was not detained for long: he noted payment on 18 October (with an allowance
    for wood from Eveleigh) and repaid that day what he had borrowed to pay the local monthly tax.
5   He added this line later.

in X & do her good And like wise her that is come, Lord, fitt her for the imployment thou hast called her unto.[1]

I have written a letter to my sonne in Cumberland Lord order its conveyance.

Octob. 16th. Received my stipend	09-15-00
And for wood of Mr Eveleigh	04-00-00

His faithfullness and trueth shall be thy shield & buckler[.] Men laboured to bereave me of this also, which I have received from the Lord.[2]

O my God Consider mens trampling pride,
that say our Lust shall be satisfied &c.[3]

Received of Mr Hoggesson his Rent	01-16-08
I had of one Mr Rowden for a booke	00-04-00
Received a booke from Mr Dennis	00-04-00
Novemb. 8 W. Webb delivered me from the Church	02-00-00
for bookes 7-18-0. By add[ition]: 18-18-2[4]	26-14-02

[fo. 24r]

November. 12th 1656 I call to mind this day, that 14 yeares agone On this day viz in the yeare 1642 I left mine house in New England which was then on a Saturday Now it is Wednesday my lecture day,[5] on the Munday following Novemb the 14th I set saile and so was brought to England, where I have beene protected preserved and provided for and my famely of whom I have had mine Eldest son taken away by death whose son is living with me, My other three (I hope George is livinge) two of them viz Patience a Widdow & Jane married in Tavistocke are living heere in Tavistocke. For heapes of mercies I doe heere set downe this remembrance with praise. Lord Consider me for I am brought very low. Remember me according to thy trueth. Thy mercies are the mercies of A God for which way is made by Jesus who hath satisfied thy Justice for lost mankind that cometh unto thee, which thou

---

[1]   This entry runs across the whole folio. 'X': Christ.

[2]   Larkham sets down a sharp note about the illegitimacy of the charges against his ministry, which had delayed payment of his stipend. He embroidered Psalm 91:4 (KJV), 'his truth shall be thy shield and buckler', with Ephesians 6:16 ('the shield of faith, wherewith ye shall be able to quench all the fiery darts of the wicked') and Acts 20:24 ('the ministry, which I have received of the Lord Jesus, to testify the gospel of the grace of God').

[3]   Exodus 15:9 (KJV): 'The enemy said, I will pursue, I will overtake, I will divide the spoil; my lust shall be satisfied upon them; I will draw my sword, my hand shall destroy them.'

[4]   £7-18s-0d and £18-18s-2d add up to £26-16s-2d (as on fo. 24r). Larkham initially entered this as the total but then corrected it to £26-14s-02d, working from the figures in the column.

[5]   George Hughes (CR), Larkham's predecessor as vicar of Tavistock, had started the Wednesday lecture. In 1659, Larkham's opponents began a rival Thursday lecture, much to Larkham's annoyance: see Introduction.

from October 17th in houskeeping & Malt fetcht October 14th & so
    Brewed and for hops. 10½ the Malt was. 5[s] 6[d] and 3s 10d of
    it was for 6 seames of turffes at 2 severall time[s]   00-16-00
paid for making T Larkhams Coate   00-01-06
for making Tom Millers 18d lent for shoes &c iis   00-03-06
To the market Oct 24 ˆ5[s] 6[d]ˆ & for mending shoes 6d & 3d &
    Tabacco 3[d]   00-06-06
Laid aside for housekeeping until Nov. 18th   00-19-08
Octob. 30 at church collection 6d Lords day communion 6d   00-01-00
for making my wives red jumpe[1]   00-01-[00]
    since Sept: 29th spent   15-15-[00]

paid for three moneths taxe more Nov 6th pretended to be from
    Dec 25th Next &c[2]   0-02-00
[f]or malt and a pricke of Tabacco. iis[3]   0-07-06
                                                                           0-09-06

[fo. 24r]

---

1   'Jump', *n*²: 'a kind of under (or undress) bodice worn by women' (*OED* - the first example cited is
    1666).
2   This entry and the next spill over into space at the foot of the left column.
3   A small roll of tobacco (*OED* 'prick', *n.* 13).

hast given me to do by thy good spirit why then should I doubt? Lord, strengthen my faith.

Novemb 16th endeth this first quarter of the 55th year of mine age	
In which I have received in all by addition	18-18-02
Besides I also received for bookes of yong Condy,[1] 06-13-06, & for	
six of the Attributes ^24[s] 6[d]^	07-18-00
	26-16-02

All which money I have spent by Reason of my Voyage to Ireland	24-19-08
to settle my daughters estate and in payinge what she owed and	
furnishing her with Mony for her occasions &c except only	
01-16-06 which remaineth in house	
The end of the first quarter Remaines	01-16-06

Munday, November the 16th beginneth the second quarter of the 55th yeare of mine Age
I had a letter from my son George.

I had paid out of my meanes at Kirton the summe of £5-7s-0d	
whereof £1-14s-6d was bestowed for tithes Shilston[2] exacted	
for the last yeere and 4d for the monthly taxe cleare &c	03-08-06
Received Dec. 10[th] for A booke of the Attributes	0- 4s
Dec. 11[th] I had of Phillippe Boye from Mrs Audry ex[ecuto]r[3]	0-10-00
1-14-6 left in house & since received	4-02-00
In all untill December 25	5-17-0
whereof cleare receipts only 10s & from Kirton 3-8-6	3-18-6

At this present I have no mony in house

Dec 29 I preached at the funerall of Edward Pine a schollre, his	Rem:
brother sent 20s but I gave backe to the bringer 2s 6d, mistaking	00-17-06
it for 1s[4]	
Mir: Dun:[5] Lord let it grow & multiply it was the first of this yeere	
Jan. 5. given	00-10-00
Jan. 6th My stipend received of Mr Eveleigh	09-15-00
Jan. 8th of Elizabeth Toller by David Condy	00-05-00
Jan 10th I had of W. Webb from the Church	01-00-00
Jan 14th I was at Kirton Received of Mr George Yong. 2 quarters	
rent. 3-12-6d allowed for halfe a yeares rent 40s & 3 months	
ground taxe 7s. cleare receipts	

---

1   Also referred to as 'Ed Condy'.
2   Not identified. This is the only reference to Shilston.
3   Tavistock PR, burials: 10 December 1656, Mrs Audrian Edgcombe. The payment was probably for a funeral sermon.
4   Tavistock PR, burials: 29 December 1656, Edward Pine.
5   Perhaps another gift from 'Miria[m] Dun*rish*' (Dunrich): see fo. 23v.

Paid for making a Gowne for my wife to Daniell Sowton	00-06-00
Item for silke and other things used about it	00-01-06
Novemb. 21 first market day of this quarter	
because one bushel of wheate was bought	00-14-00
given to a poore man this day	00-00-03
spent novemb 28th in provisions	00-04-09
spent in a journey to Exeter Dec 2 & 3 & 4 about articles &c[1]	0-09-09
Dec 5th ^to^ a distressed Gentlewoman	0-03-00
Dec 8th paid all owing to son Condy	1-19-09
Given to Mr Brownsdons boy	0-00-04
Laid out Dec 5th about the house	0-04-04
Given Dec. 11th to divers members of the church that were poore	0-06-00
Laid out in houskeeping untill Dec 20th	0-14-03
Dec. 22. 3 seames of Turffes[2]	0-02-01
Dec 23 Barber 6d Parchment xiid	0-01-06
Paid Maides wages Dec. 25th	0-10-00
For Bakinge this quarter now ended	0-01-06
Untill December 25th spent	5-17- 0[3]
Laid out by my servant Dec 26th &c	0-04- 6
Jan: 3rd laid out for victuals & corne	0-07- 6
Jan. 4 at the breaking of bread given	0-00- 6
Jan: 7th 3 seames of Turffes	0-02- 0
same day paid for Malt for 2 Brewings	0-10- 0
Delivered to my daughter for the house[4]	0-18- 0

---

[1] A visit prior to the occasion on which the commissioners issued their ruling, 14 January 1656/7 (fo. 24v).

[2] Three pack-horse loads of turf (peat, for fuel).

[3] This matches the figure noted in the opposite column.

[4] Patience Miller, at this point staying with Larkham in Tavistock.

paid for the poore untill December 15th [?]s out of mine owne
mony allowing George Pearse 14d towards the ground taxe [3]
quarters head rent 5s. & in mony. 3-10.   01-01-08

                                          Receipts   13- 9-02
                  Reckoning 10-6-8

[fo. 24v]

                                                          £   s   d
I lent my Daughter £2-10s which with £2 [*paid to*] Holcombe in
    Ireland served to end & satisfie all Demands from fr: Glanvile
    at present[1]   02-10- 0
Also I Bestowed in plate for each of my daughters & a little silver
    seale   05-00- 0
Also I delivered to Mr Short Minister of Lyme[2] for my two sisters
    Jan 15th   01-00- 0
Also I bought one yard of Alamode[3] for my wife the same time   00-04-04
Also I left with Bennet faro to give Register Smith for the order &c[4] 00-02- 6
Also I spent at Bow[5] 1s 3d, at Ex[e]ter 3s 8[d], at Kirton lyinge ther
    two nights 5s 8d   00-10- 7
More I paid Daniel Sowtone for makinge a New coate for me   00-02- 6
More for two yards of black kersie and for silke & buttons paid
    Son Condy   00-19- 0
The remaines of My Money was delivered to my daughter Patience
    to bestow which was   00-07- 9

      So at my Returne from Exeter I cleared at my accounts | 10-16- 8 |[6]

My Returne was Jan. 16th My Businesse touchinge Articles was heard Jan. 14th. I
was ordered the day following to continue. But freely offered for peace sake if the

1   The words in brackets are a conjecture. The Irish connexion suggests the daughter was Patience
    Miller. 'fr: Glanvile' could be Larkham's opponent Francis Glanville: it is not clear how he was
    involved, but elsewhere Larkham referred to Patience's debts.
2   Ames Short (*CR*), vicar of Lyme Regis until 1662. He was accused in 1661/2 of having gathered a
    church at Lyme by covenant (as Larkham had done in Tavistock).
3   'Alamode' was in use by the 1650s as a variant for 'à la mode' (fashionable), but later came to be
    the name for a fine plain silk, usually black (*DTGC*, *OED*). Larkham buys a 'yard of Alamode' and
    so here predates the first use of the word for a textile noted by the *OED* (1676).
4   This relates to the hearing of Articles against Larkham by the Devon Commissioners for the Ejection
    of Scandalous Ministers at Exeter, January 1656/7: see Introduction. Larkham noted further calls
    to appear before the commissioners in October and December 1657. The identity of 'John Smith,
    Register' is confirmed by *Naboth* p. 23, although in Larkham's handwriting here the surname could
    easily be mistaken as 'Snaith'.
5   Bow: eight miles east of Crediton, towards Exeter.
6   At the foot of the previous folio he noted a reckoning of '£10-6-8' [sic].

I gave to Dinah at her marriage Jan 8[th][1]   0- 5-[0?][2]
To my Daughter Patience Jan 12th   0- 5-[0?]
To my wife Jan. 12th I gave to her particuler use 10s for *writing*
    leases   0-10- 0
                                                                3- 2-[0?]

[fo. 24v]

[1]   Tavistock PR, marriages: 8 January 1656/7, Nathaniel Knight and Dinah Woodman, at 'Longstone'.
      Both had worked for the Larkhams. Langstone Moor is just north of Tavistock, close to Peter Tavy.
[2]   Torn from here down.

interest of Christ could be continued by my removal I would resigne to one whom Mr Stuckely of Exeter and Mr Bartlet of Beddiford should approve of and withall it was so agreed upon at last by the Comissioners and Myselfe Deo gratias.[1]

No Weapon formed against thee shall Prosper &c[2] O Lord be pleased So to order touching Tavistocke, that the interest of thy Sonne may be kept up there.

I have received in this late journey of Mr George Ivie of Kirton for
halfe the fine of the ground for a lease of three lives the sume of £160-00s-00d Humbly prayinge the Lord to dispose of my spirit concerning the same.[3]

Jan. 17th I preached at R. Keagles fathers bur[ial][4]	00-10-00
Jan 26th for rent for my ground from Chester &c	01-15-00
Hitherto received at Tavistocke £15-2s-6d and besides at Kirton cleare £4-10s-2d the paiments to the poore Tithes & Monthly taxe eatinge up the rest besids 32s kept backe for bayliffes fees who came to destraine for ancient rents to the Crowne.	
But the Tenth of what I had at Tavistocke is just £1-10s-3d. Which I have given in workes of charity as by my accounts appeareth.	
The £160 I had of Mr Ivy is in the hands of my son Condy one hundred pounds[,] and sixty David Condy keepeth[,] for which they are to be accountable at all demands	
Feb. 6th from Ed: Condy for bookes	03-00-00
My cleare receipts at Tavistocke by addition	
not accountinge what I had for bookes, or at Kirton	15- 2- 6
and from Kirton cleare receipts were only	4-10- 2
So the Lord sent this quarter nowe ended	19-12- 8

---

1   'Thanks be to God'. This and the next two entries run across the whole folio. Lewis Stucley of Exeter (*CR*) and William Bartlet of Bideford (*CR*) held congregationalist views, like Larkham. A 'copia vera' of the commissioners' order appears in *Naboth*, pp. 22–3.

2   Isaiah 54:17 (KJV): 'No weapon that is formed against thee shall prosper; and every tongue that shall rise against thee in judgment thou shalt condemn. This is the heritage of the servants of the Lord, and their righteousness is of me, saith the Lord.'

3   Larkham set out the initial 'I' of 'Ivie' with a flourish and wrote this entry across the whole folio to show its significance: he had leased out his ground at Crediton to George Ivy for a term of 'three lives' for the vast sum of £320. ('Three lives or 99 years' was a common length for a lease.) A few lines later he noted that he had divided the intial £160 between Daniel Condy (£100) and David Condy (£60), as loans. Subsequently, he received interest, and borrowed small amounts back. He had in mind that £200 of Ivy's money would be 'for my wife to maintaine her in lieu of Kirton which I leased': fo. 27r, 17 November 1657.

4   Tavistock PR, burials: 17 January 1656/7, Walter 'Keagell'.

Jan. 27th for two seames of Turfes	00-01-04
Jan. 29. My Daughter Condy had Child to ^the^ midwife[1]	00-02-06
Delivered to houskeepinge January 30th	00-08-00
paid for 2 inkhornes for the two boyes	00-00-06
January 30th halfe dosen of sope	00-01-05
To poore seamen I gave	00-00-02
Remaining of the tenths of what God sent me at Tavistocke	
for I have given already this quarter £1-9s-5d I say rests[2]	00-00-10
this was given feb.1. at the Communion	
Feb. 2nd paid for 3 moneths taxe ended June 24th next	0-02-00
delivered to my daughter to pay for Malt & to provide for the house	
untill Feb. 18th	0-19-11
for a seame of fagotts Feb. 2nd	0-01-00
Given to the woman attending my Daughter Condy	0-01-00
Bestowed on wine & Bal. Sowtons beare &c[3]	0-01-06
To two french seamen in distress. Feb. 4th	0-00-02
Feb. 9th for 2 seames of Turffes	0-01-04
for shoes for my selfe ^3s^ & the two Boyes shoes ^mending^ ˇ& to	
the bring[e]rˇ	0-07-00
No money remaineth save only	2-05-00

that £3 which I had of Ed Condy for bookes which I intend to bestow in bookes
   againe as also all other money that I have received for bookes

---

[1]   Tavistock PR: 'Joane daughter of Mr Daniell Condy borne the 29th of January 1656[/7] & baptised
   the 1 of March 1656[/57]'; buried 18 March 1656/7.

[2]   He calculated what remained ('rests') of the money set aside for charity (10d) and gave it at
   communion.

[3]   Probably Bartholomew Sowton: Larkham referred elsewhere to beer supplied by him. This entry was
   squeezed in between the others.

These Two quarters of the 55th yeare of mine age I have received by addition towards the discharge of my family & other necessary occasions Thirty eight pound ten shillings & ten pence all which I have spent & laid out & have nothinge left of it, But have borrowed of my stocke £8-14 besids [*all*] which I have spent also sithence August 18th last the begininge of this yeare 55th of mine age 38-10-10 [1]

[fo. 25r]

1656

February 17th 1656 beginneth the third quarter of the 55th yeare of my Age.
Lord be with me

Borrowed to supply my wants sithence this 55 yeare of mine age began although there be [*illegible words*][2]	8-*12*-00
Also I have spent which I had for bookes which did last untill March 24th And is sithence paid to my stocke againe	03-00-00
Also March 20th I tooke of the Money which is in the hands of David Condy to give to my Sonne George (this was paid by wrefords bill)[3]	05-00-00
And I Borrowed of my Sonne Condy 10s to give it to my Sonne George for the saddle he left behind havinge sold one horse because his man staid behind with my Son Condy (this was repaid to Sonne Condy)[4]	0-10-00

March 24th My Sonne began his journey for Cumberland, O My God & Father preserve him & bring him safe to his relations for Jesus Christs sake that I may praise thy name
Praised be God I had newes of his safe coming &c April 17th following.[5]

March 25th begins the yeare of our Lord 1657. Who can tell what a yeare may bring foorth?
He shall be called greate &c Luke the 1 ver[ses] 32-33[6]

---

1   He wrote this across both columns.
2   The manuscript is untidy here. Later, Larkham crossed out 'yeare of mine age began' (unless this is an earlier line drawn by Lane) and wrote over part of the second line, making it illegible. The total is also heavily corrected.
3   David Condy had received a loan of £60 from Larkham (noted on the previous folio). Now Larkham borrowed £5 temporarily (to give to his son, then visiting Tavistock) and soon repaid the £5 with a bill from a Crediton tenant, Philip Wreyford. Brackets have been added to the entry, to make it clearer.
4   This note was written later alongside the entry. Brackets have been added, for clarity.
5   George Larkham. This note was written later alongside the entry.
6   This, together with the next entry, runs across the whole folio. Luke 1:32–3 (KJV): 'He shall be great, and shall be called the Son of the Highest: and the Lord God shall give unto him the throne of his father David: And he shall reign over the house of Jacob for ever; and of his kingdom there shall be no end.'

[fo. 25r]

	£ s d
Inprimis for Three seames of Turffes	00-02-06
Laid out about things my daughter ^Miller^ being sicke	00-00-06½
To Ellis Bray Feb 19th for trimming[1]	00-01-00
for nailes to mend my daughter Patience chamber	00-00-02
delivered for houskeeping this first weeke	00- 8- 3½
when given 2d to a maide *brought methelin*[2]	00-00-02
Item paid for Tabacco 4d milke 4d	00-00-08
for a quart of Claret Wine February 25th	00-01-00
Feb 26th paid for a quarter of Mutton	00-01-08
delivered for houskeeping February 27th	00-08-04
Item bought quarter of pound of Tabacco	00-00-04
March the first at the Lords Supper I gave[3]	00-00-04
A seam of hard wood & of faggots [&] bought *hay*[4]	00-02-06
March. 9th 3 seams of Turfes	00-02-00
March 15th at a collection for *Clarke*[5] given	00-00-06
March 22nd at a collection for one of Maritavy	00-00-04
Expended houskeeping until March 25th	01-09-08
Hactenus spent	03-00-00

Thus farre the Lord hath holpen

Paid ^to^ old ^Bevill Wyvell^ scores for malt xs used[6]	00-10-00
paid my servants wages	00- xs-0
paid which I borrowed to pay for the saddle which I bought of	
George	00-10-00
Paid for baking last quarter	00-01-06
Item paid which I had borrowed to bestow last quarter & now is paid	00-06-06

---

1   Ellis Bray the barber: usually, the charge was 6d.
2   This is squeezed in, between other entries. The final word is unclear but may be a variant spelling of 'metheglin', spiced or medicated mead (*OED*): Larkham noted a few lines earlier that he had brought supplies to ease Patience Miller's sickness.
3   This was also the day on which his short-lived grandchild Joan Condy was baptized, according to the parish records.
4   George Larkham was visiting Tavistock (see opposite), and came from Cumberland on horseback. Here and below, his father noted expenses for hay.
5   A conjectured reading. 'Clarke' has not been identified.
6   He settled a bill of ten shillings he had run up on credit for malt.

This day The church joined with me Calling uppon the name of the Lord & we
kept it a day of solemn Humiliation &c

I received from Kirton for rents	04+17-00
& for a booke of the Attributes	00+04-00
due for my stipend this quarter	09+15-00
and for rent for my ground	01+15-00
This is all due March 25th	16- 11-00

Also when I went to Ireland last August John Sheere & others
        promised five pound but unto this day remaines due 40s

~~whereof 4ss was for a booke~~   02- 00-00

18- 11-00

This quarter Hitherto I have due (& received nothing at all) by
        addition £13-10s & from Kirton received by my sonne Condy
        which brought my Sonne on his way 04-17s Received So in all
        when I am paid it will be the full summe by addition of 18-07
        & 4s for a booke[1]

so my book and other dues (out of £18-11s-0 spent £2-0-6)
                                Remaines March 24th   £16-10s-6d

Also from Kirton arreares due before and at this March 25th cleare[2]   01-08-00
        which with the 3 pounds I had for bookes and what I had for one
        booke maketh in all   17-18-06
Since March 25th Received as followeth not due before
I had for a booke of the attributes   00-04-00
also I sold another booke of the attributes[3]   00-04-00

---

[1] He wrote this across the folio.
[2] He reverted to using two columns.
[3] Larkham's *Attributes of God* (1656).

Item paid for hay to [*illegible*] for my Sonnes horse which was unpaid
   by him   00-01-06
for one seame of wood to B: Wivile   00-01-00
                                         02-00-06

March 27: Bestowed in provision	00-12-00
March 29 Given at the Communion	00-01-00
March 31 To the Barber	00-00-06
2 seames of Turffs 16d Houskeep[ing] April 3rd 10s 8d	00-12-00
paid Will: Gee & Nat. Knight about my Garden	0-01-00
Item paid for dung 1s 6d and for carrying & to cast	-02-06
Item paid for a seame of hard wood and another of faggots	0-02-0[?][1]
Item paid for making the garden & seed besids what seeds I had of	
my daughter Miller	0-03-[??]
[*illegible*]	00-[?- ??]

---

[1]   The edge of the folio is worn towards the foot.

[fo. 25v]

Aprill 17th I laid aside the tenths of my stipend which	and of my rent of Chester
was 9-15 the tenths 19s-6d but I deducted 2s-4[d]	& Trix which was 38s
which I had given before so there Remaineth for	the tenths is 3s 6d.
works of piety and charity. 17s-02d	in all 20s 8d[1]

whereof given at a communion Aprill 26th   00-00-06
to ˆaˆ Frenchmane taken by the spaniards.   00-00-02
Item May the 14th to 4 frenchmanes   00-00-02
May 16th I delivered to my son Condy to send to my sisters at Lyme 01-00-00

The third quarter of the 55th year of mine age was ended on a Lords day May the
17th it being also this yeare vulgo Whitsunday[2]

May the 18th beginneth the last quarter of the 55th yeare of mine age.

I have received nothinge by addition since this yeare 1657 began,
    yet I have laid out & expended   06-17-10
    & given to works of charity[3]   01-02-00
Neither hath any thinge beene paid at all this yeare out of Lamerton.
    Also the 40s is unpaid which remaineth of the £5 promised when
    I went to Ireland. So that my receipts this quarter cleare by
    addition are only £11 10s. besids [£]6-5s which I had from Kirton.
    in all £17-15s Expenses in all this quarter. £13-00s-4d

            1-2-0 & 1-14-8 and 5-3-2 added. make 7-19-10[4]

I have in house £9

---

[1] Larkham's calculation of 'tenths', set aside for 'works of piety and charity', ran across the top of the folio.
[2] The only time Larkham names a traditional feast day, apart from a similar reference on fo. 41v. In June 1647 the Long Parliament had removed celebrations of Christmas, Easter and Whitsun from the nation's Christian calendar.
[3] He added this later, between the earlier entries.
[4] This is noted to the right of the previous entry, in a small hand. He noted the figure of £1-14s-8d again at the top of the right column of this folio (fo. 25v), carrying it over from 'the other side'.

[fo. 25v]

	1-14-8 on the other side
	£ s d
for mending my Breeches paid	00-00-06
for provision untill Aprill 16th	00-10-00
Aprill 16th paid for making a Coate 3s Buttons 4d	00-03-04
17th Aprill delivered for provision for the house	00-10-00
paid for a shirt for Tom Larkham	0-02-10
for 3 pound of soape ^11d^ and for silke ^9d^	00- 1-08
April 18th for a smale seame of Turfes	00-00-07
21st paid Abbot for a seame of faggots	1-00
for Malt Brewed the same day	00-05-00
April 21st delivered & spent this weeke	00-10-08
for searge 3 yards ½ buttons silke and threed	
to make T. Larkham & T.Miller coates	00-13-04
paid Daniell Sowton for making them	00-03-06
May the first delivered for the Market	00-10-00
bought of Son Condy 4 yards of cloth for a shirt	00-05-04
~~Item for sowing thread my wife delivered~~ for a seame of wood	00-01-00
Item fo[u]r yards of the former cloth for a shirt	00-05-04
for mort turpentine & wax to make salve[1]	00-00-09
May 4th 2 seames of Turffes	00-01-02
May 5th I visited Jonathan Condy bestowed to drink	00-06
May the eight in houskeeping spent	08-00
May. 11th given to men mending the high wayes	06
May 15th the last Market laid out & sugar & in fish & beare	0-08-00
I delivered to my Daughter Patience to trim & make Wascot	00-10-00

---

[1] 'Salve': ointment. 'Mort': a word for lard or pig's grease, in the South-West (*OED*). Turpentine came from coniferous resin, wax from bees.

May 18[th.] Quarta quarta ætatis 55 incipit.[1] 1657

	£	s	d

May 20th By a widdow received from a Woman Lord accept it   00-10-00
whereof 10d remains for charity for I gave 2d last week above the
    tenth of what I received last quarter and of this at the communion:
    May 24 given 6d
The other 4d with 8d more I gave to Obed Harris
May 2 and June. 1. to frenchmen I gave 2d
to a Gentleman taken by the spaniards as he was going for Ireland 6d
At a collection June 14th I gave 6d
At the communion June 21st I gave 6d
to the old woman Pope 1d July third
to Frenchmen taken by spaniards iid
to Englishman taken &c iid
From R. Glubb for a funeral sermon at the burial of his father
    P. Glub[2]   00+10-00

So deductinge 1s for the tenth out of it I find that July the 11th I have
    borrowed & do ow to my selfe yet 1s 8d which I have laid out it is
    to be allowed to me out of what I shall receive by addition heerafter.

[fo. 26r]

	£	s	d

July 14th I had of my Cosen David Condy in consideration of part
    of my stocke by him imployed[3]   01+00-00
                  whereof 1s 8d is gone already
                  in workes of charity
                  only remaineth 4d

July 16th of Mr Whiting by Aug Bond   00-05- 0
                  of which 6d is for thee
                  Lord My God

---

[1]   'The fourth quarter of the 55th year of my age begins.'
[2]   Tavistock PR, burials: 4 June 1657, Peter Glub.
[3]   Almost certainly interest on the £60 Larkham lent him in January 1656/7 from money received for
    selling a lease at Crediton to George Ivy.

	£ s d
May the 20ᵗʰ paid for a seame of wood	00-01-00
delivered to my wife for her occasions	00-10-00
May the 22ⁿᵈ Markett day laid out	00-11-00
also for Malt yesterday brewing day	00-05-00
for mending the sinke of the kitchen	00-00-10
for pairinge hedges in garden &c	00-00-04
for the Barber May the 23ʳᵈ	00-00-06
for sugar and fish the sugar to make syrrops cost 2s 8d	00-03-00
out of the 10s given me laid aside for piety & charity disposed as in	
other col:[umn]	00-00-10
spent when I plaied to Bowles May 25ᵗʰ	00-00-0*4*
laid out May 29ᵗʰ in provision & for 3 pound of sugar bought at	
Plimouth	00-13-00
Given to Obed Harris as in the other col[u]m[n]	00-01-00
May. 30 A Seame of fagotts	00-01-00
June the first to distressed frenchmen	00-00-02
More to a distressed man taken at sea &c	00-00-06
From June 5ᵗʰ in provision	00-08-00
for Dying stockens, & *clothe* for drawers & tape	00-03-06
June 9ᵗʰ I gave my Daughter Patience to paye for her white coate &	
other occas:[ions]	01-00-00
June 11ᵗʰ 2 seames of Turffes	00-01-02
for the Market June. the 12ᵗʰ & to pay debts	00-08-10
June 14ᵗʰ at a collection for a Boh:[emian] Minister	00-00-06
June 15ᵗʰ Hactenus	04-10-06

[fo. 26r]

	£ s d
June 18 paid for Malt	00+05-00
June 19ᵗʰ Market & spent this Weeke whereof at *buckland* 1s for my	
dinner[1]	0+09-09
6 seames of fagotts of W Web paid	00+06+00
paid June 20ᵗʰ for £3 of sope to Son Condy	00-00+11
June 21. At the Communion I gave	00-00+06
June 23. I spent about a goose for which I went to Bowles, & at	
night was sicke & vomited up al, God was gratious	00-01+00
paid for Baking last ¼ now ended	00-01+06
and for servants wages	00-10+00
and to my wife quarterly expenses	00-10+00
June 26ᵗʰ delivered for the Markett ˘whereof for sope June 27ᵗʰ 11d˘	00-10+06
paid a score owed for candles to W. Web	00-02+01

---

[1]   Buckland Monachorum, four miles south of Tavistock.

July 18th received of My Son Condy for the improvement of £100
    since January the 26th last past[1]   01+13- 4
                whereof the tenth is 3s 4d

July 22th I received from the Deacons   03+00-00
                whereof I gave backe
                to them the 10th viz 6s

July 25th I had of Mary Gibb   00+02-06
                whereof the tenth for piety &
                charity 3d which with 3d
                more was given at the
                Communion July the 26th

the rest of the tenthes is in a purse by it selfe. 3s 11d

My Rents from Chester & Tricks besids the head rent which they
    are to pay   01+15-00
                ˇwhereof 3s 6dˇ[2]

My stipend due also June 24th last   09+15-00
                ˇwhereof 19s 6dˇ[3]

                the tenth of these 2 sumes is
                £01-03s

July 30th at a funerall sermon I had[4]   00+10-00
                whereof 1s is for piety
                & charity

of Judah Peter a coin of Gold   whereof I put out for good   00+05-06
                workes 6d

From John Russell desiring a funerall s[ermon][5]   00+10-00
                whereof 1 shillinge is
                dedicated.

In add[ition] 4s. & 6d make 1s tenth[6]
                                          18-16-04
and on the other side received   01-00-00
                                          19-16-04

---

[1] Interest on the £100 Larkham had lent from what he received for selling the Crediton lease.
[2] The tenth to be set aside.
[3] Again, he calculated the tenth to be set aside.
[4] Tavistock PR, burials: 30 July 1657: John Voysey and Mrs Jane Cunningham.
[5] Nothing in the parish register matches this.
[6] This calculation is in tiny writing, boxed off.

June 29th. 6 po[unds] of sugar from Plimouth	00-02+06
July 3. Market day laid out for the house	00-09+09
I gave to Frenchmen taken by &c	00-00+02
to an English saylor taken at sea	00-00+02
To Mary Wills for service 10 or 11 daies	00-01+00
Delivered to be bestowed July the 10th	00-08+08
July 13. paid for shoes for Daughter Miller	00-02+08
July 16 for shoes for my selfe to Dingle	00-03+06
July 17 for Malt 2-6 & Markett 8-0	00-10+06
July 22nd given to the use of the church	00-06+08
July 24th ~~laid out for~~ provision	00-06+08
paid for 3 Moneths taxe ended June 24th which hath beene paid	
formerly	0-02+00
July 26th at the Communion	00-00+06
July 31. I lent to my daughter Miller	05-00+00
laid out in victualls & provision	00-09+09
paid for Malt. 2-6 for sope 11d	00-03+05
August 1, to a seaman taken &c	00-00+02
August 5th to 4 French taken &c	00-00+04
August 7th Market day	00-07+00
August 13 sicke at Mr Sowtons gave servants	00-01+08
Brewing this weeke paid for Malt	00-05+00
Laid out about the house & for butter	00-10+10
[*line crossed out – undecipherable*]	
as is written above in the other columne	
I gave Aug: Bond in *consider*[*a*]*tio*[*n*] of some paines about my	
Gran[d]children[1]	00-02+00
	16-19- 06

---

[1]   In earlier years, Larkham made regular payments to Augustine Bond for Thomas Larkham's schooling.

I had also of Moses Stonham[1]   00-10-00

          whereof 1s is put ap[ar]t &c

                                              20-06-04

I had in house when this quarter began £9 & received by addition
    all wayes   £20-6s-4d
I have spent £16-19s-06. as appeareth in the other columne.
So Remains. £12-06s-10d wherof one pound 10 shillings & eleven pence
    dedicated to workes of Piety is undisposed of. & the rather
    because my stipend due June last is unpaid.   it was paid since

This 17th day of August 1657 endeth the 55th yeare of mine age In which I have
received from my faithfull creatour and gratious father viis & modis[2] by addition
236-12-02 Mine annuity out of Lamerton being still unpaid as it hath beene for 3
yeares & halfe past[3]

Thus farre the Lord hath holpen me, blessing & praise & honour & glory be &c

O My father in Jesus Christ remember me poore worme and my poore relations
together with thy cause & waiting people, and thy despised handfull in Tavistocke.
                                            236-12-02

---

1   Tavistock PR, burials: 12 August 1657, Elizabeth Stoneham. On 29 November 1653 Larkham had
    lamented her 'abusive carriage' towards him (fo. 13r). Moses Stoneham served as a constable in
    Tavistock: Devon Record Office, Exeter, QS/B, 8 January 1656/7.
2   'By [all] ways and means.'
3   This summary runs across the foot of the folio.

When my stipend of £9-15 due last June 24th is paid & £1-10-00
  dedicated is deducted I shall have Remaininge this August 17th | 10-16-10 |

18 August 1657 – 17 August 1658

[fo. 26v]

Dedicated hitherto   01-10-00[1]
In house   10-16-00

August the Eighteenth 1657 beginneth the Six and Fiftieth yeare of mine age
A solemn day of humiliation was kept upon my motion at Tavistocke the 19th day.

Thus farre the Lord hath holpen me,
And his rich grace hath made me see:
O Lord my sinnes bury thou deepe
And under thy winges safe me keepe.
Me and mine I give up to God,
When failings do call for the rod:
Thy covenant Lord shall not be broke,
Thou canst not change what thou hast spoke.
Lord I beleeve increase my faith –
Lord I expect what thy word saith.

August the 31 day I began my journey For London about the recovering of mine arreares due out of Lamerton & returned (by the good hand of God) October the third yet did I not obtaine what I rod[e] for but insteede thereof was summoned in mine absence to answer to articles at Exon October the 7th. O Lord How long! m[iser]ere mei Deus[2]

October 5th Bevill Wivell Gave me upon my returne	00-10-00
I received of Mr Ivy at Kirton which was for the last paiment	160-00-00[3]
of phillip wreyford	001-00-00
A Bill upon George Pearse of ˆ10-00-00ˆ in adition I do account	
received because With it I paid my Sonne Condy £10 for	
Lancelot Hutton & allowed so much sent to my Sonne George	
Received for rent at Kirton when I went to London in September	01- 5- 0
of this 3s 6d is dedicated viz out of the 10s of B. Wivell & the 25s	
rent at Kirton that which I had of Wreyford p[aymen]t of an old debt	

So all accounts cleared betweene My God &
me I have to disspose just 4s. October 12th

---

[1]   The first two entries are noted in small handwriting above the heading for the new quarter.
[2]   'God have mercy on me.' Larkham returned from London to find a summons from 'the Commissioners for the Ejection of Scandalous and Insufficient Ministers hung up at his gate': *Naboth*, p. 5.
[3]   The second instalment of £320 for a long lease on Crediton property. £160 had been paid in January 1656/7 (fo. 24v).

[fo. 26v]

for strong water I paid[1]	00- 0- 6
for making 2 suits for the boyes	00- 5- 6
for a pound of Tabacco paid	00- 1- 0
Laid out about the house in odd things	00- 2-11
and the Market day August 21st laid out	00-08- 3
To the communion & at several times to poore *french*	0- 1- 6
Given to Mr Lanins man of Merran[2] that brought home Jane Miller	
(landed at Padstow) August the 20th	0-01- 0
for makinge T. Millers cloake & mending shoes	0- 1- 8
for sending letters to Beddiford[3] old Clogg	0- 0- 6
for 3 seames of Turffes August 25th	0- 1- 9
August 28 delivered for the Market	0- 8- 3
In my absence to London my wife laid out	
for servants wages 9s. taxe 13½d	00-10- 1½
for gathering in of apples & trimminge orchard	00- 1- 4
for mending chilldrens shoes	00- 1- 0
Laid out in houskeeping in mine absence[4]	01- 9- 3½
I gave to my sisters at Lyme[5] as I was travellinge to London	01- 0- 0
and I spent & bestowed about them & such as attended my sicke	
sister } charity	00- 8- 0
I sent to my Son George £120 by bill of exchange & order to receive	
£10 of Mr Hutton for his son, which I paid my son Condy	130- 0- 0
My wife had for Mich[a]el[mas]: quarter	
which I paid in silke bought at London[6]	00-10- 0
My journies to London & Exeter & for carriage of books & boxe	
from London & Exeter[7]	08-07- 7
a Coppy of New articles October 8th [8]	00-02- 6
my seale cost me at London	00-03- 6
Sept. 29. D[elivere]D by loan to Son Condy	20-00- 0
Octob. 9th laid out market day	0-06- 8

1   'Strong water': spirits or 'aqua vitae'; sold as a drink and as medicine (*DTGC*).
2   St Merryn, Cornwall.
3   Bideford, where Larkham's congregationalist ally William Bartlet (*CR*) was minister.
4   A single illegible word follows this on the next line.
5   Lyme Regis, Dorset (Larkham's birthplace).
6   This line he added later.
7   Larkham was away from Tavistock from 31 August to 3 October, 1657. The books he brought from London were copies of *Naboth*, 'printed for the use of the Author', which published material to prove his good standing with the London committees and Devon commissioners. A few lines later he noted 'I am out in printing Naboth besids what I have received for some 1-10-0.'
8   Larkham returned home to find a fresh summons from the Devon commissioners hung on his gate (see opposite). He paid to secure a copy of articles presented against him, presumably in Exeter to 'Register Smith', as before (see p. 142).

When I was in London I had in token for Thom: Larkham from
    Grandmoth[er] & Unckle[1]   01-00-00

Received & acquitted for improvment of *Money* from Son Condy
    untill Septemb. 29 last[2]   02-15-06

Hitherto October 19th I had in house at the begininge of this 56th
    yeare of my age and [h]ave since received of debts & every way   188-17-04
                                                                     188-17-04[3]

[fo. 27r]

If out of	188-17-04	
we deduct	181-02-05	
Remaineth	007-14-11	whereof £05 was bestowed in a Mare & old saddle &
of this 20s		bridle which I bought of Mr George Ivie of Kirton the
was sent to		other £2-14s-11d I have in house this 19th day of Octob.
T. L &c		1657. yet heere it is to be understood that of all the
		summe of 188-17-04. I have received only by addition
		05-10-6 as by Consideringe what is writte as in the
		other page may appeare[4]

October the 21 received my stipend   £09-15- 0
                    The Tenth whereof is   19s-6d and
                    the remainder in my hand made   03-00 and
                    the whole sume for my God   1-02- 6

                    The Lord direct me to dispose of it as shall
                    be most for his glory & according to Rule

                    The Tenth of the £2-15s-06d which I had of
                    my Son Condy is 5s-6½d[5] & a little more.

---

1   Richard Covert was the young Thomas Larkham's uncle on his mother's side (fo. 43v).
2   Probably another interest payment on the £100 had Larkham lent to his son, from money received
    by leasing out land at Crediton.
3   A rather scruffy summary at the foot of the left column.
4   All this is entered across the top of the folio in small writing.
5   He also wrote the figure in words, above: 'six-pence-hapenny'.

	£ s d
Paid for a New Coppy of the ffeofments of Lamerton out of the Rowles[1]	0-08- 0
I was deceived in Tabacco[2] which cost	2-00- 0
Turffes October 10th	00-01- 2
I am out in printing Naboth besids what I have received for some	1-10- 0
I Gave to my Daughter Condy a scarfe of Duicape[3]	00-15- 0
Paid for a hatt for Thom: Larkham	00-02- 4
for a shirts cloth for him also	00-02-10
for shoes and an apron for Jane Miller	00-02- 7
for Candles 15d & for the Market Oct. 16. 7[s] 8[d]	00-08-11
for buttons silke belly pert linings[4] for T.L. suite	00-04-07
for sarge loope silke for T Millers cloake[5]	00-12-02
October 17 I paid Son Condy in part of the last fifty pounds I promised with my Daughter Jane on marriage	10-00- 0
October 18 we had a Communion I gave then	00-01- 0
Given & bestowed Hactenus	181-02-05

[fo. 27r]

	£ s d
October 20th for 28 pound of Butter at 4d farthing	00-09-11
Paid for Baking Due September 29th last	00-01-06
Octob. 21 My Son Condy receiving my stipend of Mr Everleigh due Sept. 29th I added 5s to it & so paid him a second Ten pounds of the last fifty promised	10-00-00
Oct. 24, paid W. Web for 5 seames of fagots	00-05-00
Given to the poore sailor of algeres	00-00-05

---

[1] *Naboth*, p. 3, referred to Larkham's appearance before the 'Publique Trustees for Pious Uses sitting at Westminster' and their request for sight of the 'feoffment deed'.

[2] In 1669 Larkham traded in tobacco (fo. 49r). Perhaps this was an earlier venture which went wrong.

[3] 'Duicape': 'ducape', 'a plain-wove stout silk fabric', used for women's garments (*OED*, which cites the first occurrence as 1678).

[4] 'Belly-part linings': *OED* 'belly' *n* 3b, 'the part of a garment covering the belly', citing Ben Jonson (1599) 'Such a sleeve, such a shirt, belly and all.' T.L. was his grandson Tom Larkham.

[5] Thomas Miller, his other grandson.

[Oc]tober 26th Received of George Chester my rent   01-15-00
               the tenths whereof is 3s and 6d

[November] 4 Jo: Trowts wife brought ½ bushell of wheate which
    was worth 5s   00- 5-00
               of it I shall allow 6d

                                               11-15-00
& on the other side remained   5-10-06

Besids £171 from Kirton for fines Received there & here[1]   17-05-06

There remaineth the just Summe of   00-11-09
    which is paid to my sonne Condy for 5 yards of shag[,] buttons
    & silke for my study coate[2]

Non est mihi Argentum[3]

Novemb. 14th 1642 I came from New England And have beene since marvelously Cared for & holpen by the Lord (My) father, to care for my famelie which (when I left them) were as dry bones, & diverse yeares after; yet did the Lord bring them altogether againe here in England. fifteene yeares hath my good & gratious & mercifull God & father added to the daies of my Life since my being in New England, in which time he hath lift me up and Cast me Downe. I have received in stipends rents fines for leases at Kirton and in Gifts (& such waies as God hath beene pleased to provide for me by) no lesse then Two thousand Thirty sixe pound wanting just seven pence. £2035-19s-05d. This I took notice of the 12th of November 1657. That beinge the day of the moneth on which I left my famely and came to the Mouth of Paskataquake, where I staid untill the 14th day being Munday on which day the ship in which I came did sett saile.[4]

                                     Hact:[enus] auxil:[iatus] est *Dom*[*inus*]

Three Hundred Pounds I paid my wive's sister to quiett her about the meanes at Kirton:[5] About one thousand pounds in portions for my foure chilldren Thomas, Patience, George and Jane which all came to men & womens estate & were married & all had Issue[.] My eldest son Thomas Died in the East Indies, his child is living

---

[1]   The £171 is clearly written, although it seems a high figure. It was not added up with the rest but written in later (squeezed up against the £17 total). A 'fine' was a fee paid by tenants at the start of a tenancy, or with some change in the terms (*OED*).

[2]   'Just': exact, precise. 'Shag': fabric with a long pile, used for warm clothing (*DTGC*).

[3]   'I have no money.'

[4]   Larkham's experience in New England is discussed in the Introduction. 'Paskataquake' is the Piscataqua River, which now forms the border between New Hampshire and Maine.

[5]   His wife's sister, 'Sister Stone': the sisters had inherited property in Crediton from their father, George Wilton. In 1653 Larkham noted the conclusion of negotiations with 'Brother Stone' over the estate (fo. 12v).

Paid October 27 for Tenths due last December 25th (received ^by
    Mr Hale^ for the use of the Trustees for Pious Uses) & for an
    acquittance[1]   01-02-01
halfe a bushell of wheate spent of[2] J Trowt   0- 5-00
paid for New Jamping bootes & spurrleathers[3]   0- 4-00
Given to a poore woman Traveling November 4th   0-00-02
Spent in Housekeeping the remaininge part of this quarter viz untill
    Novemb: 17th   1- 7-07
paid D. Sowton for making my shagg coat   00-02-06
                                                14-9-11 spent   13-18- 2

Received this first quarter of the 55th of mine age by Addition 17-05-0 besides
    what I had of Foy & *some for &c*[4]
From Kirton in fines £171   } *profits*
                       } *leases receipts*[5]

Let me believe That God will still provide.
Though friends be few, & some are turn'd aside
Honour in God's time shall succeede my fall,
Though now my foes be greate & my friends smale.
Thy rod shall feede, thy staffe shall me sustaine,
O Lord I looke to hear that Christ doth raigne.

The frownes of men are greate I am their scorne,
Yet by thy grace I am a Saint freeborne.
Arise O God to heare thy groaning Saint,
I am allmost quitt[e] spent & like to faint
O God allwaies guide thou my tongue & pen
In pleading for thy Son with Sinfull men.
                                   Amen Amen.

---

[1]   The London-based Trustees for the Maintenance of Ministers, also known as 'Publique Trustees for
    Pious Uses'.
[2]   'Bought from'.
[3]   'Jamping': jumping. Spur-leather: 'a leather strap for securing a spur to the foot' (*OED*).
[4]   Written sideways into the binding and hard to read. He meant '56th' not 55th.
[5]   A note in bottom left corner of page, also written sideways.

with me by the name (Thomas) at the writing heereof. & Jane married & living here in Tavistocke[.] The Lord send me good Tidings of George & Patience who are farre of[f] (I hope) livinge.[1]

[fo. 27v]

1657

Novemb: 17th Heere beginneth the second quarter of the 56th Yeere[2] of mine age
In house (Besids what is owed me[)] I have made all even & have no money

This 17th day the Church kept solemnly & praised the Lord for all gratious providences. Such as were able invited to eate at their tables the rest of the members O Lord accept this sacrifice in X[3]

of all the Monies that I have received theire remaineth one hundred and fifty pound imployed by my Sonne Condy and sixty pound in the hands of my Cosen David his brother some thing is owed to me at Kirton & my horse is not yet sold. I am indebted by promise to my Son George £20 and to my sonne Condy £30, for the paiment of £10 of it I have apointed David his brother. So their will be just £200 left which is for my wife to maintaine her in lieu of Kirton which I leased.[4]

> And now Lord what wait I for my hope is in thee. Deliver me from all My transgressions: make me not the reproach of the foolish. Remember me & mine o Lord for thy goodnes In Christ Jesus, Amen, Amen[5]

	£ s d
Decemb. 3[rd] I had of T Fleshmans mother at Okehampton	00-08-06

I preached coming from Exon that day. Yesterday my busines came to hearing about the many Papers & Articles given in at severall times befor the Com[is]sion[er]s[6]

Men they mustt Doe what God above Commands,
He guids their tongues their judgement & their hands.
Unworthy Dust deserves nothing at all
but Wrath. for praise this mercy now doeth Call.
I am this farre from all my troubles freed
God grant some Comfort now may come insteede.

---

[1]	George had been in Cumberland since 1651 (fo. 4v). Patience had come to Tavistock as a widow since 1656 (fos. 22v, 23v) but had now gone away, probably back to Ireland.
[2]	Corrected from '55th'.
[3]	'X': Christ.
[4]	Larkham summarized here what had happened to the £320 he received from leasing out land at Crediton which had come to him via his wife.
[5]	The first entries to this point run across the whole folio.
[6]	Commissioners for the Ejection of Scandalous Ministers, meeting at Exeter. Many papers from the dispute came into print in the pamphlet controversy between Larkham's supporters and opponents: see Introduction.

[fo. 27v]

My Exeter journey stood[1]	00-09-00
a blacke cap for my selfe	00- 2-00
& the barber had	00-00-06
& Dr Owens Ans[wer] to Cawdry[2]	00-00-11
3 Moneths taxe paid[3]	00-01-01
Housekeeping until the 11th day of December	01-08-11
Mending T. Larkham shoes	00-00-06
for sixe seames of Turfes	00-03-10
for Paper paid	00-00-05
Malt brewed Decemb 10th	00-05-00

---

[1]   Above, he has noted: 'paid with the tenths [*illegible words*]'.

[2]   John Owen, *A review of the true nature of schism, with a vindication of the congregationall churches in England, from the imputation thereof unjustly charged on them by Mr D Cawdrey, preacher of the word at Billing in Northamptonshire* (Oxford, 1657). The copy in the Thomason Collection is marked '7ber' (September) 25.

[3]   To the left, in the margin alongside, he bracketed the word 'tenths': was he writing off his tax payment against funds set aside for 'works of piety and charity'? He annotated other items with 'tenths', below.

December the 4th I had of Mary Gibb. Wid:[ow]	00-02-06
the same day of Richarwd Dunrich	00-02-06

I borrowed upon account of Son Condy December 11th £3 paying
  him all that I owed him until then

I had of W Webb in payment of my Mare. 40s	02-00-00

of the £3 borrowed of my son Condy he alloweth what he hath
  gotten by improvement of £150 which is kept in his hand for

my wife ^the other 15s I paid in monies to him^	02-05-00

So what I owed him paid 15s December 30th

Decemb. 24th I had a letter from Mr Edward Raddon that Mine Approbaco[n]
  was past for mine augmentation Money out of Lamerton,[1] & also a letter
  from Daughter Patience The Lord give a heart to be thankfull for his rich
  grace & continued mercies, who hath hitherto disapointed myne enimies &c

Decemb 30th I had of My Cosen David Condy which owes for improving some money for me	02-00-00

I appointed him to pay my Son Condy £10 of that £60 he had of
  mine so he oweth me only fifty pound.
And I owe my Sone Condy only £20 of the last fifty for his wives
  portion

> whereof by Addition received only £4-18s-6d　　$\boxed{\text{06-18-06}}$
>   whereof Hitherto the tenths is 10s want[ing]
>   1½d or thereabout

Decemb: 31 I had a letter from my daughter Miller (praised be my God) it was 3
weekes a coming.[2] O thou God of trueth & goodnes, looke mercifull on my poore
Daughter. Amen.

I have not one Penny in house But have appointed my wife to lay out what she
hath, untill God shall be pleased to send me some money

---

[1] Raddon, an Exeter lawyer, liaised with London committees on Larkham's behalf. (He was also
Clerk of Court to the Devon Quarter Sessions: Devon Record Office, Exeter, QS1/9, Quarter
Sessions Order Book 1652-61, 13 July 1658.). The 'Publique Trustees for Pious Uses sitting at
Westminster' (the Trustees for the Maintenance of Ministers) had required Larkham to appear before
'the Commissioners for Approbation of Public Preachers sitting at White Hall'. There was a delay
while the commissioners investigated earlier charges against Larkham brought to the 'Committee
for Plundered Ministers' (which had ceased to function in 1653). For a narrative, see *Naboth*, pp.
3–5, 30–2. The decision in Larkham's favour confirmed, once again, his right to the Lamerton
augmentation of £50 a year, and secured payment – in theory – of £200 in arrears.

[2] Patience Miller was in Ireland.

given Dinah that day[1]	00-01-00
to Dennis to carry a letter	00-00-02
for a petticoat for J Miller paid to Sonne Condy	00-12-03
for soape candles & other things upon Son Condies book and some small things elswhere	00-03-04
Decemb. 15th Reparacons	00-04-09
December 18th for victualls & a letter to Plimouth for London	00-06-03
To W. Webb for Cyder	00-12-00
for wood & candles	00-10-00
for T Larkhams shoes	00-01-06
Dec. 24th paid for letters	00-01-01
for provision & at the shops & for Milke	00-07-08
To T. Miller *to Dyeit*	00-00-07
Baking 1s 6d maids w[a]g[e]s 10[d]	00-11-06
for wood paid Chapman	00-02-09
for a quire of paper	00-00-04
To my Wife I gave to bestow for her selfe	00-10-00
to the Communion[2]	00-00-06
To *Lanby* coming home with me	00-00-02

06-18-06

---

[1]   Annotated 'tenths': a gift to his former servant Dinah Knight (formerly Woodman).
[2]   He wrote 'tenths' alongside this, in the margin.

The end of the yeare 1657 according to the Almanack computation[1]

[fo. 28r]

Computation[2]

	£	s	d
Jan. 5th I had my stipend of Mr Eveleigh	09+15-00		
and insteeade of an acre of Wood	04+00-00		
Due for my Rent from Chester & Trix			
With the Lords rent[3] which I was not woont heeretofore to receive but left it in their hands to pay it for me	01+18-04		
I Borrowed of my Son Condy to build a planching[4] over my Hall, and other reparacons	1-12- 0		
and of my wife towards the repar[a]tions I had	00-09- 0		
Item I borrowed of my wife to pay for letters	00-01- 0		
Item I borrowed of Son Condy	00-08- 0		
I had for two of my Wedding Suppers[5]	00-02- 0		
Feb 10th I borrowed of son Condy	05- 0		
Item Borrowed of son Condy to pay for boards	01-10- 0		
Item Borrowed in cloth silke for a coate	01-05- 6		

So I have borrowed and and do owe otherwise unto my son Condy
in all the sume of £5 and ^6d^[,] to my my wife 10s[,] by reason of
reparations this quarter about the house I [*have engaged in*] about
which I have bestowed £05-01s-07½d[6]

Received by addition this quarter.   £15-13s-4d

I have borrowed & ow this quarter   5-10- 6

I had for one of my bookes ut supra   0- 1- 0

The Whole Sume is in all   21- 4-10[7]

1   Larkham rarely marked the year's end in December, but here remarked on the year's end by 'the Almanack computation'. In November 1653 he noted the purchase of an almanac for 1654 (fo. 13r).

2   For some reason he reiterated the last word on the previous folio (a practice found in contemporary printed books).

3   Probably 'head-rent', payable to the freeholder: on 29 September 1658 Larkham noted 6s 8d 'due for halfe yeare head rent for ground to the Earle of Bedford' (fo. 31v).

4   'Planching': planking, boarding, flooring; a word used in South-West England (*OED* 'planch').

5   *Wedding-supper* (1652).

6   In this entry, the ink is faded for the small insertion: it looks like '1s' but the sense requires 6d (to tally with the sum total borrowed, £5-10s-6d, mentioned a few lines later); Larkham's debt to Condy included the £1-5s-6d borrowed in 'cloth silke'. The words in brackets have been supplied to convey the likely sense: the original is illegible.

7   The 'whole sum' adds up to this amount, but here and immediately below (where he entered the figure again) the entries have been amended untidily.

[fo. 28r]

	£ s d
Jan 5th I paid Sonne Condy (of the £20 I owed him) another £10	10-00-00
so now I owe him only £10 of Jane's portion[1]	
Laid out about the house by my wife paid	00-08-06
Tenths for December 25th to Mr Hale and for the acquittance 4d	01-02-01
which was paid Jan 7th to Mr Hale *Rec*	
January 8th market day and paie to shops & milk	00-10-05
Jan 10th given to a collection for a man whose house was burned	
at Lamerton	00-00-06
Jan 15th Market day 8s letters 6d	00-08-06
Jan 18 untill then 7 seames of wood of William Chapman *in* 12d a	
seame	00-07-00
Jan: 22 delivered to the maid for market	00-09-06
and afterward & for sugar to Peter Trix	
paid for bringing Red Herrings[2]	00-00-11
Jan 29th Market day laid out	00-08-07
for letters from London and Ireland	10
Item for sending backe a letter Jan 29th	00-00-02
I laid out in building & repar[a]cons in this Month of January 1657	02-06-00
Janua[ry] payd for 30 *beams* to J Russell	01-10-00
for sixe foot ½ of Glasse for the forehall window ˆ& chamber & nailesˆ	0-07-01
given to maid ˆ6d & french menˆ 1d	0-00-07
I delivered to William Loveies Going in a message to Major Hale	0-02-00
Market day Feb 5th laid out for the house	0-07-05
for Two masons & one to attend them for one day & half about the	
Windowes	0-05-00
Feb the 9th to the Heliar about the eves[3]	0-00-06
paid John Sheere for a Window & worke	0-03-00
paid Daniel Sowton for making long coate	0-02-06
paid for a key for the Cupbord in Hall	0-00-04
Item paid John Sheere Feb 9th for windows	
& other worke of his man & Nailes	0-04-01
Feb. 11th paid for 3 bushells of Lime	00-03-00
for cloth & silk for a Coate for myselfe	01-05-06
Feb 12th market day 7-8 a letter sent 2d.	00-07-10
paid John Sheere for A third Window ˆ&cˆ	00-02-00
moreover allowing 1s & a fourth window	
The whole sume of expenses	21-04-06

---

1 Jane's marriage portion of £250. Larkham was paying off the last £50: £200 had been paid in 1653.
2 'Red Herrings': dried or smoked herrings (kippers).
3 'Hellier': in South-West England, a slater or tiler (*OED*).

Item allowed son Condy in paiment £2-5s-0 for improvement of money
untill March 19[th1]

Feb. 13th about 3 of the Clocke in the morninge after a sore Travell & danger in
child bearing the Lord was pleased gratiously to deliver my poore daughter
Condy, of a sore bruised child which came in an unusual manner in to the
world.[2] Blessed be the name of my God for ever

Feb 15th the Lord brought safely to my hands £20 sent by bill of Exchange from
my poore Daughter Miller for the paiment of her Debts & the use of her
children.[3] Blessed be God.

I paid	11-4d	for Tamy my daughter carried with her
and	05-7	for an under coates cloth & lace for Jean
[and]	[?-?]	~~for an upper coates cloth & lace for Jean~~
and	18-0	which was owed my wife above that 14s 6d which she had for the fowling peice
	04-3-4	is due to Martin Holman of Beddiford.
	[?–?]	*~~for what he hath lent her since her departure~~*
	5-18-3	Rem[ains] *14-1-9*.toward my Bill of what she had stood me since A Widdow.[4]

[fo. 28v]

So remaineth of the £20 which my daughter sent only   £00-13s-02d
besids the 4-3-4 which was not sent this quarter[5]

To this day of casting Account Memorandum that besides that summe of fifteene
pounds 13s and 4d which was received by Addition I had £12-5s of my Son Condy
allowed in the 10 pound I paid him

So my Receipts in all last		
quarter were	17-18-04	and before
December 24th	04-18-06	The Whole
Summe of	22-16-10	second quarter

---

1   This entry, added later alongside the total above, relates to interest on Larkham's loan of £150 to
Condy.
2   Tavistock PR, births: 13 February 1657/8, Jane Condy, daughter of Mr Daniel Condy.
3   Patience Miller (back in Ireland) and her children Tom and Jane (who stayed on in Tavistock). Her
return to Ireland is suggested by the reference to the port of Bideford on the north Devon coast, and
by Larkham's note on the next folio about money sent 'out of Ireland'.
4   Larkham noted here, against £20 received from Patience by bill of exchange, various expenses he
had incurred. 'Tammy': 'a fine worsted cloth of good quality, often with a glazed finish'. 'Fowling
piece': a light gun for shooting wildfowl. *OED*.
5   A note added later.

Non est mihi argentum. Deus providebit[1]

Lord be with thy servant this third quarter following of the 56th yeare of his age. Thus farre the Lord hath holpen blessed be God.

I gave to the midwife about Jane	00-02-06
I paid for 3 keyes It[2] to the old Cupbord	00-01-00
About this time I paid my Son Condy the last £10 of the last £50 I promised with my daughter Jane his wife so now all I promised in money is paid[3]	10-00-00

He had £7-15s and allowed £2-15s for trading upon £150 of mine untill March 25[th] next.[4]

Out of my daugher Millers Money I tooke to pay £2-15s to my son Condy besides the £2-5s I had for annuity for the quarter ended March 25[th] next. also I paid 10s I had borrowed of my *wife*

[fo. 28v]

Memorandum my Expenses and disbur[se]m[en]ts This last quarter Were 38-05-11
So I am out of Purse more then my receipts by addicon 15-09-05

Having paid £20 to my Sonne Condy beinge now out of his debt wholy, also my reparations about my house tooke 5 pound 1 shilling and 7½d I *was* holpen to money by selling of my Mare, and by receiving some money out of Ireland

Thus farre the Lord hath holpen

---

1   'I have no money. God will provide.'
2   'Item' (also), or perhaps 'iterato' (again), as a few lines earlier he had noted payment for a cupboard key.
3   The last £10 of Jane's £250 marriage portion.
4   Interest on the £150 Larkham had lent.

Tenths 10s & Tenths 1-15 al disposed of (& more)[1]

Feb 18 beginneth the third quarter of the 56th yeare of mine age

I had of W. Webb the last for my horse	01-00-00
But he promised if it proved well to give somthinge more	
I had of Mr Leere one bushel of Wheate which saved the expending	
of Ten shillings	
I made of bookes at severall times	00-01-03
sold also bookes March 19th	00-00-08

March 19th I accounted that I was indebted to Son Condy in all
    (which he paid to Mr Raddon £1-3-0 to Mr Holman 4-3-4
    & for boyes Coates ˆclothˆ buttons & thread 13-7½d)
    <u>sixe pound want but one halfepenny</u>
            to be paid (when I have money) by me, or mine executour if I dy
            before it be paid.   I paid Aprill 23rd 1658

I had from R. White of Kirton by old Holmes for a fine, March 25th	03+09-06
Due for my stipend here	09+15-00
for Rent from Chester & Trix for 1 quarter rent	1+18-04
From David Condy untill March 25th	
who had £60 to improve which now is £50	0+15-00[2]
From Kirton due March 25th and received at severall times	5+11-06
	21-09-04
Out of this deduct which I paid Son Condy	06-00-00
April 23, So there remaineth in mony to me	15-09-04
Out of which I spend as followeth[3]	

---

[1]   This note, squeezed into the right column across from the total of £22-16s-10d, appears to be a rough
     calculation that he had given away (tithed) a tenth of his income for the quarter.
[2]   Interest on Larkham's loan.
[3]   He referred forward to the list of expenses in the right column, opposite.

paid Will Webb for wood Feb 18th	00-10-00
for Malt brewed Feb. 2nd last past	00-05-00
for the Market & other provisions	00-08-01½
for 4 seames of earth for [*illegible*]	00-01-00
for setting in the Hall backe Window	00-00-06
Item for mending old glasse & nailes	00-00-06
Item to Chapman for two seames of wood	00-02-00
Feb 25th for plaisterers & renders &c[1]	00-03-06
for a bushell & halfe of haire	00-01-00
Feb 26th Market day bestowed	00-12-06
paid for carriage of letters	00-00-06
Also Feb. 27 paid Roger Row	00-04-08
Given to french men taken by Ostenders	00-00-03
March the Second Brewing day	00-05-00
Item for 2 daies worke to Roger Row	00-02-04
March 4th 3 moneths Taxe	0-01-01½
Laid out March 5th Market day	00-10-00
Laid out to Mr Andrew Raddon for the use of Mr Edward Raddon	
about orders obtained for me sent to Exeter by my Son Condy[2]	01-03-00
a paire of leatherne stockenes[3]	00-02-06
for settinge of leekes for seede to W.G.	00-00-03
About the fitting up of an old Bedstead bought of Mrs Ellis daughter	
besides timber of mine owne paid J Sheere	00-05-00
The Bedstead is now worth 25s	
To P. Chubs maide bring[ing] [*illegible*]	00-00-04
March 12th Market day laid out	00-09-06½
for making of 3 low joyesteeles[4] & boards	00-03-06
paide for a seame of wood March 13th	00-01-00
for setting of cabbidg plants	00-00-03
paid for sending money to Mr Holman	00-00-06
my sonne Condy sent the money viz	04-03-04
March 19th for the Market &c	00-09-08
Shagg & buttons & thread to make coates for 2 boyes[5]	00-13-07
maides wages & baking came unto	00-11-06
wood & candles paid to william webb	00-03-09
	11-15- 9½

---

[1] For plastering and rendering and (on the next line) horse-hair for the plaster.
[2] Edward Raddon continued to work for Larkham in business with London committees and perhaps with the Devon commissioners.
[3] 'Leather stockings': 'a kind of legging or long boot', 'boot-hose', 'boot-stocking' (*OED*).
[4] Probably 'joist-steeles', metal fixings used with joists and boards.
[5] Coats for his grandsons Thomas Larkham and Thomas Miller. 'Shag': fabric with a long pile, used for warm clothing (*DTGC*).

[fo. 30r][1]

Heere Beginneth the yeare of our Lord <u>1658</u>
March 25th

an° 1658   an° 1658[2]

aprill 20th I called to mind the birth of my deare son George on this day in the yeare 1630, and on this day God (which ordereth everythinge in the World) suffered yea ordered the comeinge to this Towne of a booke, written as it seemes principally by Nicholas Watts[.] The Authors names that owne it being written in Capitall letters shew them Capitall offenders yet ashamed to write thier names at large.[3] O my God before thee doth thy old poore servant spread this heape of trash. thou knowest it is full fraught with lies, slanders, calumnies, false accusations: and was written in extreame malice & revenge & wrath of pride[.] Therefore O Righteous God take it on the account of thy Son Jesus whose I am by ˆunion inˆ the covenant ˆof graceˆ & worke for thy names sake, that thy greate & holy name be not prophaned.

I had from my daughter Twenty pound to be added to my receipts of
    these 3 quarters past
It is now eight weekes since this yeare 1658 began, in all which time
    I have not received one penny as Minister upon any account whatsoever.

---

1   Not all the folios are marked with a number. Sometimes Larkham obliterated Lane's numbering by scoring it out or writing over the top. The foliation of the original manuscript has been followed here, even though it jumps at this point from the previous marked number (on fo. 25r). Strictly speaking this should be fo. 29. There is no evidence of a missing page.

2   This heading runs across the whole folio. Thereafter the entries are divided into two columns.

3   The book was F.G. D.P. W.G. N.W. W.H. &c, *The Tavistocke Naboth proved Nabal: in an answer unto a scandalous narrative published by Mr Tho: Larkham in the name (but without the consent) of the church of Tavistocke in Devon* (London, 1658); a riposte to the pro-Larkham *Naboth* (1657). The title-page of the Bodleian Library copy (see Plate 9) carries handwritten identifications of the authors: 'Francis Glanvile. Diggory Polwheel. Walter Godbear. Nicholas Watts. William Hore'. For this vociferous controversy in print, see Introduction. In his will, Watts set up a fund to give godly books to the poor of Tavistock, to 'testify true repentance and make some amends for those wretched idle pamphlets [I] wrote in my youthful years for my own Vindication wherein I stuck not to cast Dirt on others for the Clearing of myself'. Devon Record Office, Exeter, W1258M/LP/9/3, 'A copy of the will of Mr Nicholas Watts of Tavistock dated Feb 17th 1674'.

Paid for 2 skinnes to make Linings   00-02-00

So that the whole of layinge out this part of the third quarter of the
56th yeare of mine age addinge this 2 shillings to the 11-15-9½
mentioned in the other Columne is

                                                                      11-17- 9½
                  I have only 1½d remaining in house

[fo. 30r]

Item for making two Coates for the boyes	00-03-06
paid for making drawe[r]s of leather for my selfe and for tape[1]	00-00-11
paid for 3 weekes schooling for the boyes	00-01-00
Given to my wife for her owne use	00-10-00
March 26th Market day bestowed	00-10-00
Malt Brewed March 30th	00-05-00
Aprill the second about houskeeping	00-08-06
for a letter to Plimouth for London	00-00-02
paid for making the table in the parlour besids mine owne timber which table is worth now 14s	00-06-00
bestowed upon the masons to Drinke	00-00-06
April 9th Market day for the house	00-10-00
paid Aprill the 9th for making dublet	0 -02-06
paid for Parchment for lease	00- 1ss-
Aprill 10th paid towards the ponion end[2] of my house to the Masons	01-00-00
Given to Petronell Chubb	00-00-06
April 14th given Item to the Masons to drinke	00-00-06
Item to *Newbury* to cleanse the chamber	00-00-02
paid for letters to and fro from Plimoth which came from & were sent to Mr Raddon	00-00-06
Aprill 16th Market day laid out	00-10-00
Aprill 18th given to the communion	00-00-06
Aprill 19th for gardening and seeds	00-03-03
Aprill 23rd paid to Mr Eveleigh for rent for halfe a yeare ended March 25th last past[3]	00-06-08
[*illegible*] Dan: Condy	
Paid for mending two paire of shoes for T.L. & T.M.[4]	00-01-02

[1] Leather breeches (*OED* 'drawers' – a garment for the lower body, not restricted to underclothes until later).
[2] 'Pinion-end': in South-West England, a gable end (*OED*).
[3] 'Head-rent' due to the earl of Bedford, paid to his steward Eveleigh.
[4] Thomas Larkham and Thomas Miller.

The third quarter of the 56 yeare of Mine age is ended
the 4th and last begines by Gods Providence with a day of humiliation

Lord give thy holy Spirit to thy poor servant that asketh it &c[1]

Received hitherto in these 3 quarters now ended in fines stipends &c 252-11-08

[fo. 30v]

£9-5s-10½ in house & Trix oweth me 12s-6d / £8-13s-4½d[2]

[M]ay 19th   beginneth the 3rd quarter[3]
an° 1658   Lord send the paraclete

May the 20th of Edward Paine[4]   00-10-00
May 27 of E T wid[ow] Lord accept   00-05-00

It is to be noted that this 5 day of June John Trix oweth unto me for rent due
March 25th last past 12s 6d and one quarter more will be due next June 24th
to wit from George Chester £1-05s-10d from Trix 12s and 6d more

June 9th I called to mind with thankfullnes that this day 1652 I departed from
Exon, sad & uncertaine of issue upon the shutting of the doore of the parish
meeting upon me.[5] But the Lord carried me safe to Bristol & thence to London
& gave me good succese. Blessed be God.

---

1   An allusion to Luke 11:13.
2   This note is added in a small space at the top of the folio: he seems to have worked from the right, first making a note of the £8-13s-4½d in hand, then remembering money owed by John Trix and adding these together to make the sum 'in house'.
3   Actually the fourth quarter.
4   For a funeral sermon. Tavistock PR, burials: 15 May 1658, Walter Payne.
5   The 'riot' of 1652: see Introduction..

Aprill 23rd Market day laid out	00-09-04
26, Paid, Hockaday & Bickley It[*erato*][1] about the Ponion End of my house	01-00-00
Brewing day Aprill 27th	00-05-00
Market day April 30th	00-10-00
May the second A collection I gave	00-01-00
paid May 3rd about Heliars[2] worke	00-05-00
May 6th given to poor frenchman	00-00-03
May 7th Market day delivered	00-09-10
May 14th laid out & paid what was owed	00-11-05
	08-14-04

So endeth the third quarter of the 56th yeare of mine age in which I have laid out on the other side	11-17-09½
which being joyned to that on this side is	20-12- 1½
My receipts have beene only by all waies from kirton & heere	21-09- 4

May 18th. The end of this quarter

[fo. 30 v]

Tertia quarta Disbur[s]ments
an° 1658 day

May 19th given on day of humiliation	00-00-06
May the 20th to the Market	00-10-00
To the barber John Webb	00-00-06
To the Want-Catcher for &c[3]	00-00-06
About My Journey to Major Hale	00-09-00
paid for 3 Moneths taxe	00-01-01½
for mending timber vessell	00-00-06
for Malt May 25th	00-05-00
for the Market May the 28th	00-09-10½
for Tabacco 2 ownces	00-00-03
June 1 Paid to W. Webb for wood	00-13-06
for things from the mountebanke[4]	00-01-00
For the Market day June 4th & to pay till then	00-10-09½
June 5th bought Bookes of A. Dingle	00-12-00
for charges about preaching at Cornwood[5]	00-01-06
June 11th Market day	00-10-11
for letters too & fro to London	00-00-06
Letters to fro. June 18	00-01-07

---

[1]   'Iterato', again: he had already made a payment to the masons on 10 April.
[2]   Slaters' work.
[3]   A mole-catcher (*OED* 'want', *n*[1]: a mole).
[4]   'Mountebank': 'an itinerant charlatan who sold supposed medicines and remedies' (*OED*).
[5]   Cornwood, Devon: on the southern edge of Dartmoor, thirteen miles south-east of Tavistock.

On this very day also 1648. My poore daughter Miller was safely
delivered of her son Thomas at my house at Crediton alias Kirton[1]
Blessed be my God

June 16[th] I called to mind that this day 1652 when I was almost
hopelesse, I was setled & confirmed in the place of publick preaching
at Tavistocke by an order of the Comittee for Plund[e]red Ministers.
The Nations shall rush – but God shall rebuke them.[2]

Received of the Deacons for the use of My chamber for the Church	00-10-00
June 25[th] funerall sermon Esq Howards child[3]	01-00-00
Received of son Condy for improvement of £150 he hath of mine June 26[th]	02-05-00

June 25[th] I had a letter from London from my choice friend Mr E R.
that nothwithstanding all the unworthy carriage of M H against me,
yet it is ordered that I must have mine arreares out of Lamerton.
O My God what shall I &c. Behold thy servant, E, R.[4]

Received of David Condy for improvement of Money	01-00-00
June 26th A letter from my D: Miller blesed be God, she was in health at the writing thereof.	
A funerall sermon July the first[5]	00-08-00
July 13th a funerall sermon old Saxfen[6]	00-10-00
July 14th I received at Kirton only	00-10-06
viz of Brownscombe and P. Wrayford	
[Received] by the hand of John Hodge from J R	00-05-00
Received of John Trix for midsomer ¼ besids what he owed for *rent*	00-12-06
of George Chester for midsommer quarter	01-05-10
My stipend is also Due for that quarter	09+15-00
Received this quarter Hactenus	18-16-10

---

1   Larkham's wife and family may have stayed at Crediton while Larkham (and his son-in-law Miller)
    served with the parliamentary army. Larkham's will, 1669, mentioned 'my mansion house at Crediton
    … mortgaged to Mr Richard Covert (uncle by the mother to Thomas my … grandchild)': A. G.
    Matthews's Notes of Nonconformist Ministers' Wills, Dr Williams's Library, London, MS 38.59, fos.
    607–11 (the original in the Devon Record Office perished during the Blitz).
2   Isaiah 17:13 (KJV): 'The nations shall rush like the rushing of many waters: but God shall rebuke
    them, and they shall flee far off, and shall be chased as the chaff of the mountains before the wind,
    and like a rolling thing before the whirlwind.'
3   Tavistock PR, burials: 25 June 1658, George, the son of 'George Howard Esq.'. Larkham received
    £1 for this sermon, rather than the usual 10s.
4   'E.R.' and 'M.H.': Edward Raddon, Major Hale. Raddon acted for Larkham against Hale in the
    dispute about the Lamerton augmentation. Larkham recalled Psalm 116:12 (KJV) 'What shall I
    render unto the Lord for all his benefits toward me?' and perhaps also Deuteronomy 19:27 (KJV):
    'Remember thy servants, Abraham, Isaac, and Jacob; look not unto the stubbornness of this people,
    nor to their wickedness, nor to their sin.'
5   Tavistock PR, burials: there is no entry for 1 July but there had been burials on 28 and 30 June.
6   Tavistock PR, burials: 13 July 1658, 'William Saxffen'.

for provision for the house	00-10-09
to John Web Barber June 19th	00-00-04
to Roger Row for a weekes worke	00-07-00
Item paid him for an old shovell	00-00-06
June 22 for making a Calaminco[1] suite for my selfe paid D Sowton	00-04-00
Paid my servants wages	00-10-00
To the Communion Given June 20th	00-00-06
for a *jackecheese*[2] paid Jane Allen	00-00-06
Malt Brewed June 22nd	00-05-00
for Baking last quarter ended June 24th	00-01-06
for the Markett June 25th	00-10-06
paid for a demicaster & hatt case[3]	01-04-06
paid for 5 yards of Calaminco for a suite for my selfe & for Trimings & cloth for the boyes clothes & all that was owing upon Son Condies booke untill June 26th	2-02-00
paid for Ribbin for shoeties and bobbing[4]	00-00-06
for Pockets for my New suite	00-00-03
June 28th for 3 Moneths taxe	00-01-01½
July 2 at the Markett	00-10-00
July 9th Market day laid out	00-12-10
July 7th John Webb Barber	00-00-04
July 15th bought at Exeter books	00-06-02
spent in myne exeter journey	00-07-10
a hatt house bought at exeter of *keagle*	00-02-00
Bought the 2 boyes each of them shoes	00-03-04
July 16th Market day laid out	00-10-*04*
Item for half bushell of Malt this worth	00-02-06
	13-03-09

---

[1] 'Calamanco': 'woollen stuff from Flanders, glossy on the surface, and woven with a satin twill and chequered in the warp, so that the checks are seen on one side only' (*OED*).
[2] A conjecture: perhaps a wrapped cheese ('jacketed').
[3] 'Demicastor': inferior quality beaver fur, or a hat made from this (*OED*).
[4] 'Bobbing': 'fine cord' from a haberdasher (*OED*, 'bobbin').

[fo. 31r]

                             £   s   d

I had by the hands of George Pearse who turnd it over to My Sonne
    Condy one quarters rent from Brownscombe my tenant at Kirton   00-10-00
    So Brownscombe hath cleared all until Midsommer last

I being about (this 9ᵗʰ day of August) to take a journey to Exeter do
    signifie under my hand that my stipend of £9-15s. due from the
    Earle of Bedford for the quarter now ended June 24ᵗʰ last is unpaid

The Lord of his eye dazling grace hath looked upon me an
unworthy worme And granted me at last to Receive of mine
arreares August 11ᵗʰ   141- 3- 6[1]
                                            141-13- 6

    And on the other side   18-16-10[2]

    In all received this quarter   160-10-04[3]
    Item I received August 17ᵗʰ   23-14-*00*   of J. Pointer[4]
    finis anni 56 ætatis   184- 4-04[5]

Spent & laid out this quarter one the other syde is   21-10-8½[6]
13-3-8½ & heere *spent 9-7* in all

---

[1]   Arrears from the Lamerton augmentation.
[2]   Corrected from £17-16s-10d.
[3]   Corrected from £159-1s-4d.
[4]   An additional payment related to Lamerton.
[5]   Corrected from £183-4s-4d.
[6]   '8½' is inferred by addition, but the figure is heavily blotted and on the face of it looks like a 3; the
     shillings have been altered from 16 to 10; 'spent 9-7' is also blotted, and so a conjecture.

[fo. 31r]

To William Webb for wood	00+05-00
July 18th Given at A Communion	00+00-06
July the 19th for makinge a suite and coate for myselfe	00+07-00
To Nathaniell Knight helping about wood	0+00-06
7 yards of Calaminco for a coate	00+17-06
for buttons loops silke & triming for a cloath dublet and Breeches &c	00+13-03
Rich: Peeke bought for me a parcell of wood of Richard Spry which cost	01+17-00
July 23 Market day laid out	00+11-10
My wife is to have from Kirton of Pearse by the hands of my sonne Condy	00+10-00
July 30 brewed ½ bushell of malt	00-02-06
laid out at the market & weeke following	00-10-02
August 6th Market day laid out	00-09-00
August the 7th John Webb barber	00[00]06
August 11th sent to my sister at Lyme by Mr Short[1]	00-05-00
paid to Mr Stanbridge for orders & for his paines[2]	00-01-00
To Mr Hales man when I received the money[3]	00-02-06
My Exeter journey August 9. 10. 11. 12th stood[4]	00-09-10
August 13th the last Market of this quarter	00-10-06
	08-12-07

---

[1] Ames Short (*CR*), minister at Lyme Regis. One of Larkham's two sisters had died by this time.
[2] The 'orders' must be related to some aspect of Larkham's battles to secure his rights. Stanbridge is not mentioned again.
[3] This relates to payment by Major Hale of arrears from the Lamerton augmentation.
[4] 'Cost me'.

18 August 1658 – 17 August 1659

[fo. 31r *continued*]

18th August 1658

This yeare through many troubles I have past
And under many mercies have at last
come to the end thereof. My God hath wrought
for me and mine. My foes hath brought to nought.
Glanvill this day laid at the Churches feete
though Pompously by men brought through the streete.[1]
My Mony (almost all is paid) to me.
Many salvations God hath make me see.
This day begins my fifty seventh yeare.
Why should I either men or devills feare?
Eight time seven yeares compleate God hath me kept
In all my dangers he hath never slept.
Let me cry Lord o Lord lift thou up my voice
& give thy poore flocke moore cause to rejoice
Let me & them each day be kept by thee
Our freedom thus farr thou has made to be.
While Grills & Glanvill *under* our feete in dust
Ly mouldring, to our God singe praise we must.[2]
for further glorious workes I hope I live
More of thy spirit Lord do thou me give

          So sang Larkham the servant of the Lord
          August the 18th 1658
          His birthday in the
          <u>yeare 1602</u>

[fo. 31v]

A[e]tatis. 57
beginneth   August the 18th 1658 begins the fifty seventh of mine age[3]
an° 1658

---

[1]   Tavistock PR, burials: 'Francis Glanvill Esqr Died the 2 of August 1658 & was buried the 18 of August 1658.'
[2]   Tavistock PR, burials: 7 February 1656/7, William Grills.
[3]   After this heading at the top of the folio, the entries are in two columns.

[fo. 31r *continued*]

Anni ætatis[1]   yeerely receipts all waies &c

51 ending 1653 August 17th	216-17-01
52 ended 1654	175-11-07
53 ended 1655	112-02-10
54 ended 1656	203-12-03
55 ended 1657	236-12-02
56 Currente 1658 Maij[2] 18th	252-11-08
I began the 4th quarter on a day of humiliation Maij 19th	1197-07-07
who can tell what it may bring foorth?	

To Which let be added what the Lord sent me the first yeares after
    my returne from New England viz untill August 18 1652   1056-17- 1½
                                    I find the summe 2254- 5-05½

This hath God done, Thus farre God hath holpen.
Oh! Christ Christ! None but Christ! Nothinge but Christ!

The last quarter of this yeere I received in all my Lamerton arrears   184- 4- 4

So in all This last yeare I have received no less then 434-16-00
                        & since my coming from N.E. £2438-09s-09½d

[fo. 31v]

an° 1658 18 day of August *is* laid out

	£ s d
Bestowed in Wine this weeke	00-02-03
in Beere & Cakes among my friends	00- 0-07
About entertaining My Son Condies London friends, & his brethren	
& their *wives* ^mutton &c^	00-04-10
I gave to his two servants Marshall & Lansy to drinke	00-00-04

---

[1]   'Years of my age.'
[2]   May.

August 20 I called to mind that on this very day Anno 1602 I was baptized at Lyme Regis in the County of Dorsett where I was borne. The Lord reconcile his holy ones touching Infant baptisme.[1]

The Guilt of lust by baptismes done away,
yet its rebelling force behind doth stay.
Lord let it not in me henceforth beare sway
But buried daily more and more I pray.

	£	s	d
August 24th I preached at the buriall of Richard Peekes wives Daughter & had[2]	00+10-00		
I had also for bookes which came from London of David Condy & John Sheere[3]	00+06-00		
{I lent my Daughter Condy }			
{for Richard Burrow 40ss }[4]			
Will: Web sent me a cheese and a few Peares to bake			
Received of the Deacons for rent of the chamber for the Church	00+10-00		
Due September 29th for my stipend from the E of Bedford	09+15-00		
from George Chester rent	01+05-10		
from John Trix the younger	00+12-06		
Lent Will Chap[man] [and ?] 10s			
Sept. 25th I lent to Petronell Chubb to pay Gray his first paiment for her house	3-00-0		

Sept 29th is due for headrent at Kirton

from Mr Ivy + 10s	}+	
from John Macy for a yeare + 10s	}+	
from G Pearse halfe a yeare + 5s	}+	01-18-00
from W. Brownscombe 1 quarter 10s	}+	
from Brock & Cooper - 02s cooper paid	}+[5]	
from White & Wreyford - 01s		

from John Pointer by promise		
for the last halfe yeer out of Lamerton for the harvest 1657 past	24+15-06	
from my son Condy	02+05-00	
from my cosen David Condy[6]	00+15-00	

by addition received & due   42-06-14   Received
abating the 6s I had for bookes

---

1   Larkham was alleged to have called Anabaptists 'white devils': *Judas*, p. 18. This was an allusion to the saying 'the white devil is worse than the black' – those who claim to be as pure as the driven snow may be particularly dangerous.
2   Tavistock PR, burials: 24 August 1658, 'Elizabeth Edmond'.
3   Probably copies of *Judas*, fresh from the press. Condy and Sheere were leading members of the gathered church, which ostensibly authored the tract. The timing, in terms of the pamphlet controversy, is about right.
4   Larkham crossed out the entry after the loan was repaid.
5   This looks like a comprehensive list of his Crediton tenants. He checked off the entries when the head rent had been paid.
6   Quarterly interest payments from David and Daniel Condy.

paid for bringing bookes[1] from Exon and to John Russell paid in all	00-00-06
malt brewed this first weeke	00-02-06
August 20th Market day	00-13-04
August 22nd at a Communion given	00-10-00[2]
paid for making a Chest to John Sheere	00-08-00
paid for a Clavell[3] for a Chimney	00-04-00
August 24th for mending T. Millers shoes	00-00-08
paid my D. Condy for 4 dozen of buttons which was owed to Joan Lovers	00-01-00
August 27th Market day	00-16-04
August 28th shoes for my selfe of Dingle	00-03-06
August 30th I gave to the children it beinge the eve of Johns faire[4]	00-01-03
Sept. 1 paid J Sheere for a washing Tray[5]	00-02-06
bought 3 pound sugar & 3 p[ound] of Raisons	00-02-01½
Malt Brewed August 31. cost	00-05-00
Laid out Sept. 3. Market day	00-08-09½
paid John Sheere for a close stoole	00-05-00
paid for a Pewter pan for it[6]	00-04-06
September 7th Barber	00-00-06
Sept 10th for mending Tom Larkhams shoes	00-00-07
the same day being Market day laid out	00-07-03
Given to a sicke man Sept 13th	00-00-03
for one hundred of hatch nailes for the New laying of the New plancking over the Hall	00+00-10
for 21 boards for the apple loft & ladder	01+02-09
for Beames to beare up the boards	00+06-06
for workemans wages about the worke	00+06-09
delivered Sept. 17th for the Markett	00-10-11
That day paid for a letter from my son George	00-00-05
for mending T. Millers shoes	00-00-07
Given at the Communion Sept 19th	00-00-06
Sept. 22th ˇ& 29[thˇ] N. Knight gathered in Apples	00-01-00
Laid out last weeke in victualls & this market	00-10-06
Sept. 24th which endeth Michaell:[mas] quarters Servants wages & baking quarterly	00+11-06
Also I usuall[y] give my wife out of Kirton	00+10-00
Due for halfe yeare head rent for ground to the Earle of Bedford Sept. 29th	00+06-08

---

[1] Probably copies of *Judas* : he noted in the other column 'the books which came from London'.
[2] Larkham usually gave 6d or 1s at communion. He may have been tithing his windfall from the Lamerton arrears.
[3] 'Clavel': the lintel over a fireplace (*OED*).
[4] 'John's Fair', an annual fair which coincided with the Feast of the Beheading of John the Baptist on 29 August. This had replaced a much older fair on 29–31 August, the 'eve, feast and morrow' of St Rumon, the pre-Reformation patron saint of Tavistock Abbey.
[5] 'Tray' at this time could mean a shallow open vessel, a basin.
[6] 'Close-stool': 'a chamber utensil enclosed in a stool or box' (*OED*); Larkham listed first the stool, then the pewter chamber pot.

deduct   <u>9-15-10</u>   spent untill Sept. 29 1658

There will remaine   <u>32-11- 6</u>   when al this is paid mentioned in this
Column

[fo. 32r]

The Continuation of the first quarter of the 57th yeare of mine age[1]

October the first I tooke notice that I had an estate of £400 in money and debts &
rents now due: and over and above that summe only one pound 13 shillings and
9d this day I wrote a note of all the particulars, & praised God.[2]

October the second I prayed with & for my Daughter Condy sorely afflicted in
spiritt & she was perswaded to poure out her soule in prayer her selfe in which
performance she had wonderfull asistance, & some Cessation of the grievous
storme &c Blessed be my God &c

Lord sanctify to W. Bole his trouble & let the malignant plott against thy cause be
discovered & frustrated Let it not be in vaine that thou ^hast^ hitherto wrought for
thy greate name, & poore people, & unworthy servant

Octob. 9th I presented Judas & Elymas[3] before God &c
Lord quiet my spirit, against them, if they belong to thine election

	£ s d
Octob. 20th Received of Mr Eveleigh in lieu of an acre of wood	04+00-00

Octob. 21. Mr Howard sent me a little roll of Tabacco, O that God
   would shew him mercy
Thou art O God wonderfull in Counsell & mighty in working
   O be good to my poore Daughter Condy in the Lord X.
Octob. 21 22 I lent to Mr Willi[am] Pointer at [*illegible*] 20s
I gave £50 to My Son Condy which I thought not to have done
   untill after my decease but he was about to take somthing for
   his children & therefore of that £150 in his hand he henceforth
   oweth me only £100
~~Octob.25th Bennett King had 20s more for Mr William Pointer~~
~~In all 40s~~

David Condy oweth for an old paire of bootes	<u>00+04-00</u>
Richawrd my maide Oweth for my daughters Wascot	<u>00+07-00</u>

My in-comes by way of addition this 1 quarter of the 57th yeare of
   mine age since Sept 29 last only by addition £4 for wood   <u>46-06-10</u>

---

1   After this heading the entries are in two columns.
2   A trace of other notebooks and papers Larkham kept.
3   He had already cast Nicholas Watts as 'Judas' in print; Elymas (the sorcerer who opposed Paul at
   Paphos, Acts 13:8) might be Bole.

for mending cloathes for Jane Miller	00+00-08
Given to the boyes on Michaels: faire[1]	00+00-04
	09-15-10½

[fo. 32r]

October first day market laid out	00-09-10
And for Malt brewed this weeke	00-05-00
ˆOctob. theˆ 2nd for sweeping my Chimneyes	00-00-06
Item for a quarter of mutton	00-01-10
Octob. 7th paid 3 moneths taxe	00-01-01½
Octob. 8th Market day ˆ& at a fair 9½ˆ & to french men	00-08- 9½
Octob. 11th a paire of shoes for J Miller	00-01-10
Octob. 15th laid out in the Market	00-08-08
Octob. 16 paid for making a *Corsy*[2] roabe for Jane Miller to Dan: Sowton	00-04-06
for 7 yardes ¾ of stuffe for the said garment at 2-4d per yard to Sone Condy	00-18-01
for a *siphir* or love hood[3] for	00-03-02
for other things used about her clothes	00-04-10
and for cloth for *a smo[c]ke* for *her &c*	00-03-06
a shirt for her brother	00-02-06
a shirt for Thomas Larkham	00-02-06
given at the Communion Octob 17th	00-00-04
paid for soape & candles	00-01-06
Octob. 21 To Esquir howards boy	00-00-06
for a peice of Timber for N Hockaday bes[i]ds [*illegible*]	0-00-10
October 22 Market day laid out first	0-05-11
Paid Ag:[nes] Fleshman for 36 pound of butter	0-16-06
Octob. 22 for 3 pound of soape	0-00-11
Item laid out for victualls this weeke	00-01-09
To 2 Men bringing Cyder I gave	00-00-03
Octob. 29. Market day laid out	00-09-09
& for Malt brewed this weeke	00- 5-0[0]
November the 5th Markett day laid out	00-04-10
	06-04-09
	09-15-10½
So still Hitherto I have the above mentioned summe of £400 saving that 50 pounds of it, is since given to my Son Condy	16-00- 7½ spent in all this ¼ past

---

[1] The Michaelmas Fair in late September, like the 'John's Fair' in August and the Goose Fair in October, was part of Tavistock's annual calendar. Larkham gave his grandsons 2d apiece.

[2] 'Corsy': 'big-bodied' (*OED*).

[3] 'Siphir' or 'sipher': variant spellings of 'cipher', which can mean 'false, mock'. 'Love-hood': a hood made of thin crape or gauze material (*OED*).

It is sixteene agone that I left New England. Greate & marvellous o Lord have thy providences beene over me and mine. I am full as the moone and ready to burst &c.[1]

Thy Spirit O God hath writt the gospell-story
upon the fleshly tables of mine hearte.
Christs birth, his cradle, crosse, his grave his glory,
All's acted on that stage by th' Spirits art.
Let me not greive thy Spirit or go astray,
When it doth say to me, this is the way.

As th' Hen her chicken so has thou mine ever
gather'd, & warmd under thy blessed wings,
To do what pleaseth thee make us indeavour,
Harke how the offspring of poore Larkham sings!
Father all things for us thou doest provide
In all our woes hast still beene on our side

Sic finitur quarta prima Anni 57 ætatis

[fo. 32v]

1658

The Second Quarter of the 57th yeare of mine age beginneth Novemb.17th[2]

November the 18th I had Newes of My Daughter Patience by a letter sent to her brother in Cumberland which said letter was dated August 17th last past then she was alive blessed be my God. O my God upon all accounts behold me in X[3]

Novemb 19th I lent Will: Chapman 13s

Nov. 30. I had sight of Watts his second booke very sinfull & abusive I do humbly spread it before the Lord.[4]

Dec. 2 The Church lay before the Lord in a serious & solemne humiliation. (I will Harken what the Lord &c) and communicated in breaking of bread the Lords day Following. Dec 5th[5]

---

[1] He wrote this across the whole folio.
[2] After this heading the entries are in two columns.
[3] Christ.
[4] *A strange metamorphosis in Tavistock, or the Nabal-Naboth improved a Judas. Set forth in reply to a scurrilous pamphlet called Judas, &c* (London, [1658]), which Larkham here attributed to Nicholas Watts. The London bookseller George Thomason marked his copy 'April 27' in 1658, presumably soon after it came out (Thomason Tract E.940[2], British Library), so the delay before Larkham saw a copy is puzzling.
[5] A day of humiliation on Thursday, to prepare; followed by communion on Sunday. 'I will Harken': the allusion is probably to Jeremiah 26:1–7, a call to repentance.

[fo. 32v]

	£ s d
Laid out in expenses due last quarter	00-10-09
for Worke to Roger Row ˆ2 daies 2s-4dˆ & given ˆA 2dˆ to him also	
to a poore woman 2d	00-02-08
Item laid out in provision for the house whereof 14d was for *an*	
apple-store	00-11-03
paid W Web for a dozen of candles	00-05-00
for Malt brewed November 23ʳᵈ	[0]-05-00
November 26 Market day	00-05-04
November the 30ᵗʰ given to Jane Miller	00-00-06
for 2 hatts for the two boyes	00-07-06
December 2ⁿᵈ at a day of humiliaton	00-00-06
December 3ʳᵈ given to N Knight & laid out this weeke & this	
Market day ˇwhereof for Turffes 2 seames 1-7d 00-01-07ˇ	00-12-06
for shoes 3s for the boyes	00-03-00
Decemb 5ᵗʰ to Church Communion delivered	00-00-06
December 10ᵗʰ to John Webb Barber	00-00-06
The same day delivered for the market	00-09-09
The same day for Beefe for store	00-11-00
for making & mending wascotts	00-01-00
paid Son Condy which I borrowed to give his Nurse	00-00-06
December 17ᵗʰ Market day laid out	
ˇand a quart of metheglinˇ[1]	00-05-08

[1] 'Metheglin': 'a spiced or medicated variety of mead' (*OED*).

My Son Condy had conference with Mr Stucley Decemb. 7th about Mutuall Communion betweene the Churches: Lord set us in the hearts of thine holy ones to thy glory & our comfort.[1]

~~Decemb 13th I sent Son Condy eight pound~~

O My poore Rocky Untoward Wife!
O my unsuitablenes to her! Lord helpe.[2]

I had of R. Spry for funerall sermon[3]	00+10-00
I had of son Condy Gotten by Macy he hath of mine to trade upon	1-10-00
Received of the Deacons for the Chamber	0-10-00
Due for Rent from G. Chester	1- 5-10
Also for Rent from J Trix due	0+12-06
My stipend from Mr Eveleigh due	9+15-00
& from Mr Cosen David Condy	0+15-00

Jan 4th I paid 38 pound for the first paiment for Fords land which I tooke in my Son Condies name I am to pay £50 March 25 next & £50 more September 29th next his price was £140 but he abated (as a gift) forty shillings

of R Hawskworth his wife buried[4]	00+10-00
sold herrings for	00+09-07
viz. 2d & ½ to duntervile for 4[s] 8d the rest after 2s 6d viz. 1d & halfe	
Due Decemb. 25 from Brownscombe	00-15-00
Brownscombe paid percase[5] Macy *besids* Browns: former	
of Mr Brownsdon his wives fun: serm[on][6]	1+00-00
	Rec 17-12-11

Hitherto spent	[?]-*05-7*

---

1   Lewis Stucley (*CR*) of Exeter. Daniel Condy acted as a 'messenger' of the church. As in Tavistock, Stucley's gathered church had been split by a dispute about excommunications, which sparked a local print controversy: [Thomas Mall], *A true account of what was done by a church of Christ in Exon (whereof Mr. Lewis Stucley is pastor) the eighth day of March, 1657, when two members thereof were excommunicated* (London, 1658); Susanna Parr, *Susanna's apologie against the elders* (n.p., 1659) Lewis Stucley and Thomas Mall, like Larkham, had an uneasy relationship with the Devon Association: Halcomb, 'Social history of congregational religious practice', pp. 225–7.

2   'Rocky', as in 'unfeeling, unyielding; flinty, hard'; or difficult to manage, intractable, perverse (*OED*). In more than twenty years , Larkham made only two direct comments about his wife in his diary. The other is in June 1661, on his thirty-ninth wedding anniversary: 'For my unworthy selfe & poore wife, My father thou knowest how it is with me and her, O thy spirit is all I crave for us both, And then all will be well enough' (fo. 41v).

3   Tavistock PR, burials: 6 December 1658, 'Agnis Spry'.

4   Tavistock PR, burials: 8 January 1658/9, 'Joan Hawsworth'.

5   'Percase': as it happened (*OED*).

6   Tavistock PR, burials: 11 January 1658/9, Mrs Abigail Brownsdon.

Three seames of Turffes	00-02-04
for Malt brewed December 21	00-05-00
for letters brought & sent Dec. 24	00-00-10
laid out about the Markett then	00-05-10
paid servants Wages & gave her 1s	00-11-00
paid for baking the quarter now ended	00-01-06
paid a score at Son Condies	00-08-06
Decemb. 25th paid for the Cupboard in the hall	
besides 16d formerly for 4 keyes	00-12-00
I paid item unto John Sheere for Mr Ellies daughter for making my	
coate ^& *for thread* & b[*uttons*] & silke	00-03-04
to Jane Miller 6d Mattacots[1] children when son Condy tooke	
posession 6d	00-01-00
Decemb 31 Market day laid out	00-08-00
paid for 3 moneths taxe	00-01-00
Jan: 1 John Web Barber	00-00-06
for bringing herrings from Plimoth	00-01-06
January the second at a Communion given	00-00-06
Jan.1. For 3 pound of Soape paid	00-00-11
paid for making a deede for Fords land	00-06-00
Lost in counterfeit Money & spent in &c	00-02-00
paid for 3 seames of Turffes Jan 4	00-02-06
To Frenchman, 1d to Lansy I gave iid	00-00-03
paid for bringing home the other herrings	00-01-06
Delivered for the Markett Jan 7th	00-08-10
to Clog for a letter 3d to Marshall iid	00-00-05
To Jane Condies Nurse her little girle	00-00-06
Jan 14th delivered to the maid market day	01-02-11
Jan 20 for mending the 2 boyes shoes	00-01-02
Brewing Jan 18th Market Jan 21 & 28	[*illegible*]
Jan 22 for beare & wine [*illegible*]	[*illegible*]

---

[1] At first sight 'Mastacot', but Larkham often did not cross through double 't's, and the surname 'Mattacott' appears in Tavistock's parish register.

[fo. 33r]

<u>Remaininge out of the receipts of this quarter January 29th</u>   6- 7- 4

£ s d

spent since as in the other Columne 3-5-11 In all 14-11-6.
Remaines at the end of this quarter of the receipts   3-01-05
for the summe of the receipts was   17-12-11
And the summe of the expences was   14-11-06

So endeth the second quarter of the seven and fiftieth yeare of mine age
blessed be my God.

I love my children, doth not God love me?
And shall not I againe my God love thee?
Make Watts thy postinge vengeance for to see
That he may to the refuge city flee.[1]

The Third quarter, in it God shall me blesse:
To pray to him my mouth shall never cease:
O, thy poore handfull heere guid[e] And preserve,
That from thy blessed rules we never swerve.

Received in Malt of Bevill Wivill for the Rent of close[2] due
    March 25th   00+12-06
Received of Son Condy in full for the profitt of £100 untill
    March 25th 1659   01+10-00
Due unto me March 25th my stipend   09+15-00
from Chester this quarter for *ground*   01-05-10
from Kirton for headrent from Brownscombe Pearse and Macy   00-15-00
From William Webb for &c   01+13-00
from David Condy for the same   00+15-00
From my Tenants of Fords land   01-02-06
from the Deacons for the meeting chamber and towards the staires
    & fittinge of[3]   01+05-00

---

[1] Nicholas Watts, who led public opposition to Larkham. 'Posting': rapid, speedy. Israel provided
    'cities of refuge' for those who unwittingly killed a neighbour (Numbers 35, Joshua 20–1): thus
    Larkham allowed Watts a glimmer of hope.
[2] 'Close': probably an enclosed field (*OED*); elsewhere, Larkham referred to Wivell's 'ground'(31
    August 1659, fo. 35r).
[3] The gathered church paid rent to hold meetings in a refurbished chamber in Larkham's house.

[fo. 33r]

<u>spent Hitherto this quarter</u>	<u>11-05-07</u>[1]
Turffes 31 Jan. 18d Parchment 1s	00-02-06
for mendinge Jane Millers shoes	00-00-06
Feb: 4th a market day laid out	00-06-09
At the Communion I gave	00-00-06
for 4 yards at iis per yard for my shirt & making of it which I gave	
to Joan Miller	00-08-06
February 11th for a yeares tenths acqu[i]tt[an]ce	01-02-01
Laid out this day being Market day	00-10-00
Brewed a bushell february 18th	00-05-00
To my wife for the quarter Xtide[2]	00-10-00
to a poore man	<u>00-00-01</u>
spent in all this quarter	14-11-06

Heere beginneth the third quarter febr 16th

Inprimis given to a poore man	00-00-02
paid for two seames of Turffes	00-01-07
Febr: 18 the first market of this quarter	00-19-08
for dyeing stockens 6d & a glasse 4[d]	00-00-10
paid for a skin for Pockets to W Lovis	00-00-06
for a yard of Tape for shoeties	00-00-02
market day Feb. 25th 6[s]-6[d] Jane 4[d] Com[munion] 4[d]	00-07-02
for earth 10d & stones to bright & lyme and Pinnes & wages to the	
Helar[3] 41s 8d `& Pod 1[s]`[4]	02- 3-06
To the Drakes for Mason worke	00- 9-06
for Glasse paid John Austin	00-01-00
for Haire, Lathts,[5] Hailds & guards[6] nailes Gimies[7] Twists[8] & It[9]	
Lyme	00-13-10
given in beare at severall times	00-00-09
for stones for the staires paid	00-05-00
for Carpenters worke & boards besids what boards & Timber I had	
by me	01-17-00

---

1   The corner is torn but the last number can be calculated from figures below and opposite.
2   Christ-tide: the quarter from 25 December to 24 March.
3   'Hellier': slater, tiler (*OED*).
4   'Pod': the socket of a brace (for holding a bit), or a tool handle that could take tools of different
    gauges (*OED* 'pod' *n*² / 'pad' *n*² 18).
5   Laths and (horse) hair for plasterwork.
6   'Hailds' (holds): the mortise cavity of a lock. 'Guards': the 'wards' of a lock, i.e., the ridges inside
    designed to fit a particular key (*OED* 'guard' *n*¹⁶ pl, 'ward' *n*² 24).
7   In this context, likely to be 'gimmals' or 'gimmers' (*OED*): joints, hinges.
8   A 'twist': 'the flat part of a hinge' (*OED*).
9   'Iterato': again (he had listed lime a few lines earlier).

March 25th – 1659   18-13-10
                                                           11-05-00
                                                            7-08-10

Thus farre the Lord hath holpen.

Tis not a heape of rude bruite-beasts shall stand
When pray'r lifts up God's peoples reaching hand

Ah – fifty nine hast nothing in thy Wombe?
Oh faith presse in set thou promises home.
Father advance the Sonne that died i' th flesh,
Thy praying fainting people Lord refresh.
Thou saucy Bab'lon beware thy head[1]
Come out foule beast out of Xhrists spouses bed.
When he was slaine that did thy Master brain,
He tooke an order thou shouldst not remain.
Th'[ou] has thrust the que[e]ne into the truckle bed[2]
Tis meete (vile traytor) thou shouldst lose thy head.

              Lord grant I leave the jade[3] below
              To mount to' th' place my God shall shew.

              Ita pipiebat Larkhamus serv[us] [do]mini[4]

00-19-01
    2-08[5]

---

[1] 'Saucy' had a sharper meaning than today: 'insolent towards superiors; presumptuous' (*OED*).
     Larkham conjured here with imagery about Antichrist and the Whore of Babylon from Revelation
     17–18.
[2] In other words, the antichristian whore usurped the place of Christ's royal bride the Church.
[3] 'Jade': a pejorative term – a whore.
[4] 'So cried Larkham servant of the Lord.'
[5] Rough notes jotted in the corner, using the space around the poem.

ˇmore for iron workeˇ   00-02-05
Market day March 4ᵗʰ laid out   00-09-10
March 8ᵗʰ Brewed a bushel & halfe cost   00-07-06
Paid Son Condy in full satisfaction of all owed on his booke untill
    March 8ᵗʰ   00-18-00
March 11ᵗʰ Market day laid out given to poore man 3d   00-07-08
March 13 paid for shoes for Jane Miller   00-02-00
March 18ᵗʰ market day bestowed   00-08-03
about letters To and fro this day   00-00-06
March 21 at a fast of the church given   00-05-00
for 2 seames of Turffes   00-01-06
A Sattin Capp bought of Tranter   00-03-06
Servants wages 10s Baking 18d   00-11-06
Due for halfe yeares rent for my ground to the Earle of Bedford   00-06-08
                                                                        11-05-00

1659. March 25ᵗʰ Market day ˇwhereof a bushell of wheate 10sˇ   00-16-00
paid Aug: Bond for a weekes diet   00-02-06
March 26ᵗʰ for a swabb[1]   00-00-06
27ᵗʰ Communion day I gave   00-00-06
March 26ᵗʰ lent Petro:[nell] Chubb £3-10s so in all she oweth
    me £6-10s
paid for 2 pair of shoes for the boyes   00-03- 4

Hactenus 01-02-10 & 11-5-00[2]

---

[1] An absorbent mass of rag or other stuff, used for mopping up, cleansing (*OED*).
[2] Here he lists the total of expenses above, with the £11-5s spent since 18 February.

[fo. 33v]

the rents reckoned before *were paid*[1]

	£ s d
Received of Mrs Trowt for Her rent	00-01-08
I had at the Marriage of W. Burges[2]	00-00-09
A marriage of Peter Row[3]	00-00-08
Of John Anstis & Richard Huggins Head rent for Lady day[4] quarter	00-04-02

past this & such other Rents are not to be reckoned among the
receipts since March 25 last though since received

Aprill 14th I gave to Mr Torr schoolmaster one of My bookes of
the Attributes[5]

Lord blesse my children that are gone abroad
preserve them from all dangers on the roads
Grant that no just offence they give to any
nor be caught in snares, though they meete with many
refresh their spirits & keepe them close to thee
O Let my children Lord thy children bee.
Bring them in safty home i' th' close o' th' day,
That I the Lord be praised to thee may say.

Sic scripsi[6] – Apr. 19th
when my children were gone to Plimouth for pleasure

Aprill 25th My son departed with his wife & man servant towards his owne home[7]
The Lord send them safe for Jesus sake amen.

Praise waiteth for God upon this account also
O that my heart wer so Directed that I might keepe thy statutes.[8]

[1]   A small note entered at the top at a different time.
[2]   Tavistock PR, marriages: 5 April 1658, Walter Burgis and Martha Moses. From 29 September 1653 marriages in England been conducted by justices of the peace. Larkham's fee of 9d – far less than the 10s he usually received for funeral sermons – was probably for saying prayers.
[3]   Tavistock PR, marriages: 7 April 1658, Peter Row and Elizabeth Rundell.
[4]   25 March: Larkham usually avoided the traditional name.
[5]   Larkham's *Attributes of God* (1656).
[6]   'So I have written.'
[7]   George Larkham, returning to Cumberland.
[8]   Psalm 65:1 (KJV): 'Praise waiteth for thee, O God, in Sion.' Psalm 119:5 (KJV): 'O that my ways were directed to keep thy statutes!'

[fo. 33v]

	£ s d
March 31 for makinge Cloathes for all three chilldren[1]	00-06-00
Aprill 1 for the Markett	00-14-10
given and for the Church ^meeting^	00-00-06
April 4 for 3 moneths taxe	00-01- 0
Aprill 6th Brewed a bushell & halfe	00-07- 6
Aprill 7th at the church meeting	00-00- 6
Market day Aprill the 8th	00-14-00
gave to John Martin April 14th	00-00-06
paid for victualls that day	00-04-06
Aprill 15th laid out this Market day by Reason of my son George	
being heere	01-04-00
paid for a [illegible] for boyes[2]	00-01-00
paid for 3 moneths taxe for my land which I bought of John Ford	00-01-03
Barber Aprill the 16th	00-00-06
At the Church meeting. Apr. 16th	00-00-04
paid old Cudlip for 3 C[wt][3] of Hay	00+06-00
I had also of Mr Welshford 3 C[wt]	00+06-00
& of David Serjeant 2 C[wt]	00+04-00
for 4 seames of Turffes of Crage	00+02-06
Apr. 19th for veale Makrel & to Boyes cleansing the stable[4]	00+02-07
for gardening and seedes only	00+02-00
Aprill 22. it was market day spent	00+15-07
At the Communion Aprill 24th	00+00-06
for oates & more hay for my sour horses[5] untill April 25th	00+03-01
I gave to my daughter in law[6] the wife of my Son George to Bestow	
for her selfe & children	05+00-00
Aprill 26th paid Son Condy for all that was owed untill then	01+19-06
except for the stuffe of Janes coate which I also paid at the same	
time	00+10-00
Aprill the 29th Market day laid out	00+08-08
for letters from and to London	00+00-06
Aprill 30 paid W Webb for candles & wood	00+09-00
May. 1 at a Church meeting	00+00-06
This weeke it cost me in recreations	00+00-07
May 3rd for a bushell of Malt	00+05-00
in Lamb & fish this weeke	00+01-02
May the 7th A paire of shoes for my selfe	0 +03-06

---

1   His grandchildren Thomas and Jane Miller, and Thomas Larkham.
2   A puzzling reference, hard to decipher and make any sense of.
3   'C', formerly used for 'hundredweight' (*OED* 'cwt.').
4   The visit of Larkham's son George explains extra expense for horses (hay, cleaning the stable) and unusual food (veal, mackerel).
5   'Sour horses': 'heavy, coarse, gross' (*OED* 'sour' 9).
6   Dorothy Larkham.

Thy grace unthought unsought hath seiz'd on me,
And (Lord) my soule is breathing after thee.
This weeke there cam to mine eares a strange story
I hope the saints shall shortly see Gods glory.
By him the princes rule & kings do raigne
That Christ exalted is see would I faine.
By thine owne word through th' Spirits incubation
Set foorth the world now in a new edition.

May 9th I received by the hands of George Pearse 22s viz from
    Brownscombe 20s from Cooper 1s from wreyford and White
    each of them sixe pence which is crossed thereupon in the
    forthcoming places of each quarter.[1]
The money George Pearse had[2] was of that £50 which was
    once in the hands of David Condy
May the 11th Old John Trixes wife buried[3]   00-10-00

cleare receipts this quarter were   19-05-03   But since 59 only 11-05

spent & laid out in all this quarter   66-17-07[4]   whereof £38 was to Pearse
now ended   remai[ns] 10-11-9 of this

[fo. 34r]

The fourth quarter of The seven & fiftieth yeare of mine age beginneth
May the 18th 1659[5]

an°1659
It appeareth that of my sto[c]ke I have spent foure nobles[6] in
    housekeeping And apparrell & workes of charity more than
    I have received since September 29th last for then I had   £400 stocke
since which I gave my son Condy towards purchasing of land
    as is before mentioned the sum of   50-00-00[7]
and I have laid out in land which I bought ˆofˆ one ford £138
    whereof is paid   88-00-00
I bought of George Pearse one anuity at   38-00-00
And I have owed unto me from diverse   11-13-04

---

[1] This explains his habit of making a downstroke to form '+' when he had checked off a sum of money.
[2] Larkham purchased an annuity from Pearse for £38 (see below and opposite).
[3] Tavistock PR, burials: 11 May 1658, Joan Trix.
[4] The total of all the quarter's expenses (the sum of the interim totals £1-2s-10d, £11-5s and £54-9s-9d).
[5] After this heading the entries are in two columns.
[6] This is the only time Larkham reckoned in nobles (a coin usually valued at 6s-8d) but he did not fill out the details of what was accounted for.
[7] Below this Larkham crossed out a line ('and to my son George his wife bestowed for her selfe & chilldren 05-00-00') because he had reckoned this up elsewhere.

for a yard of ferrett for shoeties[1]	0 +00-04
Given at the church meetinge	00+00-04
Laid out the market May 6th & *also following*	0 +08-10
for Letters from and to Pli[mouth] only	0 +00-04
May 9th I laid out for an annuity of 50s per annum for 3 lives[2]	38-00-00
May 10th I gave to my wife	00-10-00
May 13th the last Market of the quarter	<u>00-12-10</u>
	54-09-09

[fo. 34r]

Inprimis given at a church meeting	00-00-06
for a Gowne for my sister & making it[3]	01-11-02
for 2 paire of drawes[4] for the boyes	00- 2- 8
for 3 pound of Sope	00-01-00
Laid out in provision the first weeke and somthinge bestowed this weeke before	00-08-11
I gave to maide washing my foote	00-00-06
recreations stood this weeke past	00-00-07
May 21st Barber	00-00-06
May the 22nd at a Communion	00-00-06
Given to poore frenchmen	00-00-02
to the Almshouse at Okhampton & Ben Kinge	00-01-01
May 27th markett day laid out	00-08-08

---

[1] 'Ferret': 'a stout tape' made of cotton or sometimes silk, used for shoelaces (*OED*).

[2] A transaction with George Pearse of Crediton. 'Three lives or 99 years' was a common term for a lease.

[3] His surviving sister (Elizabeth or Jane) had come to stay in Tavistock. Elsewhere, he described her situation as 'worse than a widow'. She returned to Lyme Regis on 30 April 1661 (fos. 40v, 41r).

[4] 'Drawers': breeches, not (at this date) undergarments (*OED*).

And I have in house remaininge & abroad in *sundry hands* 206-00-[00]

        sume of all which is 393-13- 4

217-13-04   Hactenus auxiliatus est Dominus[1]

~~Received of Em dodge 3s 4~~ formerly accounted for

I have had in Malt of Bevile Wivell so much this quarter comes unto 00+12-06

June the 10th the Lord brought safe to me my Deare daughter
Patience & her Daughter Anne Blessed be my God and father
in Jesus Christ who hath thus farre holpen me & mine. Lord
direct concerning them for thy Covenants sake.

Heere are with me Patience my daughter Thomas Jane and Anne
3 of her children. Mary her eldest child and daughter at Dublin
Lord looke on them all as within the Covenant in Jesus Christ.

Due to me my stipend at Tavistocke   09+15-00
from The Deacons for my chamber   00+10-00
for my ground this quarter is due besids what I have received of
 B. Wivile   01- 05-10
Rents of Land at Tavistocke quarterly   01- 02-06
Rents & annuities at Kirton due quarterly   01- 08-00
besides what is paid yearely ~~by some~~ of son Condy out of my
 stocke with him   01+10-00
      received or due, Hactenus 15- 11-10

I had also of my daughter Miller when she came June 10th 1659
 in Money   06+00-00
Received or due unto me   21- 11-10

        remaineth 9-02-04[2]

[fo. 34v]

June 24th mid sommerday Continues the last quarter of 57th yeare of mine age[3]
an°1659

               £ s d
June 27th At a Marriage I Had[4]   00-02-06

---

[1] 'Thus far the Lord hath holpen.'
[2] The remainder, once expenses (in the right column) had been deducted from receipts (above). Across
  the foot of the folio various notes have been crossed out and are illegible.
[3] After this heading Larkham divided the entries into two columns.
[4] Tavistock PR, marriages: 27 June 1659, Edward Burgis and Mary Martine.

spent in my journey to Lyme about my sisters businesse	01-02-09
May 30th given to a Travellour pretending Captivity by the Ostenders	
& a university man	00-01-00
In a quarter of lambe & fish June 1	00-01-04
paid for Bobbinge[1] silke sope to D. Condy	00-00-10
To Roger Row Paringe hedges	00-00-02
for victualls the Thursday ^18d^ appeares June 3 ^12-6d^	00-14-00
This weeke Past Brewing viz May 31st	00-05-00
for dressing a demicastor & new head linings[2]	00-02-00
Item bestowed in recreations this weeke past	00-00-02
June the 10th market day & the weeke past	00-12-04
The same day mending boyes shoes	00-01-02
for mending mine owne shoes	00-01-00
for sacke at the comminge of my Da:[ughter]	00-00-10
for Tabacco ^6d^ Item Mutton ^23d^ & to the man ^6d^ that brought	
my daughter from Padstow	00-02-11
June 12th Given at a church meeting	00-00-06
June 17th Market day wheate 8-10 and besides in Provision 10s	00-18-10
A bushell of Malt to brew June 20th	00-05-00
for sixe seames of Turffes	00-04-00
Item for silks ^rated[3]^ 6d & wives gowne 5s 6d paid to Daniell	
Sowton June 20th	00-06-00
for white wine Claret wormwood beere[4]	00+01-06
for dressing of a hatt for my selfe	00+00-06
due now June 24th for servants wages	00+10-00
& I usually give of Kirton rents to my wife	00+10-00
& for baking due this quarter	00+01-06
Paid to W. Webb for wood 10 seames	00+10-00
Upon my son Condies bookes for diverse things for selfe wife sister	
&c	02+19-00
paid Will: Gee for pockets for the boyes[5]	00+00-08
for halfe a pint of hott water	<u>00+00-06</u>
Spent & Laid out hitherto	<u>£12- 09-06</u>

[fo. 34v]

an°1659

	£	s	d
June 24 Laid out in market	00-	12-	4
June 27th I gave the Deacons		01-	0

---

1   Probably 'bobbin': fine cord (*OED*).
2   'Demicastor': a fur hat of some kind (*OED*), here refurbished with a new lining.
3   'Rated': valued at.
4   'Wormwood', a bitter-tasting plant, used – until forbidden by law in 1710 – for brewing ale (*DTGC*).
5   Possibly small pouches or bags, made of leather. On an earlier occasion (fo. 20r) Gee provided 'skins' for 'linings'.

for a funerall Sermon R. Hitchens[1]   00-10-00

This quarter received by addition   22-04-04[2]

Thus hath my God this first of the Ninth Seven
preserv'd me sweetely in my way to heaven.
And now my Lord what waite I further for,
The times tumultuous are, yet at thy door.
Many stand knocking that will knocke each other
if thou prevent not. Lord keep thou a brother
from sheathing of the sword in's brother's side,
Bannish formalitie malice and pride.
And let King Jesus be exalted high
And babilonish brats be made to cry.[3]
In Ta'stocke Lord appeare for thy poore folke,
in this greate egge they are a little yolke.
O looke upon us for thy covenants sake,
a vessell for thine use do thou us make.
And my poore offspring and relations all,
jewells of thine my God do thou them call.
The *fourth that's going now, beyond the seas,   *TL[4]
to give thy Spir'it to O may'st thou please.

Sic pipiebat indignissimus servus Domini.[5]

Received this yeare 57th of mine age ended

	£ s d	
1 Quarter	46-06-10	
2 quarter	17-12-11	
3 quarter	19-05-03	
Last quarter	22-04-04	I had *also* of my daughter Miller June 10th £6
	105-09-04	which maketh the said sume as is aforewritten

Receipts by addition this yeare were only £99-9s-04d[6]

---

1   Tavistock PR, burials: 25 June 1659, 'Al[i]ce Hitchens'.
2   Including the total of £21-11s-10d from the previous folio.
3   Another allusion to the Whore of Babylon, Revelation 17–18.
4   His grandson Thomas Larkham, who was about to go to France.
5   'So cried the most unworthy servant of the Lord.'
6   He inserted this line later into his summary.

June 30th paid D: Condy for bonlace[1] for capps	02- 0
July the first Market day laid out	00-13- 0
5 July 2 seams of Turffes	00-01- 3
6th paid D Sowton for Turning breeches	00- 1- 0
for cloath for shirts & bonds[2] for my selfe	00-18- 0
for cloth for drawers for T. L *with buttons*	00-01- 6
July 8 Market day & lambe yesterday	00-19-10
for making bonds & cuffes for my selfe paid	00-08
for Bondstrings for my selfe & Tom Larkham	00-00-08
Wine & Mutton July the 12th	00-01-03
for ferret ribbin[3] for shoe ties	00-00-04
July 14th a day of humiliation of the Church	00-00-06
July 15th Market day and the weeke follo[wi]ng	0-19-03
July 16th To The Barber	00-00-06
July 17th at the Comunion & another collections paid	00-10
for letters July 22nd I paid	00-00-05
Market day & the weeke following	00-09-08
for six Moneths taxe paid July 25th	00-02-06
About ^2 daies^ tilling my Orchard ^& to *Roger* Rowe 2d^ & seedes 4d	00-02-10
to poore frenchman	00-00-01
About turninge of a cloth coat for my selfe	00-02-04
July 29th Market day butter & Corne	01-04-01
at the going of Thom Larkham to Plimouth	00-01-00
July 30 for 3 paire of shoes for the 3 chilldren[4]	00-06-04
About sendinge Tom Larkham to france charges in Plimouth in all laid out at August 3rd	01-16-06
Item sent August 5th when I sent New cloathes and I paid to George Oxhenham	1-03- 6
Markett day this 5th day laid out and this weeke untill now	01-02- 0
Owed to Bevile Wivel for malt	00+10- 0
And unto my son Condy for Materialls for. T. Larkhames cloathes	01+05-11
Untill the end of this quarter & 57th yeare of mine age for the house	00+10-04
for making Hose & coate for. T. Larkham	00+02-06
for a paire of understockens for my selfe	00+03-02
7 pound of sugar at 9½d a pound	00+05-07½
for 6 pound of sope paid August the 8th	00+02-00
August 8th sent my daughter Miller	00+10-00

---

[1]   'Bone-lace' or bobbin lace, made of linen thread (*OED*). Larkham's birthplace, Lyme Regis, became famous for this in the eighteenth century. Later, he sent his grandchild Jane Miller there to learn how to make it.

[2]   'Bonds' and 'bondstrings': collars or ruffs for shirts (*OED* 'band' *n*² 4) and strings to hold them in place; used by men and women. 'Bands' were not yet a specialist item for clerics and lawyers. Larkham's portrait (Plate 1) shows him with band, bandstrings and cuffs.

[3]   Ferret ribbon: stout tape for shoelaces.

[4]   Thomas, Jane and Anne Miller. Thomas and Jane had been in Tavistock, in Larkham's household, for some time. Patience, 'my daughter Miller', arrived from Ireland with Anne in May 1659. All four returned to Ireland in November 1659 (fos. 34r, 35v).

Spent & laid out this 57th yeare of mine age

	£ s d	
quarta 1^a	16-00-07	
quarta 2^a	14-11-06	
quarta 3^a	28-17-07	whereof D. Larkham[1] had £5 a gift
last quarter	27-04-08	this last quarter my sister & daughter Miller & 3 chilldren were with me
	86-14-04	

My incomes have beene more then mine expens this yeare only £18-15 whereof 9-8s-10d is in debts made this yeare, in house 9-6-2[2]

for mending the newe chamber locke   00+00-06
                                                                         14-15-02

on the other side spent this quarter   12-09-06

                                    spent in all this quarter   27-04- 8

18 August 1659 – 17 August 1660

[fo. 35r]

August the Eighteenth 1659 beginneth the 58the Yeare of mine ag[e][1]

Ah my deare Lord do thou revive my hearte
And with thy gentle wings O stroke my smart
Blesse me this following yeare begun this day
An yeare of many mercies be' it I pray.

	£	s	d

August the twentieth of Jo Pointer in p[aymen]t[2] of mine
 augment[ation] for the yeare 1658   26-00-00
Memorandum I left in my son Condys hands five & twenty pound
 of the money I had of Pointer[3]

Tis a sad world when brethren kill each other,
Yet now there is no trusting one another
Fainted I had but that the scripture saith,
When Christ shall come, shall he on earth find faith?[4]

August the 31 I made a bargaine with B Wivill for all my ground
 for 7 yeare for £7-15s per yeare & allowed all unto Sept 29
 next receivinge of him upon allowance of Malt for
 Michael[mas] quarter.   0-12-06
which forsaid day of August I had twenty shillings more of my Son
 Condy (£24 being yet in his hand)
A funerall sermon Edward Hunt Buried Sept 26[th5]   00-10-00
of the Deacons for rent of the chamber for the quarter ended
 September 29   00-10-00
Due to me from Kirton besids arreares which have beene formerly
 mentioned each quarter from Mr Ivy & the other Tenants that
 pay yeerly. Ivy 10s. Brocke 1s. Cooper 1s. white 6d   00-12-06
from Pearse & Macy this quarter only   00-05-00
for Pearses annuity this quarter besids what they owe both in arreares   00-12-06
from Wreyford one quarters rent for barne   00-00-06
from Brownsdon on[e] quarters rent   00-10-00
my quarterly rents at Tavistocke are   01-02-06
my rent this quarter from Chester   01-05-10

---

1 After the heading across the top the entries are divided between two columns.
2 A part payment of the Lamerton augmentation for 1658: the next instalment came on 12 November 1659.
3 He quickly drew on this £25 for living expenses, as entries below show.
4 Luke 18:7–8 (KJV): 'And shall not God avenge his own elect, which cry day and night unto him, though he bear long with them? I tell you that he will avenge them speedily. Nevertheless when the Son of man cometh, shall he find faith on the earth?'
5 Tavistock PR, burials: 26 September 1659, 'Edward Hunt'.

[fo. 35r]

Inp[rimis] given to Church & poore man	00-00-09
for hat, bands & money to Tom Larkham	00-08-0[8]
August 19th Market day laid out	00-19-03
& in fish & Mutton formerly	00-01-06
& a quart of clarett wine on my birth day	00-00-08
for 2oz of Tabacco paid	00-00-03
for making a settle of *old* timber boards which I had except some	
little boards & 2 small peices of timber which John Sheare put to	00-07-00
paid for butter potted to Miria[m] Brownscombe	00-10-00
for T.Ls diet at Plimoth to T Nichols[1]	00-05-04
August 22nd for catching a Want ^to a poore man^[2]	00-00-08
August 24th delivered to my daughter miller	00-10-00
August 26th market day laid out in all	00-16-09
August 27th for making a dublet for my *selfe*	00-02-06
paid for malt brewed this August	00-05-00
~~August~~ Sept. 2 dressing on hat & hatband	00-00-10
that day market day & after for provision	00-10-11
for a New butter pott	00-00-10
for the boyes New coates making	00-01-09
for a seame of wood Sept. 5th	00-01-00
Sept. 9 Market day, about houskeeping	00-16-08
Sept. 11 Given at the communion	00-00-06
12th to Roger Row for a daies worke	00-01-02
The same 12th day Brewed Malt	00-05-00
paid Dan. Sowton for making clothes for T.M.[3]	00-04-06
Sept 16 market day & the weeke following	00-16-00
Lent also or given to my Daughter Miller	00-02-00
paid for making Joan Millers Wascot	00-01-03
for cloth & trimmings to Son Condy	00-08-00
for trimmings for T Millers cloathes	00-05-04
for 38 pound of butter of M. Charles at 5d	00-15-10
for a quart of Baral Claret[4] to Spencer	00-01-00
for provision Sept 23 Market day &c	00-14-00
paid for baking ended Sept. 29	00+01-06
my wife quarter out of Kirton Rents	00+10-00
my servants wages Due Sept. 29th	00+10-00

---

[1]   'T.L.': his grandson Tom Larkham.
[2]   Larkham paid 8d to a poor man who caught a 'want' – a mole (*OED*).
[3]   His grandson Thomas Miller.
[4]   Claret from a barrel.

my stipend due from the Earle of Bedford
09+15-00
41-16-04

I had of my money in son Condies hand at one time 10s viz Sept. 23.
& Sept. 29. I had 30s so there is yet £22 this 29ᵗʰ of September
Sept. 30 Received of son Condy for improvement of £100 which
he had of mine¹
01-10-00

October 9ᵗʰ Mr John Tikle brother by the Mother to Watts the Grand Rebell had leave to preach in Tavistocke Pulpit & partly upon his principles partly upon prejudice & partly upon his brothers interest did not preach Candidly the syncere sound word, he flew out into some gnashing expressions &c²

Lord before thy mercifull Majestie I spread it Remember thy greate name & thy poore trampled Church.

October. 11ᵗʰ I had 40s of Son Condy. Rest in his hand £20.

[fo. 35v]

[R]eceived & due on the other side this quarter
£43-06s-04d
Laid out this quarter on the other side
£15-14s-10d

October 13 of Mr Eveleigh in leiu³ of an acre of Wood
04-00-00

Watts and his Confederates have sett up a lecture in opposition to me & the Church (as I conceive) and in prosecution of this proud Rebellion, in the Hall of Mrs Glanviles house on Thursdayes; it ˆwasˆ begun October. 20 by Mr Gove, & the weeke following Seconded by Mr Polewheele. So let it prosper as it is of God, & may be for the Salvation of poore Soules.⁴

This weeke viz Munday October 24 I paid John Ford the last fifty pounds which I owed him & made over with my Son Condy about that money of Mine he had in his hand, & Received £20 of him so that now he oweth me only eighty pounds, it was £100

---

¹ A recurrent item: quarterly interest on a long-term loan.
² John Tickel (*CR*), a minister from Exeter, born and bred in Tavistock, step-brother to Larkham's fierce critic, 'Judas' Nicholas Watts.
³ 'Lieu'.
⁴ This Thursday rival to Larkham's Wednesday parish lecture is discussed in the Introduction. Andrew Gove of Peter Tavy and Digory Polewhele of Whitchurch were neighbour ministers, and members of the Devon Association (which Larkham stayed out of).

| To the Earle of Bedford due halfe yeares rent for the ground as Minister & a yeares rent for fords land | 00+07-04 |
| | 11- 03- *9* |

Sept. 29 a faire day Bestowed in gifts upon my relations	00-11-08
Sept 30 Market day Bestowed about the house	00-10-05
Octob. 2 at a Church meetinge I gave	00-00-06
October. 3 Brewing day ^a bushell & a pecke^	00-06-03
The same day paid Jo: Gay for dressing a Riding coate	00-01-00
for silke 6d & makinge up the coate againe. 2-6	00-03-00
Octob. 4 for six moneths assessment	00-02-06
Octob. 7. cloth for a coate for my selfe & silke & for making paid Dan. Sowton & Buttons	01-00-00
It was this day market day & the weeke &c	00-15-05
October 9th at the breaking of bread	00-00-06
October 14th Market day delivered to my maide	00-19-[*10*]
In all Hitherto £15-14s-10d[1]	04-11-[*01*]

[fo. 35v]

	£ s d
Given to Lansi bringing Money from Mr Eveleigh	00-00-04
October 21st Market day and some daies following	00-13-09
October 27th brewing day Malt	00-07-06
October 28th Market day	00-13-03
paid to John Ford £20 was remaining of John Pointers money in Son Condies hand £10 I had in house & £20 I had besids of Son Condy	50-00-00
Novemb: 4th Market day	00-12-*00*[2]
for making a dublett	00-02-06
for halfe a pound of Tabacco	00-01-00
To my Daughter Condies keeper I gave[3]	00-01-00
November 6th at a Communion	00-01-00
for triminge for the old dublet & a brasse button paid S Condy	00-01-06
November. 11th Market day	00-06-00
In all spent this quarter	52-19-10
£18-14s-8. & £50 paid Fords this last paim[*ent*]	

---

[1] With the £11-03s-9d already noted above.
[2] For the next few lines, the figures at the edge are obscured by the binding.
[3] Tavistock PR, births: 2 November 1659, Daniel, son of Mr Daniel Condy. Jane Condy's 'keeper': the midwife or attendant. Over the coming months Larkham gave small tokens to 'my daughter Condies nurse', 'Nurse Kelland' (fo. 36r), probably a wet-nurse.

I owe to Bevile Wivell for Malt at 3 severall times 18s-9d which is reckoned in the account of Sept. 12. October. 3rd & October 27th but is yet in my Purse because I purpose to allow it in Rent next December 25th

I have not in house (this 11th of November which is the last market day of this first quarter of the 58th yeare of mine age) ˆnow endedˆ on[e] penny, but have owed me for rents, & which I lent out of my Purse. £12-04s-08d

November 12th received out of the sheafe of Lamerton for the ˆ2ˆ
    last quarters of 1658   22-07-06

Mr Pointer Denied to pay 32s-6d because he saith	Received in all since
he laid out so much in money taxes & for the	August 18th last past with
poore charged upon mine augmentation	what is owed 69-11-10

The same time I paid my Son Condy that £20 I borrowed of him so now he hath £100 as before of mine in his hand

Novemb. 15th 1649 which is now Ten yeares since I received a greate mercy at Plimouth, of fredom from that Regiment to which I belonged upon differences about their irreligious carriage &c.[1]

Novemb. 25th I brought my poore daughter Patience & 3 children of her's Thomas
    Jane & Anne aboard the vessell bound for Ireland, O my God & my fathers
    God blesse them all, whom (probably) I shall see no more.
I delivered her in money this weeke at severall times £19 & laid out at ˆ& aboutˆ
    Plimouth £1-14-10d so about £30 more (which I hope God will make me
    able to give her) maketh her full portion of £300 and about ˆ(17) orˆ (£18) *or*
    another £19 over ˆIˆ allowed also willingly besids some *kind* of diett for her
    and her chilldren. ˆWithˆ feather pillowes & bookes which I gave unto her.
At the Funerall of Mary Dier[2]   00-10-00
From Old Redstons sonne[3]   00-11-00
I am indebted this 8th day of December
    to Jo. Sheere £5
    to William Web for wood candles & horse hire £1-6s-11d[4]
                                 In all [£6-6s-11d]

---

[1]   This entry is across both columns. In the thicket of charge and counter-charge, Larkham's opponents alleged he had been ejected as chaplain of Sir Hardress Waller's foot regiment as an 'enemy to this Common-wealth, for endeavouring to stir up the souldiers to mutinies and divisions'. Larkham insisted he left over personal differences with particular officers. *Naboth*, pp. 6, 12; *Tavistock Naboth*, pp. 21–2, *Judas*, pp. 8–9. *Tavistock Naboth* named the officers as 'Major Clerk' (Colonel John Clerke, who paid Larkham arrears of pay in 1652, fo. 9r), Captain Northcot, Lieutenant Smith and Quarter Master Lane.
[2]   Tavistock PR, burials: 23 November 1659, Mary Dier, wife of William.
[3]   Tavistock PR, burials: 5 December 1659, Nicholas Redstone.
[4]   At the foot of the folio he noted debts to Condy and another, but crossed these through once repaid.

Novemb. 14th 1659

It is now 17 yeares since I left my famely in New England & came with my Eldest Son towards England. O the mercies I have received! O the afflictions I have undergone! O the providences God hath vouchsafed!

Thus farre the Lord hath holpen me & mine,
Lord cause thy face on the Remnant to shine.

Novemb. 17 beginneth the 2 quarter of the 58th yeare of Mine age

given at a Collection at the Commemoration of Q. E comming to the crowne[1]	00-00-06
For victualls spent & used this day	00-01-07
Novemb. 18 Market day & the weeke following	00-12-10
about tilling of Beanes November 21 &c besids what I made of the pear tree 4s 6d	00-04-02
for 3 seames of Hard wood bought of J doidge	00-04-06
Brewed November 24th one bushell & a pecke	00-06-03
Friday November 25th Market day	00-07-10
about cleaving wood & mending the parlour	00-01-00
Novemb. 25th at Plimouth I gave the Barber	00-00-06

---

[1] The accession of Elizabeth I, 17 November 1558.

[fo. 36r]

	£ s d
Due now December 25th Erle[1] Bedford	09+15-00
from Bevile Wivell for rent	01+18-09
My Rents of fords land are	01-02-06
My Rents & annuity at Kirton (besids such as pay yeerely at Sept. 29th) are	1-08-00

Much is due in arreares yet unpaid

of Son Condy for imployment of Money	1+10-00
Due to me from the Deacons for chamber	0+10-00

I have Borrowed £10 of Mr Hudson by the hands of Bevile Wivill to
   be paid when I have my stipend which is due for the quarter past
I had £6 of Capt Larke upon account of the improvement of £100
   when he tooke Pixon,[2] & promised me of it £7 per annum &c

Jan 6th of J. E. a member of *us*[3]	00-10-00

This day I had a letter from my daughter Miller after 6 weekes absence, I hoped before I had opened it that she had bene safe in Ireland but perceived she is at St Ives distressed[.] I sent Mr David Condy the Mondy following Lord preserve & direct him in his journey &c[.][4] O that we might see the good of this providence, & what the Lord our father intendeth by it, Amen

Jan 18 I delivered mine acquittance to Bevile Wivell for 9-15s-00d & desired him to deliver 5s in money for the satisfaction of the £10 he borrowed of him for me[5]

---

1   'Erle' is from an earlier entry by George Lane which Larkham incorporated to stand for 'Earl'.
2   Today, Pixon Lane runs close to the centre of Tavistock on the opposite bank of the Tavy.
3   This is the only time he used this phrase, presumably for a member of the gathered church. The final
    word is hard to decipher because Larkham has written over a 'C' from George Lane.
4   Patience Miller had left Tavistock on 25 November 1659 to return to Ireland (fo. 35v).
5   This refers to £10 Larkham borrowed via Wivell from Mr Hudson ('him'), mentioned a few lines
    earlier.

To little Torr & W. Dier about Ja:[mes] Cottonlieu[1]	00-01-10
At Plimouth to my Daughter Miller in all	20-14-10
December 2nd market day laid out	00-10-11
for a letter from my son George & sending one backe	00-00-07
Decemb: 4th Communion day I gave	00-00-06
that which I owe William Webb uppon account	01-06-11
Item December 9th Market day & the weeke following	00-08-08
Dec: 16th Beef for store & for victualls &c	01-06-11
Dec. 22 brewed one bushell	00-05-*00*
Dec 23 market day laid out	00-10-*00*

[fo. 36r]

Laid out Hitherto as in the other Columne	27-07-[??][2]
Dec. 23rd for 2 seames of wood at 13d a seame	00-02-*02*
I gave to a seaman & another	00-00-0[?]
paid for servants wages	10+0-[00]
I paid my wives rents out of Kirton	00-10-00
Dec. 26 bought cloth to make shirts & stockens to send to France of	
Son Condy[3]	00+08-00
for baking last quarter ended now	00+01-06

---

1   Cottonlieu came from France to Tavistock in 8 October 1659, and left in January 1660/1. This overlapped with the time Larkham's grandson Thomas Larkham spent in France but it is not clear how these arrangements came about. On the last leaf of the manuscript (the penultimate page of entries) Larkham listed expenses for clothing and schooling Cottonlieu:

1659
October 8th Saturday
James Cottonlieu my French boy came to my house

Laid out for bringinge his Chest	00- 00-10
for horsehire to Plimouth	00- 01-00
for paper and a Primer	00+00-10
paid Austin Bond for schoolinge	00+02- 6
paid for Buttons & mending dublett	00- 00-06
March 10th he borrowed of me	00- 00-06
Item for paper at 2 several times	00+00-10
Item for schooling the second quarter	00+02-06
Item mending shoes Aprill the 5th	00- 01-00
for a Dozen & halfe of Buttons set on	00- 00-03
for schooling untill June 24th	0+ 2-00
for a quire of Paper	0+ 0- 4
July 5th Mending his shoes	0- 1- 0
August 23rd for fine white paper	0+ 0- 4
for a suite of Apparell to wit doublet breeches long coate & all things necessary	2- 8- 3
for makinge the said clothes to D.S.	00- 06-06
for schooling at Micha[e]l[mas] paid	00- 02-06
Octob. 8. for Buttons silke & work	00- 02-09
November 22 in fine Paper	00- 00-03

2   The corner is torn.
3   For Thomas Larkham, who went to France in August 1659.

O. My father	This was not done	Ordered that Mr Cosen David pay	04-00-00
Remember the		her more	
Widdow & 4	my daughter was	so remaines of her full portion only	{00-05-08
orphans for	gone from St Ives	twenty pounds which I hope God	{the journey
thy goodnes &	the day before my	will enable me to pay and blesse to	{to St Ives
Covenants sake	Cosen David came	that poore afflicted soule & sanctifie	{& letters &c[1]
in X Jesus	there	to her all her crosses & afflictions	

therefore these 2 lines }   remaines therefore in all £24
are added   }   of my daughter Millers portion

Jan 21 Alice Lambshead was buried[2]	00-10-00
Jan 24 Mr Kitto's son was buried[3]	00-10-00
Feb 8th at Stephen Cole's childs buriall[4]	00-10-00
Feb 9th at Buriall of a son of Wid Pike[5]	00-06-00

Hactenus this quarter   19-11-03

Feb. 11th I Reckoned with my son Condy and found that I owed him upon
account £17-15s-2d so I had 4s-10d which made up £18 & he promised
to pay 40s more & I p[ro]m[ise]d him to sett downe upon the bill of
£100 which he oweth me that I had received Twenty pounds, so he
oweth me only £80.

[1] These entries are in four columns across the page.
[2] Tavistock PR, burials: 23 January 1659/60, 'Alce Lamsheade'.
[3] Tavistock PR, burials: 24 January 1659/60, 'Thomas Kittow'.
[4] Tavistock PR, burials: 8 February 1659/60, 'Roger Colle', son of Stephen.
[5] Tavistock PR, burials: 10 February 1659/60, 'a son of Ann Pike, widow'.

Dec. 28. A day of humiliation for parish and Church both I gave in Publique	00-00-06
I laid out about Jo Brownsdons living £50 I had of C[apt]. Larke £10 of Son Condy as is in the lower end of the other Colume besids £6 of C[apt]. Larke as formerly is written	60-00-00
December. 30 Market day	00-08-09
Delivered to James to carry to A. Bond for schooling	00-02-06
Jan 1. Given at the Communion	00-00-06
Jan 2: 3 pound of Sope & threed 1d	00-01-00
for making Bonds & hand kierchefes & cloth for them, to be sent to France[4]	00-01-10
To a poore woman	00-00-01
for a seame of Turffes Jan. 3.	00-00-09
Jan 6 Market day & the weeke following	00-11-0*0*
paid for fraight of Herrings brought laste yeare	00-04-00
paid debts owed by my daughter Miller to severall persons in all which with what was laid out at Plimouth maketh £26-3s-9d	05-08-11

Jan 13th Market day	00-10-0
Jan 16th given to Nurse Kelland[5]	00-01-0
Jan 20 Markett day & the weeke follow[in]g	00-06-11
for stockens &c to send to France &c	00-05-10
for *Kelland*	*00*-00-06
laid out about a suite for T. Condy[6]	00-12-07
for making it 2s given T Condy 2d	00-02-02
for 8 yards of dowlas[7] for 2 shirts for my selfe of three quarter & halfe cloth	00-08-08
Jan 27 ¼ of [*illegible*] & other things	01-09-00
paid W. Gee for pockets demanded for the boyes	00-00-08
& which John Sheere laid out for T.L.[8] schooling, to Torr T Millers allowed in Son Condies notes	05-00
Item to W. Webb for 17 dozen fagots, 5 seames hard wood the fagott 6d doz in the wood the other brought home	0-16-00

4 For his grandson Thomas Larkham.
5 A nurse (wet-nurse) is mentioned often in the next few months.
6 His grandson Thomas Condy, born 8 July 1655.
7 A coarse linen cloth.
8 A payment in retrospect, as his grandson Thomas Larkham was now in France.

[fo. 36v]

	£ s d
I owe unto William Webb in all	+2+ 2+10
unto Elizabeth Toller Widdow	+0+17-00
Unto my Wife which I borrowed of her	1+10-00
Unto John Sheere Deacon	5- 00-00
	9- 09-10

& my son owes me 40s besids the £80 he hath of mine

This account I tooke Feb 11th 1659[1] when I made up my accounts for
     this second quarter of the 58th yeare of my age in which I received
     by addition £19-11-3 and disbursed 101-14-0*8*

Heere followeth for the third quarter of the 58th yeare of mine age[2]

Received of My Daughter 18d and 12d upon occasions out of that 40s
     which is in her hand
ˆFeb 13[th]ˆ my maide had 3 pound of Sope paid for of my Daughter
     Condy price 11d, I thinke.
Feb. 24 Richorwd[3] Had in Money 00-10s with which she bought
     provision for the house that day

March 3[rd] Received of Mr Pointer in p[aymen]t of the augment: for
1659[4]   15-00-00

Received March 3[rd] acounting with my Son Condy the rest of the 40s
so we ˆareˆ even & he oweth me only £80 having allowed in debts &c
£20 at severall times of the summe of £100 which I lent him

Feb. 21[st] Moonke Entred the parliament with the Secluded Members &c a strange
turne followeth thereupon, bon fires & ringing all day the Munday following Feb.
27th at Tavistocke, Speckman Mrs Glanvile's man the setter foorth of the worke,
greate joy amonge all the Rascall crue in the Towne Many drunke, threatnge

---

[1]   11 February 1659/60. Larkham's 'second quarter' ended 17 February, since he reckoned the year from
       18 August, his birthday.
[2]   Unusually, this heading is in the right column, where Larkham wanted to fill up a space. He drew a
       line across the whole folio to mark the division between quarters and put this heading above the line.
[3]   The Larkhams' new maid, after the departure of the long-serving Dinah Woodman, was 'Richorwd'
       Allen.
[4]   The Lamerton augmentation: see Introduction.

The 2 last markets of this quarter spent   00-14-0[?][1]
At a Communion on Feb 5th I gave   00-00-0[6]

Expenses this quarter past 101-*19-08*[2]

whereof [*illegible*] were in extraordinaries

[fo. 36v]

I have laid out this quarter more then I have received by addition the summe of 82-03-05d by reason of £60 about John Brownsdons living & £26 paid & to be paid & delivered to ˆ&ˆ about my daughter miller. Lord blesse her.

Inp[rimis] for 35 pounds of Bacon of B Wivile	00-16-00
for 2 paire of shoes for T Larkham	00-04-04
A paire of shoes for my selfe	00-03-06
Given to a Collection Feb 12th	00-00-06
Given to my Daughters Nurse visiting &c	00-06
for Malt Brewed February 13th last	00-05-00
Paid Pitts about Heliars[3] worke and materialls used about it	00-06-05
paid for Buttons & mending James[4] doublett	00-00-06
Laid out Feb 17th market day & that weeke paid	00-07-04
Feb. 24 laid out in the Markett	00-10-05
for 5 yards ½ cloth for a cloake for my selfe	01-13-00
March 2nd laid out in the Market ˆ& Tabaccoˆ	00-05-00
& for dyinge stockens for my selfe	00-00-06
for making cloake & silke & canvas	00-02-10
March 4th Given at the Communion	00-00-06
10th lent to James my french boy[5]	00-00-06
yesterday & this week in houskeeping	00-14-04
for 3 moneths taxe paid March 12th	00-02-00

---

[1] The edge of the folio is worn.
[2] The total can be inferred from summary of expenses on fo. 36v.
[3] 'Hellier': a slater or tiler (*OED*).
[4] James Cottonlieu.
[5] James Cottonlieu.

to burne houses. The Constable of the C my S.C.[1] abused by the rude ones,
Speckman encourageth them Polewheele Watts & that crue call it the blessed of
newes that ever came to Tavistocke.
O Horrible Blasphemy against the Gospel!

Now all is sure, for so men thinke and say,
The Cause of God & X & Saints is Low,
Arise O God heare thou thy folke that pray,
At thy presence let the mountaines downe flow.

And now this following yeare what wait I for?
Saints stand amaz'd, knocking at th' doore of hope:
They will in ashes now themselves abhorre,
Till God againe to them the doore set ope.

Let God once more (I beg) i'th mount be seene,[2]
And Lord bring downe the vulgar & prophane rout.
It shall be so, if sin do'nt intervene.
O Holy God of saints now turne about.

What tho the cause of God seeme lost? Yet sure,
Tis written that mount Sion shall endure.[3]

[fo. 37r]

March 19th Munday I had other letters from my poore Daughter Miller, bearing date
Feb. 23. & from Tom Miller (poore boy) Lord blesse him and his sisters. O love
my daughter & hers &c

Though farre from me my God they be remooved.
yet neere to thy goodnes Lord lett them be,
to lay them at thy doore it me behoov'd,
for I can't care for them Lord, thou doest see.
This widdow & her four helplesse ones,
save soules, feede bodies wrap their skin & bones.

1660 March 25th being the Lords day

The Lord's day doth, sixtieth yeare begin,
O come Lord Jesus bring foorth thy great things.
And of thy people all forgive the sinne,

---

1   'The Constable of the Court, my Son Condy'. Daniel Condy had also served as 'keep:[er] of the
     house of Correccon': Devon Record Office, Exeter, QS/1/9, Quarter Sessions Order Book, 1652–61,
     13 January 1656/7.
2   An allusion to God's appearance to Moses on Mount Sinai, Exodus 24:15–18.
3   Hebrews 12: 22–9.

Brewing day the same March 12th   00-05-00
March 16th Market day laid out   <u>00-10-10</u>

                                      Hactenus   <u>06-09-00</u>

Yesterday March 15th I had a letter from my Daughter Patience dated Feb 6th
At last through many crosse providences she with her children came safe to
Waterford in Ireland, Thanks to my God in X.[1]

This day greate feare about Jane the Daughter of my Daughter Condy neere unto
death[.][2] God was sought unto earnestly at a meeting of some brethren, to give
life to the child as a pledge & token of the resurrection of this (seemingly) dead
(or at le[a]st) dying Cause.[3]
                    March 18[th] some hope of the childs recovery

Weake flesh almost to dust was brought,
God was in prayer for her sought.
Our eyes and eares have seene & heard strange things
O when shall joyfull tidings come on wings?
Thanks to my God for some hope of the child,
Helpe thy poore ones, by worldly wise beguil'd.

[fo. 37r]

March 22   £   s   d
paid for 3 paires of shoes for children   00-06-[??][4]
paid in exchange of Pans for a kettle   00-06-[??]
paid for a cover & locke to a coffer   00-03-[??]
a journey to Plimouth & barber   00-04-[??]
March 25 Market day   00-07-[??]
for 3 pound of Sope & 6 pound of Candles   00-03-0[?]
for Tabacco & paper for James   02-09
for James schooling March 26[th]   00-02-00
paid my servant her wages   00-10-00
March 30 Market day   00-10-00
for letters from & to my Son George   00-00-10
paid the Baker this quarter   00-01-0[?]
Aprill fi[r]st to the Communion   00-00-0[?]
To my Wife out of Kirton rents   00-10-[00]
Halfe yeares rent of Earle of Bedford   00-06-0[?]

1   'X': Christ.
2   At Jane's birth, 13 February 1657/8, Larkham recorded that she was 'a sore bruised child which came
    in an unusual manner in to the world' (fo. 28r).
3   Larkham hoped her recovery would be a sign that the 'dying Cause' of the godly would revive.
4   The edge of the folio has worn away. Many of the figures on the right are missing or unclear.

That C[hrist] is Comming now flieth on wings.[1]
Let's by beleeving set to trueth a seale,
Then shall we have at last man'y a good meale.[2]

Received of Bevile Wivile for rent   01-18-09

March 25th I had a letter from my sonne George and newes of his wives save
deliverance &c

Downe then thou evill heart of unbeleife
Thy Lord & Christ is comming as a theife.[3]
Till all his friends ar[e] up & foes throwne downe,
I shall not lay aside my mourning Gowne.[4]

My Kirton Rents & annuity are   01- 08-00
my quarterly rents at Tavistocke   01- 02-06
my stipend due March 25th last past   09+15-00
of my Son Condy I had Aprill the 7th   01+04-00
                                                                 15- 8-03

Though that Francis Glanvill be dead & Gone,
Yet of vipers ther's a gen'ration.
One Ellis Crimes keepes on enormities;
& hath promoted late, slanders and lies.[5]
My God thou see'st how that my name is torne,
and state threatened; leave not my soule forlorne.
Poore Veale & Hore and Watts and Pennington
Polewhele & Gove & blind Em[m]anuell,
In all which hearts hardnes is come upon,
Rescue these poore on'es Lord from death & Hell.
Set on (o Lord) on all believer's board,
The prophesies of th' everlasting word.

Aprill 14th Marg: Dodridge Buried[6]   00-06-00

All's turned to love Crimes Row & both the Preists
seeme very joyfull all except Rude Hore,

---

[1] David sang that the Almighty, his deliverer, was 'seen upon the wings of the wind' (2 Samuel 22:11).
[2] The last line seems to have been written later and is rather a strained conclusion.
[3] A common image: 1 Thessalonians 5:2; 2 Peter 3:10; Revelation 3:3.
[4] His hope that God would triumph is tinged with the language of Psalm 30:11 (KJV), 'Thou hast
     turned for me my mourning into dancing: thou hast put off my sackcloth.'
[5] In April 1660, the burgesses of Tavistock returned 'Ellis Crymes' as one of the town's MPs for the
     Convention Parliament, although he was set aside because of a double return from the borough.
     Journal of the House of Commons: volume 8: 1660–1667 (1802), pp. 3–4: www.britishhistory.ac.uk/
     report.aspx?compid=26176 (accessed 7 March 2011).
[6] Tavistock PR, burials: 14 April 1660, 'Margaret Dotheridge'.

Aprill 2nd: 5 seames of Hard wood	00-07-0[?]
for mending James his shoes	00-01-0[?]
for the market first in Aprill	00-08-0[?]
April 6th a day of Pub:[lic] humiliation	00-00-06
Given to Walter Jay of N. England taken by the Ostenders (besids	
5ˆsˆ of the Deacon and a paire of breeches)	00-01-0[?]
Aprill 10th about my Garden in all	
the Dung was made in my stable & court	00-04-00
for Furses[1] to brew & malt	00-05-08
Aprill 13th Market day laid out	00-11-07
To 3 distressed men taken by Ostenders	00-00-09
To my Daughter Condy her Nurs. April 16th	00-01-00
Aprill 20th market ˆ6s-9dˆ & 2 seames of fagots	00-08-0[?]
Aprill 27 Market day & the weeke follow:	00-10-0[?]
Aprill 28 for 3 moneths taxe	00-02-0[?]
for fitting up a paire of Breeches paid	00-01-0[?]
for pocketts silke and buttons	00-00-0[?]
May the 4th Market day & the weeke following	00-11-1*1*
for 2 seames of Turffes May the 7th	00-01-0*0*
for building a wall between David Serjeants backside besides what	
he paid	00-09-*09*
for makinge wascott & coate for my wife	00-02-*06*
May the 6th Communion day given	00-00-*06*
May the 9th for an ordinary at lecture	00-00-*10*
May the 11th Market day	00-12-*07*
May 13th at a Collection given	00-00-*06*
	08-16-0*6*[2]
Spent as on the other side	06-09-*00*
in all this quarter spent ended May 17th	15-05-06

For sin th' avenger posteth after me,
But to the refuge citty lo I flee.[3]
Great Conquerer which had kil'd death i'th duell
Remember now ˆthineˆ owne deare ones thy jewell.

ˆMay the 16thˆ At a funerall of Luggers daughter in law[4]	00-10-0[*0*]

Received this quarter past by addition	31-04-[??]
Spent & laid out – £15-5s-6d	

---

1   'Furses': gorse flowers, used in Larkham's time (and nowadays) to make beer and wine.
2   Corrected from 7d, or the other way round.
3   Larkham alluded to Israel's 'cities of refuge' (Numbers 35:25–7), but interpreted the image typologically to refer to Christ, the 'Great Conqueror'.
4   The surname 'Luggar' appears in the parish register, but nothing corresponds to Larkham's entry here.

Lord keepe me close ˆ(I pray)ˆ to thy Beliefs
that gleamy daies may n't shutt X out of doore[1]

for Aprill 17ᵗʰ at the meeting of Justices to examine
complaints all is husht & the lecture on Wedn[e]sdaies
as formerly & I desired to admitt others to preach
which I have many yeeres offered & desired:

                                  Deus nobis hactenus hæc otia fecit[2]

[fo. 37v]

[1]660 May the eighteenth the 4ᵗʰ quarter of the 58ᵗʰ yeere of mine age

[M]ay the 18ᵗʰ day before I was out of my bed [a] letter was brought from my
daughter Miller dated this day 6 weekes viz Aprill the sixth

[L]ord my God I give thee thanks & beseech [t]hy fatherhood in Christ to blesse
guide preserve and provide for her & hers, all which are thine, and Mine also o
my God.

Rescue thine (O My God) out of their hands whose mouth talketh of vanity &
their right hand is a right hand of falsehood. Helpe Lord, Xᵗᵉ veni.[3]

June the 8ᵗʰ I sent to Mrs Martin five pounds to be in p[aymen]t of what my
daughter Miller borrowed of her husband Humphrey Martin Gent now in Ireland
if he shall so order it &c

whereas I borrowed of the Deacons £5 I have June 11ᵗʰ 1660 delivered £5 to John
Trowt to be sent to Petronel Chubb as from the Church for some time [s]he also
oweth unto me besids £1-10s. her house reedeemed from Cragg was assigned to
John Brownsdon & Son Condy & the lease as yet is in my hand.

	£	s	d
Received of son Condy due June 24ᵗʰ for he knoweth what	01	+04	0
[D]ue for my stipend	09	+15	6
[F]rom Bevile Wivell	01	+18	9
Rents at Tavistocke	01	-02	6
Rents & annuity at Kirton	01	-08	0

---

[1]   'X': Christ. 'Gleamy': 'marked by intermittent sunshine' (*OED*).
[2]   'Thus far God has made this tranquility for us.'
[3]   'Christe veni': come Christ.

[fo. 37v]

	£ s d
May the 18th market day	00-13-06
May 20th & 21 given to poore men	00-00-09
for 2 daies for Roger Row about my Garden	00-02-04
May 25th the second market day of this quarter	00-10-08
May 26 given to Daughter Condis Nurse	00-01-00
June 1 Market day laid out	00-09-04
Owed for Malt brewed May 24	00-05-00
June the 8th Market day	00-14-08
and the weeke followinge & one ordinary[1]	00-01-00
at a Collection June 10th I gave	00-00-04
June 15th market day laid out	00-12-04
for wine & Biskets on young Mr *Shrott*	00-01-01
for Malt June 16th brewed	00-05-00
June 22nd delivered to my maide to deliver to Son Condy to allow	
Bole for his horse	00-01-06
the same day market day & 8d yesterday for a legg of Mutton	00-07-08
The same day I cast up account what I owed upon son Condies	
booke & found it to be 32s-8½d whereupon deducting 24s which	
is due to me June 24th I ow unto him upon account just 8s-8½d	
Hactenus	04-06-03
The summe to be put among expenses expended in this part of the	
quarter past	01-12-08½
Paid Rich: Peeke for wood By my wife which I allowed to my wife	
June 22nd & paid it to her the same day	00-15-00
Paid Daughter Condy which she had paid A Gibb for making a coate	
for Daughter Miller	00-00-08
Paid Richord my servant her wages	00-10-00
To Nath Knight helping about wood	00-00-06

[1] Around this time, Larkham started to use the term 'ordinary' and often noted 1s spent on or at an 'ordinary' in the following months, always (when a date is given) on a Wednesday, lecture day. The shilling was probably his contribution to a collection taken at the lecture, or – less likely, but another meaning of 'ordinary' – payment for a simple meal at a tavern (*OED* 'ordinary', *n* III.11, 12).

Now Railing rude & unbredd Torr,[1]
is made a rod, though he be base.
Let none the stinking'st knave abhorr,
when God imployes him to disgrace.
Thy cause & me o Lord recover,
In dismall times let faith help over.
Let Shime'is tongue do me no harme[2]
to save me Lord stretch out thine arme.

Newes of A New attempt to remoove me out of Tavistocke July 20th
Only God guide me & deliver me.

Received this yeere the 58th of mine age.

1 quarter	69-13-10
2 quarter	19-11-03
3 quarter	31-04-03
Last quarter	15-08-03
	125-17-07 Hactenus

[fo. 38r]

July 20th I lent my sonne Condy in the morning £10 & also to his wife
   40s & £8 the Munday before in all £20 which he oweth me besid the
   £80 upon a Bill Also I paid 17s-4d to his wife which was owed upon
   my booke & made even for all untill the 20th day of July 1660.
July the 24th I gave to C[olonel]. Bennet and C[aptain]. Larke each my
   booke of the Attributes.[3]

The Orphan which was sent to france,
      lies much upon my heart.
The widdow & 4 fatherlesse
      oft make my soule to smart.[4]
My father, send some good newes,
      About these poore creatures
Thou art A tender-hearted God,
      The Scriptures this assures.

---

[1] Larkham gave 'Mr Torr', a schoolmaster, a copy of his *Attributes*, and he was one of various people
    paid to educate Tom Larkham (fos. 33v, 36v). No details of Torr's part in the campaign to oust
    Larkham survive, but it seems he was another friend turned enemy.
[2] Shime-i, who cursed King David: 2 Samuel 16:5–14.
[3] Larkham's *Attributes of God* (1656). After Larkham resigned in 1660, 'Colonel Bennet' sent a bushel
    of wheat and is probably the 'Mr Robert Bennet' who 'Came of purpose to visit me & Comfort me'
    (fo. 38v). Larke had taken a lease from Larkham at Pixon (fo. 36r).
[4] His orphaned grandson Thomas Larkham, in France; his widowed daughter Patience Miller and her
    children Thomas, Mary, Jane and Anne.

Item paid Richard Peeke for wood	00-18-06
To Roger Row about a Gutter	00-00-06
June 28th given Collection for the poore	00-00-04
June 29th Market day	00-12-06
July the first Communion day	00-00-06
paid for baking last quarter	00-01-06
To A Bond for James schooling	0-01-06
July 4th An ordinary at lecture	0-01- 0
July 5th mending James shoes	0-01- 0
July the 6th Market day &c	0-08- 0
July 9th Daughter Condies Nurse I gave	0-00- 6
an ordinary on lecture day paid	0-01- 0
for casement & mending glasse	00-04- 0
July 12th about sowing Turnip seede	00-00-10
July 13th 20th laid out Market daies	01-04-10
July 19th paid for 3 moneths Rate	00-02-00
July 20th about letters From & to my child[r]en	0-01-00
for shoes for my Daughter Patience in Ireland	
besids what I had prepared before	<u>00-06-08</u>
	11-11-03½[1]

[fo. 38r]

July 20th to poore frenchmen	00-00-[??]
Given Clogg for carryage to Bediford[2]	01-0[?- ??]
Sent by him July the 23 to Beddiford to be sent to my daughter Miller	
besids bookes & shoes in Money for tokens whereof 2s & 6d was	
of my wifes money	01-00-[??]
July 25th one lecture ordinary	00-01-0[?]
for five quire of paper	00-01-0[?]
June 28 Paid for making a coate to D S[3]	00-02-0[?]
Sent by my maide for silke & a loope	00-01-0[?]
laid out from July 27 Market day	00-11-[??]
The first August 4 seames of Tu[r]ffes	00-02-[??]
August the first given to my wife Kirton rent for the quarter due last	
Midsomer	00-10-[00]
August the 3rd Market day	00-08-[??]
Two Brewings of Malt the last whereof was July 28 brewed	00-10-0[?]
August 5th Communion day	00-00-[06]
August 6th 4 seames of Turfes	00-02-0[?]

---

[1] The corner is worn: strictly, by addition, the total is £11-11s-02d (including the interim total of £4-6s-2d above) but this is 1½d short of the total Larkham carried forward to fo. 38r. The missing 1½d may be hidden in the binding.

[2] Bideford.

[3] Daniel Sowton.

Aug. 16 I received a letter from T Larkham out of France blessed be the God of mee and mine.

Memorandum that £5 of the last £20 I lent to my Son Condy is owing to Mr Brownsdon to be paid either by him or me if he satisfie that £5 then my Son Condy oweth only £15 besides what upon a bond remaines due viz. £80.

August the 17th 1660 endeth the eight and fiftieth year of myne age. L. D.[1]

The day being Market day left not one penny in my posession			
But owing to me as followeth	£	s	d
from Mr John Pointer	35	00	00
Received in Gold rated at 23s per pound £11-10[2]			
from son Condy (besids £5 to Mr Brownsdon) to me	95+	00	00
Received £5 August 31 to the other £90 I added 10, for an anuity of £8 per ann[um] out of his Mill[s]			
from Mr Larke remaines of a bill due unto me[3]	44	10	00
from George Chester for one yeeres rent	05	03	04
from Thomas Tillam upon account for rent &c			
received Sept 5	01+	07	05
from John Martin remaines for rent due	00	10	00
from Eme doidge[4] remaines due for rent	00	10	00
Received 6s-8d Sept 21			
Arreares of Rent due at Kirton as per note	03	13	06

From Mrs Kath: Martin which I sent to her – unlesse her husband in Ireland allow it upon my daughter Millers account &c   05-00-00
it seemes this was allowed in Ireland by my daughter Miller to her husband[5]

                                                                          190-14-03

I also laid out for Petronell Chubb to preserve her house, but at last   06-10-00
had £5 of the Churches stocke, something is due for the Chamber   she saith
& if they give it wholy to me it will be fitt enough in case God   it is £7
make her able to pay all or any   I have
    forgotten

---

1   'L.D.': 'Laus Deo', praise to God. He entered this and the following summary across the whole page.
2   Larkham added comments to his summary, to the right: here and below these comments are indented.
3   Payment for Larke's lease at Pixon (fo. 36r). Larkham had difficulty getting money from him (fo. 41r).
4   Emma Doidge.
5   Humphrey Martin.

August 10ᵗʰ Market day & the weeke following ending 17ᵗʰ Market   00-17-[??]
An ordinary August 15ᵗʰ among the Ministers   00-01-00

& on the other side   £11-11s- 03½d   04-12-0[?]

In all laid out this quarter   16-03-05½

I have received   135-17-07   this yeare past

& have laid out   065-07-07½   besides what I have bestowed in buying lease or
                                land & laid out about my daughter Patience

Hactenus auxiliatus est Do[m]i[nus]¹

---

¹   'Thus far the Lord hath holpen.'

<u>197-04-03</u>
of this 10s
is owed for
malt to
B.[W.][1]

So the sume of My estate is   <u>196-14-03</u>
which is all in
others hands

---

[1]   Bevil Wivell.

18 August 1660 – 16 April 1661

[fo. 38v]

[A]ugust the Eighteenth 1660 beginneth the 59th yeere of mine age[1]

Christs Resting day in grave, begins this year[2]
The nine and fiftieth of my sinful life.
Let me see that grave where lay my Lord Deare
That betweene God and me ended all strife.
My sins in his grave's buried with his dolours,
O keepe me now from flyinge from my colours.[3]

      Christ's buriall was part of's humiliation,
      He seemed then a while both lost & dead
      So doth his cause now seeme' an abhomination
      Pride and prophanesse holding up their head.

Let the Lords day begin to dawne (O Christ) I pray,   sic pipiebat Larkhamus[4]
Tis night and Darke (God knoweth) O When shall I see day? Aug. 18° 1660

John Brownsdon Thomas fleshman sent each of them three seames of Turffes.
John Trowt sent three seemes of Moares[5]
Elizabeth Toller. August 28. a Roasting pigg
August 31. I received of my Son Condy in accounting for James his
    clothes and for butter paid Mary Charles, & in money in all the
    summe of £5. so he oweth me £10 & £80 he paying as he hath
    promised what is owed John Brownsdon.
~~This day I borrowed of my wife Twenty shillings~~ paid the 5th of September
[S]ept. 7 David Condies wife 2 Couple of Chickens

	£ s d
[S]ept. 10 Mary Pointer Wid[ow] buried[6]	00-12-00
[S]ept. 12th from Mrs Whiting by John Sheere	00-05-00

[S]ept. 15th I had a letter from my son George, Lord looke on him
& the day before from T. Miller. Lord blesse my children &c

---

1   The heading is across the top of the folio.
2   Saturday 18 August 1660.
3   'Dolours': griefs, sorrows. 'Colours': as in regimental colours, but here meaning betrayal of Christ.
4   'So cried Larkham.'
5   'Seem': a variant of 'seam', a horse-load. 'Moare' ('more'): in the South-West, a word for a root or
   tree stump (*OED*).
6   Tavistock PR, burials: 10 September 1660, Mary Poynter.

[fo. 38v]

The widdow & 4 fatherles,[1]
Lord take of them the charge
keepe the poore Orphan now in france[2]
from cunninge out at Large.
make them (Lord) lovers of the trueth
teach them to feare thee in their youth

Be thou a husband & father
unto them Lord I pray
provide for their soules & bodies
all needfull things each day
keepe them (o Lord) from sin & shame
Teach them (father) to love thy name

Owed formerly for Malt & paid this ¼	00-10-00
August 23rd Brewing day Malt	00-05-00
August 24th Market day & shop paid for many smale things owed to R. Hitchins	00-16-04
for 54 p[ounds] of Butter paid to Mary Charles	01-00-00
Paid for a suite & coate & making for James[3]	02-14-09
& for Trappe upon the small prophets[4]	00-12-00
August 29: At an ordinary among the Ministers	00-01-00
August 31th Market day	00-08-05
I had a letter from france by Bristoll paid post	00-00-06
To poore seamen & the Com[m][un[ion] Sept. 2	00-00-06
Sept. 4 to John Webb Barber	00-00-06
Sept. 5 an ordinary at the lecture	00-01-00
Sept. 7th Market day ending the weeke	00-10-05
Sept. 11. A pound of Tabacco	00-02-00
Sept. 14th Market day laid out	00-10-08
Sept. 15th I had home my cyder & gave the bringers	00-00-06
Sep 16th for gathering apples & sent to Nats Wife[5]	00-00-10

---

[1] His widowed daughter Patience and her four children.
[2] His grandson Thomas Larkham.
[3] Here and in the list of expenses below, 'James' is James Cottonlieu.
[4] John Trapp, *A commentary or exposition upon the XII minor prophets* (London, 1654).
[5] Nathaniel Knight, who worked in the Larkhams' garden, had married Dinah Woodman, their maid, 8 January 1656/7.

Will Webb powned & prest[1] my Apples & sent me a Caske of
    32 gallons & added 7 Gallons ½ to fill it up.
Mary Gibb a dish of butter. Mary Web a quince. & 7[2] & 7
    quinces Miria[m] Brownsdon 3 chicken[.] Eula[lia] Condy
    2 chicken. John Trowt 2 chickens
Allowed Bevile Wivell for Malt 20s which was spent this
    quarter past in money Received 18s. 9d In all   01-18-09
Sept. 29. Mary Charles a pound of butter & a partridge.
Octob. 4. W. Giles daughter buried[3]   00-08-00
Eliz. Toller October 5th. 2 pullets.
[The] wife of Richard Peeke a good cheese.
[Oct] 8. I had of Son Condy   01-04-0
[I] bought an annuity out of *his* Milles [*torn*] have quarterly 40s
    & owe him only £10[4]

[fo. 39r]

I borrowed 26s of my wife & had for bookes sold & wood &c 7s & 2d which
mak[e]th my accounts even u[ntil] the 13th day of October having also had that
halfe crowne of Son Condy which I gave Mr Leere for [*illegible*] about his Tenement & Tucking Milles which I am to pay £100 for, I thinke my Son Condy desires
the bal[*ance*][5]

I have laid out hitherto £8-7s-3d more then I have received this quarter by addition.

I have not one penny in house nor my wife of whom I borrowed 26s ut supra [*illegible*]

I have newes of a Warrant out against me to appeare next 6th day October the 19th
befor five justices empowered by an act to take *oaths* against me about my being
outed of the place of preach-[*er*]

---

1   'Powned & prest': pounded and pressed.
2   The number is repeated.
3   Tavistock PR, burials: 4 October 1660, Mary Gyles.
4   After this the last line, including the total, is illegible: the bottom edge of the page has worn away.
5   This entry runs across the whole page at the top. A 'tucking-mill' is a West of England term for a
    fulling mill ('a mill in which cloth is fulled or milled by being beaten with wooden mallets … and
    cleansed with soap or fuller's earth', *OED*). Larkham took out an annuity of £8 a year against the
    mills (fo. 39v).

about letters from & to my son George	00-00-08
Sept 23 Market day ending the weeke	00-10-09
27th Peter County had for Physicke & labour	00-15-00
28th Market day endeth the week laid out	00-11-03
paid for Baking this quarter past	00-01-06
Servants Wages paid	00-10-00
for a brewing in September	00-05-00
paid for a chaire with a Coveringe	00-12-00
paid for James schooling this quarter	00-02-06
Barber John Webb. October 3rd	00-00-06
October 5th Market day laid out	00-06-08
Octob 7th at the Communion I gave	00-00-06
8th Poll Money[1] 8s & to Sister & *servant* 1s	00-09-00
for Buttons silke for James 1s 9d Sope 11d	00-02-08
for mending James clothes to D. Sowton	00-01-08
October 12th Market day ending this weeke	00-11-08
[?] £12-15s-*09*d spent hitherto	12-15-*09*

[fo. 39r]

---

[1] 'Poll money': tax. Larkham's sister (Elizabeth or Jane) had come to Tavistock in May 1659.

Octob. 18 of Mrs Trowt for Mich:[aelmas] quarter   00-01-0

Octob. 19th I was before the Justices (5) of them about my confirmation or the contrary nothing Concluded on but my Binding over to the assizes, & to bring my Counsell next friday

The Lords day Oct. 21.
I left mine imployment of preaching in feare & upon demand of the Patron[1]

In Patience (Soule) be content, X shall raigne
His Rod & staffe shall me & mine sustaine.
Is living gone? do friends begin to hid[e]?
Do not distrust (take heed) God will provide.
No power or hate can hurt those that are his
to such as trust in God nought comes amisse.

my stumbling reason let faith help me over.
and eke[2] my doubting shaking soule recover
Sathan hath cast many a fie'ry dart.
Which but for faith would surely kill my heart
Concerning ordinances guide me now,
Lest I be found a breaker of my vow.

---

from one Rich Dunrish of Beare or buckland[3] 4 chickens by B Kinge
Novemb. 1. Received £9-1-8 of Mr Hogson & allowed 13s-4 for Rent
   by Bevill Wivill   09-15-00
I paid my wife 26s which I had borrowed & 20s-6d which I had
   borrowed of Son Condy   14-04-05
                                        by adition
                                        Hactenus

---

[1] Larkham, cited before commissioners on 19 October 1660 and bound over to appear at the Assizes, was not formally ejected but resigned as vicar of Tavistock at the insistence of the earl of Bedford. He drew a thick line beneath this entry and wrote the verses below, side by side across the folio.
[2] 'Eke': also, too, moreover (*OED*).
[3] Within ten miles of Tavistock, to the south, are Bere Alston, Bere Ferrers, Buckland Monachorum and Buckland Abbey.

A Numerous Crew come on to sweare & stare
(thronging so thicke & threefold in upon me)
That neither sober nor yet civill are,
that if faith presse not in they will undo me.
Deceitfull Jacob, also vile Vivian,
And drunken Nosworthy by church cast out[1]
With tagg and ragg of many a wicked man
intend with me to have a lusty bout.
But Lord thy holy booke rich things Containes;
Let faith compound some sov'raigne for heart-paines

O pow[e]rfull faith whose every smallest grain
sends all my guilt of sin, that long hath stood
and layes them on him that died not in vain
to drowne them in the sea of's precious blood
my foes are many feirce and desperate
like th'builders of proud Babels towres of ol[d][2]
Lord they will talke & do at th'highest rate
theyle sweare & raile & scoffe & jeere & scold
But he that taught all fingers fight can quell[3]
Even Christ that in my heart by faith doth dwell

for ¼ pound of spanish Tabacco	00-00-09
for an ordinarie on the lecture day	00-01-00
laid out Market day October the 19th	00-10-0[?]
for a letter from sonne George	00-00-0[?][4]
October 22th for a moneths taxe	00-01-0[?]
October 26th market day laid out	00-05-06
Octob. 31. An ordinary & 2d besides	00-01-02
Novemb. 1. paid a yeares rent for the ground, it was abated in my stipend[5]	00-13-04
for 2oz of Tabacco the same day	00-00-03
for 3 pound of sope paid. Son Condy Nov. 1 when I paid all that had beene borrowed upon Market daies & made even	00-00-11[6]
Laid out this week in *housekeeping* & victualls	00-02-02
Spent Hitherto November. 1 from August 18th last past the summe	14-11-07

---

[1] Larkham referred to opposition from John Jacob and Richard Vivian, former royalist soldiers, in *Naboth*, pp. 17, 19. Nosworthy may be the drunken church member identified in *Tavistock Naboth*, p. 75. All three served as churchwardens around this time: Nosworthy (1660), Vivian (1661), Jacob (1662). Devon Record Office, Exeter, 482A/PV1, Tavistock Vestry Minutes 1660–1740.
[2] The tower of Babel, Genesis 11:3–9.
[3] Psalm 144:1–2 (KJV): 'Blessed be the Lord my strength, which teacheth my hands to war, and my fingers to fight … who subdueth my people under me.'
[4] The edge is worn.
[5] This relates to the entry opposite for 1 November: Larkham received his stipend of £9-15s-00d by a payment of '£9-1-8 of Mr Hogson & allowed 13s-4 for Rent by Bevill Wivill.'
[6] Below this a single entry has been crossed out (and is illegible).

Nov. 1. Hitherto Received by addition 14-4-5
which with 7s-2d I had for bookes sold & wood spared maketh   £14-11s-7d

Novemb. 7th the Deacons brought to me   01-00-00

I owe Son Condy £10 to make up that £90 which he owed to me
    £100 for which I have made to me an anuity of £8 for some
    lives[1] & have delivered his bond
Novemb. 8. I had a letter & a Cheese from Ireland Blessed be
    God for my daughters life & Lord let this prayer for thy
    direction & speciall providence about the busines she writes
    of be allwaies before thee
Nov. 12. Peternell Chubb acknowlegeth £7 she owed which
    I thought had been but £6-10s & so had formerly writt
                  Received in all hitherto   £15-11-7d

              Paid for rents last quarter besids arrears   3- 1-4

[fo. 39v]

The second quarter of the 59th yeare of Mine age   1660[2]

[No]vemb. 19th I gave to the Midwife that [de]livered my daughter
    Condy &c[3]   00-02-06
[I] gave to the woman attending   00-01-00
[Pai]d for writing about Tucking Mill[4]   00-03-00
[N]ovemb the 23 first market daye   00-10-00
I gave to Conall[5] Bennets man   01-00
[Paid] Peter County the younger about *tenth*   01-00
Novemb. 30 Market day   00-05-06
December 1 I paid to My Son Condy that £10 which I owed him
    about the £8 annuity out of the Mills in Dolvin   10-00-00
December the second Communion day   00-00-06
December 4. Brewing day.   00-05-00
Decem. 7th I delivered & laid out this weeke ended this Market day   00-06-03
[G]iven to my servant extraordinary   00-00-06
December 14th Barber   00-00-06
the same day Market day   00+08-11
[f]or a letter from my Son George   00+00-05

---

1   This is the term of the annuity, vaguely expressed.
2   A heading across the whole page.
3   Tavistock PR, baptisms: Patience, daughter of Mr Daniel Condy, born 18 November 1660, baptised
    12 January 1660/1.
4   For legal paperwork about the annuity he had raised against the mill.
5   Colonel.

Item November the 2nd Market day &c	00-09-*07*
Novemb. 4. Communion day	00-00-06
November 8th brewing day not paid	00-05-*00*
Given to Clog for bringing cheese & letter[1]	00-01-00
November 9th Market day	0-11-00
At Mr *Wis.* house I gave	0-00-0[?]
To Mrs Martin for Daughter Patience[2]	5-00-*00*
To John Hodge his son November 12	0-00-0[?]
November 16th market day laid out	0-06-[*00*]
In all laid out this quarter	6-*14*-[*01*]

with the £5 for my daughter 21-05-08[3]

[fo. 39v]

The last quarter I received 14s & 1d lesse then I spent besids £5
    to Mrs Martin for my daughter   But the arreares of Rents due
    last September which are £3-01s-4d will (if paid) make £2-7s- 3d
    more then my expenses except Mrs Martins five pound[s]
Col: Bennet sent me a bushell of wheate
John Russell a very good Turky.
Mary Charles a wood-dove.
December. 3rd Mr Robert Bennet Came of purpose to visit me &
    Comfort me &c
John son of Rich: Pecke sent Two woodcocks. Dec. [*5th*]
Decemb 6th I had of my Son Condy from Kirton of Macy, Ivy,
    & Wreyford 10s & 10s & 2s for ˆaˆ yeares rent   ended Sept 29th
    last past.   01+02-00
Due more (besids 3-13-6 arreares befor Sept. 29th last) 18s-6d in   00-18- 06
    all £4-12s This only besids arreares I say when it is paid but
    Dec. 7th not paid
neither yet the £3-13s-6d arreares which I put to my account of
    August 17th last past
John Brownsdons wife sent me A Capon Dec. 14th
And Dec. 19 Ribbs of Beefe – by himselfe

Besids arreares as is aforesaid there is due to me December 25th as followeth

---

1   These came from his daughter Patience Miller in Ireland. On 23 July 1660 Clog had carried shoes,
   books and money for Larkham to the port of Bideford, for passage to Ireland (fo. 38r).
2   Katherine Martin's husband, Humphrey, was in Ireland.
3   £21-05s-08d: the sum of £14-11s-07d and £6-14s-01d.

My son's displac'd, with faith let's feete be shod,
With Noah & Enoch to walke with God.[1]

Dec. 17. My Da. C[2] Marriage day I had some *friends* & a quart of wine	00+01- 6
Dec 21 Market day laid out	00+05-10
paid for James his schooling	00+02-06
Due for my maides quarter	00+10-00
& for baking last quarter now ended	00+01-06
Due also by promise out of the Rents at Kirton for 2 quarters ended. Dec. 25th unto my wife to be allowed to Son Condy towards the paiment for the plate for his child[3]	01+00-00
Dec. 26 on an ordinary &c	00+01-00
Dec 28 Market day	00+04-11
Jan 2 an ordinary at lecture	00+01-00
Jan. 4 Market day	00+07-04½
Brewing day last Munday which was the 31 day of december	00-05-00[4]
allowed for head rent for Austins house	00-00-04
paid for a quarter of beefe to Son Condy	00-09-00
to William Cole for James his schooling	00-01-03
for Tabacco 6d & shoulder of Mutton 10d	00-01-04
Paid to William Web lent: T Larkham[5]	00-10-00
Deli:[vered] to James french boy[6] in all with the [?] 6d I paid for going with his chest to Plimoth	01-08-00
[?] bringin[g] Trunke home & [?]	00-03-04
[*This*] day Jan. 11 Market day	00-06-10
Spent Hitherto	18- 6- 9½

---

1   Hebrews 11:5–7 and Genesis 5:24, 6:9 (KJV). George Larkham (*CR*) ceased to preach on 26 August 1660 and was ejected by commissioners sitting at Cockermouth 15 November 1660. He continued as pastor of the congregational church there until his death in 1700.
2   Daughter (Jane) Condy's wedding anniversary.
3   For the newly born Patience Condy.
4   In the left column between this entry and the next, he wrote the words 'Upon the Returne of Thom: Larkham … ' which preface the poem in the right column, opposite. His expenses have been listed without interruption here.
5   Larkham's grandson.
6   James Cottonlieu.

Inp[rimis] from John Martin for this quarter	00-06-08
from T. Tilla[m] for this quarter & a Capon	00-07-08
from Eme doidge for this quarter	00+03-04
from John Austine for this quarter	00+04-02
All these in arreares also. Martin 16s- 8d and Tillam 6s-8d: Em	
~~Doidge 6s-8d Austin 4s-6d~~	
Mrs Trowt without arreares only this quarter	00+01-08
Due from Will Brownsdon for this quarter	00-10-00
from George Pear[s]e for annuity & rent	00-15-00
from John Macy	00+-2-06
from Phillip Wreyford for the barne	00-00-06
besids the above mentioned arreares viz from Pearse £3-9s.	[02-11-06
Brownscombe £1 White. 1s, Brocke 1s & Cooper one shilling. due Sept 29. last	
Received of the Deacons Decemb. 24th	01+00-0[0]
Received of Son Condy for anuity of the Mills in Dolvin the 8th day of January.	02-00-00[1]

Upon the Returne of Thom: Larkham out of France who came home the 5th day of January at night 1660 I wrote the day following these verses

> Blest be my God The Orphan is come safe
> On the fifth of th' eleventh thou made'st me laugh
> Lord love him for thy Cov'enants sake I pray
> And send help to thy folke without delay.
> Amen let be, it shall be, God hath said.
> Shortly thy foes (O God) shall be well paid.[2]

Jan 18th I was made a prisoner by C. Howard & had a guard of 6 souldiers put into my house & the Munday following was conveyed by six troopers to the Provost Marshall at Exon [*returned not*] untill Aprill 11th 84 Daies in all[3]

---

[1] He entered this last note beneath the verse about his grandson, below.
[2] Larkham's grandson Thomas had gone to France in August 1659, around the same time as the 'French boy' James Cottonlieu came to Tavistock. When Thomas returned to Tavistock, James left for France (see the entries below).
[3] 'C.' Howard: colonel or captain. The foot of the folio is ragged: the bracketed words are a conjecture.

17 April – 23 June 1661

[fo. 40r][1]

Farwell accounts about worldly affaires,
Hell hath deflow'rd the earth farwell those cares.
Alas my God the world is devill ridden,
Let my soule still (I wish) with God be hidden
Methinks my trading with the world should stop
Alas my God keepes a well furnish'd shop.
The Land's all Egipt now and Egipts curse
is over all the world, if not much worse.
For Beelzebub with his cur'st swarming braine,
Hath all things fly-blowne on hills in plaine.[2]
ther's nothing that is sweete but Saviours flesh
(All's dogs meate else,) with it Lord me refresh.
Deare God who hath bewitch't me that I can't
Deny this courting whorish world a grant?
   Let faith in these darke times make conscience good,
   and that well drest shall be my dayly food.

Written by Thomas Larkham (a
partiall prisoner & kept out by
violence & oppress[ion] of the
place of publiq[ue] preaching) the
17th day of Aprill 1661

O Remember thy saints
for greife my heart now fai[nts]
Plucke downe thy cruell fo[es]
When God will help who kno[ws]

During the time of mine imprisonment my Sonne Condy took car[e] to furnish my family at home & me a prisoner with Money.

He chargeth himselfe with	02-11-05	Received of George Pearse in woo[d]
with £22-12s Received out of	22-12-00	from J Pointer for the yeare 165[9]
Lamerton		
And alloweth for anuity out of	02-00-00	the Milles stane in Dolv[in][3]
Milles		
Due March 25th 1661 Summe is 27-03-05		
He chargeth me with particulars	21-00-00	upon his booke &c
So at my returne Aprill 11th	6-03-05	is comming to me from him

Besids this spent out of mine owne estate Diverse men & Women sent tokens of their love to me the particulars I wrote out & cannot now find, the Lord grant that it may be for the furtherance of their profit & abound to their account respectively. Thou Lord knowest them by name & what they did in way of Communicating with mine affliction And I do humbly beg thy Majestie in X Jesus to accept of the worke of faith & labour of love of all those thy poore ones that had care of me in that my distress

Amen Amen.

---

1   At this point Larkham abandoned his two column structure and for the next few weeks wrote entries across the folio; so this short section of the diary (17 April – 23 June 1661, fos. 40r-41v) is presented on continuous not facing pages.
2   'Egypt' recalls the Israelites' unfaithfulness and a return to the bondage from which God had freed them (Hosea 8:13–14, the Lord will 'remember their iniquity … they shall return to Egypt. For Israel hath forgotten his Maker'). Beelzebub is 'the prince of devils' (Matthew 12:24). Originally Larkham wrote 'mountains' instead of 'hills' but crossed it out – it did not scan.
3   Condy's costs for supplying a millstone were allowed instead of paying Larkham his annuity income.

[fo. 40v]

[W]hereas Aprill the 11th at my returne from Exon I accounted
[wi]th my son Condy & left in his hand £6-3s-5d. Since my
Servant tooke [of] Money to pay her Wages & for housekeeping
& seeds & Gardning &c

[*illegible*] So Aprill 27th I made all even and Received   03-16-04d of my Son
                                                                                  Condy

And I had in house (affor I had paid My Wife all due out 01-02-02
of Kirton untill March 25th last and also the rents for
Mr Leeres mills untill then and also [I] Sent & paid
halfe a yeares rent for the vicaradge ground[).]¹   04-18-06 in house
                                                                                  April the
                                                                                  27th 1661

[So I] was out of debt to all except £45 due to Mr Leere   Besids this said sume
for first paiment for my Mills taken in my Son   there is owing to me
Condies name   from my Tenants &c²

                                                          £   s   d

Inprimis from George Pearse & William Brownscombe
    Due last March 25th £3-07s-07d and £01-00-00 in all   04+07-07
from Phillip Wreyford halfe yeares rent for the little barne 00-01-00
for Cooper 01-00 Brocke 01s & white 01s headrent³
Due last September 29th & to be paid then but is owing   00-03-00
From John Austine for this quarter due March 25th   00+04-02   + R July 5th
                                                                                  for this &
                                                                                  the next
                                                                                  quarter

from Eme doidge⁴ due for one quarter ended *that* same
    time   00-03-04
from John Martin due to me upon account March last   01-10-00
from Thomas Tillam 3 quarters & a Capon last Xtide   01+01-00   R May 18th
From one Gliddon that dwelt with old Tillam   00-07-06
from old Tillam due February 2nd last past but May 3rd
    next he is to pay £1-17s-6d for this quarter will then
    be out againe⁵   01-10-00
                                                                  09-07-07

---

1   This appears again towards the foot of the folio, in Larkham's reckoning of money owed to him
    (which he admitted he was unlikely to see). He had paid £3-17s-06d 'head-rent' on the vicarage land,
    to the earl of Bedford as freeholder, up to 25 March 1661.
2   Besides the £4-18s-6d 'in house', Larkham was due rents in Crediton and Tavistock, itemised in the
    next entries.
3   'Head-rent': the rent payable to Larkham as freeholder.
4   Emma Doidge.
5   Tillam would be in debt again (*OED*, 'out' *adv.* 26).

Also George Chester oweth me for rent   05-03-04
And Petronell Chubb [oweth] to me &c   07-00-00
Josias Reede & George Brocke promised £6
    for Reedes life upon Brocks house in
    reversion &c the leases are ready due 10s   Received
    for them, & for the fine £6. In all   06+10-00 [£]6-7s in full
                                  28-00-11

Also out of the sheafe of Lamerton for the
    yeare 1660   50-00-00
Also for the rent of the ground belonging to
    the Minister for I paid the headrent untill
    March 25th last upon demand   03-17-06
Also for Wood-Money due last Sept. 29th   04-00-00
Besids half a yeares stipend due March 25th
    last & detained   19-10-00[1]
There is due unto me March 25th last past   105-08-05

But I do never expect all of it[.] I do referre all to the pleasure of God who hath revived my languishing spirit often, & raised up sicke children, & caused to be found things lost & not thought to be found, & freed me from my late long imprisonment.

O that the salvation &c Psalme 14 vs 7.[2] For my selfe, It is the Lord &c 1 Sam Cap.3. v. 18[3]

My sister worse then a widdow,[4] the orphan of my eldest Son, the fatherlesse ones of my Eldest daughter & her also. The famelies of my son George & Daughter Jane I give up unto the love & mercy wisdom & allmightines trueth & faithfullnes of the eternall & blessed God in Jesus X. O Lord take them for thine owne &c Good father in Jesus Christ consider thy cause, people, me & my relations

                                                  Amen amen

[1] Larkham reckoned he was owed half a year's stipend, but the period this covers is not clear. He expected payment on 25 March 1661. His manuscript contains no clear evidence of what was agreed about his stipend, or about tenure of the vicarage, when he resigned as vicar. Previously, he had recorded payment of his stipend for the quarter ended 25 March 1659/60 (fo. 37r), payment still due for the quarter ended 24 June 1660 (fo. 37v), and a payment made on 1 November 1660, just after he resigned (fo. 38r).

[2] Psalm 14:7 (KJV): 'Oh that the salvation of Israel were come out of Zion! When the Lord bringeth back the captivity of his people, Jacob shall rejoice, and Israel shall be glad.'

[3] Larkham addressed to himself the words of Eli to Samuel, 1 Samuel 3:18 (KJV): 'It is the Lord: let him do what seemeth him good.'

[4] His surviving sister, Elizabeth or Jane Larkham, who had come from Lyme Regis to stay in Tavistock two years earlier: see the next entry (fo. 41r) and various references soon after 18 May 1659 (fo. 34r). She seems to have been an elderly spinster, 'worse than a widdow'.

[fo. 41r]

Aprill the 30th I sent away my sister by drake to Exeter and so to Lyme whence she came 2 yeares since[.] I gave her 20s and paid Drake for carriage of herselfe & goods to Exeter –10s

The Saturday following I rode to Dartmouth with my Grand child[1] thinking to have placed him there or at Totnes & so to have ridden Eastward But God otherwise disposed I came back very lame upon Tuesd[a]y the 7th of May with the expence in that journey of about 20s

$$£ \quad s \quad d$$

There grow due to me May 3rd from old Tillam for the Mills which
    were bought of Mr Leere (besides one quarterly rent due before)
    for from Feb. 2nd he the said Tillam   ˆonly *received*ˆ 01-17-6
    Tooke the dwelling house also that Gliddon had formerly
on friday 10th of May Capt Larke was with me I being in my bed lame
    and he promised me faithfully that at midsommer he would pay the
    Money unpaid upon a bill obligatory of 200 pound if he do so he is
    to have up his bond[2] That which he is to pay me is (after the rate of
    our agreement out of Pixon) £45-00s-00d which if it be honestly
    paid June 24th next the whole bill obligatory is to be yeilded up

The 17th day of May 1661 endeth the third quarter of the 59th yeare of mine age.
on which my son Condy had a letter from Son George *[3]

Tertii Mensis 18° vulgo (May) 1661 beginneth the ending quarter of
this sad yeare.

The day on which X lay dead in his grave,
with me began this nine & fiftieth yeare.
And what Lord do I of thy goodnes crave?
Only that thou say (Son) be of good cheare.

If heaven smite what though men raile & scoule
Well let them barke I'me sure they can not bite
Such as in God trust and on him do rowle.[4]
Men, do your worst you can but show your spigh[t][5]

---

1   Thomas Larkham.
2   'Have up': to summon, to call to account (*OED*, 'have' *v.* 16b).
3   Larkham marked this with a star.
4   'Rowle': rely, entrust, cast oneself on God; a usage based on the Hebrew text behind verses such as Psalms 22:8 and 37:5, and Proverbs 16:3 (*OED*, 'roll', *v*² 10).
5   'Spite'.

	My Sixtieth yeare begins on the first day,	Lord can the eye
Sic scripsit T.L.	Christ's cause shall rise againe, O come away.	that reads be dry?
vinctus in Domino[1]	All wo'nt prove Gold that glisters in that day.	Reader stop heere
	Many shall be found base that preach & pray.	& drop a teare.
		O my soule burne
		in love, & mourne
Jehovah Jehovah	Happy is he who my Lord finds well doing	Till thy Lord rise
Elshaddai Elshaddai.	that backe againe to Egipt is not going.	fill heaven with cries

The 3rd Moneth (vulgo May) the 23 day From one a clocke in the morning, at which time I arose out of my bed, the Lord was pleased to afflict me with most sharpe paines of the chollicke the like paine (I do not remember) I ever felt. But by use of meanes, vomiting clistering[2] &c I received ease. And the 24th day at 4 of the clocke in the morning arose, read, sang, prayed & praised God with my family

Even so o Lord let it be with thy (seemingly) Dying Church & Cause Revive thy worke &c Amen

The 25th about the same time in the Night my extreame paine came again & sent for a physician who gave me a clister which wrought very much, this second time the Lord hath eased mee[.] the day following being the Lords day I praised God & spake to such as came to visit me

May 27th I Resolved upon giving over houskeeping

May the 31. 1661. Mr Browne minister,[3] with his wife & 3 chilldren came to Tavis-tocke, great joy [&c] manifestations of it by ridinge runninge ringing among super-stitious ignorant prophane people (The *peop[le]* of God som[e]thing sad[de]ned ^at their^ sacrificing to *th[ese]*[4] oathes, lies & persecutions Habbacuk. 1. 16.[5] But thy old despised servant is bold in X *to expect* & pray as it is *yet* justified *with* & for thine to expect thy faithful*ness*[6]

[fo. 41v]

yet Mr Browne Bruised[7] came in ^to Towne,^ the Wagon (as is said) in which he came with his Wife & children overturning or breakinge. So He preached not at all the Lords day following tho[ugh] (ut vulgo dicitur) Whit Sunday neither was any other at all that day in Publicke. I went with Some scores in the afternoone to Sanford Spiny[8] & there preached the word of God

---

1 'Thus wrote Thomas Larkham, a prisoner of the Lord.'
2 'Clyster', *v*.: to treat with a 'clyster', 'an enema or suppository' (*OED*).
3 Samuel Browne: Tavistock PR, burials: 7 August 1661, '[ ] Browne, child of Mr Samuel B. vicar'.
4 Two blots of red wax make it hard to read this line and the next.
5 Habbakkuk 1:16 (KJV): 'Therefore they sacrifice unto their net, and burne incense unto their drag: because by them their portion is fat, and their meat plenteous.'
6 Larkham perhaps had in mind a verse like Hebrews 10:13 (KJV): 'From henceforth expecting till his enemies be made his footstool.' The foot of the folio is badly worn, so the last line is indistinct.
7 Larkham turned a surname entered earlier by George Lane ('Braser') into 'Bruised'.
8 Sampford Spiney, four miles south-east of Tavistock, which has a parish church.

	£ s d
The Munday I gave John County who had taken paines with	
me in my Late grevous fitts of the Cholicke. 10s, & a quart of	00-11-04
wine 16d	

I Also tooke into consideration that this very day viz June 3rd in anno Domini. 1622
I was married at Shobrooke & have lived in that estate full 39 yeeres In which time
I have seene & enjoyed Marvellous providences vouchsafed to me & mine. I Now
humbly Lay before my father the Orphan of my Eldest Son who hath neither father
mother brother or sister, Lord take him in X & love him[.] And next My Sonne
George his wife & children I humbly present to my God & father[.] And also My
two daughters Patience & Jane with their's, O Lord love them[.] For my unworthy
selfe & poore wife, My father thou knowest how it is with me and her, O thy spirit
is all I crave for us both, And then all will be well enough[1]

The fortieth yeare beginneth now   And now father what waite I for
of my married condition: Standing and knocking at thy doore?
Lord turne thee to thy wonted grace   I stand & knocke at th' doore of hope,
And that with expedition   Lord let the doore of Love fly ope.

Who walkes in Christ can never go astray
My soule get in, walke on in this good way.
Peace let me have, thy peace Lord to me give
Let thy sweete calmes my troubled heart releive.

June 10th I passed an account with my sonne in law Daniel Condy & Received of
him three & twenty shillings & two pence allowing sixteene shillings & ten pence
which I owed him upon his booke & so that 40s which would have beene due for an
anuity out of the Mills in Dolvin is paid before hand, which I should not have had
untill midsommer next. So now no more is due untill September 29th next comming
if my terme so long continues then 40s more will be due.

Ita est, By me Thom Larkham

June 20th I earnestly commended to the Lord my God & father the afflicted condition
of my poore daughter Patience from ˆwhomeˆ I received lately a letter which was
dated May the 22nd last: Deare father looke on her & her poore fatherlesse ones I
likewise mentioned my son Condy now (I hope) safe in London, Lord be with him
&c but especially I commended to the Lord his greate cause now bleeding

Let it Rise, Let it Rise, let it revive O Lord for thy truethes sake.

Amen Amen Amen

---

[1]   Larkham had married Patience Wilton at Shobrooke, Devon. The only other personal reference to his
wife – in marked contrast to the affectionate comments he lavished on his children – was in December
1658: 'O My poore Rocky Untoward Wife! O my unsuitablenes to her! Lord helpe' (fo. 32v).

24 June – 17 August 1661

[fo. 42r]

June the 24th midsommer day 1661 Due to me for rents as followeth[1]

	s d	
Inprimis from Thomas Tillam	06-08	
from Eme dodge[2] for 2 quarters	06-08	
from Mrs Trowt for one quarter	01-08+	
from John Austin & Huggins 2 quarters	08+04+	
from John Martin upon account due paid	36-08	
from Paine for the garden plot at mills	03+00+	
Arreares from Tillam for the Mille	60-06	
from Gliddon due last February	7-06	
Tillams quarter will be ended August 1 Next		
	138s-00	6-18-00[3]

June 27th Capt Larke paid me £30 and William Webb was appointed to pay me £10 sometime this weeke and he himselfe *promised* to pay me £5 at his Returne to Tavistocke, and so I delivered up to him his bond of £200 for the paiment of £100 which had laine longe broken in my hand[4]

June 27 & 28th I paid Mr Leere the £45 remaining upon the first bill he had £5 Aprill 4th last past

The latter of these daies in June was a blacke day for the people of God at Tavestocke. Thou has seene it for thou Beholdest mischeife and spite to requite it with thy hand: The poore committeth himselfe to thee thou art the helper of the fatherlesse Breake thou the arme of the wicked and the evill man, seeke out his wickednesse till thou find none[5]

July the 4th I dinned with Mr Bazzet a french man at Serjeants & was at Mr Counties to see him with him and another frenchmen. I dranke much Wine this day I am apt to be vaine[6] when occasion is given, Lord remitt & helpe[.] I spent in Wine £00-03s-02d[.] the Next Morning July the 5th I sent for John Web who trimmed me I gave him 00-00-06[7]

---

[1] After this first entry across the top of the folio, he split the entries between rents due in Tavistock (on the left) and in Crediton (on the right, opposite).

[2] Emma Doidge.

[3] The total in shillings converted to pounds, shillings and pence.

[4] 'Broken': incomplete (*OED*, 'broken', *ppl. a.* 14).

[5] Larkham gave no details about why this was such a black day, but wrote out Psalm 10: 14–15 (KJV) verbatim: 'Thou hast seen it; for thou beholdest mischief and spite, to requite it with thy hand: the poor committeth himself unto thee; thou art the helper of the fatherless. Break thou the arm of the wicked and the evil man: seek out his wickedness till thou find none.'

[6] 'Vaine': foolish, silly, thoughtless (*OED*).

[7] John Web, Larkham's barber.

[fo. 42r]

	£ s d
Inprimis at Kirton from Pearse	05+02-07
From William Brownscombe	00-10-00
From John Macy one Quarter	00-02-06
from Phillip Wreyford for 3 quarters	00-01-06
from Cooper, Brock & Whit[e] due Sept last	00-03-00
Next Sept. 29th will be due *It*[1] from Brock 1s Cooper 1s White *6d*	05-19-07

---

[1] This word (written over an entry by Lane) is perhaps an abbreviation for the Latin '*iterato*': again, likewise.

This day my sone Condy writes from London that my son George had written to him out of Cumberland that he hath not missed to preach not so much as one Lords day since he was ejected.[1]

Thanks be to God my sone is well	For he is yong and like to faint
& yet boldly rings Aarons bell:[2]	He'is but a yong though sincere saint,
Lord pitty me his poore father	But I am old and good for nought
yet pitty him Lord I had rather	yet am I with Jesus blood bought

> O thou salve of all mercy, behold thy peoples misery,
> shut not thine eares against our cry.

Thom Larkham pipiebat[3] July 6th 1661

July The Ninth Tuesday William Webb paid me £10 for Captaine Larke

Lord remember &c[4]

O that God would once againe once againe[5] restore the glory to England.

Amen Amen Amen

July 15. 16th Roger Row for work had 02s-04d.   What is the signe that I shall goe
and July 17 William Web had for wood 04-00   againe to the house of the Lord?

July. 19th in letters from London some hope was manifested of some indulgence to be granted to the people of God. Lift up thine eies to the hills who will for me my helpe commeth from the Lord which made heaven and earth.[6] Lord I have none to go unto but thy Majesty who art my father in Christ/:

August. 1°. (Tillam being dead) Nicholas Gill tooke to the Mills & is to pay 40s quarterly, but if he thrive not on them, I am to abate (10s) at the end of the yeare

Deare God! who hath Bewitc'hd me that I Can't	
Give to thy gratious offered X a ready grante?	
The Whole World is to him a ragged shred,	Augusti 7° 1661
The greatest Potentate is but one single threed	
Surely the Worlds credit can't longe hold good	
Tis mark methinks that it so long with me hath stood.[7]	

---

1   George Larkham, ejected on 15 November 1660 by commissioners at Cockermouth, but pastor to the congregational church there until his death in 1700 (CR).
2   Exodus 28:34–5: Aaron's priestly robe had a bell attached, so 'his sound shall be heard when he goeth in unto the holy place before the Lord' (KJV). Larkham interpreted this typologically, to mean preaching.
3   'Cried.'
4   Perhaps Larkham had in mind a prayer for the late-payer Larke which paraphrased the thief's words to Christ on the Cross: 'Lord, remember [him] when thou comest into thy kingdom' (Luke 23:42).
5   Larkham reiterated 'once again'.
6   Psalm 121:1–2 (KJV): 'I will lift up mine eyes unto the hills, from whence cometh my help. My help cometh from the Lord, which made heaven and earth'.
7   'X': Christ. 'Mark': worthy of note, remarkable.

August the 6th *Botten* belonging to Kelland came & required me to goe with him but having nothing to shew but an old Parole[1] I did not goe with him he gave many threates & dep[ar]ted But what will come of it I know no[t]

Lord I betake me to thy grace
Mine enimies sorely me chase
But let me see thy gratious fac[e]

---

[1] 'An old parole': a document setting out conditions for the release of a prisoner, presumably dating from the time Larkham came out of prison in April 1661.

18 August 1661 – 17 August 1662

[fo. 42v]

August the 18th beginneth the sixtieth yeare of mine age   <u>1661</u>

August the 22nd Rod[e] to Exeter Assizes, and was Putt of[f] in regard of my *heare[in]ges* of the indictments untill Lent Assises. Hearing of Waite laid for me I Rode toward Cumberland where the Lord preserved me in health & saf[e]ty.[1]

I Returned to Tavistocke March the first 166½ And am now living in the house of my Son Condy together with My Wife.[2]

	£ s d
March 7th I Received of Eustace Pike who hath bought Martins Right[3]	00-06-08
March 10th of Emē Doadge[4] ~~Received~~	
she acknowledgeth March 25th will be due 6-8d it[erato]	00-10-00
I received also of Samuell *Hutch* at Kirton for 2 quarters ended last	
December the 25th he bou*gh*t out the right of George Pearse of	
Kirton	00-05-00
March 10th I cast up account with my Son Condy	
& find he oweth me upon account the summe of	13-00-00
He having left unpaid to Mr *Leere* which I ordered him to pay the	
summe of £16 which I am to pay for he hath paid him only £34 at	
severall paiments of that last £50 for his Mills. & £1-15s for a	
horse that Thomas Larkham rode away with me upon	
Received of John Austine for Rent untill Dec. 25th allowing 14d for	
mending glasse at Gills Mil	00-08-04
March 15th I had Brought to me by J.S. a Deacon of the Church some	
money in a purse which at my returne viz March 19th I told and	
found to be. 5-10-6. I had of Mrs. W. 5s. & of R.D. 2s more ˇand	
of M.G. 1sˇ [5]	
in all I had	05-18-06

---

1   From the time-gap (there is no gap in the text), it seems the manuscript stayed in Tavistock when Larkham went North. Nothing is known of what transpired in Cumberland. He began to make entries again a week after his return.

2   Until this point, he left no clear record of where he had lived since his resignation in October 1660. Perhaps he stayed on in the vicarage until just before his successor Samuel Browne arrived on 31 May 1661: in January 1660/1 he spoke of being guarded in 'my house' (fo. 39v); in late April he was making arrangements for his sister and grandson to be accommodated elsewhere (fo. 41r), as if in anticipation of a move. On 27 May he 'resolved upon giving over housekeeping' (fo. 41r).

3   Pike took over a lease or tenancy, probably from John Martin.

4   Emma Doidge.

5   'J.S.' is almost certainly John Sheere; the others are perhaps Mary Webb ('Mrs W'), Richard Dunrish ('R.D.') and Mary Gibb ('M.G.'), who had all given him gifts before.

[fo. 42v]

	£ s d
paid for shoeing my horse to Thomas Carter March 8th	00-01-04

At my Returne to Tavistocke From Cumberland I delivered to
    Lancelott Hutton viz besids the 40s given by his brother (I wrote
    of) 2s-6[d] from his mother and 1s from his sister Fellows, the
    letters written by them were lost with many other things of mine
    owne in my Portmantio*e*,[1] of which I can heare no newes   02-03-0[?]

I laid out for glasse at Leeres Mills hinted in the other columne   £0- 1s-2d

My Son Condy havinge undertaken to satisfy Mr Leere £16 I am
    indebted unto him three pounds. I expended in fees &c about my
    two enditements. 52s & in charges 12s-4d in all my Exeter journey
    stood me. £3-4s-8d

March the 19th I paid the abovemention[ed] three pound to my
    Da[ughter] Condy, so now I owe not anythinge unto him.[2] I also
    paid for 3 Moneths taxe for the mill 1s[.] the 3 shillings demanded
    for fords land I refused to pay, because no more was paid by me
    when I enjoyed the vicaridge

Now free I am, how long God only knows
O what a Croaking's made by Carrie Crowes[3]
Lord let me once more heare the turtles voi*ce*
the singing of the birds most rare & choi*ce*
Pitty Poore England that lies in the Dus[t]
Scowre off hir drosse cleanse your poor peoples ῾rust῾
Beare up the spiritts of all thy holy ones
their prayers heare & pitty Lord their gr*oanes*

---

1   Portmanteau.
2   Larkham paid his daughter Jane Condy £3 to settle his debt of £3 to her husband Daniel Condy.
3   'Carrie Crowes': 'carre-crows', carrion crows.

I acknowledge to be satisfied [in] my annuity out of the Milles in
    Dolvin from S[on] C[ondy] untill March 25th 1662   02-00-00
    which I received upon account for my Wives diet this quarter
    untill the said day from Xtide last[.] all is even hitherto

I have beene in Bonds & under imprisonment in both Goales viz at the Castle &
Southgate & under the Marshalls power at an Inne in Exeter & upon recognisances
with sureties from October 19th 1660 untill March 17th 1661 which is about one
whole yeare & 21 weekes[.] In which time all my meanes hath beene kept from
^me^ & for time due before to the value ^in all^ of neere £200. & yet unreasonable
taxes above any man upon that little temporall meanes I have in Tavistocke. These
things I lay before the Righteous judge

Written March 19th 166½

God exacteth of thee lesse then thy iniquity deserveth. Job. 11. 6.[1] I know Lord
that your judgments are right Ps. 119 v.75[2]

When God bringe Saints into a low estate,
it is to humble them, & raise their faith,
& make them pray at a very high Rate
& to discover base heartes. The word saith.
also, the enimy must vent his spleene
& X in straights more cleerely will be seene[3]

Take heed my soule lest thy poore spirit do sinke
That God is Israels God still do thou thinke

[fo. 43r]

1662[4]

1662   The Yeare of our Lord   1662 March 25th Beginneth March 25th

I live in hope that I may see this yeare,
something to fill the Saints hands with good cheare.

£ s d

March the 26th I paid my son Condy for diet since my cominge home
    March 1st   00-10-00
Also I delivered to him to make satisfaction to Mr Brownsdon for
    his horse   04-00-00

---

1   Job 11:6 (KJV): 'God exacteth of thee less than thine iniquity deserveth.'
2   Psalm 119:75 (KJV): 'I know, O Lord, that thy judgments are right, and that thou in faithfulness hath
    afflicted me.'
3   In difficulty, Christ will be seen more clearly.
4   The initial entries run across the whole folio.

This day ends 61 come sixty two,
Let God arise in his peoples defence.
And on thy foes o Lord let fall woe woe.
And likewise let them be driven farr hence
No pitty have ˆtheyˆ shewed in this sad day
but of all sorts of folke have made a prey

>   What time I am afraid I'll trust in God,
>   and till he burne it, humbly kisse the rod.
>
> written March. 24. 1661

[fo. 43r]

Sent by Step[hen] Rundle to Phi:[lip] Doidge for Dressinge my horse   00-01-00
    while he was here
Note that of the money mentioned in the other columne to be Received
    of Petronell Chubb that which was properly myne owne was 30s as
    I thought & [not] 40s as she said for I had £6 in all which should have
    beene £6-10s or £7. what was above was money of the Churches by
    consent remitted to me in regard of my many troubles & expences.
Aprill 14ᵗʰ I sent to Ralph Carter by Lanti for drenches &c for my horse 00-05-00
    (which now is sold to Stephen Rundle)[1]

---

[1]   Larkham sold his horse after the journey from Cumberland to Tavistock. 'Lanti' (or 'Lansy') was a
servant in Daniel Condy's household. 'Drench': a dose of medicine for an animal (*OED*).

It is agreed Betweene us this 26th day of March 1662 that my Son Condy hence forward have for my Diet while I live in his house the full benefitt of the Milles which I bought of Mr Leere he paying hence forward all rates and taxes and the Lords Rent. And that *if* befor such time his owne Milles and so the anuity out of the Milles in Dolvin are to goe for my wives Diett in like manner paid so all is even betweene us untill this time. The Milles were taken of Mr Leere in his name I trusting him to do as I shall order at all times with them. Blessed be my God who hath hitherto provided for me & d[elivere]d me[1]

	£ s d
March 27 Received of S Condy for N. Gill[2]	01-00-00
Aprill 2[nd] Petronell Chubb brought unto me £5-19s-10d insteede of	
£6 desiring that the rest due might be remitted which I granted &	
delivered up her writings	5-19-10
I received this weeke of Mrs Trowt for rent	0-01-08
of Eustace Peeke for lady day quarter	0-06-08

Aprill the 12th I accounted with Nicholas Gill and He resteth in my debt upon the Whole 18s. ^Rec. 12s^ and so in the presenc[e] of Nich: Watts I delivered up the tenantship of the said Nich: Gill to my Son Condy to whom will be due one quarter. May 3rd Next and for the plott of ground at Midsommer 3s which he with Francis *Bucher* tooke unto March 25th last

Can these bones live? Abba father all things are possible unto thee.[3] O the scattered churches. Helpe Lord.

It is in satisfaction of my Diet at the house of my Son Condy that I do yeild up these Milles, & so long to continue.

May. 23. John Edgcombe of Lamerton havinge beene sicke & neere
    unto death upon recovery came to me & gave &c   05s-00d

July 4[th] I received £45 of the kinsman of John Brownsdon in p[ar]t of pay for my right in Rodge which is £65. So he is to pay £20 more September 29[th] next cominge if the businesse be effected with the Lord about the change of the life,[4] otherwise I am to pay backe the foresaid £45, I have given with my Son Condy a bill obligatory for it. which said £45 with £14 (which was in my son Condy's keeping before) & 20s more delivered this day Maketh £60. which lyeth in my Son Condyes hand £50 for Tom Larkham's Master if he be bound, & £10 for my Son George which he tooke up for me in Cumberland the other £20 (if I have it) £10 of it is to satisfie a debt I owe which John Brownsdon procead[ed][5] for me the other is left for my occasions.[6]

---

1   Larkham assigned to his son-in-law the annuity of £8 a year from the mills (which had been bought in Condy's name), to pay for 'diet' for himself and his wife. The mills had been bought in August 1660 (fos. 38r, 39r, 38v).
2   At this point the entries divide into two columns.
3   Ezekiel 37:3, Mark 14:36 (KJV).
4   In other words, if a change in the lease could be agreed with the earl of Bedford's agent.
5   Carried forward.
6   'Occasions': personal requirements.

Thus farr the Lord hath holpen blessed be his name.

	s d
Jane Miller came out of Ireland to Tavistocke	
June 14th 1662. Paid Cosen Davy Condy which he gave her at Barnstable	
when he first saw her	01-00
paid John Duntervile for bringing her to Tavistocke	03-00
paid for mending 2 paire of shoes	01-02
paid Daniell Sowton for worke about her cloathes	02-06
paid for stuffe[1] & lace & other things for ˆaˆ Wascott for her	07-04
given to her in money	00-06
paid Roger Charles for her Diett untill July the 16th	08-00
paid for 4 yards of doul[a]s[2] for a smocke & for threade	02-08
It[erato] for Diet to Roger Charles for 5 weekes ended August the 20th	10-00
	01-16-02

Thus endeth the sixtieth yeare of Mine age August 18th 1662

Thus farre the Lord hath holpen me,
And's his love in Christ hath made me see,
His holy name still praised be.

---

1   'Stuff': used for a various textiles but especially for worsteds, made from twisted woollen yarn (*DTGC*).
2   'Dowlas': coarse linen cloth.

The business about Rodge was effected July 7[th] & I am to have £20 paid me Sept. 29[th] next & the bill I gave is yeil[d]ed up to me & I have delivered up mine assignment to J *Brough* & cancelled it. So my right in Rodge is Sold.

July 21° I delivered £10 to Mr Syndry of London to be paid to Mr Wilson upon my S[on] C[ondy's] account He is partner with Mr Richard Bate.[1] & was paid the £8 laid out formerly about the horse I brought out of Cumberland.

July 25[th] my Son Condy wrote to Mr Rich: Bate to pay £50 to one Mr Dan: Arthur Merchant in London by order from T. Larkh[a]mes Master Received in a letter with intelligence that the busines is effected and a copy of the Indenture & a bond of *£500* for me [to] seale which I have done & sent it backe &[c][2]

sic finitur 60° annus ætatis[3]

---

1   Probably the London haberdashers David Syndry and Richard Bate, who traded together and with the West Country: wills, National Archives, London, PROB4/25780 and PROB11/309.

2   In his will, proved 9 March 1669/70, Larkham by-passed Tom Larkham as his heir, 'with some sadnes', because of his 'miscarriage which I hope he beginneth to see'. Tom had been in Barbados and was about to put to sea again. Larkham had been forced to mortgage his house at Crediton, chiefly to 'buy apparell & necessaries to set forth the said Thomas Larkham the second time that he might be able to live in this world' (A. G. Matthews's Notes of Nonconformist Ministers' Wills, Dr Williams's Library, London, MS 38.59, fos. 607–11). The younger Thomas Larkham's will, 21 June 1685, described him as 'of St Martins Orgars in the Citty of London Merchant' (National Archives, PROB11/382).

3   'So comes to an end the 60th year of my age.'

18 August 1662 – 17 August 1664

[fo. 43v]

1662
August the Eighteene beginneth the one and Sixtieth yeare of mine age

The saddest weeke that ever England saw
Witnesses slaine by vertue of a Law.[1]
Many fall off in this sad day of triall,
God's cause meetes now with many a deniall.
All proves not gold that glister'd and was specious,[2]
All are not found to have that faith that's pretious.
Yesterday ended godly men's preaching
that do refuse traditions of men's teaching.
Enter the the Mattins of Bartholomew
Lord keepe thy poore saints from the bloody crew.
Let not the cruell make it suche a day
as 'twas in 72[3] O Lord I pray.
Bury in Christs grave our sinnes with his dolours
Reduce poore soules that have fled from their colours[4]
Lord make amend of this sad dismall story,
And let thy praying people see thy glory.

Sept. 16th Mir:[iam] Brownsdon in acknowledgment of her duty
    though I could not do the office of a Pastor gave me the first
    pay I received since March 15th last past anno ætatis 61°   £00-10s-00d

October 18th I tooke Notice that I had laid out about Jane Miller since her
    comminge out of Ireland £2-10s-02d I say fifty shills fifty shillings & 2d

November 12th 1662 It is full 20 yeares since I left my house in new England
    and came to the havens mouth at Pascataquak and so tooke shippinge & came
    thence

O Gratious God thou has beene good to me
and mine. Thy deare son thou has made me see
For evermore thy name Lord praised be

---

[1] Larkham's poem marked not only his birthday but also the deadline for subscription under the Act
    of Uniformity, St Bartholomew's Day, 24 August 1662.
[2] 'Glister': glitter. 'Specious': fair and pleasing to the eye.
[3] The St Bartholomew's Day Massacre, 24 August 1572, which saw thousands of Huguenots die in
    France.
[4] 'Dolours': griefs, sorrows. 'Reduce': bring back, lead back, restore. 'Fled from their colours': a
    metaphor for betrayal of principle (literally to desert a regimental standard). *OED*.

[fo. 43v]

O God shall wicked men putt out our light?
We have deserv'd it Lord that's very right.
But lett trueth's pillars ^stand^ still firm and fast,
And blow away her foes with a strong blast.
In England let some still call on thy name
till flowres forget to breath & fire to flame.
The Light's puffd out (deare Lord) that shin'd so bright
And now in England tis a pitteous night
Descend (our Joshua) with all thy Might
And set thy churches and cause now at right.
Bless me and mine this following yeare I pray
Come Lord and comfort me O come away
Thou know'st all things thou know'st that I abhorr
my worthlesse selfe for loving thee no more.

	£ s d
September 16th I paid my daughter Condy which her husband paid for 3 moneths taxe for fords land	00-01-00
paid for 2 weekes diet for Jane Miller	00-04-00
Oct. 8 paid for cloth for a halfe shirt for my selfe	00-02-06
Item for 4 yards for a smocke & 1d thred for Jane Miller	03-05
for a paire of bodies[1] for her	00-01-08
for Peniston[2] inckle[3] gallo[o]n[4] thread for a Wascott	00-02-01
for a New paire of shoes for her	00-02-06
paid for Jane Miller for Trimming for A Melley[5] Wascot (given her by her Aunt Condy)	00-03-01
I sent to my sister at Lyme Decemb. 6th by my S[on] C[ondy] who delivered it to Mr Hart of Lyme	00-10-0[0]

---

[1] 'A pair of bodies': a bodice (OED).
[2] 'Peniston': a coarse woollen cloth used for garments or linings, named after a Yorkshire village (OED).
[3] 'Inkle', linen tape used for fastenings (OED).
[4] 'Galloon': 'narrow, close-woven ribbon or braid, of gold, silver, or silk thread, used for trimming of apparel' (OED).
[5] 'Mellay': 'a cloth made of wools dyed in different shades or colours and mixed before being spun', cf. medley (OED).

Received of Em doidge in p[ar]t of pay for 2 quarters	00-05-00
Received from Kirton by my Son Condy which Walter White brought	
to him which he had gathered of my Rents	2- 2- 6
Jan. 20[1] George Chester brought me of that £5-3-4d he oweth me	01- 0- 0
J.S. brought from M.W. Jan 21st [2]	00- 5- 0

Feb. 22nd late at night I departed upon a report of a warant &c
    returned to my quarters April 3rd late at night spent this time   01- 9- 0
at my returne G.O. gave me[3]   00- 5- 0

I was in all absent from my quarters 40 daies[4]

Aprill 8th about 3 of the clocke in the morninge I departed from Tavistocke 1663 and returned not untill Aprill the 25th 1664 so I was absent one whole yeare and 2 weekes & 3 daies[.] In mine absence the Earle of Bedford by his steward forced away my Milles which I bought of Mr Leere who had a lease from the said Earle & assigned it to me for £100. But besides the charges of a suite & Mr Eveleighs bill to the summe of about £7 they abated me £30 [*illegible*] I paid. Lord give repentance & consider me.

[fo. 44r]

Be favourable O Lord unto Sion Build thou the walls of Jerusalem[5]   an° 1664

May the 5th 1664 I wrote these words that I might in writing be thinkinge upon God Who never yet failed me, no nor never wil Lord I beleeve help thou myne unbeleife.[6]

---

1   20 January 1662/3. Larkham's entries at this time were intermittent.
2   Probably John Sheere and Mary Webb.
3   Perhaps George Oxenham.
4   Larkham made few entries in 1663, when for most of the time he was away from Tavistock (without his notebook). At some point in 1663 he added to a calculation made in 1611 by George Lane (fo. 'F'v). Lane added up the years from Adam to his own time: 5,585 years, 6 months and 10 days. This he deducted from 6,000 (in the judgment of many, the Millennium would come 6,000 years after Creation). In 1663, Larkham brought the calculation up to date, looking forward to the dawn of God's judgment:

$$
\begin{array}{r}
5585\text{-}06\text{-}10 \\
\text{From 1611: Unto 1663 (when I wrote this last line) is} \quad \underline{53\text{-}\ 0\text{-}\ 0} \ [sic] \\
5638\text{-}\ 6\text{-}10
\end{array}
$$

5   Psalm 51:18 (KJV): 'Do good in thy good pleasure unto Zion: build thou the walls of Jerusalem.'
6   Mark 9:24 (KJV): 'Lord, I believe; help thou mine unbelief.'

My Son Condy hath in his hand of mine   10-00-0[0]
    besids the £10 I owed to drake *procured* by J Brownsdon which
    he also is to pay when it is demanded
Given to Jane Burrow when my D[aughter] had child   0- 2- 6
Decemb. 23. I cleared the shop booke of my Son Condy. and now I
    owe him nothing but ut supra he has the above written summe of
    £10 & hath lent it to S. Rundle
Given among the servants of Son Condy   00-04-0[0]
& among others & toyes for the children of Cosen Davy & the little
    ones heere   00-03-0[0]

clearin[g] Aprill 6th¹ My Son Condies book & paid what he laid out
    for my horse he oweth me of the abovementioned £10 only   3- 3-1[?]

After my returne ^viz^ May the second 1664 I cast up all accounts with my son
Condy & he is debtour to me the summe of just thirty pound & which he saith is in
Stephen Rundles hand – twenty pound with said £50 I do owe unto Richard Covet
of London unckle by the Mother side to Thomas Larkham &c²

Three of my Grandchildren stood me this yeare about £30. viz Thomas Larkham
Thomas Miller & Jane Miller[.] One I sent to the Barbadoes the other to Venice,
and the maide I placed at Lyme to learne to make bon lace.³ O Lord in mercy make
provision for my poore offspringe that I may rejoice in thy trueth.

[fo. 44r]

Save me my God I humbly pray
O to my requeste o say not nay
Men have me vext without a cause
Thy word they slight & plead proud lawes⁴
My offsprings poore ^are^ in distresse
this yeare of *them there came amesse*⁵
Thus farre thou *had* cared for mee
thy faithfulnes Lord make me see⁶

¹ 6 April 1663.
² The younger Thomas Larkham left £5 to 'my uncle Richard Covett', to buy him mourning: 'Will
   of Thomas Larkham, Merchant of Saint Martin Orgar, City of London', 20 June 1685 (National
   Archives, PROB11/382).
³ 'Bone-lace' or bobbin lace, made of linen thread. Lyme Regis became famous for lace in the
   eighteenth century but at this point the industry was in its infancy.
⁴ Larkham may have had in mind the First Conventicle Act (May 1664) which prohibited gatherings
   of more than five people for worship unless it conformed to the liturgy of the Church of England.
⁵ 'Amiss'? Larkham has written over Lane's earlier entries.
⁶ Beneath this he (or George Lane before him) entered roughly 'X X X', to mark off the space. It is
   unlikely that here 'X' stands for 'Christ'.

Aprill 30th 1664 Quadraginta minie sunt Mihi
Et preterea circiter 26s of Money besids. D.G.[1]

I had beene at home but 3 daies, before Newes came to me that Mary Miller another
Grandchild was come to me she came Aprill 28th 1664 bringing very sad Tidings of
her Mother My eldest daughter. O my God pitty her & provide for her, & give her
a sanctified use of thine afflicting hand Amen. Hactenus auxiliatus est Do[m]i[n]us

	£ s d
May 10th 1664 paid to J sheere for making shelves for my bookes &	
for boards ^July afterwards I sett some in the Entry & some went	
to the makinge of the side table in the parlour^[2]	00-07-06
I gave to Mary Miller at her departure May 16th 1664 20s & paid for	
horse hire 2s-6d	01-02-06
Also in linnen charges in Peticoate & say apron[3] &c I paid to my	
Son Condy ^for her^	01-03-08
I sent to Lyme 2 Wascots cloth & galloon lace for one, & a taffety	
hood one Wascot & galloon my sister oweth me for 8s-6d the	
other *Amee Potter* 7s-6d the hood J. Miller[4]	01-00-00
	3-13- 8

July 4th. 1664 I came to dwell in the house sometime of Mr Grills because of the
straitnes of the Roome at my Son Condies. O my God, stay thy Rod, Bow my
will, blesse me still[5]

In the hands of my Son Condy there is one other £30. In all he hath £60.
The Rest of the £40 above mentioned viz Aprill 30th to be in my
   hand is bestowed ut supra *Lost* some, & in some small parcelles
   of houshold stuffe £2-3s-7d ^& houskeeping spent untill July
   18th^ & in a horse   4- 2- 9

   All even untill July the 8th 1664

my horse was sold againe to Jerome Penny who oweth me for him £4-10s   paid[6]

[1] 'April 30th 1664 Forty pounds are mine and moreover about 26s of money besides. Glory to God.'
    D[eo] G[loria].
[2] Written later, between the lines.
[3] 'Say': 'a cloth of fine texture resembling serge, probably of wool' (*OED*).
[4] 'Amy Potter' is a conjecture. She and Larkham's sister were charged for the waistcoats but he seems
    to have sent Jane Miller the hood as a gift. 'Wastcots': waistcoats. 'Galloon-lace': 'narrow, close-
    woven ribbon or braid, of gold, silver, or silk thread, used for trimming'. 'Taffety': taffeta (used for
    various fabrics with a sheen, often silk or linen). *OED*.
[5] In 1662, the house of 'Mr John Grills' was said to have three hearths: Devon Record Office
    QS/79/1/32, Hearth Tax Return for [town and parish of] Tavistock, 1662. By this time the Condys
    had six children (fo. 45r).
[6] Added later.

	£	s	d
Received of Eustice Pike for midsomer quarter	0-	6-	8
the Deacons brought me at severall times £2 & Mrs *Whits*[1] 5s	2-	5-	0

And from G. Ox[enham]. formerly viz June 26th I had 5s & M.F.
    widdow 2s[2]   0- 7- 0

Mr Leere sent me July the 18. halfe a bushell of wheate worth[3]

J. Hodges wife Butter & [*illegible*] 1s

D.S. 2 fowles.

G. Oxe[n]ha[m]s wife chicken

July 20th John Brownsdon A pecke of wheat & E. Toller Butter

Kate Hitchens sugar & *raisons*

I had also formerly of. C.B.[4] when I was at his house   0-10- 0

To this add the money I had of Jerome Penhay for my horse   4-10- 0

Received August 13th of John Austin for rent allowinge 8d for head
    rent to the Lord of the Burrough for 2 yeares last Micha[e]lmas.
    he paid me for 3 quarters en[d]ed June 24th   0-11-10
                                    8-10-06

    when 5-15-4 the summe in the other columne is deducted out of
the 8-10-6 mentioned in this columne, then remaines 2-15-4[5] To
begin this following yeare for maintenance of me & mine

---

1   Perhaps the 'Mrs White' who sent 5s by 'J S' (John Sheere, deacon) in February 1664/5 (fo. 45v).

2   The identity of widow 'M.F.' is unknown.

3   Larkham did not fill out the value but bracketed this entry clumsily with the gifts of food noted below.

4   'C.B.': perhaps Colonel Robert Bennet.

5   This should be £2-15s-2d. Larkham rarely made a slip, but here repeated '15-4' from the previous line.

for 2 quarts of olives paid July the 19th to y[*oung*] Pet[er] County	0+2-0d
Cotton 15 yards Inckle 2 peices. thread an *oz*. Rings 3 Dozen – all about a paire of curtaines & valence & the makinge of them[1]	0+18-0
I had a greene Rugg from Son Condy	0+16-6
Given by me to Piety or charitie at several times in Communion taken	0+ 4-0
About the house these weekes past untill July. 25th called St James day	0+10-2
I owe for *other* ˆthings and forˆ woosted & spinninge to my daughter Condy	0+08-4
until August the third spent every way	0+09-0
Item spent untill August 17th & for letters from London	0+8-10
Item for worke & houshold stuffe to J Sheere	1+10-*0*
Item for a hatt to Stephen Toller which my daughter Condy bought for me	0- 8-6
Sic finitur Annus 62us vitae meae	5-15-4

---

[1] 'Inkle': linen tape for fastenings, here used to make curtains and valances.

18 August 1664 – 17 August 1665

[fo. 44r *continued*]

August the 18th 1664 beginneth the 63rd yeare of mine age

When shall thy kingdome come? Father thine cry,
Send forth thy light & trueth or else we die.
We waite & looke hard for a good reply,
come comfort us in this our misery.
           To see Christ inthronized, tis our hearts desire
           O Jesus King of Saints make speede trim up thy quire,
That Halelujahs may be sung in praise,
When thou (Jehovah) thy low cause shall raise.

[fo. 44v]

1664 ætatis 63   I Began this Sixty Third yeere of my age with prayer

a[u]gust 18th day
I began to reade the Bible this morning in the family from Genesis &c

The mony past in the other page as due to my Son Condy I do keepe in my hand
    untill we come to account for anuity of the Mills in dolvine, & for £60 of mine
    in his hand

So I owe £2-11s-04d to my Son Condy   which is charged in the other page
                                  in the Columne of disbursment*s*
which with 2-15- 4 besids which I have in house
maketh just 5- 6-08   £ s d
                   I say I have in house in all 05-06-08
    whereof (as is above written) 2-11-4 is owed to my Son Condy

August. 27 Received of my Daughter Condy, as from Em[ma] doidge
    long ago[.] Received of John Doidge (as he affirmes) by her   00-05-00
Sept. 6th Em[ma] Doidge brought 9s-6d all is paid untill midsommer
    last I allowed her 6d for 2 yeares rent paid to the Portreeve[1]   00-09-06

Sept. 28th Received of S Condy upon account for the Anuity of the
    Mi[l]les &c paying all upon his booke except for the hatt of which
    he knew not the price   0-15-00
                                             6-16-02

---

1 'Portreeve': the 'boroughreeve' or 'Lord of the Borough', the chief executive officer of the town,
    elected from the Court Leet. Tavistock was governed as a manor within the estates of the earl of
    Bedford, through the Court Leet, where the earl's steward presided (Hopkins, 'Thomas Larkham's
    Tavistock', pp. 157–66).

[fo. 44r *continued*]

Men by their trades expect to be maintain'd
But tis my lot by faith to be sustained.
This following yeare is Climactericall
under thy foreapointments I must crawle.
Thou God & father of my Lord & Christ
I daily waite to have my soule dismist
But faine I desir[e] thee to remove thy rod
And breake in peices all thy foes, O God.[1]

[fo. 44v]

paid for knitting worst[ed] stockens to my ^wife^	0- 2- 0[2]
spent unto August 26th	0- 5- 4
untill Sept the first & second	0- 5- 8
for sacke 1s 4d bunnes 6d Sept.14th	0- 1-10
paid Sept 16th to the shop of St:[ephen] Rundle	0- 2- 4
spent in houskeepinge untill then	0-10- 0
spent untill Michaelmas	0-06- 6
paid for clothes ^carriage^ by Drake	0- *0*- 9
Given at Hexworthy[3] to servants	0- 0- *1*
given to [*illegible*] when I had the horse of Steven Rundle	0- 0-02
Untill Sept 29th	1-14-08

Hactenus auxiliatus est Dominus
Tu qui fecisti ut experirer angustias multas
et malas, rursus vitae restitues me: et ex abyssis
terrae reduces me. //vox fidei//[4]

Sept. 29 laid out in toyes for children	00-00-06
30th for letters p[er] post & from Plimouth	00-00-09
October 3rd paid Mrs County a quarters rent	00-15-*00*

---

[1] Larkham once again wrote verses to mark his birthday, and set lofty spiritual sentiments (on the left) alongside personal aspirations (on the right). He took the common view that the 63rd year of life was the 'grand climacteric', a particularly critical and dangerous time (*OED*, 'climacterical').

[2] The binding is tight: the italicized figures are conjectured.

[3] Thirteen miles east of Tavistock, on Dartmoor.

[4] 'Thus far the Lord hath holpen. "Thou, which hast shewed me great and sore troubles, shalt quicken me again, and shalt bring me up again from the depths of the earth": the voice of faith.' Larkham recalled Psalm 70:20 (here cited from KJV).

The above mentioned summe of £2-11s-4d which I owed to my son
   Condy being allowed to me upon account ut supra (except for a
   Hatt which I am to pay for when Steven Toller sends the price
   of it) and the 1-14-8 in the other Columne deducted I have in
   house Sept. 29ᵗʰ   5-01-06

Sept. 30. D.C. & J.S. brought unto me[1]   0-15-00
Octob. 3ʳᵈ Received of S.R[2] for improvement of Money untill
   Sep. 29ᵗʰ last   0-15-00
Octob. 4 received of Eustace Peeke for Michaelmas quarters rent   0-06-08
                                                                             6-17-02

               whereof laid out for rent, wages, baking &c which
               belongeth to the former quarter 1-2-3d remaineth
               hitherto in house towards expenses henceforward   £5-14-11

Oct 17ᵗʰ
I had of S.M.*B*   1-00-00
I had of C.R.B   0-10-00
I had for a Collection 5-5d to be dd to DD[3]   0-05-05

Octob. 19ᵗʰ whereas Thomas Tillam owed me for rent for 14 quarters
   due last Michaelmas £4-13s-4d and for 3 capons for 3 yeares last
   Xtide[4] 3s in all £4-16s-4d. I received this day by the hands of his
   wife three pound in payment & allowed 3s which he laid out (as
   he saith) for 3 months taxe. I say received   £3-03-00
               Since October the 4ᵗʰ Summa Hactenus of receipts   10-10-04[5]

Octob. 26ᵗʰ. T. Miller my Grandchild came to me.
   My father shew what with him I shall do,
   and still shew me the way that I shall go.

Received of the Tenement in Bannawell[6] for rent   0- 3- 4
   there is yet due for 2 quarters more 3s-4d
                                                                            10-13- 8

1   David Condy and John Sheere, deacons of the church (usually identified either by initials or as
    'the deacons'). He first noted that these two brought money in August 1658 (fo. 31v). In 1672,
    Condy's house was licensed for worship under the Declaration of Indulgence: 'The howse of Dav:
    Coude at Tavestock' (congregational) and 'the new meeting house of David Condy at Tavystock in
    Devon' (presbyterian). G. Lyon Turner, *Original records of early nonconformity under persecution
    and indulgence*, 3 vols. (London, 1911–14), I, pp. 540, 566.
2   Stephen Rundle.
3   'S.M.B.' not identified, but a further gift of 10s is noted on fo. 45v . 'C.R.B' may be Colonel Robert
    Bennet. 'To be dd to DD' is perhaps 'to be delivered to the deacons' (he uses 'DDⁿˢ' on fo. 46r).
4   'Christ-tide': the quarter from 25 December to 24 March.
5   A tiny note alongside reads (possibly) '£9-0s-0d after Oct 21'.
6   John Wynne's map of 1752 marks 'Bannawell' on the site of today's Bannawell Street, Tavistock.
    'Tavistock 1752: the Tavistock Wynne Map Heritage Project', www.tavistock1752.co.uk.

paid Richawrd for a quarters wages	00-05-00
October 4 paid for Baking last quarter to E.P.[1]	00-01-00
	01-02-03

first weeke of this quarter ended the 7th day of October In which I spent	00+05-0[?][2]
paid son Condy for letters from London	00+00-1[?]
for 14 seames of turfs bought of T. Flesh[man]	00+10-0[?]
given to 2 collections	00+01-0[?]
Laid out from ˆthence toˆ Octob. 14th	00+03-0[?]
Given to a house where I lodged	00+00-0[?]
from October 14th to October 21	00+ 5-0[?]
October 20 given where I lodged a night	00+00-0[?]
October 21 begins another weeke laid out	00+02- 9
Summa Hactenus	[??-10 -??][3]

October 22 paid Cosen Rundle owed on his booke for smaleware[4]	00+01-06
paid (for little table folded double) to J Sheere	00+07-06
I gave to Mart[in] his man bringing it home	00+00-04
October 28 delivered for the market	00+03-02
	00-12 - 6

Oct. 29 paid D.S.[5] for makinge a dublet & breeches for. T. Miller		00+03-0[?]
for Pockets paid William Gee		00+00-0[?]
~~the cloth 10s other things~~ [illegible] 6s		~~00-16- 00~~
the odde groate[6] I delivered to Miller		00+00- 4
so I laid out just 20s upon him at first		
I paid for sugar & other things to S. Rundle		00+03-10
Paid for halfe a Sa[l]mon		00+01-03
November 4th laid out for provision		00-04-11
for sacke 8d. & strong beere at times		00+00-11
for a weekes pay to the Monthly taxe		00+00-01
November 11th Market day untill the next		00+05-00
Item delivered Nov 18th 2-4 & for capers 8d	00+03-00	
November 21 at a collection		0+ 0-06
November 24th paid Mr County		10+ 0-00
the same day being market & for the weeke untill Nex[t] market		0+04-10
paid for writing about the Apothe[cary]		00+ 2-00
kept for sacke at the conclusion &c		00+ 0-09

---

1 Eustace Peeke.
2 The pence column is hidden in the binding.
3 The figures have been heavily corrected and the binding is tight.
4 'Small-wares': haberdashery, wools (*OED*).
5 Daniel Sowton.
6 'Groat': 4d.

November 25th Received a debt of John Co[u]nty which was allowed in payment of £10	02-16- 0
Item Cos[en] Stephen Rundle paid for me which I am to account for when we come to account & is received of him	00-04- 0
Received out of the shop this first broken weeke besides 13d laid out in sugar & paper for the shop whereof my part is 6d ob.[1]	0- 4- 9
	3- 4- 9

> Adsit amoenitas Jehovae Dei nostri
> nobis; & opus manˆuˆum nostrarum
> institue in nobis: ipsum (inquam) opus
> manuum nostrarum institue./[2]

[fo. 45r][3]

november 18 1664

At the beg[inni]nge of this quarter remained	£7-12s-8d
Hactenus Received for this 2nd quarter	£3- 4s-9d

November 29th I had of my son Condy upon account which I borrowed	01-00-00
Received of D.C. & JS the same day[4]	01-00-00
Taken this weeke in the shop ended Dec 3rd for my part besides what paid for candles & bladders and in paper my part 10d	00-16-06
	13-13-11

Dec. 6th my S[on] C[ondy] being at Exon faire I invited his wife my daughter to supper & I beheld her & her 6 children according to Psal: 128.6. I saw then the only son of my eldest (undone) daughter (whom God hath preserved from many dangers). Let the other part be hastened: Peace upon Israel.[5]

Dec. 8. from my Tenants at Kirton by S[on] C[ondy]   2-17-06

Dec. 10th I was called up in the morninge at 4 a clocke to see the blazing starr. A signe (doubtlesse) of Gods displeasure for Englands sinnes.[6]

---

1 'ob': a halfpenny.
2 Larkham echoed Psalm 90:17 (KJV): 'And let the beauty of the Lord our God be upon us: and establish thou the work of our hands upon us; yea (I say), the work of our hands establish thou it.'
3 The upper third of this folio contains accounts by George Lane (1598), crossed through.
4 David Condy and John Sheere, as deacons of the church (see the similar entry on fo. 44v).
5 Larkham cited Psalm 128:6 (KJV): 'Yea, thou shalt see thy children's children, and peace upon Israel.' The first part of the psalm had been fulfilled: he looked on his grandchildren (including Thomas Miller). The second part – peace in Israel – was yet to come. His widowed daughter Patience seems to have been 'undone' by an unsuitable marriage: see 'Daughter Harries' (fo. 47r).
6 The great comet of 1664 is mentioned in records from around the world. English observers included Samuel Pepys and Isaac Newton. See http://www.pepysdiary.com/archive/1664/12/15.

paid for chimney Money[1]

00- *2-00*
10-13-01[2]

[fo. 45r]

Of this 2nd quarter on *the* other sid[e][3]

£10-13s-1d

From Novemb. 28th 1664 laid out
Inprimis for beare for wormwood beare | 00+01-08
I paid the odd 9d of the 33 pound 8s & 9d which remained due to
    Mr County | 00+00-09
Lent to T. Miller when he bought shoes | 00+01-10
Item for my smale barrell of table beare[4] | 00+00-07
Novemb. 29. 16 pound of Oile of Bayes[5] at 16d per pound 21s-4d
    [and] A pot of honey 2s-6d my part | 00+11-11
for a dripping pan of Earth[6] | 00+00-06
for mending the shoes of T. Miller | 00+00-08
December the 2nd market day delivered to bestow | 00+05-06
Dec. 4th at a collection I gave | 00+00-06
Dec. 6 my S[on] C[ondy] sent to Lyme to my sister & Jane Miller[7]
    which I allowed to him | 0+05-00
Item lent Tom Miller to send to his sister Jane | 0+01-00
Dec. 9th paid to Mr John County in p[ar]t it[erato][8] | 3+08-00
Dec. 9th laid out in the market &c | 0+05-11
Dec. 14th paid all due upon his shop booke for T. Millers cloathes, &
    my wives & other smale things | 2+05-09
Item paid him for my hatt he bought of S. Toller for me | 0+08-06

---

1   Hearth Tax.
2   The last line of the folio (with the total) is badly worn. The figure is supplied from Larkham's cross-reference on fo. 45r.
3   At the foot of fo. 44v.
4   'Table beer': weaker than strong beer or porter, stronger than small beer (*OED*).
5   'Oile of Bayes': the berries of the bay tree, used to make a butter-like substance (*OED*).
6   A ceramic pan to catch 'dripping' from roasting meat.
7   His granddaughter, sent to Lyme Regis to learn how to make bone-lace: see fo. 43v.
8   Here these common abbreviations could stand for 'part' or 'payment', and 'item' or 'iterato' (again).

Taken in the shop this weeke ended Dec 10th ^mint^[1]	00-11-00
besides my part laid out in Grommell[2] seede. 13d ob.[3]	
Received of Son Condy for anuity of the Mills	02-00-00
& for improvement of £60 from Mich. to Xtide[4]	00-18-00
Decemb 15th Received of Son Condy	15-00-00
Dec 16th I had of Ed Pike for rent out of Bannawell	00-03-04
Decemb. 17 Received this week out of the shop my part	
of things discharged that have beene bought in	00-11-00
Dec. 19th Rec of Em doidge for Michael:[mas] quarter	00-03-04
Dec. 22 Received of Son Condy more	15-00-00
Dec. 24. Received this weeke now ended out of the shop	00-10-00
Dec 27 Received of Eustace Peeke for a quarters rent	00-06-08
Dec. 29 Received of S: R[5] for improvement of Money this quarter	
past besides 4s I had Novemb. 25th last past	00-05-09
Dec. 31 out of the shop besids 2s-6d laid out for my part	00-05-00
Received & taken of my stocke	52-05-06[6]

I have in house
Jan. 2 only   9s-6d

[fo. 45v]

	£ s d
an° 1664 day[7]	
January the 2nd I had in house	00-09-06
January the 7th I borrowed of Son Condy	[illegible
^this is allowed before the £12-5s^	figures][8]
Received the same day of J Austin ^Rent^ for 2 quarters ended	
Dec 29th	00-08-04
Received out of the shop this weeke	00-04-06
Jan. 14. from C.B by Azarell[9] I had	01-00-00
O my God, accept Comfort, Blesse &c	
Guid[e] and direct thy servants.	
Jan 14 at Night out of the shop for this weeke	00-04-06

---

1 'Mint': actual money.
2 'Grommell': 'gromwell', 'the common name for any of the plants of the genus *Lithospermum* …
   characterized by hard stony seeds … formerly much used in medicine' (*OED*).
3 'ob': a halfpenny.
4 From Michaelmas to Christ-tide.
5 Stephen Rundle.
6 This was the total from the start of the quarter (including the interim total of £13-13s-11d).
7 As was his habit, Larkham kept 'an°' and 'day' from George Lane's original heading, but altered
   '1598' to the current year and crossed through the surname that headed Lane's column.
8 He crossed out the figures after he repaid the debt to Condy.
9 Azarel Condy, his granddaughter. 'C.B': possibly Colonel Bennet. An illegible line of text (crossed
   through) follows this.

Item paid Mrs Elizab. Rundle owing for smale ware[1]   0+04-00
Item paid Mr John County which I received of S[on] C[ondy]   15+00-00
Item paid for a quart of Brandy   00+01-00
Paid William Webb for wood   00+12-06
Dec. 16ᵗʰ Market day laid out   00+05-11
Dec 20 paid Daughter Condy for [e]*ll* canvas & inckle for Millers
    ˆaprons²   0+01-04
Item for an almanacke. iiᵈ & for sirrups &c for stopp[i]ng in
    stomakes 10d   +01-00
Item for beare taken in & sent for December 20ᵗʰ   00+00-08
paid the last £15 to Mr Jo[hn] County   15-00-00
Dec. 23ʳᵈ delivered for market & the week following   00-05-06
paid Eustace Peeke for baking the last quarter   00-01-00
paid Cosen Rundles shop booke Dec. 29ᵗʰ   00-02-05
the same day delivered & paid laid out about the house this weeke
    past, the more for some guests   00-*06*-06
to Mr John Counties man & maid servant each 6d   00-01-00
to Mrs County for rent ˆ15[s]ˆ *tokens paid* ˆ5[s]ˆ
    & Tom Miller ˆfor one wage 18dˆ³   01-01-06
for a paire of spectacles & case for my wife   00-00-06
Spent untill Jan. 1. | 51-16-00 | 51-16-*00*

[fo. 45v]

anᵒ 1664 day £ s d
January the 6ᵗʰ for me from Plimouth   00-04-04
Laid out in the market & provision this weeke   06-08
given to W. Webs maid that bro[ught] a Turky   00-00-04
Item laid out in provision untill Jan. 16ᵗʰ   00-04-00
Item paid D.S. for making cloathes for my wife   00-03-*00*
Item D.S *fortsat* dimitter⁴ & Tape & made drawers for me   00-00-06
given to Azarell bringing a token from C.B.⁵   00-00-06
paid for Beare taken in three times   00-01-09
Item for a quart of Brandy 11d & in strong Beare 7d   00-01-06
Item delivered to pay for milke breade fruite, & to bestow this market
    day Jan 20ᵗʰ   00-06-06
Jan 22 given at a Collection   00-00-06

---

1   Haberdashery, wools (*OED*).
2   Aprons for Tom Miller, for work at the apothecary. 'Ell': 45 inches of canvas. 'Inkle': linen tape.
3   The first payment to Tom Miller for his work at the shop.
4   'Dimity', a strong cotton fabric used for making 'drawers' (a garment for the lower body, not
   necessarily underwear) amongst other things. It was common to categorize fabric by a descriptor
   related to its origin. At this point 'dimity' usually came from Lancashire, but the word conjectured
   as 'forstat' may refer to 'Fostat', the suburb of Cairo from which 'fustian' (a similar coarse cotton
   cloth) perhaps took its name. The word 'dimity' itself may be derived from 'Damietta', an Egyptian
   port. (See *DTGC* 'dimity', 'fustian'.) 'D.S.': Daniel Sowton, tailor.
5   Azarel, his granddaughter; 'C.B.' perhaps Colonel Robert Bennet (this parallels an entry opposite).

Jan. 20. a widdow M.G.[1] (Lord accept it) brought	00-01-00
Jan. 21 Received out of the shop this weeke	00-06-00
Jan. 28 Received out of the shopp	00-10-00
Feb. 4 from Mrs White by J S.[2]	00-05-00
the same day out of the shop	00-07-06
Feb 11th I cast up account with my daughter Condy and owe upon account which is for so much received of Son Condy[3]	12-05-04
Feb 11th I Received out of the shop	00-6s-6d
Received from London & so allowed as from Mr King by Mr Chappell paid or to be paid to Mr Syndry & is deducted as at so much paid to Son Condy	02-13-0
I had to keepe for T. Miller Feb 11th 13s-6d in New Money besids £2-3s when ^53s^ is paid by Mr Chappell & allowinge 10s laid out by his unckle Condy for him	0-13-6
From J S.[4] Feb.11 at night	0-10-0
	19-18-8[5]

I have in house to begin the third quarter just 46s   £2-6s   £2-06s-00d
and in New money which is T M[6] - 13-6d besids 43s expected from
  London for him 10s of the 53s being paid by me to his unckle.

	Received since
Feb. 18 out of the shopp	00-08-00
Feb 20 I had out of the shop in the begining of the weeke	00-06-00
Feb 25th Item received out of the shop the sam[e] weeke	00-04-00
Feb 27th borrowed of Son Condy	00-05-00
Feb 28th I had of my Son Condy	00-05-02
So he oweth me upon account £17 if he Receive £2-13s from London otherwise he oweth but £14-07s to me out of the money had *of* mine which was in all £30 for I received in paiment for my wives Wascot soape silke & thread	00-04-06
out of the Apothecary shop March 3rd friday	00-05-00
Item the 4th day out of the Shop	00-05-00

---

[1] Probably Mary Gibb.

[2] John Sheere, deacon.

[3] Around this time, on the penultimate folio of the manuscript, Larkham also 'cast up accounts' for linen:

  What I have in house. Feb. 1664 of linnen
    4 paire of sheetes ordinary for use
    3 paire of better sheetes
    7 paire & an odd one of Pillowbeares
    one diaper table clothes. 2 diaper table napkins
    2 larger table clothes of fine canvas & 12 table napkins
    2 little canvas table clothes & 5 old table Napkins & 3 old Towelles
   At Lyme 2 paire of sheetes 1 paire of Pillowbeares
    6 Table napkins & 3 hand Towelles
   these things with other goods were brought home in Aprill 1665 & Jane Miller returned home.

[4] John Sheere, deacon.

[5] This should be £20-4s-8d, 6s more. Possibly he overlooked 6s (the 6s-6d had been heavily corrected).

[6] Thomas Miller's.

Jan. 27. Market day laid out this weeke & now	00-02-10
Feb. 1. paid for 3 seames of Hard wood	00-04-00
Feb. 3rd market laid out this weeke & Now	00-03-08
Item the same day for a pecke of wheate	00-01-08
Item for 2 seames of Turffes	00-01-08
Item paid William Web for 2 seames of hard stickes	00-02-07
Feb. 10th Market day. 5s-1d. 1s-3d	00-06-04
Feb. 11th to the Boy when he trimmed me	00-00-06
paid Mr Pearse for goods bought of him which was sent to the	
barbadoes & for charges for my part, he adventuringe the other	09-01-04
paid my daughter Condy for the halfe of another parcel which was	
sent to the Barbados	3-09-00[1]
~~to barber charged in the house for the boy~~	~~00-10-00~~[2]
Item which was for shirts & smockes thread inckle sope	01-02-00
[*other words illegible (deleted)*]	
Feb. 17th the last market of this second quarter of the 63rd yeare of	
my age ˆIˆ laid out to pay debts to shops & for beare	0-04-00
	16-19- 2

Feb the 18th (which is tomorrow if I live so long)	I lived untill the day
beginneth the 3rd quarter of the 63rd yeare of mine age	following God be praised

paid for Bacon 6 pound good weight	00-02-06
Delivered to T. Miller to pay for goods for the shop	02-10-00
given to servants when I lodged from home Feb. 21	00-00-08
laid out this week. 10d 6d & 5s-6d & 2s 1s Feb. 25th	00-09-10
for making a night wascot for my wife	00-00-08
Feb. 27 paid my part in Hogs grease for the shop	00-05-04
& to Thomas Miller I delivered upon account	00-01-00
Feb. 28 paid for shagg for my wives night wascot & Galloon lace[3]	00-03-08
& for soape 8d. & for silke & threed 2d	00-00-10
Mutton. 15d oyle 5d market & owed 3s-6d & 18d	00-06-08
March 5th to a collection	00-00-04
March. 10th market day & for this weeke past	00-04-10
[*blot*] paid Lanti[4] (which he saith) he sent to Lyme	00-05-00
for a Letter from S.G.[5] 5d & shoes for wife. 2s-3d	00-02-08
had for a pint of Canary[6] given to Mr T Pointer	00-00-06
March 17th market day & the weeke past	00-06-11
paid for an electuary[7] for stopping in my stomake	00-04-06

[1] Larkham had sent one of his grandsons to Barbados in 1664: see fo. 43v.
[2] Larkham crossed out this line, then marked it 'stet', i.e. let it stand.
[3] A 'night waistcoat' for warmth, made of 'shag' (long-piled fabric). 'Galloon lace' was narrow ribbon or braid of gold or silver or silk thread (*OED*).
[4] Lanti or Lansy, Daniel Condy's serrvant.
[5] Probably 'Son George' (Larkham).
[6] 'Canary wine': 'a light sweet wine from the Canary Islands' (*OED*).
[7] 'Electuary': 'a medicinal compound in which the ingredients were bound with honey or some equivalent syrup, or with wine' (*DTGC*).

March 7th from T. M.[1]	00-02- 6
March the 10th A.E.[2] of Lamerton gave me	00-05-00
March the 11th out of the Apothecary shop cleere receipts	00-10-04
March 13 of Em dodge for Xtid quarter[3] last abating 3d which was laid out for the head rent	00-03-01
March 17th of S. M. B[4]	00-10-00
March 18[th] endeth this weeke Rent of the shop	01-14-00
March 21 Received of T Tillam (who [*oweth*] me March 25[th] next 20s)	01-06-08
	06-14-03

[fo. 46r]

March 25[th] beginneth the yeare 1665
and Continueth the third quarter of the sixty third yeare of mine age if
the Lord will Mis[ere]re mei et meorum[5]

an° 1665 this day, In house, £3-vs[6] remaineth.

March the 25[th] Received out of the shopp	01-00-00
Received of Stephen Rundle out of moneys he hath	00-09-09
Received of Eustace Peeke for last quarters rent	00-06-08
March 31. received out of the shopp	01-05-00
Aprill 7[th] out of the shopp	16-06
Received of Mr John Conte for the boyes ^Diet^ Diet untill March 25th last past his part[7]	01-00-00
Untill Aprill 12th receipts	08-02-11[8]

	£	s	d
My Son Condy delivered to Richard Drake upon my account to pay for the Casting of the greate Mortar[9] and is acknowledged to be received by me			04-00-00

1　Thomas Miller.
2　Not identified.
3　Emma Doidge, for Christ-tide quarter (25 Devember–24 March).
4　Not identified. In October 1664 this person had given Larkham £1 (fo. 44v).
5　The heading runs across the whole folio. The Latin phrase, written over Lane's heading, means 'Have mercy on me and mine'.
6　'£3-5s.'
7　County's share in Thomas Miller's maintenance. The line beneath this is illegible (deleted).
8　This total is hard to make any sense of: the figures for receipts above add up to £4-19s-11d; with the interim total in the left column of the previous folio (£6-14s-03d) the total should be £11-14s-02d.
9　'Great Mortar': a phrase in common use. Apothecaries had mortars and pestles of different sizes and materials (metal, stone, wood) for grinding different substances (*DTGC*). This one was of cast metal – brass or iron. In his list of expenses for the shop Larkham referred to payment for his part of 'the greate Morter & Pestell' (see Appendix 3); below, Larkham referred to the purchase of an 'iron pestle' (fo. 47r).

This weeke ended March 24th which was market day spent & laid
    out in provisions

<u>00-09-04</u>
<u>05-15-05</u>

Hactenus auxiliatus est Do[m]i[n]us[1]

[fo. 46r]

an° 1665 day	£	s	d
March 25 paid Richawd[2]	00	05	00
Delivered to Thom Miller to his use	00	06	00
Item delivered in full satisfaction of wages for the ¼	00	01	06
To St[ephen] Rundles shop. 3s wood & sacke 2s	00	05	00[3]
paid Mrs Contes for a ¼ for my house now ended	00	15	00
Laid out about wine for *Kirton Cosens*	00	03	*02*
Item this weeke ended March the 31st	00	08	00
paid for Baking the last quarter	00	01	00
for a digestive drinke & syrrup of violets[4]	00	01	09
for chymny mony paid Aprill 2nd	00	02	00
given to a collection April. 3rd	00	00	06
for hard[wood] & fagots of each one seame	00	02	06
Item laid out this weeke ended. Aprill 7th	00	07	06
Lent to T Miller. 4.6. & laid out untill Aprill 12th. 2s-6d	00	07	00
Paid for my part of the great Mortar & for bringing from Exeter, for rent for the shop and garden & for my part in pretious stones[5]	04	17	00
Untill Aprill 12th Disbursements all even	08	02	11

---

[1]   A frequent comment: 'Thus far the Lord hath holpen.'
[2]   Richawd Allen, the Larkhams' maid.
[3]   The next line has been deleted and is illegible.
[4]   'Syrup of violets': made from flowers, 'to cool any heat or distemperature in the body, either inwardly or outwardly' (*DTGC*).
[5]   Stones like lapis lazuli, which contained sulphur, were used in small quantities in medicine (*DTGC*).

Aprill 14th received out of the shop £1-12s whereof paid for my
    part in 3 quarters of a lb of sugar £1-11s received cleere   00-01-00
I allowed my selfe againe out of the London money that 4-6 I lent.
    T. Miller   00-04-06

Aprill. 15 I have in all in my Custody of T. Millers   ~~I had a shilling of him I have~~
    mony new [word crossed out] just 1s   ~~17s of his of new money~~

all accounts ballanced untill this daye
The same day I received of Son Condy   03-03-00
    And casting accounts & paying all his demands He hath of mine
    in his hand just £10
Received since upon account 20s whereof T. Miller allowed 10s
    which Mr Davies of Waterford delivered to Patience my
    Daughter[1]   1-00-00
Aprill. 22th received out of the shop, besids disbursements &
    paiments for necessaries & debts   <u>00-16-00</u>
                                   <u>08-04-06</u>[2]

Aprill 24th I remembered with thankfullnes the Lords preserving me now a whole
    yeare since my last returne (after a long absence) for feare of enimies. O my
    father heare the cry and pity the condition of a poore father in regard of his
    children and childrens children. Amen Amen.[3]

I have in house. £4-17s-08d & 17s of ˆT Millersˆ new money in
    p[ar]t of pay of 20s, whereof his mother had 10s. ut supra.[4] In all   5-14-08
I have againe the 3s ˆfrom T Millerˆ & allowed in paiment of
    money the 20s I lent Mr Contie   1-03-00
Received in allowance of paiment of S. Rundle   20-00-00
Received my part of the debts upon the booke which I sold to Mr
    John Contie for £10   05-00-00
Received in money towards my paiment & discharge of rent &
    wages &c June 24th next which is wholy to be discharged from
    Apr. 25th by me.   01-10-00
Received for my part of what was sold to Mr Kelly out of the shop
    & towards all paiments & for all reckonings betweene Mr Countie
    & me untill April 25th 1665.   <u>01-02- 4</u>
                  Now the shop is wholy mine.   <u>34-10- 0</u>

Aprill 26th I had out of my shopp   00-11-00
Item at the end of the same week April 29th   00-14-06
I received then of DD^{ns} O mi Deus accipias oro[5]   03-00-00

---

1   Below this he crossed out three lines, now illegible, about a debt (subsequently repaid).
2   This should be £9-4s-06d.
3   This entry runs across both columns, left and right
4   This entry also runs across both columns.
5   'O my God, accept, I pray.' 'DD^{ns}' is probably an abbreviation for deacons: he received £3 from the
    church.

	£ s d
paid for 3 moneths assessment	00-01-00
Paid. R. Drake for bringinge Jane Miller &c	
who came Aprill the 12th towards evens	00-04-00

paid for 3 moneths assessment — 00-01-00

Paid. R. Drake for bringinge Jane Miller &c
    who came Aprill the 12th towards evens — 00-04-00

spent about house & paid to shops untill Aprill 15th — 00-09-11

Aprill. 15th I put among T. Millers money in full quittance out of the
    London £2-13s. paying all his debts for clothes, barbers boxe &
    4 ob[1] owed me and one New shilling to make up his money 17s — 00-02-06

of which 10s was allowed in that 20s Mr Davies paid to his mother
    the other I gave to her which [illegible words, crossed out] — 00-10-00

So T. Miller oweth me 3s because I delivered him another 10s Aprill
    the 18th when I lent 20s to the Dr as he did that cost — 01-03-00

untill Aprill 21 being market day, & that day in victualls beere fish
    Brandy & other necessaries — 00-13-05

for 3 pints of white wine to make an Apoth:[2] for J: Miller — 00-01-02

Aprill 22 for a paire of leatherin Buf[f]g[l]oves[3] paid — 00-02-00

Aprill 25th paid Mr John Contie in p[ar]t for his moyety[4] of the
    Apoth:[ecary] shop — 33-10-0

spent since in wine & beere for this part of the weeke past and for
    Phisicke for Jane Miller (besids my part) before I tooke the whole
    which was allowed to Mr Contie for the whole besides the white
    wine (ut supra) was 8s — 00-06-07

Laid out this weeke ended Aprill 29th more — 00-07-04½

paid John Sheere for a standing Bedstead — 00-10-00

Item paid for carriage of beddin[g] & Trunkes &c — 00-10-09

Item paid T. Miller for halfe wages for this quarter — 00-10-00

Delivered to my Daughter Condy to send to sister at Lyme — 00-07-04

for R. Row about my Garden & for some seedes — 00-01-06½

Laid out this weeke ended May the 5th — 00-14-11

for a matt for a bed paid Anthony Mathews — 00-00-10

paid for 4 dozen of Peta[5] to Mr Wats 3s wood & Turffes 3s-1d — 00- 6-01

Item for beere and provision this weeke ended May 12th — 00-12-06

& to provide for the house untill May 18th which begins the last
    quarter of the 63rd yeare of mine age — 04-[??- ??][6]

                                        spent [illegible] — [??- ??- ??]

---

1   'ob': halfpenny.
2   'Apothecary' in the now obsolete sense, 'a treatment by drugs' (OED).
3   'Letherin': 'leathern' (OED). 'Buff-gloves' is a conjecture.
4   A part-payment for the 'moiety' (half) of the shop belonging to County.
5   Peat (OED).
6   The edges of the manuscript are worn.

May the 6th out of the shop received	01-12-11
May the 9th I Tooke out of the money chest in the shop	00-11-00
May the 9th received for rent out of Bannawell	00-03-04
Item at the ende of the weeke received out of the shop	00-10-00
In all 41-12-09	07-02-09

[fo. 46v]

1665   If the Lord will May the 18th beginneth the fourth quarter
of the Sixty and third yeare of mine age[1]

an° 1665 day

Hactenus auxiliatus est Dominus.
Deus, docuisti me a pueritia[m] mea[m], et
huc usq[ue] indicavi mirabilia tua. quare
etiam tantisper dum senex & canus sum Deus,
ne derelinquas me, &c.[2]

I have £3-18s-^10d^ in house remaining of what hath already beene
sent me from God I say 3 pound 15s & 10d. Hitherto &c

May the 19th Received out of the shop.	01-06-06
I had of S.R. before he paid Mr John Contie	00-03-00
Received of S. Condy. May 25th	10-00-00
May 27th Received this weeke out of the shop	02-09-00
May 29th of S.M.B.	00-10-00
	14-08-06

This day it was told me that yesterday the 28th of May yong Preston of Maritavy
officiating at Tavestocke pronounced me Excom: by authoritie from yong Fulwood
now Ar[ch]Deacon of Totnes. Consider O Lord these fooles and pitty them for they
know not what they doe. Suffer not thy greate name to be (SO) taken in vaine.[3]

Received out of the shop this weeke with Mr Conties bills June 3rd	2-12- 9
Received out of the shop this weeke June 10th & in allowance to	
Mr Contee of medicines	1-15- 0

---

1   The heading runs across the top of the folio.
2   'Thus far the Lord hath holpen. God, you have taught me from my childhood, and until now all the
time I have pointed out your wonderful works. Why therefore so long as I am old and white-haired,
may you not, O God, abandon me.' Larkham recalled Psalm 71:17–18 (KJV): 'O God, thou hast
taught me from my youth: and hitherto have I declared thy wondrous works. Now also when I am
old and grayheaded, O God, forsake me not; until I have shewed thy strength unto this generation,
and thy power to every one that is to come.'
3   Luke 23:24 and Exodus 20:7 (KJV). 'SO' is Larkham's stress. The Diocese of Exeter's Episcopal
Return, 1665, reported that in 'Tavistock … Tho: Larkeham thence ejected … stands Excommunicate'
(Lyon Turner, *Original records*, I, p. 179).

[fo. 46v]

I have paid for a paire of shoes for Jane Miller 2s-10d & for mending ˆan old paireˆ 6d	00-03-04
I paid Mr *wascot* for candlestick[,] Pint, and halfe Pynts for the shop of lattin[1]	00-01-00
to the Pewter for halfe a pint, quarter of a pint & halfe quarter of a pint of pewter	00-01-00
paid Cos. Steven Rundle for the other part of sugar the other part being paid for on account before	01-11-00
for a paire of shoes for myselfe	00-04-00
for a new skillet & an iron frame	00-04-08
paid for little juggs for the shopp	00-00-10
Laid out this first weeke & paid at shopps	00-09-07
May 25th paid to Mr John Countie	10-00-00
Laid out this second ˆweekeˆ and paid at shops	00-10-00
May the 28th at a collect[i]on	00-00-04
May 30th paid D. Sowton for making a Wascot for my wife of Calaminco[2] & for stuffing & Bone &c	00-05-00
this weeke ended June 8th laid out	00-14-06
June 2nd I gave to Jane Miller a new halfe crowne	00-02-06
June 3rd paid to Mr County in p[ar]t[3] of what I owe I owe ˆhimˆ only £5 this day. Besids Dennyes Bills unpaid	06-00-00
Paid Mr Countie more June 9th in medicines	01-00-00
Laid out this weeke which will ende June 15th	00-09-03
and for wood & turffes the same 15th day of June	00-02-03
from June 15th unto the two & twentieth Day	00-07-00[4]
June 19th given to Thomas Miller part of his wages	00-05-00
June 20th paid one Moneths taxe for Fords land	00-00-04
Laid out the same time for Mrs Countie for a moneths taxe	00-00-*10*
Paid to Mr Countie in medicines	00-09-11
paid to Thomas Miller in full for midsomer quarter[5]	00-05-00
from June 22nd unto the end of that weeke	00-08-02

---

[1] 'Lattin': 'latten', 'a mixed metal of yellow colour … identical with or closely resembling brass' (*OED*).

[2] 'Calamanco': 'woollen stuff from Flanders, glossy on the surface, and woven with a satin twill and chequered in the warp, so that the checks are seen on one side only' (*OED*).

[3] Or 'p[aymen]t'.

[4] Below this he deleted a line of text.

[5] This completed the part payment noted a few lines earlier.

June 17th out of the shop (besides also the soap sugar & other things paid for) cleere	0-13- 0
June 24th 25s-6d & allowed for medicines which Mr John Contee had this weeke in all 9s-11d the whole of this weekes receipts	1-15- 5
June 27. Received of Eustace Peeke	0-06- 8[1]
out of the shop I had this June 27th[2]	0-04- 6
Item John Bennet paid which he owed to the shop	0-01-06
Item from Killington[3] June 28 (with that last lent to Mr Contee)	0-08-00
Item June 30th in Phys.[icall][4] druggs for Mr Contee Received	0-05-01
Item out of the shop the same day	0-13- 0
Received of Son Condy upon account	1-10- 0
Received out of the shop viz from Killington 11[s]-6d allowing 9d I paid for roses	0-10- 9

I heard June the 6th that my Daughter Patience was at Appledore.[5]
O Lord Helpe

Item July the eight I had out of the shopp	0-06-02
Received of J.S.	0-15-00
July 10th Received of John Austine for 2 quarters rent ended at Midso[mme]r allowing 4d paid for head rent for the last yeare ended last Michaelmas	0-08-00
my daughter Miller delivered to me at her coming with Clogg July 12th 16s whereof I paid him for bringing her from Bideford.^&c^ 2s-6d rest[6]	0-13-06
I had of T. Miller which he tooke at Killington	0-07-06
Received more at the end of the weeke out of the shop	00-14-00
from Killington for medicines. July the 19th	00-06- 9
I had to drinke wine of R.H. [illegible words]	00-01- 0
I had of Mr Moore for my quilted wascots stuff[7]	01-00- 0
received out of the shop this weeke	00-10- 0
Killington & the shop went to paying. Cos. Rundle 7s-10d which was owed for things about the shop & August 5th 5s of receipts appointed to pay W. Web for roses brought me from M[rs] *Whiting*[8]	0- 5-*00*
Received out of the shop & from Killington this weeke	00-19-10
	[?- ?- ?][9]

1 Rental income.
2 Larkham bracketed this and the following four items together.
3 'Killington': probably Callington, Cornwall, eight miles south-west of Tavistock. In 1665, Larkham made frequent reference to money from Killington, where his grandson Thomas Miller seems to have been running an apothecary as a subsidiary to the Tavistock business.
4 'Physicall': medical. He used the same phrase unabbreviated elsewhere.
5 Appledore, close to the port of Bideford: a landing point in north Devon for ships from Ireland.
6 'Rest': remainder.
7 Fabric.
8 Perhaps 'Mrs White' who sent 5s in February 1664/65 (fo. 45v).
9 At the foot, the folio has worn away.

Item for a seame of Hard wood	00-01-06
Item to Mrs Contie to make up midsomer quarter	00-14-0[?]
paid for baking this quarter ended June 24th	00-01-00
paid Richawrd my servant for midsomer quarter 0	0-05-00
paid to Mr Contie which he borrowed of T. Miller at Killington	00-05-0[?]
paid to Mr Contie June 30th in Physicall druggs	00-05-0[?]
paid Cos Rundle upon Mr Counties order & to his account	00-10-0[?]
paid for a post letter from London & plimouth	00-00-0[?]
for Houshold expenses untill the sixth of July	00-11-0[?]
for bringing 2 cheeses from Beddiford paid old Clog	00-00-02
paid July the 7th to Stephen Rundles shop for *food* spice candles	
soape vineger which was owed	00-02-*02*
for household expenses untill July 13th	00-09-02
Item allowed to Mr Contie in medicines	00-06-00
July 19th paid for wood & turffes	00-02-06
for household expences untill July the 20th	00-09-02
Item to the shop for smale ware. Paid in the same weeke also ˆtoˆ	
S Rundle	00-01-07
July the 22nd paid 3 moneths taxe	00-01-*08*
July 27th paid Mr Contee in money whereof 7s-6d was for rent of	
the shop for a quarter ended last midsomer	00-17-*09*
	30-16-*05*

and 4s rest to pay of the £5 & 6s for moneys *Received*	
the odd 9d was allowed in *somthinge* of the shop	
All is even (except Denies Bills[1]) this present 27th July	
laid out this weeke in housekeeping July 27th	00-06-08
paid for 10 pound of coarse sugar to Mr Hernaman	00-05-00
August 3rd. Housekeeping 10s-10d. 10s untill August 10th	
11s-7d the last weeke	01-12-[05]
Sic finitur annus 63rd ætatis mea[2]	33-00-06

---

[1]   Henry Denny, who had provided supplies for the apothecary shop.
[2]   'So the 63rd year of my age comes to an end.'

18 August 1665 – 17 November 1669

[fo. 47r]

August the 18th 1665 Beginneth the 64th yeare of mye Age[1]
if I live untill the end of the yeare I shall see strange things.

Remaineth in house £02-05s-05d towards housekeeping
and expenses hence forward

O Christ which of the Church art the true Head
Raise up thy slaine witnesses from the dead.
Do thou Restore the nation Lord wee Cry
we pray we weepe we waite for a reply
cheare up our dropping hearts, drinke of the brooke
Lift up thy head, for thee we daily looke.

Receipts henceforward of all sorts.[2]

	£ s d
Allowed T. Miller for a [*illegible (deleted)*] he had to his owne use ^8d^ a ^little^ barrell he sold [*illegible (deleted)*]	0- 1-0
[*illegible (deleted)*]Received out of the shop at some odd times & lent to T Miller p[ar]tly[3]	0- 3-6
August 18[th] Received by William Dingle from Will Brownscombe for 2 quarters ended last March 25[th]	1- 0-0
from John Ma*cy* for 3 [*quarters*] untill Mids:[ummer]	0- 7-6
from S. Hi*mi*sh for a yeare ended Next Mich:	0-10-0
August 19[th] out of the shop	0-10-6
August 26[th] out of the shop	0-16-6
Sept the second out of the shop	0-13-6
Hactenus by Addition Rec[eived].	4-02-6
Sept. 9th out of the shop	0-05-6
At my returne Sept: 26 havinge beene absent 12 daies from home I received out of the shop for 2 weekes	0-16-0
Allowed in clearing accounts with my Son Condy for a quarters rent out of the Milles in Dolvin	2-00-0

---

1 This entry and the next run across the whole folio. 'Mye' has a line over it: perhaps 'myne'.
2 Exceptionally, Larkham organized this folio into three tightly packed columns. Most folios contain up to 800 words, but here Larkham squeezed in 1,350. He headed the columns 'Receipts henceforward of all sorts', 'Disbursments for clothes wages wood and such like things' and 'Disbursements about the house only'. This is the left column of three: for the quarter to 17 November 1665 the other two parallel columns are opposite and (to fit Larkham's entries into constraints of an edition) appear sequentially rather than side by side.
3 Or 'particularly'.

[fo. 47r]

{make hast   One halfe day more ˆourˆ Saviour Christ replyed
{o Beloved   Behold I quickly come. Tho now defyed
{come Lord Jesus   Ile rise and my friends shall get up with me,
{come quickly   my foes shall downe, this all shall shortly see.
{why is his Chariot   Downe Archtheife that hast robd on Gods highway
{so long in coming?   shall not God heare his Saints that daily pray?![1]

Disbursments for clothes wages wood and such like things[2]

paid for making a wascot for Jane Miller of stuffe[3]	00-02-06
Item for making a sarge[4] one	00-01-06
Item paid debts for. T Miller & allowed what he owed in p[ar]t[5] of Wages	00-04-06
paid J.S[6] for exchanging my truckle bed for a halfe head *bedstead* & a shelf in the parlour	00-02-00
humbly presented at a meeting[7]	00-00-06
for 3 seames of Turffs	00-02-06
for one seame of faggotts	00-01-00
A paire of shoes for Daughter Patience	00-02-10
for Alamode[8] for my Daughter Patience	00-08-06
for dowles[9] for 2 shifts for her	00-08-03

[1] Another poem probably written around this time appears on the penultimate page of the manuscript, following a note of expenses for the Apothecary shop dated 27 July 1665 (Appendix 3):

> O God faile not to build up thy Sion,
> destroy them that to it ˆdareˆ say fie on.
> O Lord make hast come quickly tarry not
> for all the world thy great workes have forgot.

[2] Middle column. The right column is listed below, not alongside this material as it is in the manuscript.
[3] 'Stuff': woven material (*OED*).
[4] 'Serge': woollen fabric (*OED*).
[5] Or 'p[aymen]t'.
[6] John Sheere.
[7] Probably a church meeting.
[8] 'Alamode': thin and glossy black silk (*OED* 'à la mode').
[9] 'Dowlas': coarse linen.

Received of Daughter Harries[1] which came out of the shopp
   allowing what she had laid out in mine absence untill
     November the 20[th]   5-17-9
Item of Eustace Peeke ¼ s rent   0- 6-8
I owe my Son Condy upon account (allowinge this quarter for the
   Milles in Dolvin which I have received ˆut supraˆ £5   5- 0-0
Received of John Brownsdon   0-10-0
Sent of some members of the Church By David Condy   0-16-6

                          Remaines & receipts in all   22- 0-4[2]

---

[1] Probably Patience, who came back to Tavistock and helped in the shop along with Thomas Miller. She had remarried, it seems disastrously. Larkham's will (written in June 1668) specified: 'My apothecary ware and utensils shall remain to the use of Patience my undone daughter yet so as it be managed … for her use that her husband may not have the wasting of it as he hath the rest of her estate'. A. G. Matthews's Notes of Nonconformist Ministers' Wills, Dr Williams's Library, London, MS 38.59, fos. 607–11.

[2] This is the quarterly total, comprising £15-12s-5d (the unstated sum of the receipts immediately above), the previous interim total of £4-2s-6d, and £2-5s-5d he had 'in house' on 18 August 1665.

paid Daughter Condy for midsommer ¼ for her garden August 26	00-02-06
for 2 Petticoats makinge	00-01-00
for my New coate & turninge my long coate & breeches	00-04-00
paid my wife upon T. Millers account	00-03-00
Item paid Bennet Sargent for making of Tho: Millers coate	00-03-00
Item for making a Wascot for my wife	00-01-08
Item in fair paid for. D.[aughter] Condies children	00-01-06[1]
Item to my wife to buy spectacles	00-00-04
Item for a steeling Iron[2]	00-01-04
August 29th for bringinge my Picture &c	01-00
& more for hooping of a barrel	00-00-08
Sept: 2nd for dowles for a ½ shirt[3] & threed	00-03-00
Item 2 frames for pictures & coates of armes	00-03-06
Item for making my daughter Patience wascot	00-01-04
for cloth for a smocke for Anne Miller[4]	00-02-06
for 2 heating irons for a steele for linnen	00-11
for New fitting my second Picture[5]	00-10-00
for mending mine owne shoes	00-00-03
Item lent T. Miller to helpe pay for shoes	00-00-06
paid a debt to Son Condy for Tho. Miller	00-16-10

whereof 9s is remaining due to him out of his quarters wages ended
    Sept. 29th so he oweth me 7s 10d towards his next quarter
    Dec 25th

Item paid him[6] for Jane Miller	00-13-02
Item paid him for other wages for my selfe & Daughter Miller[7]	02-18-06
paid Cosen Rundle for. T Miller	<u>01-02- 6</u>

    T. Miller at Xtide next (allowing 20s to him for this ¼)
    will owe me 10s-4d   <u>7- 7-01</u>[8]

Disbursments about the house only.[9]

August the 18th beginneth (being friday) the first weeke & ending.
    August 24th I delivered for this weekes expences whereof 17d
    was spent by my selfe in wine beare & *paid* about rent charges   00-10-07

---

[1] Jane Condy had six children: Larkham gave them 3d apiece. Tavistock's 'Goosey Fair', which began in the twelfth century and nowadays falls on the second Wednesday in October, used to run over three days from 29 to 31 August.

[2] A flat-iron in Devon dialect (*OED*).

[3] 'Half-shirt': a shirt front for a man or chemisette for women (*OED*).

[4] 'Smock' at this time meant 'a woman's undergarment; a shift or chemise' (OED). Larkham's granddaughter Anne had presumably come over with her mother Patience from Ireland.

[5] Larkham referred here and above to various pictures and coats of arms, but only one portrait of Larkham exists, engraved as a frontispiece for *Wedding-supper* (1652): see Plate 1.

[6] Daniel, 'Son Condy'.

[7] Probably 'Daughter Harries' on the previous page. He reverted here to her previous surname.

[8] This should be £9-7s-1d.

[9] Right column.

November the 18th
beginneth the second quarter of the 64th yeare of Mine age.

Remaines towards next quarter	01-15-08
Received out of the shop in my absence until January the 6th	3-08-06
besids what was laid out about my lease in Mine absence & for rent	
& an Iron pest[le]	2-01- 6
of Mrs Whitinge[3]	0-05- 0
Item by Cosen David some tokens[4]	0-12- 6
Jan 7th Received of Mr Brownsdon	0-10- 0
	8-05- 2
Tokens I received since	0- 5- 0
Received owed to the shop	0- 0- 4

---

[3] 'Mrs White' or 'Whitinge' had by this time sent 5s on several occasions.
[4] David Condy: the 'tokens' may have been from Larkham's flock.

& paid to the shop this weeke for ˆcandlesˆ soape & such like things

since	00-01-06
August 25. I tooke for expences this following weeke in all	0-05-05
Sept. 1 to the 8th 6s-6d besids 2s left of the last week	0-06-06
Sept. 8th beginneth the 4th weeke[1]	0-08-06
Sept 15th beginneth the 5th weeke laid forth to be expended	00-10-00
spent in my absence and at home untill Sept. 22nd ended[2]	0-04-00

untill November 20th all paid out of shopp receipts as followeth

laid out for a coate for Daughter Patience	9- 0
paid for baking last ¼ ended Sept. 29th	0- 1- 0
paid for rent for the garden	0- 2- 6
Paid Mrs County ¼s rent	0-15- 0
paid Richawrd for her ¼	0- 5- 0
paid for 3 Moneths taxe	0-01- 0
paid for spectacles & case	0-00- 6
paid for sugar to Dan Sowton	1-05- 0
paid for a Tray & Hogsgrease	0-07- 6
paid for carriage to Drake[3]	0-12- 6
paid for Polts[4]	0-04- 6
spent among servants	0-09- 0
laid out about the house 8 weekes untill Novem 20th	2- 8- 7
	10-07-07[5]
on the other Columne	7-07- *1*
	17-14-*08*
paid to Mrs Alice Contie for a quarter beforehand	02-10-*00*

November the 18th begineth the second ¼ for
expences about the house

			£ s d
Receipts with remains[6]	22- 0- 4[7]	Inprimis to 2 servants of C.S.R[8]	00-01-00
Disbursments of all kinds	20-04- 8[9]	Item where I lay next to the maide[10]	00-00-06

---

[1] A Friday. Larkham's custom was still to start the week with the weekday his birthday fell on.
[2] Larkham gave no clue about his whereabouts over the following two months.
[3] Larkham's payment to Drake suggests that part of his journey, at least, went east to Exeter and Lyme Regis: many entries show Drake carried goods and passengers that way, whereas 'old Clogg' plied the route to Bideford.
[4] 'Polts': probably 'pestles' for the apothecary shop rather than leeks for planting in his garden – though Larkham had sown leeks in earlier times (for both senses, see *OED*).
[5] This should be £9-7s-7d.
[6] 'Remainders'.
[7] Total receipts, carried over from the foot of the left column.
[8] Perhaps 'Cosen Steven Rundle'.
[9] Total disbursements of £17-14s-08d, listed in the two columns and summed up in the right column, below, and a further £2-10s paid to Mrs County.
[10] This is not an unlikely gift from Larkham to a bedfellow: a comma is required after 'next', and for 'lay' read 'stayed'.

I have by me Jan 18th £2 & 6d[1]

[fo. 47v][2]

	£	s	d
I have borrowed of Son Condy when I bought my horse & saddle after	2-00-		0
More Received since Diverse wayes	0-05-		8
February 20th I cleared my receipts	2-	0-	6
putting that on the other side to this which maketh just the sume of[3]	4-	6-	2

And so much as disbursed as in the other columne

---

[1]   This he centred at the foot of the folio, beneath all three columns.

[2]   Fo. 47v gives a picture of Larkham's fortunes after the Five Mile Act (October 1665) came into force. Under the Act, a nonconformist like Larkham risked a fine of £40 if he came within five miles of his former parish. The Diocese of Exeter's Episcopal Return in 1665 for Tavistock had already listed him as 'ejected', 'stands Excommunicate' (Lyon Turner, *Original records*, I, p. 179). On this folio, Larkham's entries are sporadic. The first entries follow from his reckoning on 18 January 1665/6, which was also the date he gave up the apothecary shop (see Appendix 3). He made jottings (not full accounts) in late February, after a month away from Tavistock in which he visited Liskeard, Cornwall. After this he made brief entries in May and July 1666, then nothing until April 1667 and nothing again until September 1667. He seems to have left the notebook in Tavistock and made brief entries on intermittent visits. On 30 September (at the foot of the right column) he marked his return to live in the town after 'many years' of 'wanderings'. Apart from the references to Liskeard he made no mention of where he had been. He put some of his apothecary utensils into store. Also, he bought a horse: a clear sign of plans to travel, to go by earlier horse-trading in the 1650s. Larkham's entries became more regular again after December 1667: it is unlikely to be a coincidence that this is the time when the earl of Clarendon's fall eased pressure on nonconformists.

[3]   'On': in the manuscript, 'one'. 'Just': exactly, precisely.

Remaines in my hand	01-15- 8	
Remaines upon account Jan 11ᵗʰ. in my hands I lodginge at my son Condys house	£4-02s-8d	paid for rent to Mr Contie 01-02-06
Received since as in the other Columne	0- 5- 4 4- 8- 0	

paid for rent to Mr Contie   01-02-06

Item for the garden to my   00-02-06
   Daughter Condy
Item for an Iron Pott paid   0-05-06
+ among servants when   0- 0-07
   ˆBrandy 4d givenˆ
I *have payed*¹ untill Jan 8ᵗʰ   0-06-00
laid out about my house   2-03-03²
given at Mr Sowton's to
   servants   00-00-08
          4-02-*10*

given to Daughter Patience   £2-00-[??]
paid Daniel Sowton for her   0- 6-[??]
given to servants   0-[??-??]

I have by me Jan 18ᵗʰ £2 & 6d³

[fo. 47v]

	£ s d
Feb. 15ᵗʰ paid for a little Nagg⁴	03-00-0[?]
Item Feb. 16ᵗʰ for a Saddle Bridle & girts⁵	00-12-00
since January the 18ᵗʰ in all laid out	
Item paid for mending my dublett at liscard⁶	0-01-0[?]
Item paid for making my ston gray coate to. W.R.⁷	0-02-0[?]⁸
Item paid for makinge gray sarge drawers	0-00-0[?]
Given at Liscard at severall times to the men & maidservants	0-06-0[?]
at Mrs Pomroyes & Cap*t* [*illegible*] each 6d⁹	0-01-00
I gave to my Wife at my depture from her Jan 20ᵗʰ	0-02-06
Hactenus Feb. 20ᵗʰ 1665/6	4-06-02

---

¹   A conjecture: the text is unclear.
²   From here downwards the edge is worn.
³   This appears at the foot of the folio beneath the three columns (for clarity, it is here as well as opposite).
⁴   A small horse or pony, not necessarily (as nowadays) old and feeble (*OED*).
⁵   'Girt': a saddle-girth, a leather strap to secure the saddle (*OED*).
⁶   Liskeard, Cornwall, fifteen miles from Tavistock.
⁷   Not identified.
⁸   Above and below Larkham crossed out lines of text. The binding is tight and hides the pence here.
⁹   'Pomroy' or 'Pomery' is a historic Liskeard surname. The second name is illegible – Kalnoith?

I have now in house other waies received which is by me   <u>0-15- 6</u>

What is received out of the Apothecaries shop hath satisfied many
   debts owing by my daughter Patience. viz
      to Richard Hitchins   0-14- 0
      to Cosen David for things bought of him   1-00- 4½
      to Cosen Rundle for goods & what she laid out   2-10- 0
      And also which was owed to Mr Contie   20-00- 0
Also given to my Daughter & her son out of the shop about or neere <u>1- 0- 0</u>
                                            25- 4- 4½

Sent to my Daughter Patience by Clogg a paire of shoes[1]   0- 2-10

May 28th for some daies thenceforward I tooke account of my Sons
   Apothecary shop & Received of Cosen Elizabeth Rundle, &
   Richawd for Hogs grease[2]   0-19-0

All Mr Contees debts are summed up Hactenus for Apothecary ware & some
Houshold stuffe & he is indebted to my son George in £40 to be paid £5 quarterly,
one ^£5 ^ should have beene paid last March. 25th as he promised but failed[.] for
the other £35[,] 7 Bills are in my Son Condies hand of £5 each Bill. Nothing as yet
paid. The £10 be due June 24th

                                              £   s   d
July. 2nd. 1666. I paid Mrs Contee for the rent of her Chambers untill
   September following from the time of my putting of myne
   Apothecaries things there[3]   00-10-00

April the 8th 1667[4] I paid Mrs Contee for halfe yeares rent for her
   chambers ended March 25th last past & so the yeare is ended
   & the chambers left   00-10-00
My Son Condy And I made even of all accounts untill March the
   18th last past. So I owed him nothinge *then*[5]
Received in utensils & Apothecary druggs of J. Contee,
   the 4 first five pounds   20-00-00
So he oweth yet £20 to my Son george. The whole of that so
   received with all that lay in Cousin Rundles house & other

1   Patience Miller had returned to Ireland: Larkham used Clogg to send goods to her via Bideford.
2   These two entries in May 1666 are the first since February 1665/6. He had made over the shop to his
   son George (see Appendix 3).
3   Larkham handed over the Apothecary in January 1665/6. He initially put utensils in store but then
   sold some off piecemeal and in his will left the rest to his daughter Patience (see fo. 47r).
4   The first entry since 2 July 1666. In these few entries in April 1667, Larkham settled his affairs,
   probably in anticipation of a further absence from Tavistock. He made no use of the manuscript until
   30 September 1667, when he made a solemn entry to mark his return to the town.
5   This sentence has been scored through lightly.

The rest that is owing out of the shopp is £35-*02s*-8½d besids
    debts upon the shop Booke & Mr Polewheels Bill.[1]

	£ s d
& the old debt owed to Mr Contee is all satisfied,	
& he yet oweth me	31-04-03½
& His brother Peter[2] oweth me	03-01-11½
Cosen David remaineth debtor to me	00-14-03½
Thomas Carter	00-01-02
Feb. 20th 1665/6	35-01 08½
	35-01 08½
for fuell from Mr J. Contee	00-09-06½
for fuell from A Bond	00-09-09

---

[1] At a later date Larkham crossed out the debts recorded here. 'Mr Polewheel': Digory Polewhele, one of Larkham's critics in the 1650s?

[2] Peter County.

things to the value of £55 was delivered to Thomas Miller in
Aprill 1667 & he is to make the best of it who hath a shop at
ockhampton & is to pay me or mine five pound yeerly for
11 yeare the first paiment next lady day.

Having wandred under the hand of providence many yeares
I came Sept. 30th 1667 to Take a Chamber to live in Tavistocke.

I paid for one quarters rent to Mrs Contee ended December 25th
ˆput in the next page to accountˆ
                ˇand paid Richord for her attendance untill Nov. 7thˇ
                                        (ˆ& spent this quarter besids. 1-5-10ˆ)[1]

Thomas Miller hath remooved his dwelling to Tavistocke this quarter & hath
        taken a part of his old shop &c[2]

                                        spent hactenus £1-5s-10d[3]

[fo. 48r]

1667/8

ano 1667/8 day[4]

Decemb 25 I have in house[5]	£vi 6d
Dec. 28th Received in earnest of Eustace Pike in the assurance of	
£8 for his sons life upon a tenem[en]t	00-01-00
I received to mak[e] up the £8 from Pike	07-19-00
Item for the first paiment of my horse	00-15-00
	14-15-06
1667/8 January 12th I was at *holye Communion*[6]	
Received by gift Jan: 17th of Mr Brownsdon	00-10-00
February the 17th of George Oxenham	00-05-00
Feb: 17th from Collonell Bennett Received	00-15-00
	16-05-06

---

[1]   He made only a fragmentary record of expenses in the autumn of 1667. (The total for incidental expenses is reiterated at the foot of the column.)

[2]   From the entry in April 1667, Thomas Miller may have been trading at Okehampton. Earlier, he had helped Larkham in Tavistock. (By the autumn he had come back to the town and perhaps worked alongside his mother Patience (to whom Larkham bequeathed his apothecary utensils).

[3]   Below this the edge is worn. One or two words are illegible.

[4]   Larkham (as usual) adapted George Lane's earlier heading, amending the year.

[5]   On this new folio, Larkham made the first detailed entries since January 1665/6, for the quarter from 25 December 1667. On 12 January 1667/8 – for almost the first time since his resignation in 1660 – he mentioned communion. Not long afterwards, he referred to a baptism (25 March 1668). It is likely that he celebrated these sacraments with his nonconformist congregation. The fall of the earl of Clarendon in December 1667 had eased pressure, even though though the First Conventicle Act remained in force. (The Act prohibited worship by more than five people unless it conformed to the Book of Common Prayer. It expired on 1 March 1669.)

[6]   This important entry is almost illegible because Larkham wrote over an earlier entry by Lane, but the celebration of 'the ordinance of the Lords Supper' is confirmed by the entry opposite.

[fo. 48r]

an° 1667

Inprimis was paid to Mrs Conte as ^quarters rent^	00-05s-00
January the first to Thom Condy bringing a shirt for a gift from his mother	00-01-00
The same day I gave to my wife	00-02-06
I gave to John Couch & to Mary *Gove*[1]	00- 1-*00*
Item to eliz[a]beth Keagle	00-00-06
Item to Elizabeth Condy bringing *Brandy*	00-00-06
Jan 4th paid Dan Sowton for making a coate	00-01-06
Jan: 7th I gave to Margery Knight who had attended me many weekes &c	00-02-06
Also the same day given in Nutts &c	00-00-04
Jan: 8th lying at Mr Sowtons gave servants	00-00-08
Jan. 9th. 10th. 11th lying at Mr Brownsdons gave	00-00-10
Item at the ordinance of the Lords Supper	00-00-06
Item since given to servants & children	00-02-08
untill this present 27th of January	00-19-06
Jan: 28. whereas I had given Richord Allen a pottage[2] I tooke it againe and gave her in mony	00-05-00
Laid out about provision ^& sacke^ this weeke	00- 2- 6
paid Em:[anuel] frost for a firepan & tongs	0- 2-00
for A skillet paid Kat Pennington	0- 2- 0
for a handle & leggs for the skillet	0- 0- 8

---

[1] Unclear: a conjecture.

[2] 'Pottage' usually means soup or a stew. Larkham probably meant a pottage-dish: he had paid her in kind when he had no money, but could now pay her 5s in cash.

I spent & bestowed this quarter ended March 25th 1668 ˆ& for rent
  & wagesˆ besids Wood & turffes sent by John Sheere which I
  have not yet reckoned with him about   05-15-06

I was taken sicke March 21 in the Morninge & a Physician was sent for viz Mr J.
Contee to whom my Daughter Condy gave 10s which I have not yet accounted with
her about, besids apothecaries Bills yet unpaid

	£ s d
I have in house at this present[1]	10-10-00
and (which I had) of E F[2]	00-01-06
of Amy Oxenham *C* Baptized March 25th [3]	00-02-06

Aprill 1. my Son Condy and ˆIˆ accounted
  He had Received Since our last in December of Eustace Peeke
  13-4 & of Dingle 3s-4 and I was on the booke for A shirt,
  wheate sope & what was paid Peeke for baking 13-1d
  so I had in money to cleare the acco[unt]   00-03-07[4]

---

[1] Larkham started the new year (as commonly reckoned in the old calendar) with a note of how much
    he had in hand. For the quarter 25 March – 24 June 1668 Larkham itemized his income but made a
    general summary of expenses (which follows below). In the manuscript, the column opposite these
    receipts is filled up with his account of expenses for the previous quarter, ending 24 March.
[2] Probably Emmanuel Frost, who paid a similar amount on other occasions.
[3] Before 1660, when he held the parish living, Larkham noted fees for funeral sermons but nothing for
    baptisms. Now, in his nonconformist ministry, he recorded a gift of 2s-6d.
[4] In other words, Larkham's accumulated debts to Daniel Condy amounted to 13s-1d, so he set this off
    against 16s-8d Condy owed him in rents. Strictly speaking, this entry belongs to the previous quarter.

Bestowed in ˆcloame[1] &ˆ provision about my hoˆuˆskeeping 5-6 & to
    Steven Goad 4d   0- 5-10

                                                        00-18-00

Laid out Feb 7th unto the end of the weeke as followeth. 8s-4d
    crocke frying pan heaters for a steele 2s-4d   00-10-08

for a Bottom to an old warminge pan   00-04-03

Feb. 12. paid Cosin Eliz Rundle for a barrell for beere   00-02-00

From thence 6s to her shop & Feb. 14 delivered to Jone 4d[2]   0-05-08

Item paid for cloam viz driping pan chafing dish pipkin   0-00-08

Item to Em: frost for a roasting iron & Brandinge & Toasting iron   0-02-10

& mony to be laid out this weeke 12s-2d   0-12-02

untill March 1st 1667/8 laid out in all   01-18-00[3]

March 12th I paid Lancelot Hutton   00-05-00
    which he had delivered to my Daughter Patience

Item the same day for mending my Watch   00-03-00

taken out for houshold expenses untill March 25th   01-02-00

Item paid Joan my servant for wages to March 25th 1668   00-05-00

Item to Mrs Contee for rent for odde time   00-05- 0

Hactenus auxiliatus est Deus, summa.   05-15- 6[4]

---

[1] 'Cloam': earthenware (*OED*).
[2] He sent 6s to the shop and his servant Joan received 4d in change.
[3] The figures total £1-7s-2d, so he has added in extra expenditure, unlisted.
[4] 'Thus far the Lord hath holpen'. £5-15s-6d is the sum of his interim totals (£0-19s-6d, £0-18s-0d, £1-18s-0d) together with the expenses listed since 12 March 1667/8.

Aprill 10th 1668 I had of Mr Brownsdon	00-10-00
April 11th from Mrs Roberts by Temp.[erance] Edgcomb	00-05-00
the same time by the same from Mrs Pomroy	00-02-06
April 13th Received of T Miller	01-05-00
April 17 of David C & J Sheere[1]	02-10-00
June the 8th following they brought a Note of the names &c & more in money[2]	00-16-00
March June 24 I received for the annuity of my Son Condy, from the time of my housekeeping	03-04-00
& also upon account the rent of Austin & Huggins	<u>00-16-08</u>
	<u>20-06-09</u>

of this I delivered to my Daughter Condy to lend in her name to T. Miller	01-10-00
And what is laid out about. T Larkham	05-02-04
& the rest is spent in houskeeping & rent & servants wages & upon my selfe	05-15-09[3]

[fo. 48v][4]

June 24th all expences for cloathes for. T.L. & makinge them (though paid since yet accounted for) and servants wages & house rent. I had remaininge in house just £8 to live upon.

Received by S.[on]C.[ondy] from Kirton tenants July the 18th[5]	3- 4-0
from J Bisset & Mary in tokens	0-10-0
from Mr Brownsdon	0-10-0

---

[1] David Condy and John Sheere, deacons of the church.
[2] A list of supporters or subscribers, and more gifts for Larkham as pastor.
[3] These three entries, for the quarter ending 24 June 1668, total £12-8s-01d. Taken from sum of receipts above (£20-6s-9d) this left a remainder of £7-18s-8d, close to the £8 Larkham noted (at the top of the next folio, fo. 48r) he had 'in house' on 24 June 1668. In the column opposite, he made a separate note of what he had spent in rent and wages, and itemized further what he had spent on his grandson Thomas Larkham. At this point Larkham entered information intermittently and without the consistency and detail of earlier years.
[4] The top third of folio is taken up with George Lane's accounts from 1598, for 'Mr Hurds' and 'Mr Griffine'. Larkham drew a line beneath this. He started his entries across whole page, switched briefly to two columns and then reverted to writing across the whole page.
[5] Five entries here list receipts until the end of August: rents from Crediton; gifts from the Bissets and Brownsdon; more from the sale of apothecary utensils. Strictly speaking, the money from the Deacons belongs to the the new quarter and new year which Larkham began on his birthday, 18 August 1668, but the structure became much looser at this point, when he 'gave up housekeeping' and moved in with Daniel and Jane Condy.

paid this quarter ended June 24th for rent	00-15-00

paid this quarter ended June 24th for rent   00-15-00
for servants wages   00-10-00
And for T Larkhams acco[unt] to son Condy (he abating 2-6d upon
    the cloake stufe)   04-06-00
& he had in money of me & a handkerchefe   00-05-00
and paid for a band for him to C[osen] Eli:[zabeth] Rundle   00-01-00
Item paid Dan. Sowton for making clothes for him   08-[??]¹

[fo. 48v]

paid for a bottle of surfett water² from Plimouth   00-01-08
and for mendinge mine old blacke coate   00-01-00
paid for baking last quarter ended June. 24th   00-00-09
July 27th I paid Richord for helping in Jones absence   00-01-08
July 19th & 26th given at Three church meetings³   00-01-04
Barber July 30 trim[m]ing me   00-00-06
August. 14. A token sent to Azarel Condy   00-02-06
D[elivere]D to. T Larkham to buy necessaries   01-10-00⁴

---

¹ The corner has worn away. The amount Larkham spent on clothing for his grandson amounts to at least £6, more than the £5-2s-4d noted opposite. 'Stuffe': fabric. 'Band': a neck-band or collar for a shirt (*OED*).

² 'Surfeit-water': a medicinal drink to cure 'surfeit', i.e. excessive indulgence or a digestive disorder, or a fever or fits (*OED*).

³ These dates fell on Sundays.

⁴ He did not sum up these expenses.

Received for Apothec[arie]s Bottles & weights   9s-7d
August 29[th] of the Deacons   01-00-0[1]

August 18[th] beginneth the 67[th] yeare of myne age.
   I have in house Nine pound just.[2]
August the last I gave over housekeepinge & went to live with my Son Condy

October 1 I paid Mr Contee for rent for 2 Moneths 10s & in polts & glasses [&]
   for chi[m]ney mon[ey] ˆ1sˆ Item for the quarter ended at Xtide for the chamber
   in which I kept my goods – paid 5s to Mrs Contie[3]

I passed an account with my Son Condy unto March 25[th] 1669 allowing him £8
   for mine & my Wives Diet (besids mine own expences) and what he laid out
   for Thomas Larkham to sett foret[h] to sea & gave over my rents of Tavistock
   to be by him received & am satisfied of the annuity in Dolvin & out of the said
   rents until the said March 25th & for the £60 he was to pay for the highrents
   & there is due to me upon all accounts £25-18s-8d. All upon his books
   discharged.
Hence forward he is to pay me Out of the Mills in Dolvin quarterly 40 shillings &
   out of the lands in Tavistock During mine & my wives life quarterly – 22s 6d.

March 27th 1669 I have in my keeping Nine [pounds] Ten shillings. whereof £8-5s
   was received for bookes I sold to Mr Quicke a Minister living at Plimouth.[4]

Aprill the 8th I had brought by J.S.[5]   £2- 0s-0d
Aprill the 10th I paid my Son Condy which he laid out for Physick
   to Mr Yong the Apothecary at Plimouth   0- 3- 4
Aprill the 14th of M[r] J. B.[6]   0-10- 0[7]

---

1   Larkham's recording and reckoning were at this point not an exact science: he did not sum up either
   income or expenses. At the start of the next quarter he noted he had £9 'in house'. (The actual total
   of the figures here is £12-13s-7d, with expenses of £1-18s-9d, leaving a balance of £10-14s-10d.)
2   He made fragmentary entries for year August 1668–9.
3   He traded in apothecary utensils to pay part of his rent. 'Polts': pestles. 'Xtide': Christ-tide.
4   He made a fresh effort to record receipts from 25 March 1669 (the start of a new year) but faltered
   before the end of April. The nonconformist John Quick (CR, ODNB) tended George Hughes (CR) at
   his deathbed and had his own funeral sermon preached by Dr Daniel Williams. Quick's manuscripts
   are now in Dr Williams's Library, London. It is not known how these papers came into the collection
   (I am grateful to the director, Dr David Wykes, for advice on this), but it is intriguing to speculate
   that some of Larkham's books, too, might have found their way from Quick's study to the Library.
5   John Sheere.
6   John Brownsdon.
7   Larkham mixed up his record of receipts with an expense, for physic. On the next folio he carried
   over from here a total of £10-15s-0d: £8-5s-0d (from the sale of books), £2 (from Sheere), 10s (from
   Brownsdon).

[fo. 49r]

Item from J Sheere Aprill 24th [1]	£1- 7s-6d
& from Peter Glubb	0- 2-06
From Mrs Jane Roberts	0- 5-0
from Kirton for Rent I had from S Condy	
from Mr Ivie 9s from Brownscombe £2 from Macy 07-6	2-16- 6
From Capt Gloake	0-15- 0
from Mr Joan[2] & Mary Bissett each 5s	0-10- 0
from Mr Brownsdon at my return from *Stow*[3]	0-10- 0
from Cosen Elizabeth Rundle *Gold*[4] yielded	0- 5- 6
	6-12- 0[5]
and on the other side I had in all	10-15- 0[6]
	17-7s [00]

Besids what I laid out for Tabacco & horse

Remaineth in Money in my house August 18th	£4-2s-1d

August the 18th 1669 beginneth the sixtieth & eight year of myne age.

Thy Church (My God) with strife and heart division is rent & torne
   O come play the Physician.
O come and take of that poore pittance left of parts[7]
   for I of all am quitt bereft.
If any aske whose witt & parts are these which yet remaine
   they'r thine Lord if thou please
Possesse my hearte that so when strangers come,
   I answer may God hath t'ane all the roome

---

1   These continue his account of receipts from foot of the previous folio.
2   John.
3   Not identified: possibilities are Pedrockstow, Devon (north of Okehampton on the road from Tavistock to Bideford); Padstow, Cornwall (formerly known as Petroc-stowe); or Stowe House, Kilkhampton, Cornwall.
4   Or perhaps £6: Larkham's handwriting is poor here.
5   A total for receipts since 24 April (without taking into account entries on the previous folio).
6   This figure he carried over from the previous page (fo. 48v).
7   'Parts' (which Larkham abbreviated as 'pts'): personal qualities or attributes, especially intellectual; abilities, gifts, talents (*OED* 'part', n[1], 15).

[fo. 49r]

Sent about Tobacco	10- 4- 8
Item to Thomas Miller	3- 0- 0
Item charges about horse & Tabacco	2-06
bought a horse cost	3-10s-[0]
	16-17-02

sent to son George	20-00-00

Re[c]koned with Son Condy all even between us Hitherto	19- 7- 0[1]
	16-17- 2
	2-09-10

<hr>

[1] He recorded no further details.

	£ s d
The Wife of G. Oxenham gave to me	00-01-00
Received of John Sheere deacon a gratuity	01-16-00
from Mr Brownsdon	00-10-00
from Em[m]anuell frost	00- 1-06
from Mathew Cudlip. Novemb. 13th	0- 2-00
	2-10- 6
Received this quarter ended Nov. 17th	£6-12- 7

Where[a]s I laid out about freeing of Tabacco for T.M & for charges
   about bringin[g]e it to Tavistocke   13-17-04
I have received for Tabacco & the caske in which it was brought
   from Virginea   14-01-03[1]

---

[1]   This relates to notes in the previous quarter about trade in tobacco undertaken with his grandson
      Thomas Miller (T.M.). The outlay noted earlier (£13-7s-2d) and here (£13-17s-04d) do not match,
      but from this final reckoning it seems Larkham still made 3s-11d profit.

	£ s d
paid P Doidge for fetching water from Lamerton[1]	00-03-00
paid the Barber for Trimming me	00-00-06
for sugar for my Eringo rootes[2]	00-00-10
for 2 oz of E[r]ingo rootes bought at Plimouth	00-00-10
for sacke at severall times unto Sept. 10	00-02-09
paid for making clothes & mend[in]ge for Daughter Miller	00-02-06
paid for a barber trim[ming] me	00-00-06
for Almonds & waters for Almond milke[3]	00-01-02
for sugar used about it	00-00-10
Laid out in Houskeeping untill Michaelmas	02-17-10½
And which Richard gave Daughter Miller at her dep[ar]ture[4]	00-05-00
Laid out since in houskeeping untill November 17th	1-13-01½
Also all is paid which was upon Son Condies booke	01-06-08
	06-06- 7[5]

Novemb. 17th beginneth the 2nd quarter of the 68th yeare of mine age

Laid out to the Barber	0- 0-6[6]

---

[1] 'Lamerton water' is not mentioned elsewhere: possibly a kind of 'strong water', or 'aqua vitae'; sold as a drink and as medicine (*DTGC*).

[2] 'Eringo': eryngo-root, a sweetmeat made of the candied root of Sea Holly (*OED*).

[3] 'Almond-milk': made of blanched almonds and sugared water, used in medicine as an emollient (*OED*).

[4] Perhaps travelling over to Ireland again; 'Richard', Larkham's maid Richawd Allen.

[5] Larkham's total (£6-6s-7d) is 9s short of the actual total (£6-15s-7d).

[6] Larkham's last entry – for his habitual sixpenny trim at the barber's – was a month before his death. He was buried on 23 December 1669 (Tavistock PR, burials) and his will was proved 9 March 1669/70 (*CR*). George Larkham took the manuscript to Cumberland and began his entries on the next folio in September 1670: the third writer to use this paper book.

2

Naboth, in a narrative and complaint of the church of God … at Tavistock in Devon (London, 1657)

NABOTH,

In a

Narrative and Complaint

Of the

Church of God which is in Christ Jesus,

AT

Tavistock in *Devon*; and especially of and concerning Mr. *Thomas Larkham*, Publick Teacher and
Pastor of a despised oppressed handful of the sheep
of Christ there;

Humbly presented to the Churches of Christ, and to
the Magistracy and Ministry of the Nation
in this Common-wealth.

---

*So I returned and considered all the oppressions that are done under
the Sun, and behold the tears of such as were oppressed, and they
had no comforter : and on the side of their oppressors* there was
power, but they had no comforter, Eccles. 4.1.

And the men of Belial *witnessed against him, even against* Naboth
in the presence of his people, saying, Naboth *did blaspheme God
and the King,* I King. 21. 13.

LONDON,

Printed for the use of the Author, 1657.

A Narrative and Complaint of the

Church of Tavistock *in* Devon.

Humbly presented to the Churches of Christ, and to

the Magistracy and Ministry of the Nation in this

Commonwealth.[1]

It hath been the pleasure of God, for ends best known to his holiness, justice and wisdom, to permit a people at *Tavistocke* in *Devon*, that desire to live holily, to be for divers years persecuted, oppressed, and opposed in all their endeavours to promote Religion, and the publick welfare of that place, by the contrivances, stirrings, prosecutions and actings of an opposite party, prevalent in the said place: which carriage, although we cannot be so blind as to excuse it, and acquit it altogether from that enmity that is in men unto the waies of the Lord and Gospel mysteries : yet had we rather impute it to those unquenchable animosities which have unhappily been set on fire and burn most fiercely in the breast of one especially, most eminent (civilly) in that place. Alas! God know[s] the[at] we are loth [p. 2] to provoke : it is not the intent of these papers so to do: but rather to plead our innocency, and to give satisfaction to all the people of God, to whom the report of our stirs and broils for these eight or nine years last past hath come and likewise to beg their prayers for us, and their advice and counsel to us, that we may do nothing offensive, uncomely, or of ill report, or which may make the Cross of Christ of none effect. Our state is as followeth.

We lived divers years in a sad vacancy of the means of salvation and the Ordinances, by reason of the removal of our former Minister Mr. *George Hughes* to

---

[1] *Naboth* was the first salvo fired in the pamphlet battle between Larkham and his opponents in the late 1650s (a discussion of this controversy is provided in the Introduction). Larkham spent September 1657 in London. He saw *Naboth* through the press and brought copies home: 'My journies to London & Exeter & for carriage of bookes and boxe from London & Exeter 8-07-7'; 'I am out in printing Naboth … 1-10-0' (Diary, fo. 26v). The book presented itself as the voice of the Tavistock church (with only the last pages 'An Addition written by me Thomas Larkham my self, and in my own name only') but Larkham had much to do with it. The tract, 'printed for the use of the Author', presented evidence for his integrity to public gaze, in light of yet another summons to appear before the Devon Commissioners for the Ejection of Scandalous Ministers. First, *Naboth* presented an account of the 'stirs and broils' Larkham and his flock had endured. Then came articles presented at various times to the commissioners against Larkham, with a line-by-line refutation, and an account of Larkham's recent dealings with London committees (the Trustees for the Maintenance of Ministers and Commissioners for the Approbation of Public Preachers). Much was made of the Devon Commissioners' earlier decision (in January 1656/7) to accept Larkham's offer to make peace. Larkham had offered to resign in favour of a new minister nominated by Lewis Stucley and William Bartlet (fellow congregationalists and his closest allies in Devon). The tract printed letters from the Tavistock church to Stucley and Bartlet, seeking advice, with Stucley's reply – in essence, that he could think of no one better than Larkham to secure 'the foundations of Church-Government' in Tavistock. *Naboth* identified Larkham with Naboth the faithful Jezreelite, who refused to surrender his vineyard to the evil ruler Ahab (1 Kings 21). Naboth lost his vineyard and his life in a set-up by Ahab's wife, who brought 'base fellows' to accuse him of cursing God and king. The story pivoted on false accusations. It was only a small step from Naboth's vineyard to Larkham and the 'vineyard' of Tavistock's church. The only copy of *Naboth* known to survive is in the Wallace Notestein collection at the Library of the College of Wooster, Ohio.

Plimouth ten miles distant from us.[2] We often besought the Lord that our eyes might once more see such a publick Teacher as wee might take comfort in. It pleased our gracious God to hear us, and to send us by his providence (the Regiment of Sir *Hardress Waller* having their Head-quarters in our Town) one, whom the Lord hath been pleased to keep, even almost miraculously among us for many years, notwithstanding the wrath of pride, silence of neighbour Ministers, and scandalous reports thick and threefold that have assaulted him.[3]

Neither should ordinary injuries and abuses have opened our mouthes to complain, or stirred our pens to write, had we not perceived that even Brethren and men in power that pretend to know much of God and to act highly for the advancement of the Kingdom or Christ, had also joyned (alas!) against us though (we hope) unwittingly, and great abuse shewed them, from such as care little (the Lord pitty them) what they say or swear.

The troubles that our Minister hath suffered have been many and great; and many of us have (besides a sympathy common to us all) felt the effects of mens malice, pride and prophaneness in a very great measure.[4] Witness those conventings, bindings over to Sessions and Assizes, Indictments, unjust laying of rates, and taxes, oppositions in Parish-meetings of equal and just proposals, turning honest men out of places of employment, (no cause being alledged) substituting in their stead, wicked, idle, drunken persons : and generally the making good of that Scripture saying, *He that abstained from wickedness* [p. 3] *maketh himself a prey.*[5] But of all afflictions none comparable to this, That whereas upon the detainment of the livlyhood of Mr. *Thomas Larkham*, our publique Teacher, by the contrivances of the enemies of God and Goodness, he, flies for succour and reparation to such as can and ought to right him; He is used as poor sheep that come to thorny bushes for shelter, who have not only their fleeces taken, at least in part, but also their very flesh rent and torn on their bodies: so hath he been one and again dealt withall by such as Satans wiles and mens malice and subtility have made to act, (though we are apt to hope against their principles if they knew it,) even against the Lord Jesus Christ and his Crown and Scepter at *Tavistock*.

For whereas in the composition of Sir *John Glanvile*,[6] the Rectory of *Lamerton* the next Parish to *Tavistock*, is enfeoffed to certain Trustees for uses, the first and principal whereof is for the raising of the first fifty pounds out of it, for the preaching Minister of *Tavistock* for the time being to be yearly paid for ever; which

2   George Hughes (*CR*, *ODNB*), left Tavistock in 1643 during the Civil War, and moved to Plymouth. By 1657, Hughes had become the foremost presbyterian in the county, and a leading light in the Devon Association (which Larkham stayed out of). Tension between 'Hugonites' and 'Larkamites' contributed to tension in Tavistock: see Introduction.

3   Larkham himself, who arrived in Tavistock with Waller's regiment, as a chaplain: see Introduction.

4   For comment on these vicissitudes (elaborated further, *Naboth*, pp. 2–6), see Introduction.

5   Isaiah 59:15 (KJV): 'Yea, truth faileth; and he that departeth from evil maketh himself a prey: and the Lord saw it, and it displeased him that there was no judgment.'

6   Sir John Glanville, Speaker of the House of Commons, impeached in 1644 for his loyalty to the king and later charged £3,000 as a penalty. As part of the settlement, £50 was diverted from the rectory of Lamerton parish to the vicar of Tavistock. Glanville's father (John) and mother (Alice Skerret) came from prominent Tavistock families. See Stuart Handley, 'Glanville, Sir John, the younger (1585/6–1661)' and J. A. Hamilton (rev. David Ibbetson) 'Glanville, John (1542–1600)', *ODNB*. Francis Glanville, Sir John's nephew, became one of Larkham's most vociferous opponents: Harold J. Hopkins, 'Thomas Larkham's Tavistock: change and continuity in an English town, 1600–1670', Ph.D. dissertation, University of Austin at Texas, 1981, pp. 130–2, 232.

also divers years hath been paid to Mr. *Larkham* : Occasion is taken from an Ordinance of the Protectour and Council, to bring this Rectory into the hands of the Publique Trustees for pious uses sitting at *Westminster*,[7] and a prohibition issued out to stop payment of any money raised out of the said Rectory without special order from them. Whereupon Mr. *Larkham* our Minister makes his address to the said Trustees, and hath access and audience, and this answer that he get the feoffment deed and shew his title.[8] Which accordingly being done and his right evident, (he being many years ago presented by the Patron, and confirmed by an order of the Committee for plundred Ministers)[.][9] Yet it is further said by the Clerk to the foresaid publique Trustees, that he must make his address to the Commissioners for Approbation of publique Preachers sitting at *White Hall*.[10] This also was done, and a Petition with an attestation presented in the name of Mr. *Larkham*, our Reverend and Godly Minister, though not by him (for both he and we thought his long labouring in the Ministry and faithful acting in the cause of the Common-wealth above many of his ranck and employment, known sufficiency, and godly and [p. 4] unblamable conversation, would have gotten an easie and speedy pass.) But the Commissioners some of them had letters and informations of articles that had been exhibited to the Committee for plundred Ministers (whilst it was in being) and one of them talks of Two bastards, one in new *England*, and another in old *England*; and another talks of cursing of one in publique, and much ado. So that now it appears necessary for the said Mr. *Larkham* to come to the Commissioners in person, which accordingly he did: but not being able to bear the accusations and untrue reports of slanderous tongues and pens, his spirit was moved to speak such words as he hath no cause to glory in, for they were passionate recriminations and reflexions, which he hath since professed his sorrow for, and dare not justifie himself in. And so Mr. *Larkham* departed for that time with a purpose to trouble them no more. But upon advice of godly ones, his friends, he came again, exhibiting a letter from the Church in New *England* concerning their satisfaction according to rule, and containing also sweet brotherly advice to the said Mr. *Larkham*, to labour and pray for a sanctified use of the afflictive dispensation, as by the letter it self appeared: also he had obtained from the (Now) Lord General *Disbrow* a Certificate of great use touching the rejection

---

7   The 'Public Trustees for Pious Uses': the Trustees for the Maintenance of Ministers ('Trustees for Providing Maintenance for Preaching Ministers and other Pious Uses'). From September 1654 this committee took over from the parliamentary Committee for Plundered Ministers, which ceased to exist when Cromwell ejected the Rump Parliament in April 1653. Ann Hughes, '"The public profession of these nations": the national church in Interregnum England', in *Religion in Revolutionary England*, ed. Christopher Durston and Judith Maltby (Manchester and New York, 2006), p. 97; W. A. Shaw, *A history of the English church during the Civil Wars and under the Commonwealth, 1640–1660*, 2 vols. (London, 1900), II, pp. 230–2.

8   In October 1657 Larkham noted he had paid 8s 'for a New Coppy of the ffeofments of Lamerton out of the Rowles' (Diary, fo. 26v).

9   The Committee for Plundered Ministers had been established by the Long Parliament in 1642–3 to provide for 'poor plundered' ministers forced out by royalist forces. It gathered other functions to it, including the approval of presentations to vacant livings and examination of 'scandalous' clergy. Shaw, *History of the English church*, II, pp. 193, 197–8.

10   The Commissioners for Approbation of Public Preachers (commonly known as 'Triers'), who from March 1653/4 approved all appointments to parish livings: Hughes, '"The public profession of these nations": the national church in Interregnum England', pp. 97–9; Shaw, *History of the English church*, II, p. 265. Normally, applicants presented 'certificates' to prove their fitness for office. The controversy over the Lamerton augmentation meant Larkham was asked to appear in person.

of the articles out of the Committee aforesaid, in which the said Honourable person had been a special actor, having been at *Tavistock*, and enquiring narrowly into the causes of those stirs and differences that were among us.[11]

Upon the said second address he was referred to a conference with Mr. *Caryl* & Mr. *Manton*,[12] who signified to him in the withdrawing chamber at *White-Hall* very sweetly and brotherly that some reports had come to the Commissioners ears, of some practises and carriage divers years ago unbecoming the Gospel of Christ, &c. Surely no Christian soul can chuse but approve of such behaviour as this was; and no doubt but some suitable answers were made to these Reverend men. And the result of all was, that they were satisfied in many things, that Mr. *Larkham* should trouble himself no more, but appoint one about three weeks after to call with their Register of the approbation so far as Mr. *Larkham* understood them (as he professeth, and we [p. 5] cannot but believe him.) Mr. *Larkham* hereupon having appointed a friend to call with the Register, and also to perfect his business with the Trustees, afterward returns for *Devon*, not supposing what since fell out. For behold in stead of this order to receive his livelyhood, here is an order from the Commissioners for ejection of scandalous and insufficient Ministers,[13] hung up at his Gate, (where formerly a horse head with a black-cloth, about it, a knave of spades fastened to it all hanging to a little Gibbet had formerly been put.) There surely was the Commissioners order put by one *William Hore* of *Tavistock*, who had been formerly for his wicked and unchristian walking rejected by the people of God, and was now united to the open enemies of God, to prosecute the said Minister, and oppose those very waies which he had formerly for a time walked in, as to men. And surely experience teaches us, that none usually are such desperate persecutors, as Revolters and Apostates; such a wofull man is this *Hore* become, whom we leave to the Lord.[14]

And because the loud noise of Articles against our Ministers hath made many prejudiced ones, whom we would be loth to place on the left hand among the Goats,[15] to be almost deaf in the other ear against all lawfull defences that have been made; and also forasmuch as what is gotten upon the wings of common report, is not possible to be fully called in by verbal discourses, hardly at all so as to leave

---

11 For Larkham's history in New England, see the Introduction. In 1655 John Disbrowe [Desborough] became Cromwell's agent for military rule in the South-West, as Major-General of Gloucester, Somerset, Wiltshire, Dorset, Devon and Cornwall: see Stephen K. Roberts, 'Disbrowe , John (*bap.* 1608, *d.* 1680)', *ODNB*; Christopher Durston, *Cromwell's major-generals: godly government during the English Revolution* (Manchester, 2001).

12 Joseph Caryl and Thomas Manton, both appointed in 1654 as commissioners for the Approbation of Public Preachers: *CR, ODNB*.

13 In August 1654, Cromwell issued an ordinance to establish, in each county, commissioners for the Ejection of Scandalous Ministers (commonly known as 'Ejectors'): Hughes, '"The public profession of these nations": the national church in Interregnum England', pp. 99–102; Shaw, *History of the English church*, II, p. 247. The precise chronology of the events *Naboth* reports is hard to establish, but Larkham noted 'articles' and hearings before the Devon Commissioners in December 1656 and January 1657 (Diary, fos. 24r, 24v); another summons to appear in October 1657, apparently with a successful outcome when he met the commissioners in early December (fos. 26v, 27v). On 24 December 1657, he had news from London that the 'Triers' had approved his tenure at Tavistock, so the Lamerton money would come (fo. 27v). *Naboth* came out in the run-up to his appearance before the commissioners in December 1657.

14 Hore appeared in a poem Larkham wrote in 1656 about opponents 'that me vexe full sore' (Diary, fo. 23r). His initials appeared on the title-page of *Tavistock Naboth*, where a vivid account of his excommunication by Larkham can be found (p. 16).

15 Matthew 25:33.

no scar[;] it hath been thought necessary, that as well [as] the Articles that have been exhibited from time to time against him (so far as the copies of them are come to our hands) as also some other Providences and Transactions should be made publique[.] Here followeth a true copy under the hand of *John Smith* Register to the Commissioners of ejection, &c, sitting at *Exeter* in *Devon*. The first parcel whereof are pretended to be the same which were exhibited to the Committee for plundred Ministers, and with that very title is the copy by one of us taken from the hands of the foresaid Register, and his Fee demanded, and paid for the said copy, which is as followeth. [p. 6]

*Articles Exhibeted to the Right Honourable
the Committee for plundered Ministers,*[16]
against Tho. Larkham, Clerk.

1. The said *Tho. Larkham* hath often upbraided the present Government now established by Parliament with scandalous words.
2. He being of late years Chaplain to Sir *Hardress Waller*, was by a Councel of War of the said Regiment, taken to be as enemy to this Common-wealth, for endeavouring to stir up the souldiers to mutinies and divisions.
3. He is a common rayler, calling in the Pulpit the inhabitants of the Parish of *Tavistock* by several scandalous and opprobrious names, as dogs, snarling curs, swine, grunting swine, serpents, vipers, devils, rogues, ragged rogues, rascals, scabs, ninnihammers, purquinions, fools, squint-eyed fools, sons of witches, knaves, a pack of knaves, the devils dishclouts, with frequent and horrid curses and imprecations, saying to one as he was going out of the church, Goe and the curse of God go with thee; and to the Congregation, God pour on you and yours the vials of his wrath.
4. He hath been a sower of discord and hatred in all places wheresoever he hath been, as also of a proud and turbulent spirit in all his actions; as may witness, his behaviour at *Northam* in *Devon*, and *Greenwich* in *Kent*, and *New England*; and being therefore taxed before the Commissioners of *Devon* for sequestration, for the same, said that he was thereunto sent; following the example of his Master, who came not to bring peace, but the sword.[17]
5. He said in a Sermon, that God and the Devil did cast lots, and the greatest part fell to the Devils share, which were cursed Caveliers. [p. 7]

Additional Articles unto the former
1. Mr *Larkham* left his charge for eight or nine moneths together, and took the charge of another place in the North of *England*, and received near an £100 for his preaching there, and afterward coming home, he went to Law for those profits which grew due in his absence, although he left none to supply his place in his absence; beside divers other *London* journeys also, and now hath made a voyage into *Ireland*, without making any provision for us.[18]

---

16 Articles presented against Larkham early in his time at Tavistock, before this committee ceased its work in April 1653.
17 A reference to Matthew 10:34.
18 This charge relates to Larkham's absence in Cumberland, 1651–2, and his visit to Ireland in the summer of 1656.

2.   Mr. *Tho. Larkham* the 16. of *Decem.* 1655. did deliver in the pulpit these words following, That they that now had the power in their hands, were drunk with the blood of Kings, and made themselves fat with the flesh of Nobles, and having entered into the Lands and possessions of Deans and Chapters, did now sit still, and let reformation go back to its old beggarly rudiments.

3.   He is often reviling of the Ministers, sometimes calling them Time-stealers, Truth-stealers, and Tithe-stealers, shaken-cleanlies, green-heads,[19] novices, cramd Turkey Cocks, and that the laying on of never so many of their slovenly hands cannot make a Minister; and that if the Devil had a child to be baptised, they would baptize it; and many of them fed the people with drie gobbets;[20] he made out his meaning thus; Suppose I should invite one of you to eat at my house, and should cut out the meat and chew it in my mouth, and then throw it into yours, after I had suckt out the juice of it; even so do they. And at another time he said, You shall have a Claw-back[21] Priest come to the bed-side of this dying neighbour, in hope to have the pots, and puddings, and the chine-pieces,[22] and should tell him he was a good man, and that he himself was as *Michaias, &c.*[23]

4.   He advised Mr. *Condy* to strike out the Legacy he had given his son *Edmond Condy* upon his will, and instead therefore would give him two pence to buy an halter.[24] [p. 8]

5.   He told us once in the Pulpit, that he met with one by the water side that said, that none but the scum came to hear him, and then added, now if ye can pack up this, do you.

6.   He hath often denied himself to be the Parish Minister and said, that he did as much hate *Parochus* as *Metropolitanus*; and this in the Pulpit, That if the Parish could get a good Minister before the twenty ninth day of *September* next, he would resign up the place.

7.   He said in the Pulpit that he had ten in his Church that should pray with any ten in fourty miles round about.

8.   He brings in many ridiculous rimes and impertinent stories in his Sermons, very unbefitting the seriousness which becomes one that hath to deal in the name of God about the salvation of souls.

9.   He said once in the Pulpit, That Antichrist was come over from *Rome* to *Edenburg*, and from thence to *London*, as from thence to *Exeter*, and that as a Thief pursued by a *Hue and Cry*, gets into a Justice of peace his house; And what officer dares go there to seek him?

Copia vera.

John Smith Register

---

[19] 'Green head': simpleton (*OED*).
[20] 'Gobbet': a piece of raw flesh (*OED*).
[21] 'Claw-back': a sycophant, parasite (*OED*).
[22] Probably 'china-pieces'.
[23] 'Michaias' (Micah) delivered a message against those who tried to silence God's prophets: 'Woe to them that devise iniquity … "Prophesy ye not", say they to them that prophesy' (Micah 2:1, 6, KJV).
[24] The detail is elaborated in *Tavistock Naboth* (pp. 34, 74–5) which described Edmond Condy as once an Elder of the church, but now cast out. His younger brother Daniel was Larkham's son-in-law. Larkham was alleged to have tried to manipulate Edmond and their father to profit Daniel.

[p. 9]

Additional Articles

Mr. *Larkham* said since his coming home from *Ireland*; that the Devil was an Orthodox divine, and that he had more Orthodox Divinity in him then half the Ministers of Christendom.

Also he said, that Religion was never so in fashion as it is now; for it is an easie matter for a man to come into an office under the States, either to be an Excise-man or Customer, or to get a place in the Army, and then write great lines, and call in the Countrey about them at their pleasure.

Also he hath often said formerly, that there was not a jot of grace in those words of Christs prayer which he made to his Father before his Passion, *If it be possible let this cup pass from me.*[25]

That God hath an ugly face.[26]

Also he said formerly, That if Christ should come to question him of what judgement he was of, he should be at a loss to make him an answer, neither should we hastily know of what judgement he was of.

Also those Ministers which were put in to preach in his absence being in *Ireland*, he said they were the sons of *Edom*; and gave God thanks for those that carried on his work in his absence, and did threaten them of his Church-members for leaving his private meetings, and for their going to the publick Ordinance, and for the hearing those men, they were to give satisfaction to the Church before they should communicate.

Also, Mr. *Larkham* would have left our Parish and his charge there, if that he could have got an hundred and fifty pound or a little less assured on him in *Ireland*: this was his proffer there: for the testimony hereof we do desire that *Francis Glanvile*[27] may be examined, who is here present.

Mr. *Larkham* did say to one Mr. *John Pointer* one of the antientest Magistrates of our Town and Parish of *Tavistock*,[28] as he was going forth of the Church after the exercise was ended [p. 10] upon a Market day, at least three or four hundred people then present, *The Curse of God go with thee*; to the great astonishment and amazement of the people, and scandal to Religion.

Mr. *Larkham* doth now groan under a mighty burden, which he will patiently bear, until God or the Devil do remove the burden from him.

The Town is deprived of the assistance of the neighbour Ministers, because Mr. *Larkham* hath so much scandalized them.[29]

Thus you have the Articles, which one would think should have answered themselves, and rather have drawn (at least) frowns and checks upon the Promoters, then so many weary and troublesome journeys to so many of us, beside the experience

---

[25] Matthew 26:39.

[26] This charge perhaps came from a misconstrual of Larkham's preaching on the attributes of God.

[27] Glanville, one of Larkham's principal opponents, came from a leading Tavistock family.

[28] Pointer was prominent in the Court Leet, and took a lead in denying Larkham the Lamerton money (Diary, fo. 'B'v).

[29] Larkham's relations with local clergy, and tension over their lack of access to the Tavistock pulpit, are discussed in the Introduction.

of much money (there not being sometimes a full *Quorum* of Commissioners when we attended.) We have gotten a Copy of Mr *Larkhams* hasty defence, which (he hath professed) had it not been for the sake of the people of God, and to keep up the interest of Christ in *Tavistock*, so long as it shall please God to make use of him to that end, he would never have put pen to paper, to have vouchsafed to have made. The following answers are word for word as they were given in, save only That whereas one which was then a Persecutor, is since convinced of the evil of his waies, and hath bewailed his miscarriage thereabout; it was thought fit to silence his name, which the adverse party will publish fast enough about the Countrey, who have obtained a Copy of this answer following from the Register of the Court aforesaid, for that and all evil uses Satan shall teach them to make of it. [p. 11]

> *The defence of* Thomas Larkham
> *Minister of* Tavistock *concerning*
> *certain Articles of charge delivered*
> *against him to the Commissioners of*
> *Devon, for ejecting scandalous and*
> *insufficient Ministers.*

Imprimis, To the title of the first parcel of Articles, He saith that it is not true that these five mentioned are either all or the very same that were exhibited to the Committee for plundred Ministers, for that three are wholly left out, to wit the sixth, seventh and eight. And the third hath an addition of one pretended reproachfull Phrase more, to wit, *The devils dishclouts*.[30] And the fifth is quite altered in the substance of the sense thereof, and much shorter in regard of the matter of the charge therein contained, whereby may be easily gathered, that untruths great store are to be expected in the other Rapsodies, called additional Articles.

But whatsoever the Articles were, they were fully prosecuted; and the business came to a hearing in the said Committee, and the defendant was acquitted as he can make appear. And this might serve (as the Defendant conceives with submissions to better Judgements) for the routing of the forlorn hope in this onset. But for further satisfaction, if it should seem good to this Court to proceed upon those Articles, The Respondent saith to the first, It is a malitious forged calumniation. And if times should alter to the mind of his Prosecutors (which God of this mercy to his people forbid) He hath cause to think he should be deal with all by his Accusers upon other terms: it being known to all the countrey how deeply he hath been engaged in all these late revolutions against the party that prosecuted him [p. 12] then (and most of them yet are the same) And for the Interest of Christ and his people. To the second, he saith it is utterly false; for the differences agitated at that council of war articulate were particular between this Defendant and some officers of Sir *Hardress Wallers* Regiment, whereof he the Respondent then was Chaplain.

To the Calumnistions and merry Ale-house jigs of the third, he saith it was fully heard before the Committee aforementioned; and for the phrases, some of them he knoweth not the english of them, other some are Scripture words; and the accusation of horrid curses and imprecations is very devilish, and that the instances will shew.

---

[30] 'Dish-clout': literally, a cloth used for washing dishes, but also a contemptuous metaphor for weakness (*OED*) – the proverbial 'wet rag'.

For in Answer to the first, This Defendant saith that *John Pointer* for drunkeness rejectd by the Church, flying in the face of the censure, and deriding it and threatening its overthrow, was wished to be more sensible of the censure, & to take heed left the curse of God did fall upon him, or to that effect; which this Defendant cannot punctually remember, it being near seven years since; during all which time he the said *Pointer* hath continued an Opposer of the waies and people of God. And for the other pretended curse, what man alive hath patience enough to see such shameless Behaviour and not to be moved! The words spoken by this Defendant were these, (as is printed in the 122 *pag[e]* of his treatise called The wedding supper, in an admonition or use, *and as this is a sin* (to wit, what was spoken of before) *that God bears, so also all your affronts* and scoffs *and provocations, especially your fitting your tickets and libels of contention and strife to be read on Lords dayes, and usually on such of them, as the Church use to receive the Lords Supper upon; that you may fill up the measure of your sin, and God pour on you & yours the vials of his wrath, which most certainly he will, if repentance prevent not.*[31] Is this a curse? To the fourth, This Defendant humbly desireth that the gross deceitfulness of this Brute *Godbear*, the composer of this article, may be noted. This defendant did in his presence aske the Commissioners for Sequestration, whether he ever were questioned by them, as is alleadged in this article? He the said *Walter Godbear* prevented them, raving and crying out, I taxed you, I taxed you, before these Commissioners, &c.[32] And if this may pass, any Varlet may abuse men before [p. 13] Judges, and after swear that they were questioned before such Judges. But did men know what oaths contrary to his own knowledge and conscience (this Defendant is perswaded) and most evidently false, this monster of men hath taken, they would think him scarce fit to be allowed a witness against any man, much less in this cause wherein his malice to the defendant rings in all the Countrey round about the place of his dwelling. The matter of the Article is false and caluminatory.

To the fifth, Besides the falseness and opprobriousness of it, This Defendant prayeth that notice may be taken of the alteration of it, though it be pretended to be the same that was exhibited to the Committee for plundred Ministers. Here it is, *That God and the Devil did cast lots, and the greatest part fell to the Devils share, which were cursed Cavaliers.* But formerly, it was alleadged thus, *He preached that God and the Devil did cast lots, and that he and his party (wherein are Caveliers of all sorts, Drunkards, Whore-masters,* &c.*) fell to Gods lot, and all those that were not of his party to the Devils, calling ordinarily the Sons of* Belial,[33] *all that opposed him.* This Defendant saith, that both these so cross, are not likely to be true in any rational mans eyes; but the truth is, they are the Product of a venomous enraged Spirit.

These Articles *are all answered* by *Nicholas Wats*,[34] and attested by *William Hore* with divers others, although now the said *Wats* and *Hore*, being rejected by

---

[31] This occurred in a section where Larkham addressed the theme 'cruel or unworthy dealing against the Ministers of the Gospel is a sin that God takes special notice of', which he interpreted in relation to the withholding of the Lamerton augmentation of £50 a year (*Wedding-supper*, pp. 119–23).

[32] Walter Godbeare, a Tavistock clothier, whose initials appeared on the title-page of *Tavistock Naboth*. He and John Pointer had a running dispute with Larkham over the Lamerton money (Diary, fo. 'B'v).

[33] 2 Samuel 2:12 (KJV): 'Now the sons of Eli were sons of Belial; they knew not the Lord.'

[34] Marginal note: 'Mr. *Wats* seemeth to relent also; It is hoped and desired God will help him against his many temptations.' Nicholas Watts, friend turned enemy, was the 'Judas' of Larkham's *Judas hanging himselfe* (London, 1658). Larkham regarded Watts as the chief author of *Tavistock Naboth*.

the Church for their scandalous and unsaintlike walking, are grown as bad (if not worse) as those men whom they then accounted very bad, and looked upon as malitious Persecutors.

So much for the forlorn Hope, brought up to begin the fight. [p. 14]

Answers to the additional Articles unto the former.

To the first, This Defendant answered, that not one sentence in the Article is true; But men deal in making Articles, as Atturneys do in drawing declarations. True it is, that upon the detaining of £150 by *John Pointer* and *Walter Godbear*, two of the present Prosecutors, He went to his Son a Minister about five years since, last August the fourth, having an invitation from the Commissioners for the Ministry for the four Northern Countries to come and help them; and by his appointment the pulpit at *Tavistock* was furnished untill September 29 following. And the Defendant did preach in the North divers moneths, and would willingly have left *Tavistock*, because of the implacable malice of *Francis Glanvile* Esquire, *John Jacob*, and other late Officers in the late Kings Army and one *Godbear* an excise man by commission from Sir *Richard Greenvile*.[35] But upon many letters from the Inhabitants that would not part with him (which this Defendant still hath accounted the most considerable, because of their piety and known Integrity to the Commonwealth) He this Defendant came to *London* and upon advice with Godly Ministers, & with an order of re-establishment from the Committee for plundred Ministers, returned again. But by order from Mr. *Glanvile* then a Justice of Peace, the doors of the parish-Church were kept shut on the Lords day and upon the causing of them to be opened many godly men were endited for a supposed riot, but upon traverse thereof acquitted. And also true it is that Mr. *Westlake* did procure an order from *Haberdashers-Hall*, for what money was due out of the sheaf of *Lamerton*. But yet after much trouble and the expence of above 40 pound by the Defendant, much was detained, and some paid to one *Agas* a pretended Minister, even then when this articulate officiated himself.[36] The other suggestions are utterly false concerning going to *Ireland* without making Provision, *&c.* [p. 15]

The second of these Articles which hath a superstitious Christmas man for the Author, one *Gove*,[37] is far otherwise set down then the Articulate spake. True it is that about the time articulate, these words or to this sense, were spoken in prayer by this Defendant, *Lord, which hast given the necks of thine and our enemies into our*

---

35 Glanville and Godbeare have already been mentioned. John Jacob had been a major in the royalist army (*Naboth*, p. 19). Sir Richard Greenvile (1600–59) defected from the parliamentary army to the king's forces and led the siege of Plymouth (*ODNB*).

36 'Mr Westlake' acted for Larkham to claim the Lamerton arrears: in May 1653 he paid 'Mr Westlakes Bills' for 'Commitees plunder[ed] & Haberdashers hall' (Diary, fo. 11v). The Committee for Advance of Money met at Haberdashers Hall, London. 'Agas': perhaps Benjamin Agas (*CR, ODNB*), rector of Chenies, Buckinghamshire (1648–63), or a relative. The parish of Chenies had close ties with the earl of Bedford, as did Tavistock.

37 Alexander Gove of Tavistock, who fell out with Larkham over funeral arrangements for his daughter Loveday Gove (buried 22 January 1654/5, Tavistock PR). Gove had wanted his nephew Andrew Gove, minister of Peter Tavy, to preach the funeral sermon. Larkham allegedly told Gove that as long as the usual 10s fee came to him (not Andrew Gove) he would agree. Gove signed several articles of complaint against Larkham. *Tavistock Naboth*, pp. 27, 28, 41, 71.

hands, and fed thy servants now in power with the flesh of Kings, and Captains, and Nobles, and mighty men &c.[38] *grant that they may look to thy Work thou hast put into their hands, and may not sit still and let things run back to their old beggarly rudiments.* And that this *Gove* doth it out of malice, it is evident by what he spake to one that said he would make the same prayer, that he should complain of him to Authority, to whom *Gove* said, *No Sr. you are my friend, I will not trouble you.* And this *Respondent* humbly prayeth, that his known Integrity in all these late revolutions to the late cause first contended for touching reformation, and the liberties of the Commons in this Common-wealth, may not be questioned upon malitious suggestions of such as were in actual employment in the Kings party, as (they) were Generally that oppose this Defendant, even every one except one that was a mercenary trooper for the Parliament, and some then young and unfit for actual service, who yet were carried in to the quarters of the adverse party for protection, &c. To the third, The articulate saith; That saving the last charge in it, *That he himself was as Michaias,*[39] [(]with the &c. at the end which seems to the Defendant to be unfit to be put into an Article of charge) and saving that the Article is fumbled together, out of malice in the Composer, one *Wats* who hath said he would make the Defendant odious among Ministers, and hath endeavoured it many waies, in satisfaction and service of his unruly lusts and revengefull Spirit; saving (as is said) these things, The Defendant owneth the matter of the Article, having had occasion from the entertainment of wandring Priests, some *Irish* and some other which he could name, to prophane the holy Ordinances of the Lord Jesus, to declare against them and their practices. Some spending the time in reading and singing, and then reading of forms, and the confession of faith, and some scraps of the antiquated Liturgy, and baptizing child in Ale-houses, and being drunk at the very time [p. 16] (as this Defendant hath been enformed and doth believe) some having scarce clothes to their backs; which this Defendant hopeth no godly able Minister is driven unto in these times of encouragement for such as are any way deserving, and some on Lords daies in the afternoon not preaching at all, but spending the time in reading, and singing, and saying of prayers. Other-some youths and boyes that have spent a year or two at the University and learned to swagger and prate a little, taking upon them to speak evil of the thing that they understand not, who having neither book-divinity, nor the experiences of the work of Gods spirit, get into Pulpits, and pronounce the people of God accursed that refuse to joyn them in their absurd, ridiculous and prophane performances: Some patching up dry, discourses out of books, in which, as to them, no juice remained. Some crying peace, peace to all people, whom this Defendant (tis like) may have termed claw-back Priests. But that this Defendant should intend, or did ever speak any word tending to the dishonour of godly learned Ministers fitted in any measure for that high employment of dispensing the word of the Kingdom, is a great calumny cast upon him by this wretched Apostate, the Composer of this rude charge. And the Defendant alleadgeth for himself that he hath often manifested in publique that high esteem which he hath of all Orthodox and pious Ministers,

---

[38] 2 Samuel 22:41, 'Thou hast also given me the necks of mine enemies, that I might destroy them that hate me'; Revelation 19:18, 'That ye may eat the flesh of kings, and the flesh of captains, and the flesh of mighty men, and the flesh of horses, and of them that sit on them, and the flesh of all men, both free and bond, both small and great' (KJV).

[39] Michaias: see n. 23.

though differing from him in judgement in some things (as he confessed (some whom he doth highly honour) are). And therefore humbly prayeth that neither you his Judges, nor any Reverend Ministers of Christ will entertain these slanders and calumnies brought upon him, and he is persuaded, at least hopeth God will not suffer any to swear to every phrase alleadged to be by him used in this Article, or to affirm things so to be, as according to the breed of the Composer is unworthily set forth.

To the fourth, It is answered that surely it could be no good advice, and if the Defendant did give such advice, he was not well advised. But he believeth, he that hath contributed this poor portion to this stock of Articles, will hardly swear it though his offering to swear false for one of Mr. *Condie's* Son, if he would have permitted him (this Defendant hopeth it was [p. 17] rather from rash confidence then otherwise, which he hath often shewen) may give some ground to doubt, that he hath need of one to give him advice to watch over his boysterous, rude and confident spirit, and to blot out that Article and instead thereof to write it was a mistake. Something was spoken by way of discourse of one in *London*, that gave two pence by will to each of those Judges that declared the paying of ship money long ago to be lawfull (as he this Defendant hath been put in mind by some present, for it was quite out of his mind that he said anything like the matter articulate) This is playing smal Game -------- will have a finger in the pye also.

The fifth Article is a perillous one. The truth is this, One *Richard Vivion* (a younger brother to a Gentleman that hath another spirit) a late Captain in the Kings Army[40] assaulted this Defendant as he was walking alone in a close near the Town of T*avistock*, he the said Captain *Vivion* having no business in that place, but coming of purpose to quarrel (if not to do worse) with this Defendant. Many uncivil and opprobrious words he spake, scarce fit to be mentioned; among some of the best, *Thou didst preach last Sunday a base rascally scandalous seditious Sermon.* To whom this Defendant replyed, that many approved this preaching that had as good Judgement as he (or to that effect) He the said Captain *Vivion* replyed, *that none heard him but the scum of the Town*, To whom this Defendant said, (smiling) that sometimes the scum was the best and uppermost as in a milk Pan, and so after some discourse, left him and went another way to avoid him. Now that a Congregation of two or three thousand Hearers, should be so reproached, drew from the Defendant an expression to that sense articulate, though not in that sense the Prosecutors would have it understood, which shews how apt malice is to put an ill construction upon a Christian advise, because these words which shewed how hard it was, were added. Can any one necessarily make those words to signifie an exhortation to revenge? Surely, they must have more Logick, then any of the Prosecutors (or their well-willers) have, to do that.

To the sixth, He saith he always writeth himself Minister of or at *Tavistock*, and yet often saith, not so as to administer seals [p. 18] of the Covenant to all, not Parish-Pastor to all. As for the addition about *Parochus*, &c. it is an addition and false, though it be no great matter, if he had said so (he supposeth) For the rest in

---

40   Probably one of the Vyvyan family, who supported the royalist cause. The births and deaths of various
     children of Richard Vivian, 'gent', appear in Tavistock PR, 1654–60. In October 1660, Larkham
     wrote a poem which named 'vile Vivian' as an opponent (Diary, fo. 39r): although 'vile' was deployed
     as an adjective, it is unlikely to be a coincidence that 'Vyell Vyvyan' was the eldest son of the Vyvyan
     family. See Anne Duffin, 'Vyvyan, Sir Richard, first baronet (1613–1665)', *ODNB*.

this Article, it is answered to it, That he will at all times make good what he hath said: But his Prosecutors have not considered that it becometh not such as are least esteemed in the Church to Judge, &c. I *Cor.* 6. much less as are open enemies to the power of Godliness, or obstinate sinners, or perfidious Revolters from their solemn Covenants, and engagements made, and often renewed before the Lord and his People.[41]

To the seventh, He saith that he well remembreth on a day of solemn humiliation appointed for the Nation, having performed exercises of religion suitable unto the day, unto weariness, in the close he prayed all that were desirous further to seek God, to come to his house where (though he could not, being tired out) others would carry on the work, and he might say, He blessed god that there were many that God had given good abilities unto to pray, and to this effect. And this Defendant professeth, that were it not out of respect to Authority, he should disdain to vouchsafe an answer to such absurd abusive Lyers and slanderers. *The common* Epethite[42] of one of them in the Town, being *Lying Wats*.

To the eighth, He craveth that the instances be brought; the commentary annexed is hypocritical, and befitting the foresaid *Wats*.

To the last he knoweth not that ever he mentioned the words as they are set down, but if he did, he seeth not the scandal of them, or the use of that Article, save only to perform *Wats* his promise or threat to make this Defendant odious among all the Ministers of the Country. *Godbears* work is to make this Defendant an Object of the despite of *Cavaliers*. *Wats* laboureth to render him odious among Ministers and Professors of Religion, in the strictest use of that word Professor. *Goves* malice (above his wit to order the matter) is to make him an enemie to the present Power. *Pointer* serves Mr. *Glanvile's* displeasure against this Defendant, being indebted to him, &c. [p. 19]

To the last paper of gibble gable

He answereth that it deserveth not an answer, save only that patch taken out of the first sort about *John Pointer*, which is answered unto before. As for that ridiculous flourish of his being one of the antientest Magistrates of the Town and Parish of *Tavistock*; This Defendant saith, it is beyond the memory of man to know any Magistrates in *Tavistock*, except Justices of peace of the County. True it is, that the silly people of the Town account the eight men that take accounts by custom, to be Masters of the town. And of late since such were by a faction of Malignants, as are enemies to godliness, and to the present Government, and poor indigent fellows, chosen; they have assumed to them power to chuse Parish-officers[43] contrary to Law and Ordinances of Parliament (as particularly about Church-Wardens, so called) and have been countenanced in opposition to the rigid faction (as Mr. *Glanvile* calls the godly) by the said Mr. *Glanvile*, who hath caused much trouble to honest men, and much expence of money. And this Defendant becomes a Petitioner to such of the Commissioners as are Justices of the peace, to have an eye (as Fathers of

---

[41] 1 Corinthians 6:1–11: Paul berated members of the Corinthian church for divisions and law suits.

[42] 'Epithet'.

[43] Marginal note: '*John Jacob* hath lately been chosen by a prophane Malignant party to be one of the Masters of our Town, who was in the late Kings Army a Major, and stands bound, and paid his tenth, &c.' Larkham named 'deceitfull Jacob' as one of his opponents in a poem of October 1660 (Diary, fo. 39r). Jacob served as a churchwarden in 1662.

their Country) to our Town and Parish: Wherein, to be godly, or to have been for the Parliament formerly, is accounted a sufficient cause to be kept out of offices, notwithstanding present Authority hath ordained the clean contrary. The whole in that Paragraph is a heap of untruths, and scarce two true words in it in all, surely not one true sentence. But for more full satisfaction, although this defendant is verily persuaded that there it not one assertion candidly set down, but something either redundant or deficient, yet if all were true, it would rather render this defendant weak and injudicious, then scandalous. Particularly, He saith now, that the Devil is more Orthodox then many Priests and Ministers in Christendom. And that Religion is in fashion (blessed be God) and that it an easie matter for men upon the score of Religion to abuse such as love Religion: as for the rest of [p. 20] the non sence, he believeth it is fitter for his absurd adversaries to write in Articles, then for him to utter as they are written.

The substance of that of the desire of our Lord Jesus, none but an Ignoramus will question. He referreth himself to what he hath caused to be Printed and presented to the Universitie of *Cambridge*.[44]

That about Gods ugly face, was first taken up by the husband of one *Christian Stevens*, a silly ignorant superstitious woman, and he a wretched enemy, and now as simply bound in this bundle of folly. But the Defendant never said nor thought that God had an ugly face. But hath often used Anthropopathies, as doth the Holy Ghost in Scripture to set out God frowning, scorning, tearing or plaguing wicked men, and blesseth himself at this folly of his adversaries.

Concerning the next silly scrap, he thinks malice was more plentiful then matter, to make his adversaries to play such small game: This Defendant knows not to what end he should speak as is articulate, or to what end this should be put into a charge.

But to the terrible charge which followed, He answereth that one *Digory Pole-wheel* that preacheth at *White-Church*,[45] being gotten up into this Defendants Pulpit, pronounceth the people of God accursed, and their prayer and preaching that refused to hear him, whom they knew no reason why they should hear for he had no call either of God or men to preach at that time: since (some say) he hath been Ordained by divers Ministers, 'Tis possible some words might be spoken by this Defendant, which the prosecutors would make the world believe were intended against this Mr. *Pole-wheel*. The rest he need not be ashamed to own, though much of it be stark false, for he pleaded with divers about some, that he thought did intend well in going to the Parish-meeting house, when that hundreds of choice Christians met elsewhere, and had assistance to carry on the work, for whom he still blesseth God.

That about *Ireland* is a ridiculous untruth, and that Varlet *Francis Glanvile* hath said to some, that this Defendant might have had £300 a year if he would have staid. [p. 21]

That about *John Pointer* hath been answered unto before.

That of groaning under a burden, &c. shews their wickedness that cause it, and it is not articled that Mr. *Larkham* said any such thing.

The town is deprived of many unworthy men that would fain be begging and speaking what they understand not: Godly men have liberty if they please with

44 Larkham's *The attributes of God* (London, 1656).

45 Digory Polewhele, minister at Whitchurch, whose initials appeared on the title-page of *Tavistock Naboth*. Polewhele and other neighbour ministers had joined the Devon Association, while Larkham had not: Shaw, *History of the English church*, II, p. 449.

thanks to speak in the name of the Lord, of which about *Tavistock* the number is small, the Lord make it greater if it be his blessed will. Well at last to hearing it comes, but not until the chief Gentleman disaffected to our Minister, and such as are in Congregational Communication with him, had had a journey to *London*: Who was heard to say at a Gentleman's house in *London*, holding a letter or paper in his hand, and speaking of our Minister Mr. *Larkham, Here is that shall out him.* And it hath been credibly, though privately reported, that a letter was brought from a great man in *London* to a great man in *Exeter* to this purpose, though it prevailed not then. And we are more apt to grieve that any good Gentleman should be so abused by mis-informations (as *David* himself was by a *Ziba* against good *Mephibosheth*[46]) then to have hard thoughts of them: being perswaded, that if those Worthies that have had their ears abused, did but know the truth of things as we do, they would give little thanks to their impudencies that would make them to serve the satisfaction of their unruly lusts, by wronging the innocent, and discouraging good people from well doing.

Here is would require much time to acquaint the Reader with the brags and boasts, scoffs and scorns, threats, menaces and blasphemies, wherewith the streets of our Town ecchoed by the scum of people; talk was of ringing the Bells upon the news of Mr. *Larkhams* ejection, of which they were cock-sure, for a Post was sent from *Exeter* of purpose to hasten away witnesses to attend the service of an angry Gentleman in this expedition. In the meanwhile that little remnant of Christs sheep, prayed and fasted, and wept before the Lords, that were designed to be scattered upon the smiting of their Shepherd. And when all hopes failed (for it was a design that was not on foot) [p. 22] God stepped in: and the result of all was, to perswade Mr. *Larkham* for peace sake to yield up his place: whose answer was, that if the interest of Christ might be kept on foot in *Tavistock*, he would at any time resign to such a person as was thought fit by any of his judgement for the succeeding of him the said Mr. *Larkham*. And thereupon Mr. *Stucley* Minister at *Exeter*, and Mr. *Bartlet* Minister of *Bideford*[47] were agreed upon all sides, and an Order thereupon made, which gave some little content to the adverse party, who hoped that now it would not be long ere they should have their lusts satisfied. The Order followed as it was drawn up after Mr. *Larkham's* departure.

By the Commissioners for the ejecting of scandalous Ministers and Schoolmasters

in the County of *Devon* at *Exon*, the 15. Day of *January*, 1656.

Upon the Exhibition of Articles against Mr. Tho Larkham *Minister of* Tavistock, *and examination of diverse witnesses for proof of the same, It is Ordered that the said Mr.* Larkham *do continue the supply of the cure of* Tavistock *aforesaid, until Mr.* Lewis Stucley *Minister of the Gospel at* Exon, *and Mr.* William Bartlet, *Minister of the Gospel at* Bideford *shall make choice of a fit person to supply the said cure, and to succeed the said Mr.* Larkham *in the work of the Ministry at* Tavistock *aforesaid; unto which the said Mr.* Larkham *(for peace sake) hath freely consented, and prom-*

---

[46] 2 Samuel 16:1–4, 19:24–30: Ziba lied to the fugitive King David, saying Mephibosheth had been unfaithful to him, and as a result received Mephibosheth's estate.

[47] Lewis Stucley (*CR*) and William Bartlet (*CR*, *ODNB*) who were, like Larkham, congregationalists.

ised to resign his right, title and interest in the said Vicarage or Donative (or both) *of* Tavistock *aforesaid into the hands of the Earl of* Bedford *the Patron thereof.* [p. 23] *That the said person so chosen, nominated and approved of by the said Mr.* Stucley *and Mr.* Bartlet, *may be presented by the said Earl of* Bedford *to the said Vicarage or Donative (or both) for his Legal institution and induction thereunto.*

John Copleston.

Jo. Blackmore.

Jo Elford.

James Pearse.

Copia vera.

John Smith Register.[48]

But when tidings was come to the generality of the Godly party that prayed at home, while some accompanied their Pastor to *Exon*, they were much stirred in Spirit, and after great debate, craved a true and full relation of what was done in the business: for the insultings of ungodly men were very great, and the report flew over all the County, that Mr. *Larkham* of *Tavistock* was put out.

And (to be short) they speedily dispatched three chosen men with a Letter to *Exeter* to Mr. *Stucley*, to be communicated to Mr. *Bartlet*, which here followeth. To which after some pause and consideration, that Reverend and holy Servant of Christ in the Gospel Mr. *Stucley*, wrote back an answer: which we hope to publish to the Churches will not be offensive or displeasing to that blessed Servant of God. For necessity calls for it, sith wicked men will not be quiet and wait the conveniences of changing Ministers, which is not of so light concernment as men unskilful in the things of God imagine. [p. 24]

To the Reverend Mr. Lewis Stucley, *Pastor of the Church of* Exon;
and Mr. William Bartlet, *Pastor of the Church of* Bideford.

Reverend Sirs,

It hath pleased our gracious Father, for such ends as are best known to himself, of later to suffer our Reverend Pastor causlesly to be molested by restless and unsanctified Spirits, yea Articled against before the Commissioners for ejecting scandalous Ministers, &c. which after hearing and examining of witnesses against him, (to be short) was Cleared and Acquitted of the Crimes laid to his charge: the two main ones then insisted on being dis-affection to the present Government, and negligence in his Ministry, in which we are easily induced to perswade ourselves that

---

[48] Larkham made a note of 2s-6d paid to 'Register Smith' for the copy of an order: Diary, fo. 24v. John Copleston, John Blackmore, John Elford and James Pearse all served as Justices of the Peace in the 1650s (Devon Record Office, Exeter, QS28/7–12) but here also acted as county commissioners for the Ejection of Scandalous Ministers, 'Ejectors'. Elford frequently took evidence at Tavistock alongside Larkham's opponent, Francis Glanville JP.

the malice of his wicked Persecutor did out-run their wit. But not many daies ago there came by Providence into our hands a Copy of the Order which was made by the aforesaid Commissioners, &c. relating to our Pastor; the which Order one of you (we presume) cannot but be acquainted with: the substance whereof is, that he do continue the said Cure until Mr. Lewis *Stucley* and Mr. *William Bartlet* shall make choice of a fit person to succeed him, to which is added, *unto which the said Mr. Larkham hath freely consented for peace sake*: As soon, Reverend Sirs, as our eyes saw this, for satisfaction about the latter clause, we made some of us our addresses to our Pastor, desiring him to examining his words, how far he was engaged to make a Surrender or resignation of his Cure unto another. (as is intimated in the Order.) But after deliberation, he told us that the Register was not candid in the composition of what was the result of the business [p. 25] and that he did no farther promise to lay down his Interest and consent to have another in his place, as his Successor, than that it might be satisfactory to the Church and people of Christ here. Nor was this spoken (as we apprehended him) from any desire to lay down his Pastoral charge, and to quit the cure before God should, according to Scripture rule, give him a call there-from, but only to testifie to the world, that outward advantages were not the Loadstone that held him here; and he still professes, would the Church of Christ give him a Relaxation, he should think himself freed from a great burden, and as a token of his thankfulness, would give £20 to the poor of the Church at his departure. That, Reverend sirs, which we are so exceedingly offended at, & for which we are so deep[l]y afflicted, is, that the Commissioners should think it so light a thing, to separate betwixt a Pastor and a People, and that they should take from the Church that Authority which King Jesus hath put into her own hands, to elect her own officers. However, we look on it as a specal Providence, that the care of our society is cast into your hands, of whom we have no other reason to Judge but that ye will give unto the Church that which is hers. And whereas it is inserted upon the order, that the said Mr. *Larkham* hath freely consented hereto for peace sake: we do boldly affirm, upon the many years experience, we have had of the Implacability, and diabolical restlessness of Malignant spirits against the scepter of Christ in this place, that nothing less is expected by us, than a New war upon his removal; and without question those very hands which were ready to ring the bels for Joy, and those unhallowed tongues, which have exceedingly blasphemed God and his People upon the news of the last weeks Transactions at *Exon*, will be as ready (upon the least crossing of their lusts and sinful humours) not only to Article against another (if God should give him to us) to defame him in his Reputation, and obstruct his maintenance, but (if it be in their power) also to deprive him of his life; for the malice of wretches in *Tavistock* against the Power of Godliness, is exceeding deadly. If the intent of the Order be to strike up a peace betwixt us and these, we answer in the words of *Jehu*, What peace so long, &c.[49] or in the words of the Apostle, what communion [p. 26] hath Christ with *Belial*, &c.[50] But lest it should be suggested (for we are very jealous) that the differences of *Tavistock* are between Saints and Saints, and the intent of the order is to compose the breaches among them; We further answer, besides such as have been lately cast out for gross miscarriages, we know

---

[49] 2 Kings 9:22 (KJV): 'And it came to pass, when Joram saw Jehu, that he said, Is it peace, Jehu? And he answered, What peace, so long as the whoredoms of thy mother Jezebel and her witchcrafts are so many?'

[50] 2 Corinthians 6:15 (KJV): 'What concord hath Christ with Belial?'

not two in the place that ever had the face of Religion that are at a profest distance from us; yea, so tender are we in this respect, that to prefer peace among such, we scruple not to give the right-hand of fellowship unto such who differ in judgement from us, as to circumstances. But were it true, that in *Tavistock*, two or three Professors or more there were which were discontented; We humbly conceive it far more requisite that such declare the causes thereof, that they may be satisfied than that in a preposterous manner, the Interest of Jesus Christ should vail Bonnet[51] to the lawless lusts of men. Reverend Sirs, (because we will not be too tedious) we cannot as yet but look on Mr. *Larkham* as our Pastor, and the legal Minister of *Tavistock*, though if ungodly ones could have brought their malice to effect, they would have caused his removal, to his great Infamy, and Non-capacitated him for future service in the Church of Christ. These shall be sure to answer this one day at the Tribunal seat of Christ without repentance: and now again their eyes are unto you; the hopes of all such as are enemies to Christ in this place, fetch their breath from the power the Commissioners in the order have entrusted you with; but we trust (yea are very confident) that you will be tender of the Church of Christ, and not intrude (nor suffer to be intruded what in you lies) on us or on the place, such an one as will either stop the charriot-wheels of Reformation here, or make us drive on with the slower pace. As the high Priest answered *Pilate* in another case, We have no King but *Caesar*.[52] So say we[.] we have, we desire none to go in and out before us in the work of a Pastor, but him which God hath already given us, of whose Ministry we are the Seals, at least the greatest number of us; And for a further Testimony of God owning him, we affirm that eight persons have acknowledged in the presence of God and us, that by his Ministry, since his coming home from *Ireland*, they have been plucked as so many fire-brands out of [p. 27] the fire, half burnt, and two other which were under the censure of the Church, have humbly since desired reconciliation. Honoured Srs. let us not incur your check to shew our zeal in the behalf of him, to whom next to Christ we owe no Relation so much love and thankfulness; the heavenly streams of consolation which have dropped from his Ministry, and by which we have been refreshed, do make us willing to undergo the greatest difficulties, and to deny our selves the sweetest wordly peace for the enjoyment of him; therefore we humbly desire you, (as you tender the exaltation of Christ his Interest in this place, as you would be loth to administer matter of offence to the spouse of Christ, and as you would be unwilling to have the blood of souls lie crying at your doors) to weigh the groanings of this despised handfull, and have no fellowship with suth *[sic]* as say in this the time of *Jerusalems* affliction, Down, down with it even to the ground.[53] We trust these few lines will find Acceptance; we leave them to your consideration; and if you will honour us so far as to give a Return in answer, we shall humbly thank you: In the Interim you and the people God hath given you, shall be on our hearts at the throne of grace; the which is also begged of you by us, who are the weakest of all Saints.

This Letter was subscribed by *John Leer, Daniel Condy, John Brownsdon,*

---

51 'Vail bonnet': doff the cap, 'take off the bonnet in token of respect' (*OED*, 'bonnet', v).

52 John 19:15.

53 Psalm 74:7 (KJV): 'They have cast fire into thy sanctuary, they have defiled by casting down the dwelling place of thy name to the ground.'

Richard Peek, William Web, Emanuel Frost;[54] with above fifty other. And this following Postscript was added.

This was freely consented to by the whole Church, and subscribed by as many as we could speak withall in so short a time, save only (for some causes) we thought it not expedient to acquaint our Pastor herewith, but only in general that we would write. And we have desired Mr. *John Leer, David Condy,* and *August Bond*[55] to be the Bearers hereof, and to make a further declaration of our mind unto you.

Tavistock Jan. 24. 1657. [p. 28]

To my beloved friends the Church of
Christ in Tavistock *these present.*

Honoured in the Lord,
I thought ere this I might have enjoyed an opportunity of assuring you how welcome your Messengers were to me and the more, because of those blessed breathings of the Spirit with which they and your paper were filled. It may not be expected that I should particularly speak to the contents of your Letter; I desire to be excused if I forbear to answer the desires of some of you in this thing: Only be assured that I shall with much tenderness consider your affairs, and shall do my utmost endeavours to furnish you with one so qualified, as that you may not be tempted to warp from your principles, but rather may be confirmed in them: If I know my own heart, I hate the intruding any person that shall with hay and stubble hazard the work of Christ in *Tavistock*, and shall rather forbear the naming of any one to your Town, then such as may pull up the foundations of Church-Government. I think it a vanity to move for any to succeed Mr. *Larkham*, until I have an assurance from the Earl of *Bedford* that he will settle him, and until the Town, or your selves, shall manifest some expedient how he may subsist there, and therefore think it not strange if you hear not from me until I hear from the Patron. I thought it my duty so far to open myself to you, and had given you this sooner, but that ever since your friends were here, I have laboured under bodily indispositions; which are so many that they hasten me to tell you that I am

4. *Feb.*   *Your very true Friend to serve you*
Exon 1656   *in the work of Christ*
                              Lewis Stucley

[p. 29]
Thus it hath pleased the God and Father of our Lord Jesus Christ to hear us and help us hitherto: Thus far the Lord hath holpen us.[56] Now it came into the mind of our Minister to make a journey to *London* about his arrears due out of *Lamerton*, this being the 4. year of his being unpaid his £50 *per annum*. And surely would we have consented he would long ago have quitted his publick relation as National Teacher to this place: but we still saw God blessing his Ministry for the bringing in of souls, of which scarce another to us known hath such a black box out of heaven,

---

[54] These names appear many times in Larkham's diary.
[55] David Condy, brother to Daniel; Augustine Bond, schoolmaster to Larkham's grandson.
[56] 'Thus far the Lord hath holpen us': Larkham's frequent refrain in the diary, recalling 1 Samuel 7:12.

though hundreds get the approbation, which yet we hear, (to our great grief, rather that things are so carried, then for anything else) is to this experienced Minister of Jesus Christ denied. What men have to say against him walketh in darkness, and must come under the head of whispering or backbiting: for if Laws either of God or men might take place, things could not be as they are. But designs are on foot to demolish the glorious building at *Tavistock*: God grant other places to prepare for the like sawce for their Dainties (as we have had and are like to have) with and after ours. But he is All-sufficient.

[p. 30]

An Addition written by me Thomas Larkham
my self, and in my own name only.

I know right well, that for evil actions, and things unjustifiable, the best Apology is Repentance, Satisfaction, and a doing so no more: and to that end to strike (in the help of the holy Spirit) at the root of that sin in the soul which hath prevailed: else upon the least temptation there will be a returning to folly again. Yet must we not play the Devils with ourselves, nor be over wicked either with *Cain* and *Judas*, above the mercy of a God; or by consenting to the exorbitant waies which some men of great pretended zeal and holiness would have us walk in, cause more dishonour to Religion.

Upon occasion I was walking in *White-hall* yard, with one Mr. *John Baker* (now of his Highness guard) who lived in the same Plantation I lived in, in *New England*;[57] and (I am confident) is able to say more evil of me then all *Adams* sons in the world, from the rising of the Sun unto the going down thereof. I desired him towards the latter end of *September*, when (as I said) I was walking with him in the place aforesaid, to ask whether the Commissioners, (to wit for approbation, &c.) sate or no. The party of whom he enquired, was the door-keeper of the Chamber of Tryal. He seeing him with me in the Court walking before, said to this purpose, (as I have it from Mr. *Bakers* mouth) If you ask because of Mr. *Larkham*, I can assure you his business is ended, and it is ordered that his [p. 31] writings be delivered up unto him, which was one of the desires he made in his paper delivered to Mr. *Peters*.[58] And after some further talk he said to Mr. *Baker*, to this effect he spake as near as I can remember what was told me. The business was an hour and half debating; and the villanies laid to his charge in *New England*, and since in *Old England*, are so many and great, that the Commissioners have resolved not to approve of him. I repeated by way of question the word {villanies} whether that word were used; and he replyed, yea, he used that very word. I asked of him what villanies he knew by me? He told me, If I may be suffered to speak, I will quit you from all harm that

---

57 John Baker, like Larkham, had been at Dover (Northam), New Hampshire: Susan Hardman Moore, *Pilgrims: New World settlers and the call of home* (New Haven and London, 2007), pp. 145 n. 18, 154.

58 Hugh Peter, like Baker, had known Larkham in New England. He had been sent to Northam to arbitrate in the dispute between Larkham and Hanserd Knollys: *The journal of John Winthrop 1630–1649*, ed. Richard S. Dunn, James Savage and Laetitia Yeandle (Cambridge, MA, 1996), pp. 349–50. Hardman Moore, *Pilgrims*, pp. 61–2; Carla Gardina Pestana, 'Peter, Hugh (*bap.* 1598, *d.* 1660)', *ODNB*.

can come to you for anything done in *New England* by you. And he further said, I will justifie, that whereas some say it was proved in *New England* that you had a base child by your servant, that it was never proved, though I was at the transaction of all business both before the Church and Magistrate. And she solemnly avouched that neither you nor she herself knew of her being with child when you came from *New England.* (Which is now fifteen years ago.) And that one *Joseph Austin* a man-servant in the house was vehemently suspected to be the Father of it. But withal the said (being exceedingly threatned by Captain *Wiggen* your known adversary) that it was yours, and this is the cuttingst word I can say. So far Mr. *Baker.* I have been faithful in my Narration, if any doubt they may enquire.[59]

But that no stone might be left unturned to preserve the honour of those truly Godly Commissioners, that act meerly upon the account of providing Teachers for this poor untoward Nation, and from my desire withal to keep up the interest of Christ in *Tavistock*, and to procure two hundred pounds arrears out of *Lamerton* due unto me, (my necessities calling for it, and Law giving it to me) which by mens malice, and other providences occasionally hath been, and is yet kept from me: I went again to the Commissioners for approbation, and told all the truth, and how I had been from time to time prosecuted, and was now again in mine absence from home, summoned to appear the seventh of the next Month *September* upon farther Articles (so called) as mine intelligence signified to me. [p. 32] Whereupon they seemed doubtful (chiefly my Countryman Mr. *Bond*)[60] what those further Articles might be, and gave me this answer after consultation, that because I lay charges in the City, I were best to repair home, and to give an account in time, what the Articles were, and the result of the proceedings of the Commissioners, and to send up that under the hand of the Register of that Court at *Exon*, with a Certificate and Attestation annexed for mine abilities and godly conversation: and that thereupon I should have their approbation for the obtaining of mine arrears, and the further enjoying the augmentation of *Lamerton*, (for so it is now become, being formerly a settled annuity) without any personal attendance. Against which fair, and Christian, and brotherly determination, I have nothing to say: only (as I said then) I might have chosen whether I would have acquainted them with that news, whereby occasion was taken of putting off the approbation, which otherwise (possibly) I might have attained, and by means thereof, have obtained an Order for the Trustees sitting at *Westminster* to have received mine arrears due unto me. But Gods time is the best time. The Lord sanctifie unto me all his dispensations, and give such an issue to the prayers of his poor despised ones at *Tavistock*, and the long troubles, travels, toils and tossings of me his most worthy servant in the Gospel of his Son, as to his good, and gracious, just and holy pleasure and wisdom shall seem good.

Amen.

---

[59] Joseph Austin, a man-servant in the Larkham household in Dover, has not been located in other sources. Thomas Wiggin managed the trading post at Dover and was mired in the disputes there: Winthrop, *Journal*, pp. 58n, 284–5.

[60] Perhaps the lawyer John Bond – like Larkham, the son of a Dorset linen draper – Master of Trinity Hall (Larkham's former college), and a member of Inner Temple. Stephen Wright, 'Bond, John (1612–1676)', *ODNB*.

[p. 33]

Postscript

The Reader is to take notice, that of all the former Articles, only two were insisted upon, which were referred either to the head of disaffection to the Government, or to negligence; the rest were exhibited to make a noise; no proofs offered at all to divers of them. ———The Author sent for the other Articles he is to answer unto the next Moneth, but the Register denyeth to give a Copy of them, (as by Letter he is informed.) And withall that one, a Minister, saith, he did not now fear Mr. Larkham's ejection, because all the Commissioners were Presbyterians. It is hoped this will be taken notice of, as also the design that is on foot now in Devon *against the honest party.*

FINIS.

Judas hanging himselfe: or Naboths false accuser intangled in his own testimony. Set forth in a rejoinder of the church of Christ in Tavistock, to a scurrillous pamphlet published lately by N. W. &c ([London], 1658)

JUDAS Hanging Himselfe:

OR

NABOTHS

FALSE ACCUSER

INTANGLED

in his own

TESTIMONY.

Set forth in a Rejoinder of the Church of Christ in *Tavistock*, *Devon*, to a scurrillous pamphlet published lately by *N.W, &c.* once a Member but since a persecutor of the said Church.

Written chiefly for the undeceiving of such as have been or may be too credulous thereof; by giving them a Character of the man in his sundry contradictions, slanders, lies and untruths (besides opprobrious and uncivil language) which swarm, for multitude like the frogs of *Ægypt, almost* in every page of his book.

The tongue deviseth mischiefs, like a sharp raysor working deceitfully. Thou lovest evil more than good, and lying rather than to speak Righteousnesse. Thou lovest all devouring words, O thou deceitful tongue, Psal 52. 2, 3, 4.

Out of thine own mouth will I judge thee, thou wicked servant, Luke 19. 22.

And Judas also ... stood with them, John 18. 5.

Amara persecutio in cruore martyrum, amarior in pugna
Hæreticorum, amarissima in malis moribus domesticorum. *Ad:*
Omnis malus aut ideo vivit ut corrigatur, aut ideo ut per illum
bonus Exerceatur. *Aug.*

Printed for the use of the Authors. 1658.

THE
PREFACE

Whereas there hath not many dayes ago been published unto the World an Invective Pamphlet in answer to our Naboth *or* Narrative *of Complaint (heretofore presented to the Magistracy and Ministry of this Nation, to undeceive them from that prejudice which the Enemies of Christ and his interest in this place had begotten amongst some of them, at least against him who is our Reverend Pastour) which said Invective hath been set out by five pair of Capital Letters, viz. FG. DP. WG. NW. WH.[1] all which (if we mistake them not, for they enforceth us to play at blinde mans buffe) have been no new-found enemies to the person of our Pastour, and to the Vin-yard which the Lords right hand hath planted in this place, and two of them in a most eminent manner; which said two (Represented by NW. WH) once in Communion with us, but now Apostates, do with brazen sore heads and undaunted spiri[t]s in this the day of their Rebellion Combine with the three former, as* Herod *and* Pontius Pilate *(which once were at variance among themselves, but since agreed) to pass sentence upon this Church and Pastour thereof, (a thing that may not pass for a Novelty in those dayes, neither indeed hath it been looked on as a Wonder in former* [sig. A2v] *Generations, if we begin to reckon from the first Reformation begun by Christ himself).*

We thought it no less then our duty for the prevension of that Credit which (possibly) his violent accusations might enforce from the simplicity of the Reader, and that we might give our Testimony to all the Churches of Christ concerning Mr. Thomas Larkham our Reverend Pastour, whom the Lord by his mighty power and stretched out arm (for we can attribute it to nothing else) hath [been] for divers years last past as it were Miraculously preserved from the raging and Implacable malice both of such as are down-right prophane, and those which for their obstinate carriage under Admonitions have formerly been cast forth this Church (whatever their smoothing Apologies pretend to the contrary:) For those considerations and divers others, we say, We thought it our duty to send abroad these papers into the world as a check-mate to accompany the other Libellous Pamphlet wherever it

---

[1] *Judas* was the third of four rounds in the pamphlet bout between Larkham and his opponents in the late 1650s. A discussion of the controversy and its the hinterland is provided in the Introduction. Larkham's opponents had replied to *Naboth* with *Tavistock Naboth* (London, 1658). Only the authors' initials appeared on the title-page, but the Bodleian's copy (see Plate 9) has been annotated to fill these out: 'Francis Glanvile. Diggory Polwheel. Walter Godbear. Nicholas Watts. William Hore'. Larkham replied with *Judas*, casting Watts in the *rôle*: once a dear disciple, now a betrayer. The first quotation from Augustine on the title-page spoke to the theme: 'Bitter is persecution in the blood of martyrs, more bitter in the battle of the heretics, most bitter in the evil of those of my household'. The second set it all in the context of Providence: 'Every wicked man lives either so that he may be corrected, or so that a good man may be trained by him'. After *Judas*, Larkham's opponents had the last word in *A strange metamorphosis in Tavistock* (London, [1658]). In this tract, *Judas*, Larkham presented evidence that in the past his relations with his flock – especially Watts – had been good. A critique of *Tavistock Naboth* followed: 99 points, no less. The rest focussed on refuting charges laid by ex-members of the gathered church. Only two copies of *Judas* appear to survive, in the Wallace Notestein Collection at the Library of the College of Wooster, Ohio, and at University College London.

wanders, or as a counter-poyson against that venomous Infection it hath engendered in our Westerne Air.

Wee shall not spend much time, nor waste much paper in finding out the principal Authour of that sordid book, neither indeed shall we take upon us peremptorily to determine who they all are that stand in the Title Page so cloathed in Capital Letters. It is sufficient to our purpose that we know who was the chief contriver; and for the rest, (if we mistake them not) as they added the least part to those many scores of slaunders which are in the Book asserted, so are we as willing to passe them by with the least observance. And therefore we shall contest neither with great nor small, but only with NW. alias Nicholas Watts, the undoubted pen-man thereof, which to prove so, were but to be prodigal of paper, sith some of us have had it from his own mouth, and from the mouth of his Allies and intimate Acquaintance, as being very suspitious (it seems)that our folly would have mis-fathered his elaborate piece upon another, and so have robbed him of his so Gaped-for Acclamations.

Now, because the Accuser hath most sadly represented this our much injured Pastour unto the world, and hath strongly endoavoured to make him unto all the countrey round about, a common Butt of obloquie and reproach. And because men are ever held unfit to [sig. A3] *speak in their own behalf (so incredulous is the world, as always to turn a deaf ear to what Apologies soever (though never so just) are made by men in their own particular causes. And because we are who are in Church Relation with him are reported and that most slanderously by this false Accuser in one page of his book, to be* men engaged to his will, *and therefore (possibly) might be thought (by such who are two credulous) too partial in the evidences we give of both the one and the other, we have judged it the best way in undeceiving the world, and setting them aright in their judgements about the said* Mr. Larkham, *to make the Manuscripts of this Accuser no less then Judge in the present controversy. And to this end we shall do little else at present (for if the Lord will, and other Churches advise, we shall take another time to answer the book in a more particular way) then summon forth his own papers, Certificates, answers to Articles, &c. (which he himself since prosecutes in an opposit way) that were contracted by himself, and signed with his own hand, to stand up as so many individuate witnesses to the acquitting of the said* Mr. Larkham *against his slanderous charges from the time of his first acquaintance with him until the time nearly of his rejection, and to the sentencing of the said N.W. (himself) as a Notorious slanderer.*[2] *As for what other contumelies this accuser since his rejection from Church-Communion hath raked together, we hope the ingenuity of the impartial Reader will impute rather unto malice than matter unto the satisfaction of his lust of revenge, rather then to the truth of the accusation.*

If the inquisitive Reader be willing to have an account from us why there had not been a more ample and distinct handling of these matters of charge. We answer thus,

First, That , at present it is not so much as intended by us to give the Reader satisfaction unto all those innumerable slanders, lies and untruths with which the accusers book is swolne (though to many no doubt we may) because that work is referred (as was hinted before) to another opportunity. Nor

---

2   Marginal note: 'Nec enim lex justior ulla est quam necis artifices arte perire sua.' (There is no law more just than that slaughterers perish by their own devices.)

Secondly, Is the end of our appearance in publick view so much to shew our own Attestations for our Pastour, as to produce the former attestations of his accuser, leaving it to the ingenuous Reader whether most credit to the man either when [sig. A3v] *he was in Church relation may be given, or to him since he hath (under his distemper of malice) prov'd himself a persecutor.*

3 *That these papers are not the product of weeks but only of dayes, The Accusers Libel (for a great part thereof by his own confession) a work of years. The great disproportion therefore in the time of their composure cannot admit that we should make so distinct and thorow a progress. And the reason why we have made so surreptitious an adventure into the world, is that jealously we have least that vene-mous pamephlet contract too much prejudice in the breasts of some, and be an occasion that the name and wayes of God be blasphemed by others, ere these papers came to light.*

If any man list to have any further account from us touching this matter (though what is said we hope might satisfie) we shall answer with Mariano Silesio,[3] *when being on a time importun'd by two compleat curtezans to write a Poem in the praise of beauty, he thus replies,* That he could go neer to paint them out, but he thought his pencil might well be spar'd, for they knew better how to paint themselves. *Not to detain the Reader with any longer Preface, we shall first give him the copies of such papers as upon sundry occasions were composed by the pen of the (now) accuser himself, one onely drawn up by another, to which yet we have his hand. All which might serve as a sufficient Vindicative of* Mr Larkham *from most of these contumelious charges of late, exhibited to the world against him.*

[p. 4]

This first Paper containeth in it the desire of the Church to Mr. *Thomas Larkham*, upon his offer to leave the place upon some discouragement taken by occasion of a complaint made by some Enemies to one in authority against him.

To our Reverend Pastor Mr. Thomas Larkham *Minister of the Gospel in* Tavistock.

We the inhabitants of the Town and Parish of *Stavistock* [sic], whose names are subscribed, having bowed our knees to the Father of our Lord Jesus Christ, of whom the whole family in heaven and earth is named, that he would grant us according to the riches of his mercy, (after so long and sad a vacancy of the misteries of salvation to this poor ignorant place, wherein are so many hundred souls that know not the right hand from their left in matters of Religion,) that our eyes might once more see such a teacher as we might take comfort in: *And now having our Petitions at last answered in such a way as we must needs confess it is the Lords own doing.* Now for as much as we understand that of late there hath been a certain paper drawn up, and sent to the Right Honourable Col. *Desbrow*,[4] by those whose minds are dark-

---

3   Mariano Silesio, Florentine poet and statesman (d. 1368), known in English for *The Arcadian princesse* (London, 1635).
4   John Disbrowe (*ODNB*).

ened (through the ignorance that is in them,) *to quench the Gospel light among us,
and rob us of those comforts, which we now enjoy*, do beseech you in the bowels of
Jesus Christ not to be disheartned in your labour of love in this work of the Lord
amongst us, professing that *we whose hearts have been oft warmed by those sweet
discoveries of the Love of God, which by the Assistance of his own spirit you have
held forth unto us*, do resolve in the strength of Christ to stick close unto you in
defending you against all injurious practices whatsoever [p. 5] in the Prosecution of
your Ministery, desiring you to finish that building for God which you have begun,
that the enemies themselves being convinced (if it be the will of God) of the loveli-
ness thereof may at length come in and cry Grace, Grace unto it.

This was subscribed by *Nicolas Watts*, who was also the composer of it, *Sep.
23. 1650.*

*At the same time also there was a Certiticate or Attestation subscribed by many, and
among the rest by N W. as followeth.*
> To all in Authority within this Common wealth whom
> these presents many any way concern.

These are to certifie (with all due respect) that whereas about six or eight of our
parish of *Tavistock* have drawn up a writing against *our Reverend, godly, learned
and Orthodox Minister,* Mr. Thomas Larkham, *(whom in much mercy as a return to
prayers God hath sent among as)* in which writing (as we are informed) they lay
to his charge rayling, and have particulariz'd some particular reproachful names,
and some other Accusations besides (the particulars whereof we cannot learn) We
for our parts (tho constant hearers of the said Mr. *Larkham*) *never heard any other
words out of the Pulpit, proceeding from, or saw any carriage or behaviour in him,
then that which well becometh a Minister of the Gospel of Christ* (so far as we can
judge,) and we shall think it *a very great judgement of God and loss to the Town
and Parish. If he should depart, or be removed from us.*

And we further certifie that his chiefest and most opposers[5] are men ill-affected
to the present Government, who take offence at his zealous and careful observance
of the Acts and Ordinances of the Parliament of *England* that come unto his hands.

This was dated Sept. 23. 1650.

[p. 7][6]
A Letter written by Nicho. Wats, *to Mr.* L *being in* Cumberland, *for his return which
was subscribed by the members of the Church, together with himself.*

Mr. *Larkham,* and our ever honoured Pastor,
Yours of the 25. of *August* came to our hands last *Friday*, in which taking notice of
Gods gracious providence over you in so long and dangerous a journey, an abundant
cause hath been administred unto us to bless God in your behalf. As concerning the
Church, we do by these certifie, that our affections towards you are the same that
ever they were; *and for opposers unto truth and godliness (as long as there is a
devil, and that devil hath instruments, the Church of God must never look to be free)*
but for ours, you know they are serpents without stings, all their actions consisting
in sitting still. However, Gods Church that hath the Moon under her feet is out of

---

5   Marginal note: 'He means Mr. F.G. [Francis Glanville] with whom he stands now in the title page.'
6   The pagination jumps at this point.

their reach, and for their seeking out for a Minister (which you mention in yours) we are likely to be as long without, as formerly we have been, unless God in his providence do otherwise provide for us: wherefore our joint and hearty desire is, that you will consider of our condition in your absence, and that by changing your thoughts of deferring your return until Winter be over, you would hasten to be with us before Winter come on. We have no more to do for present (besides our Petitioning the God of mercies *to hasten you again in mercy to us*) but onely to request you, that if you have not already, you would in your return take such course (which we are confident you may easily do) that the business of *Lammerton* may be settled, so that for the future, the enemy may not have the least opportunity to molest your quiet. Thus having exprest our desires, we do commend you, our selves, and our present estate into the hands of him that is able to do more exceedingly abundant then we are able either to ask or think.[7] Dated, *8 Sept. 1651.*

Transactions after Mr. L. his return from Cumberland, *upon the Call of the Church in* Tavistock.

In the moneth of *May, 1652.* God brought our Pastour safe to *Tavistock* about the middle of the week, who upon the Lords day following preached in publick, both in the Morning and Afternoon without opposition, Notwithstanding, one Mr. *Agas* was upon tryal entertained as their Minister some weeks before. But the *Wednesday* following, when Mr *L.* thought to have preached his usual Lecture, the doors of the Parish Meeting-house were shut against him; which caused him forthwith to return to *London*, and to make complaint hereof to the Committee for Plundred Ministers; by whom after a long debate, he was settled and confirmed, as by their Order, of the 16. *June, 1652.* appeareth; a Copy whereof is here given, word for word. [p. 8]

By the Committee for Plundred Ministers, June 16, 1652.
"Upon consideration had of the Petition of the Inhabitants of *Tavistock*, in the County of *Devon*, and forasmuch as Mr. *Thomas Larkham*, Minister of the said Church (having discontinued the service of the Cure of the said Church for divers moneths now past) was imployed in the service of the Parliament: It is ordered that the said Mr. *Larkham* be settled and confirmed in the said Church and Vicaridge thereof; and that he do continue to officiate the Cure thereof as Vicar, and possess, enjoy, receive, and take to his own use the Titles, Rents, duties and profits thereto belonging, till further order shall be taken in the premisses, And all person and persons are required to yield all due obedience hereunto accordingly, And the Sheriff and Justices of Peace in the said County, or any or either of them, are hereby authorized and impowered to see the said Mr. *Larkham* settled in the quiet and peaceable possession thereof, and to remove all impediments and obstructions that may disturb his said possession."

Notwithstanding which Order, the doors were again shut up, *June 27.* being the Lords day, in the year aforesaid; one of which was forced open, at Mr *Ls.* request, and the desire of the Parishioners there present, The Constable of the Hundred, and four other petty Constables of the Town and Parish of *Tavistock* being among them.

---

7 Ephesians 3:20 (KJV): 'Now unto him that is able to do exceeding abundantly above all that we ask or think.'

Whereupon divers *godly men* were bound over by Mr. *Glanvil*, and another Justice
of the Peace, the *Tuesday* following, upon a supposed riot, which after an Endict-
ment was traversed, were with Mr. *L* acquitted (who onely voluntarily appeared
among them that were bound over) yet was Indicted with them. And also Articles
were exhibited against Mr. *L* into the Committee for plundred Ministers, to which
Mr. *L* gave in answers which were accompanied with attestations of the members of
the Church drawn up by the pen of *Nicholas Wats,* which here follow.

> *The humble Attestation of the members of the Church of God at* Tavistock
> *annexed to the answers of Mr.* Larkham *their Reverend Pastor, unto the eight*
> *Articles exhibited unto this honourable Committee against him.*

We whose names are hereunto subscribed, that have been constant hearers of our
Reverend Pastor, Mr. *Thomas Larkham*, during that time he hath been in *Tavistock*
(it being four years) *never heard him speak any thing in all that time in disparage-
ment of this present Government* (under which God of his mercy hath been pleased
to place us) but he hath constantly, as often as any opportunity hath been presented,
manifested himself both in publique and private, *as sincere and faithful a vindi-
cator of their most just proceedings* as any (we are perswaded) this Common-wealth
yields.

To the second, wherein it is asserted that he was taken to be an enemie to the
Common wealth by a Council of War, being under the Regiment of Sir *Hardresse
Waller*, we which hereunto have subscribed [p. 9] have seen a fair dismission under
the hand of the above said *Sr. H. Waller* with an order to receive his arrears: And
as far as ever we could hear *the differences between him and his opponents were
only personal*. If it were otherwise, we cannot but admire that their own reputation
had not hindered his enemies from inserting this; sith some of those, which are his
greatest Adversaries, were at that time labouring with him to come and take the
charge of this place.

To the third, (that he is a common Raylor, &c.) and that backt with a large Catalogue of names[8] (some whereof *we are confident he never used in his life, nor ever
knew the meaning of*) and for the rest, we referre you to his sermons printed on the
22. of *March*, whence they have pickt one here and another there, we shall say the
less of this, because we find *few words therein which are not in scripture*, and for
the rest, the Book will answer for itself: as for that passage, God pour on you and
yours the vials of his wrath, he that reads the 22. page, will find the sence farre
otherwise then there set down. Lastly as to that he said to one, go, and the curse of
God go with thee, we do certifie you, *That man was a member of the Church and
cast out for drunkeness, what was therein done, was, (as we conceive) under a far
other consideration then in the Article is suggested.*

To the fourth, That he hath been a sower of discord and hatred in all Parishes
where he hath been, &c. If they knew this, why did they so much labour his setling

---

8   Marginal note: 'The Accuser meanes the word *Ninhihammer* and *Purquinion*, as can be proved by
     many present at the drawing up of this Attestation.' 'Ninnyhammer': 'a blockhead, a fool or braggart'
     (*OED*). 'Purquinion' (pur-quinion) is perhaps a word Larkham coined to sum up his opponents – the
     five authors of *Tavistock Naboth* – as a pack of five knaves. 'Pur' was a jack or knave at cards, and
     had currency as a prefix for nonsense words; a 'quinion' is a set of five things (*OED*). The book
     referred to in the text is Larkham's *The wedding-supper* (1652).

here. All that we say is, that *we have seen and he can shew certificates from* Northam, *his Church in* Lewisham, *and New*-England, *as speak him to have abundant respect and honour, answerable to those parts, holiness of live, and gravity, which since his living among us, we have had good evidence of.*

To the fifth, He preached that god and the Devil did cast lots, &c: is so ridiculous, as we hope hath vanity and folly enough in it to convince any man that *such words could not come from such a man as he is,* But for that venomous aspersion of a whole Church it cannot (we are confident) but receive a frown from *Mordecai* that God hath set at sterne.[9] Concerning the charge, we dare say as once a Martyr did, they shall one day answer for it unto Christ and us, &c.[10]

As to that Article of Gathering a Tumultuous rout, &c. We whose names are here-unto subscribed being then present do certifie that our Pastour having an order from this honourable Committee to preach the Gospel in this Town, Came on the 27. of *June* being the Lords day, and finding the doors shut in that day of worship and in the hour of prayer, one only there did open a little wicket and put back the shutter of one of the great doors, that so the publique worship, of God might not be hindred, & those many hundreds, which were come to hear, some 3. or 4. Miles from their dwellings, might not come to that place, as sometimes the children of the Nobles of *Israel* did unto the pits of water and return ashamed. Nevertheless, we are persuaded that could *Mr. Larkham* have preached in the Church-yard, which was hinderd by a great fall of rain that time, or have gotten a room that would have contained those multitudes that were come there to hear him, the door had not then been opened: But [p. 10] that rain then falling, and an Act of Parliament for the keeping of a fast the Wednesday following to be read that day, it was by the Conestable of the hundred and diverse other Constables then present thought fitter to have the door opened.

As for that charge of upbraiding the Justices, We who were then present do affirme, *that we heard not one word drop from him, which had not the stamp of truth and soberness. Neither was he summon'd before them for his Ryotous carriage (as is very slaunderously asserted,)* but went there onely to intreat them for those men which were accused for setting open the door of the publique meeting house, (of which some of them were not present when it was done.) And what was done by any of the rest of those honest Christians, that are through envy tossed from Justices to sessions, and from sessions to the Assises for setting open a door of the publique meeting-house, it was we are perswaded, from an hearty desire in them that the Ministry of *Mr. Larkham, which had through the free grace of the father of mercies been effectual on their souls for the revealing of his Son in them,* might have the like successe on those many hundred souls that were come to hear the mind of God revealed in the dispensation of his word; And therefore in their names we humbly beseech the Honourable Committee that these poor men may be released from that burden which is laid upon them for this their work and labour of love unto poor souls. *Which had undon them utterly if they had not been holpen by their godly Neighbours,* and that by your order the handling of the business the next Assises, to which time it is put off again may be presented, and that the honour of this committee may be by yourselves vindicated , and the contemners thereof punished, which by shutting up the Church doors occasioned these troubles.

---

[9] The story of Mordecai is in the book of Esther, but the allusion is unclear. 'At stern': behind, at the rear of the ship.

[10] The source of this quotation has not been found.

Unto the last, *Although the behaviour and carriage of our Minister, for the time of his living among us,* (which hath been upward of 4. yeares) *hath been (and yet is) such as hath not administered the least ground of Imagination that there is any of the least possible truth in that scandalous Article.* Yet we thought it our duty for the glory of God, and the credit of the Church (which both hereby are laid at stake among us) to enquire into the said business with the Narrowest scrutinie; And do finde upon examination, that he never went beyond sea but twice in his life, The first time whereof was 13. yeares since when he went with his wife, and whole familie to *New England,* (Necessitated thereunto by the persecutions of the Bishops) whence he returned about 10 yeares since. The other time, when being Chaplaine General to the Army of the Lord *Viscount Lisle* (then Lord Lieutenant General of *Ireland*) he went with him in that expedition, And with him returned again.

Thus have we presumed, (According to our apprehended duty) to annex our Attestations unto the answer of the Pastour, that so (his Integrity being vindicated, and the Caluminators of him, And of the Church of God receiving as unto Justice shall appertain,) his Arreares due out of the sheafe of *Lammerton* by grant of Parliament unto the preaching Minister of *Tavistock,* which he now is, and hath been for diverse [p. 11] years) may be ordered by this committee to be paid unto him, *and we have the happiness to enjoy him still.*

Here followeth a certificate of the penning of the said Watts *on the behalf of the persons endited upon a supposed riot, and subscribed by himself and above* 40, *others, &c.*

These are to certifie with all due submission and respect [to] those in Authority whom it may concern, that *David Condy, Augustine Bond, Thomas Thorne, & John Sheere* members of the Church of God in *Tavistock* are of a quiet, peaceable, and Gospel conversation and we are perswaded in our consciences, that if they did set open the doore of the publique meeting house the 27. *June* last past being the Lords day, (an act which we are Confident is not true of some,) it was done only from a principle of zeal to the glory of God, for that *Mr. Thomas Larkham,* Pastour of the Church there was prepared to preach, *who had been an Instrument in the hand of God to bring most of them and diverse others in this place out of the powers of darkness into the kingdom of his dear Son.*[11]

Lastly, here is a certificate drawn up by N.W. *concerning Mr. L. whom in his Booke he so much vilifieth, &c.*

These are to certifie those whom it may concern that Sir *Hardress Wallers* Regiment came into our Town of *Tavistock* in the beginning of *April* 1648, of which said Regiment *Mr. Thomas Larkham* was then Chaplain, *since which time he hath preached in our Parish Church with acceptation to all godly people, and been of a spotless and unblemished conversation amongst us,* neither have we had any other setled Minister these five years last past. In witness we have hereunto subscribed our names this fifth of *May* 1654.

---

11 Colossians 1:13 (KJV): 'Who hath delivered us from the power of darkness, and hath translated us into the kingdom of his dear Son.'

Here the Reader may take notice that this certificate was composed the same yeer wherein he[12] was cast out.

Observations by comparing those papers with sundry passages in the scandalous Book penned by N.W.

First. He condemneth *Mr. L* for using *Reviling, reyling, scandalous and oppro-brious words and names.*[13] And yet defendeth and pleaded for him against this charge in an answer to the same Article. See his Attest. to the third Article.

2. He chargeth *Mr. L.* with *ingratitude*, and accuseth him with *Bending his bow against God himself, &c.* for complaining of oppositions against godliness, &c.[14]

Yet in a letter written by him to *Mr. L* he acknowledgeth there are in this place oppositions to truth and Godliness affirming that as long as there is a Devil and that Devil hath Instruments, the Church of God must never look to be free. See his letter of the 8. *September* 1651. Besides his own complaints of his many sufferings.[15] [p. 12]

3. He makes it a crime to attribute our persecutions to *One {Civilly} eminent.*[16]

Yet none so forward as the said *N.W.* both to write to and against that Gent: which he hints at, yea to pray against in dayes of solemn fasting and prayer; And his lavish tongue and pen have not ceased to make him (whom Mr. *L.* sayeth only to be {Civilly} Eminent) Eminently, —— to instance but in a certif. of the 23. *September* 1650.

4. He chargeth Mr. L. with the knowledge of the word *Ninnihammer.*[17] He affirmes boldly in an answer to the same accusation drawn up with his own pen that he was Confident Mr. *L.* never used the word in this life, and did never know the meaning thereof. See *N. Ws.* Attest to the 3. Article, And we are perswaded he knew not what the meaning thereof was, till being asked by Mr. *Fowel*[18] what it meant, he thus answeared, being informed by some of his adversaries. They say it is in times worse, &c. And this is well remembered by Mr. *W. P.*[19] who was then present.

5. He accuseth Mr. *L* to be a *common rayler in the Pulpit.*[20] He, *viz. N. W.* puts under his hand, with others, that though constant hearers of the said Mr. *L.* they and he among the rest never heard any other words spoken by him in the Pulpit than that which well becommeth a Minister of the Gospel. See Certiff. *Sept.* 23. 1650. And that he hath preached with Acceptation to all godly people. See Certiff. *May* 5. 1654, not many moneths before his Rejection.

---

[12] Nicholas Watts.

[13] Marginal note: [*Tavistock Naboth*] 'pag. 2.'

[14] Marginal note: [*Tavistock Naboth*] 'pag. 4.' 'Bending his bow against God himself': an allusion rather than a direct citation, with a verse like Psalm 11:2 in mind – 'the wicked bend their bow against the upright'.

[15] Marginal note: '*N.Ws.* Attestation read to the first charge.'

[16] Marginal note: [*Tavistock Naboth*] 'Pag. 5.'

[17] Marginal note: [*Tavistock Naboth*] 'Pag. 6.'

[18] Edmund or William Fowell: both served as JPs in the 1650s (Devon Record Office, Exeter, QS28/7–12).

[19] Possibly Walter Peeke, the only person with these initials listed in Tavistock's 'Composition of Tithes 1651', Devon Record Office, Exeter, W1258/Add/12/2.

[20] Marginal note: [*Tavistock Naboth*] 'Pag. 7. 23. See *N.W.* Attest to the 3. Article.'

6.   He labours to cast an *Odium* on the *Ministry* of *Mr. L* by a flattering commendation (as if he were acting upon a stage) given to the Ministry of Mr. *Geo. Hughes,* of whom we should be loath to speak evil, as much as himself, let his pretences be never so specious.[21]   Yet hath he in conference professed that a more able Gospel-preacher then Mr. *L* was not in the West of *England*, and particularly he hath said in a *depraving way*, that Mr. *Hughes* was not worthy to carry his books, witness *W.W.*[22]

7.   He enters a demur (as he termes it) to our assertion, that *God sent Mr. L. among us as a return to our prayer, and in mercy*, and that he, *viz.* Mr. L. came as a *punishment to be our Minister*, &c.[23] yet writes with his own hand that he came in answer to their petitions, and that the hearts of Gods people here had been often warmed with the sweet discoveries, &c. and many more expressions quite contrary to what now he writes: See the call of the Church of *Sept.* 23. 1650. And in another paper of the same date, he asserteth that his, *viz.* Mr. *L.* his removal, would (as he with others thought) be a very great judgement of God, and loss to this Town and Parish, *viz. Tavistock.*

8.   He affirms Mr. *L. by Sir* Hardresse Waller *to be turned out of his Chaplains place;*[24] and pretends a *dateless* order, in the 22. pag. of his book.

Yet puts it under his own hand, that he saw a fair dismissions signed by the said Sir *Hardresse.* See *N. Ws.* Attest. to the second Article.

9.   He affirms that the *Causa sine quâ non* of his coming as a Minister among us, was his being turned out of the Army for misdemeanours.[25] [p. 13]

Yet he wonders that the reputation of such as once prosecuted Mr. *L.* upon the same charge had not hindred them from inserting this, sith some of those which are his greatest adversaries were at that time labouring with him to come and take charge of this place. See *N. Ws.* Attest. to the second Article.

10.   He affirms *Mr.* L. *to be cast out of the Army for animating distempers, and other high misdemeanours,* &c.[26]

Yet in an answer of his to the same charge saith, that the differences which then were betwixt him and some of the Army were onely personal. And were not the pen of this Accuser prejudiced, it could tell you of a Certificate (which he saw under the hand of an eminent Gentleman, that was an eye and an ear witness at these transactions) to the contrary.

11.   He insinuates a dislike of Mr. *L.* his causing of the doors to be opened on the Lords day.[27]

Yet he approveth and pleaded for *Mr. L* in that very act. See his Attest. to the 6. Article.

12.   He gives an imperfect, yea a false account of the affair touching the pretended Riot. And therein not only vents his own prejudice, but endeavours to fasten the same on others, with a *let wise men judge, wee'l make no comments.*

{*a.*} Let the Reader compare the relation he gives of the pretended Riot, in his

---

[21] Marginal note: [*Tavistock Naboth*] 'Pap. 9.'
[22] Marginal note: 'Mrs *R N. WB.*', not identified. 'W.W.' is probably William Web, a stalwart 'Larkamite'.
[23] Marginal note: [*Tavistock Naboth*] 'pag 9.'
[24] Marginal note: [*Tavistock Naboth*] 'pag 9.'
[25] Marginal note: [*Tavistock Naboth*] 'pag 9.'
[26] Marginal note: [*Tavistock Naboth*] 'pag. 9.'
[27] Marginal note: [*Tavistock Naboth*] 'Pag. 11.'

11. Page, with what he sayes of it in his Attest. To the 6. Article, And wise men will judge him a notorious hypocrite.[28]

13. He affirms, that {*b*} *Mr. L. was convented before some Justice of the Peace, for breaking open of the Church doors.*[29]

Yet affirmeth under his own hand, that this is a very slanderous assertion, and that his being with the Justices was voluntary, and the end thereof to intercede for others that were indeed therein concerned. See his Attest. to the very same charge.

14. He affirmeth, *that* I. Pointer *was cursed by Mr. L. as he went out of the Meeting house, and that in his heat of passion.*[30]

Yet affirms, that this man was then cast out for drunkeness; and this to be far from an act of scandal, it being a matter of another nature then is suggested. See his Attest. in answer of the 3. Article.

15. He justifies the matter of that Article, *viz.* {*c*} *God and the devil did cast lots.*[31]

Yet in answer to the same Article, thus he saith; *That this charge is so ridiculous, that it hath vanity and folly enough in it to convince any man, that such words could not come from such a man as he is.* See his Attest. to the 5. Article.

16. He makes it a ground of his pretended disowning of Mr. *L. as Pastor,* that Mr. *L. speaks against the eight men.*[32]

Yet at the same time was he an enemy to the said office, and hath oft promised himself no rest till he had used his utmost to rout them out which were gotten into it, for that they used an office against Law, and to the damnifying of the welfare of the said place; *I. S. W. L. D.C.* can testifie to this, and many others.[33] [p. 14]

17. He makes it another ground of his pretended disowning the Pastor, for that he was *often changing the Government of the said Church.*[34]

Yet we all know, that in those seeming variations of Government in the Church, the Pastor never did anything without the consent and approbation of the said *N. W.* and of the whole Church. And so far was he from ever manifesting the least distaste (to our remembrance) of what was ever done, that he was commonly the prime agent in all those changes which now he *wickedly* calls *Protean.*[35]

18. Another ground of his pretended disowning of Mr. *L* for his Pastor is, that he said, *Go and God go with thee, &c.*

Yet confesseth the words were spoken but six weeks before the date of his book, himself cast out of the Church about three years before. See 64. page.

---

[28] Marginal note: [*Tavistock Naboth*] 'Pag.11', and '*a*. The testimony of an enemy is strong against himself: To turn the point of his own sword into his own bowels, is an allowed way of clearest victory.'

[29] Marginal note: [*Tavistock Naboth*] 'Pag. 11', and '*b* Contra scientiam peccavit, qui contra Conscien-[ti]am peccavit.' ('He who has sinned against conscience, has sinned against knowledge.')

[30] Marginal note: [*Tavistock Naboth*] 'Pag. 15.' 'I. Pointer': John Pointer.

[31] Marginal note: [*Tavistock Naboth*] 'Pag. 25' and '*c* That which a man condemns in another, may justly be applied to his self-condemnation if he be guilty of the same crime.'

[32] Marginal note: [*Tavistock Naboth*] 'Pag. 63.' Tavistock's 'eight men': see Introduction.

[33] '*I. S. W. L. D. C.*': probably John Sheere and David or Daniel Condy; 'W.L.' unknown.

[34] Marginal note: [*Tavistock Naboth*] 'Pag. 66.'

[35] Marginal note: [*Tavistock Naboth*] 'Pag 64.' 'The Reader may take notice of 20 such wicked shifts in his shewing the ground of his departure.' *Tavistock Naboth* (p. 66) claimed Larkham changed the form of church discipline constantly so that the church took 'Protean' shapes: the character of Tavistock's gathered church is discussed in the Introduction.

19.   He calls that act of some members of the Church in opening the doors of the Meeting-house, *a Riot*.[36]

Yet his conscience and all the Countrey knows, that the Judge on the Bench, when the matter was tryed at an Assizes, did declare it to be a legal Act.[37]

20.   He calls it Mr. *L. his Riot*.[38]

He saith he is a slanderer (*in effect*) that saith it. See the Attest. of the said *N. W.* in answer to that charge.

21.   He affirmes that *New-England Corner on the exchange*[39] *or any Haven Town in the Contrey which holds trade with those parts can ordinarily furnish you with enough to satisfie any one in the man* (he meanes with matter of disgrace.)

Yet in his Attest. to the 5. Article thus he saith, *We have seen and we can shew certificates from* Northam, *his Church in* Lewisham *and New-England & speakes him to have abundant respect and honour answerable to those parts, holiness of life and gravity, which since his living among us, he gave good evidence of.*

Reader, might we but take the same liberty to insult against this false accuser, as he hath often in the satisfaction of his lusts, almost in every page of his Book; no doubt we might be quits with him: But indeed this is rather matter of lamentation; and therefore having wearied ourselves in this unpleasant taske which we have been forced unto, least we should be quit[e] tyred out, before we have gotten through those dirty and stinking lies, slanders and obliquies that yet remain to be taken notice of, we have thought it meet to forbear to take notice of any more contradictions although (would we blot more paper) we believe we might many more. And therefore in the next place we shall give a Catalogue of his lies and untruths.

1.   The first Untruth we take notice of is in the title page, wherein he saith, *Published in the name but without the consent of the Church,* meaning our *Naboth.* To this we thus answer, That the Publication of the said Narrative was the Churches act. And 'twere a Riddle therefore to say it was without their consent.

2.   He saith Mr. *L. put forth the Book in the names of such as solemnly have disowned it*.[40] To this we answer. (1) That we know not of any that [p. 15] now or ever did disown it[.] (2) if any might disown it in his presence (which yet our Charity cannot possibly believe concerning them) they were such as were not at the Church-meeting when the Publication of the said Narrative was agreed on, or by such as were first disowned by the Church, whereof this accuser nameth one in the margent of his third Page.

3.   He saith *Mr. L.* was summoned by the Commissioners to answer to Articles of *grosse scandal* given in against him.[41] 'Tis untrue, The Commissioners did acquit him from scandal. 'Twere indeed to make the Commissioners scandalous in acquitting him if this charge had been true.

4.   He saith *Mr. L.* did own the Book to be his, and afterward disowned it.[42] 'Tis untrue, for he still owned the latter part of his Book which he put out in his own

---

36   Marginal note: [*Tavistock Naboth*] 'Pag. 66.'
37   Marginal note: 'See 11. pag of his Book.'
38   Marginal note: [*Tavistock Naboth*] 'Pag. 66. Pag. 17.'
39   The location at the Exchange in London where New England merchants gathered.
40   Marginal note: [*Tavistock Naboth*] 'Epist[le] to Read[er].'
41   Marginal note: [*Tavistock Naboth*] 'pag. 3.'
42   Marginal note: 'Ibid.'

name. The former part thereof he seemed to disown, because it was not so much his particular as the Churches act.

5.   He saith, we must add, which is sufficient alone for the Confirmation of this truth (*viz*, his lye) that several members of his Church (he meaneth us) have ingenously confessed, &c. Professing themselves to be ashamed of it (*viz.* our Narrative,) And in the margent quotes these letters. *IL. RS. WC. AT. IN. SB. AD. FC. MT. TS. IA. RH. RB.*[43] 'Tis untrue, for we have talked with (we suppose) all that are in Communion with us to whom these letters may be referred, and they deny that ever they spake such words that might but savour of such an accusation, but do affirme the contrary, and now are in this rejoinder with us against this false-Accuser.

6.   He affirms that Mr. *L.* did procure an Agent to come from *Exon* hither on purpose to sequester the Estates of some of his Parishoners.[44] Untrue, for he (whom we cannot but believe) procured no such Agent for that purpose, we have inquired into this matter, and finde it the sixth lye.

7.   He saith one *Joshua Webber*[45] *now with God, &c, on his death-bed rang him such a peal in his ear, &c.* No such a peal (as this accuser would make the world believe) was rung in the Pastours ears, when he was in his death-bed, unless the sound thereof should reach as far as *London* where then the Pastour was, And he was dead and buried long ere the said Mr. *L.* knew thereof. But possibly by death-bed he means the bed whereon he dyed, and whereon he lay many years before.

8.   He saith, that the said *Joshua* laid down his Eldership,[46] Untrue. We all know that he never laid it down.

9.   He affirmes that Mr. *L.* spoke somewhat upon Oath, whereof he accuseth him to be regardlesse.[47] Untrue; for we do know *Mr. L.* was not sworne in that business at all.

10.   He affirmes that seventeen members were suspended at a clap.[48] Untrue; we know the contrary.

11.   He affirmeth the letter written to Mr. *Bartlet* and Mr. *Stucley* (which is inserted in the Narrative) to be written by Mr. L.[49] Untrue; [p. 16] for it was written by a member of the Church, and the said Mr. L. did not contribute a syllable thereto. Had not this Accuser been notoriously uncharitable, he might have been otherwise satisfied from the Postscript. Take notice, Reader, that he be-lyes Mr. L. with this very charge in 3. or 4. places of his pamphlet.

12.   He affirmes Mr. *L.* to be convented before a Justice of the peace in the business of the pretended Riot.[50] Untrue. He was indeed present with some which were convented; but his comming there was voluntary.

---

43   Marginal note: 'page, Ibid.' Some of the people behind the initials can be unmasked from the riposte by Larkham's opponents (although their narrative, rather muddled, adds others too): Richard Sowton,. Will Cole, Agnes Trowte, John Nosworthy, Stephen Bonny, Fra[ncis] Gibb [FC?], Mary Trowte (or Margaret Toller), Thomas Sowton, John Anstice, Richard Hitchins, (*Strange metamorphosis*, p. 13).
44   Marginal note: [*Tavistock Naboth*] 'Pag 6'.
45   Webber's story was important to Larkham's opponents but nothing more is known of him.
46   Marginal note: 'Ibid.' On 'offices' in Tavistock's gathered church, see Introduction.
47   Marginal note: 'Ibid.'
48   Marginal note: [*Tavistock Naboth*] 'pag. 7.'
49   Marginal note: [*Tavistock Naboth*] 'Pag 9. Visam fera sævit in umbram.' (A wild beast rages at its own shadow.)
50   Marginal note: [*Tavistock Naboth*] 'page 11.'

13.   He further saith, that the said Mr. L. was bound over at the General Sessions for breaking open the Church doors. Untrue. He was not bound over at all.

14.   He said that such as were bound over were acquited from a Riot by the Mediation of some friends that thought it only a misdemeanor. Untrue. Although they were acquited from the Riot, yet was it not by the mediation of friends, for it passed a tryal before Judge *Atkins*: And a Jury of 12. men could not make it either a Riot or Misdemeanor.[51]

15.   He saith Mr. L. hath as small reason to complaine as any man, &c. and that since his first Residence among us hath scarce paid twenty shillings to all rates and taxes whatsoever.[52] Untrue. For at one time for 3. moneths rate, he payed ten shillings and six pence (tho he be the first of any Minister (we know of) that ever was rated,) And so proportionably (if not exceeding his proportion) hath paid for diverse years, and to this day doth pay his proportion assessed.

16.   He saith, that the Bell-ringer was sent for to speak with the Church-wardens. Untrue; They had placed in the room of this godly poor man two men (one of which if not the other a bloudy Souldier in the late Kings Army, and that remains disaffected to this day) before the said Bell-ringer saw the messenger. Besides they sent not for the man, but for thy key of the tow[e]r-door to be delivered to the others.

17.   He saith, the Church-wardens put in too others because the wife of the said Bell-ringer said, her husband could not come, &c. Untrue; The other two were put in before, as Mr. F. G.[53] himself said unto the Bell-ringer.

18.   He saith that there were horrible miscarriages laid in to the Commissioners and proved against Mr. L.[54] Untrue; the Commissioners which were in number ten, acquitted the said Mr. L. therefrom, and could not find any thing to come within compasse of scandal.

19.   He affirmes that Mr. L. did say these words. In the name of our Lord Jesus Christ, I do here excommunicate *William Hore* of *Tavistock &c.*[55] Untrue; All we know that he was excommunicated long before. And the words *I do* and *of Tavistock* are forged. And what was said was but a declaration of what was done by the Church before. We know who swoar falsly in this.

20.   He would make the World believe that Mr. *Godbear* was not the Composer of the Article there spoken of, and that the said *Godbear* [p. 17] never saw the said Article till it was brought him by one *W. K.* alias *Pointer.*[56] Untrue; for the said *W.K. alias P* was in *London* at the time of the composing of that Article, and he never saw it till the said Mr. *G.* sent it him with others under his own hand. Some of us have seen the same under his own hand, and Mr *W. K. alias P* can shew it to any one that is desirous.

21.   He saith, that they *viz.* himself, and *W. H. were rejected not for their scandalous and Unsaint-like walking.* And saith withal that *the Conscience of Mr. L.*

---

[51] For the riot in 1652, and the legal proceedings which culminated in an appearance at Exeter Assizes, see the Introduction.

[52] Marginal note: [*Tavistock Naboth*] 'page 12.'

[53] Francis Glanville.

[54] Marginal note: [*Tavistock Naboth*] 'page 13.'

[55] Marginal note: [*Tavistock Naboth*] 'page 16.'

[56] Marginal note: [*Tavistock Naboth*] 'page 24.'

knows it to be an abominable slaunder.[57] Untrue; We all testifie that they were rejected by the Church for that very cause.

22.   He saith that *Mr. L.* at a General Church-meeting laid down his Pastoral office.[58] Untrue; He laid not down his Office, but only suspended the execution of that Office till some gave satisfaction for their miscarriages, which for the present was an occasion of a General disturbance.

23.   He saith that the ground of their leaving the Pastour was the enjoyning of the Church to the subscription of a paper.[59] Untrue; The said *N. Wats* was under admonition before, And there was not so much as a tender made him of the paper, because of the admonition aforesaid.

24.   He saith, that the other, *viz.* W. B.,[60] spoken of before, joined with *Mr.* L. again: whereby he would make the world believe, that he the said W. B. went off with him because he would not subscribe the paper before mentioned. Untrue; He did not go off with him, but subscribed the paper, and joined with us in his just rejection, and was present with us when we noted this lye.

25.   Again he inserts the name of W. B. to an Article, about *Mr.* L. leaving his charge for 8. or 9. moneths together. Untrue; The said W. B. saith he subscribed no such Article, neither knew he how long *Mr.* L. was absent; for he being then no inhabitant here, was unacquainted with that affair.

26.   He saith that not one sentence of the first of the additional article is false:[61] we know the contrary, And shall in their particulars evince it, as followes.

He saith that *Mr.* L. took the charge of another place in the North of *England.*[62] Untrue; He took the charge of no particular place, but was by the Commissioners licensed for the time he was there to preach w[h]ere he pleased himself.

27.   He saith, that neither Mr. L. not any other by his procurement more than one Lords day supplied this place (meaning the Cure of *Tavistock*) until the 18. *July* following. Untrue, He preached in *May,* and would have preached still from that time, had not the malice of some ungodly men hindred it, by shutting up the Church doors, which occasioned a journey to *London:* But at his return which was the 27. *June* he preached again. The lye therefore is apparent, for the Accuser saith that the place was not supplied till the 18. of *July.*

28.   He saith Mr. L. made a voyage into *Ireland* without making any provision for us. Untrue; He left order with the Church to improve [p. 18] their Interest in getting of Ministers here, and particularly ordered his Son in Law to distribute what charges he should be at in the procuring of them. Which he faithfully did till by a mis-information given in by the Enemies of Mr. L. to the Commissioners, *viz.* that the Cure was not provided for. They thereupon desired other Ministers to officiate till Mr. Ls. return.

29.   He saith, We have our eyes in our heads,[63] yet never saw the Church-doors open until the comming of the Ministers by the appointment of the Commissioners,

[57] Marginal note: [*Tavistock Naboth*] 'page 2.'
[58] Marginal note: [*Tavistock Naboth*] 'page 26.'
[59] Marginal note: [*Tavistock Naboth*] 'ibidem.'
[60] William Bole.
[61] Marginal note: [*Tavistock Naboth*] 'page 27.'
[62] Marginal note: [*Tavistock Naboth*] 'Ibidem.'
[63] Marginal note: [*Tavistock Naboth*] 'page 28. Oculos quos culpa clausit, pœna aperiet.' ('The eyes which sin has closed, punishment will open.')

save only once or twice when some Anabaptists got into the Pulpit, &c. Untrue; Ye saw and heard *Mr. Polwheel*[64] preach one Lords day in the after-noon, who yet was not appointed thereunto by the Commissioners at that time.

30.   He saith that Mr. L. hath called Anabaptists *white Divils.* We that are as intimate with him (and ever were) as he, and that are constant waiters on his Ministrie cannot but Judge this to be an untruth.[65]

31.   He saith, That Mr. L. said the Anabaptists bring in damnable Heresies. We Judge this as true as the other. Indeed, he hath said no lesse of *Ranters, Quakers, &c.*

32.   He saith, that the words charged on *Mr. L. were not charged as delivered in prayer.*[66] Untrue, *A.G.* swoar in the presence of above twenty that can attest it, that they were delivered in prayer.

33.   He would make the world believe that he did not say that *he would make Mr. L. odious among Ministers, and calleth for proofe.*[67] Now to rubb up his memory, let him but aske of Mr. *Stonham*[68] and *Francis Gibbes*, and they will tell him, That besides the former allegation, *he said he would vex the very Spurin of him.*[69]

34.   He saith, *We know not a Minister, no not in all* England, *that giveth him the right hand of fellowship, or desires any familiarity or acquaintance with him.*[70] Answ. Saving that it is well put in, *We know not*, we must look on it as an untruth, both in *Devon*, much more in all *England* there are, that both give him the right hand of fellowship (to our knowledge) and that do desire familiarity with him; witness Mr. *Gove*, who in the name of divers Ministers of this Country, did desire him to be of the association.[71] Besides, were there none that *gave him the right hand, &c.* how came he to obtain his approbation lately, in order to the obtaining his arrears due from *Lammerton*?

35.   He saith in the Article, that Mr. *L.* should say, that he himself was as *Michaias*, which Mr. *L.* denies in his answer, whereupon this replier saith, that he hath again and again compared himself to *Michaias* in the Pulpit, thought now he deny it to the press;[72] it is a very untruth, in plain words, a *lye*, that Mr. *L.* ever said the words, either as it is charged in the Article, or impudently recharged in the reply,

---

64   Digory Polewhele, minister at Whitchurch.

65   Marginal note: 'This was only put in to performe his promise of making him odious among all sorts of people.' 'White Devils': an allusion to the saying 'the white devil is worse than the black' (those who claim to be as pure as the driven snow may be particularly dangerous).

66   Marginal note: [*Tavistock Naboth*] 'page 29.' 'A.G.': probably Alexander Gove.

67   Marginal note: [*Tavistock Naboth*] 'page 31.'

68   Moses Stoneham, whose testimony was invoked again in *Strange metamorphosis* (p. 24). Larkham noted in 1653, 'November the 27 being the Lords day upon ocasion of the unworthy carridg of Elizabeth the wife of Moses Stoneham I resolved by the helpe of Christ to avoide such provocations and after groaninge yesterday & last night I … Received some hope of greate good by her abusive carriage. Am*en*' (Diary, fo. 13r).

69   'Spurin': the meaning is unclear. (Possibly 'spurring' – inciting, provoking?)

70   Marginal note: [*Tavistock Naboth*] 'page 31'.

71   Andrew Gove, minister of Peter Tavy and a member of the Devon Association (W. A. Shaw, *A history of the English church during the Civil Wars and under the Commmowealth, 1640–1660*, 2 vols. (London, 1990), II, p. 449); uncle to Alexander Gove (*Tavistock Naboth*, p. 71).

72   The marginal note is obscured: the paper is damaged. 'Michaias' (Micah) delivered a message against those who tried to silence God's prophets: 'Woe to them that devise iniquity … "Prophesy ye not", say they to them that prophesy' (Micah 2:1, 6).

though it be true he hath made use of that Scripture often upon fit occasion, and that (as we judge) to good purpose.

36. His wit will not serve the turn, though he make so many shifts, and leave no stone unturned; for it is an untruth, that Mr. L. doth not disclaim the accusation of his saying, that *he was as Michaias* in the pulpit;[73] [p. 19] for although as this unshaken and loose pen that changeth phrases, affirmeth with boyish squibs, *he doth but for manners sake refuse it in the Press,* yet it is evident and known, that it was denied in his answers given in to the Commissioners, and not a witness was produced to the proof of any part of that third Article.

37. As for another untruth (which should first have been noted, but that lies do so croud in upon one anothers back, that we know not which to answer first) *that Mr. L. and his Article would soon shake hands,* &c.[74] Let Mr. Ls. answer to this Article be read as he gave it in, and not by piece-meal, as this replier takes notice of it, and it will appear that these words do contain in them another untruth, as we said before.

38. He saith these words, in reply to our Narrative. *But makes he no more ado of cursing men in publique, we knew before he doth not in his passion* &c.[75] We answer, this is both a lie and a slander too; for we that have been constant hearers of Mr. L. never heard him curse any man in publique, either in passion, or out of passion. If it were a thing so common with him, as this Accuser insinuates, undoubtedly one or other of us might have heard it as well as either of them.

39. He saith, that the information of Mr. L. *cursing one*, fell short that he that said that might have said three[76] (he meaneth that Mr. L. hath cursed) this is another wicked lye, and horrible slander; we all say we should have known it, being constant Hearers, and this that wretched man testifieth under his own hand, as may be seen in his Attestation to the third answer of the Article, as they were first given in to the Committee for Plundred Ministers.

40. He saith, the first of these was Mr. *J. Pointer* (*viz.* which Mr. L. cursed)[77] this is an untruth; *N. W.* hath given it under his hand to be false, before he turned persecutor, and none averr'd it upon oath but only *J. P.* himself, neither before the Commissioners empowered by the Committee for plundred Ministers, not before the Commissioners for Ejection, &c. for it pleased Mr. L. his adversaries, to prosecute him upon the same Articles twice, though there were four or five years between; in all which time, their malice could not be quenched.

41. He saith, the next man that he cursed, was old *Henry Green;*[78] this also is a most slanderous lye, for the truth is, this person in the midst of a Sermon upon the Lords day, taking up his Crutches, and clapping on his hat, turned his back on Mr. L. went out muttering in the face of the Congregation and said with a loud voice to the said Mr. L. *leave your lying, leave your railing*, for which he was set in the Stocks, and after by *John Elford* Esq, a Justice of the Peace, for this disturbance threatned

---

[73] The marginal note is missing because of paper damage.

[74] Marginal note: [*Tavistock Naboth*] 'Ibidem.'

[75] Marginal note: [*Tavistock Naboth*] 'Page 15.'

[76] Marginal note: 'Ibid.'

[77] Marginal note:' Ibid.'

[78] Marginal note: 'Ibid.' The Quarter Sessions ordered Tavistock's churchwardens to take care of the infirm Green, whose allowance had recently been withheld: Devon Record Office, QS1/9, 11 January 1652/3. Larkham travelled to Exeter for this Sessions week: Diary, fo. 11r.

to be sent unto the Goal; but upon Mr. *Larkhams* intreaty, because he was a poor lame man, was onely enjoyned to make an open confession the next Lords day in the same place, for his miscarriage, as it was by the aforesaid Justice set down in writing, which accordingly was done.

42.   He saith, that two or three dayes after the said *Green* had sent a Letter to the said Mr. L. he was by him turned out of the Church. This is an untruth, for he had many weeks time allowed him to be humbled for his many miscarriages, for which he had been dealt with by the Church; [p. 20] and after at least two moneths time, was for his obstinacy by the whole Church, laid aside as a person hardned and incureable.

43.   He saith, *William Hore was another that was by Mr. L. cursed.*[79] This likewise is another untruth, for Mr. L. onely declared that he had been by the Church, for his Unsaint-like carriage and obstinacy rejected, which was done above two years before; And this declaration was made upon the wicked deriding of the word Excommunication, in these words: *Your Excommunication will reach as far as a man will throw an horse.*

44.   He saith, upon Mr. L. going into the North, that there was but one years augmentation due;[80] upon examination we find this a very lye.

45.   He saith that Mr. L. *is not regarded in his words where he is known.*[81] Untrue; His words have been regarded by you heretofore, and especially by your wife, who (unless she bely'd her self) hath confessed to be converted by them. Your malice cannot blot the impression they have made upon the hearts of many that can say you are herein a slanderer.

46.   He saith, that *he left Mr. L.* Untrue; The Church rejected him ere he left the Pastor.

47.   He saith, That *Mr. L. should say on a Lecture day, That he did as verily believe the Gospel to be from the devil, as the Presbyterian Government from Jesus Christ.*[82] This we cannot but judge to be an abominable slander, sith not one of all our society can remember anything in the least that might look like it.

48.   He saith, that *Mr. L. came to the house of* W. B. *desiring him to go with him and deal with* Mr Condy, &c[83] Untrue, for Mr. L. came not to his house as it is suggested.

49.   *Nor did he desire* W. B. *to go with him,* as hinted.

50.   *Nor did they go away together.* So that the Reader may perceive three lyes as a clap, taken notice first of all by *W. B.* himself.

51.   He saith, That *W. B. affirmeth there was not any discourse of the Judge about Ship-money.*[84] Untrue; He the said W. B. saith, that he always told them otherwise; and soe of us can say, that therein he spake no other than the truth.

52.   He saith, that Mr. L. advised Mr. *Condy* to strike out the piece of Plate, and the Tucking-mill out of his Will, and give it to his Son *Daniel*, &c.[85] Untrue. These words were not spoken, as it can be cleared by such as were present; nor was there

---

[79] Marginal note: [*Tavistock Naboth*] 'Page 16.'
[80] Marginal note: [*Tavistock Naboth*] 'Page 18.'
[81] Marginal note: [*Tavistock Naboth*] 'Page 31.' Nicholas Watts' wife was Mary.
[82] Marginal note: [*Tavistock Naboth*] 'Page 32.'
[83] Marginal note: [*Tavistock Naboth*] 'Page 33.' 'W.B.': perhaps William Bole.
[84] Marginal note: [*Tavistock Naboth*] 'Page 34.'
[85] Marginal note: 'Ibid.' Daniel Condy, Larkham's son-in-law.

such Unchristian advice given, though the malice of this Accuser hath trimmed up a compleat tale.

54.   As for the long tale he hath in three whole pages, about Mr. Ls. bragging that *he had ten in his Church that could pray with any ten in fourty miles round about;* and that he *spake these words upon a Lords day in the Afternoon, drawing towards the close of his Sermon.*[86] We that are constant Hearers of the said Mr. L. do affirm, that we remember not these words so spoken as is alleadged, but rather as is set forth by Mr. *L.* in his answer to the Article: yet nevertheless, should Mr. L. so far forget himself (which we believe is an untruth) yet of all men, *Nicholas Watts* is most unfit to tax him for this, who hath been generally known to brag [p. 21] of his own ability in prayer and preaching most ridiculously, and he was once heard to say by some of us, in a boasting way, That *he would preach with Mr.* Joseph Edgcumbe *under leg; who is a Minister in* Devon.[87]

55.   He saith, That *many hundred hands would be given him from persons of the most considerable quality in the place, to testifie unto the world, that they never so much as heard of any such thing before it fell from Mr.* Ls *scandalous pen; and that such as are sincerely godly, and endued with civility, would acquit him therefrom* (he means from being accounted a lyar.) Untrue; for long before it dropt from the pen of the said Mr. L. it hath been reported by many to us: we might instance in such as not are most intimate with him; *Mr. D.P. J.P. M.T.* &c.[88] but we shall not produce more Capital letters, your own Book, had it a tongue, would be as 99. witnesses, to prove you a man free of your words in that kind.

56.   He insinuates, that some witnesses were sworn to the 9. Article in the second papers, *viz.* He said once in the pulpit, that Antichrist was come over from *Rome,* &c.[89] Untrue; No witnesses swore to any such thing, and therefore that reference (to use a conceit of his own) serves onely to make up a ly——ne.

57.   He saith, *Mr. L.* hath given to the Devil an ample Attestation, In saying the Devil is an Orthodox Divine, and that all Christendom never heard such a thing before; and brands it for a down right lye at least in his apprehension.[90]

We answer, that in our apprehension to *believe,* is more then to be orthodox, and yet saith the Apostle *James, The devils also believe,* 2 Jam. 19.[91] Were *James* alive, possibly this Accuser would tell him as he doth *Mr. L.* that *the devil is much beholding to him for saying he did believe.*

58.   He saith, that *Mr. L.* once used that expressions, *viz.* That *that part of Christs prayer, If it be possible ,&c. had not a rag of grace in them.*[92] Untrue; he never said so of those words; but indeed hath said, that that nauseating of the Cup, did proceed from Christs creaturely wit, and was not the voice of the Spirit, or to that effect; for he hath oft expressed himself in various termes, wherein both the

---

[86]   Marginal note: [*Tavistock Naboth*] 'Pag 37, 38, 39.'

[87]   Joseph Edgcumbe: not identified, but Edgcombes belonged to the Tavistock church.

[88]   '*Mr. D.P. J.P .M.T.*': Digory Polewhele, John Pointer and (perhaps) Mary Trowte or Margaret Toller.

[89]   Marginal note: [*Tavistock Naboth*] 'Page 41.'

[90]   Marginal note: [*Tavistock Naboth*] 'Page 42.'

[91]   James 2:19 (KJV): 'Thou believest that there is one God; thou doest well: the devils also believe, and tremble.'

[92]   Marginal note: [*Tavistock Naboth*] 'Page 45.' The reference is to Christ's prayer in Gethesemane: 'O my Father, if it be possible, let this cup pass from me: nevertheless not as I will, but as thou wilt' (Matthew 26:39).

Commissioners as well as our selves were very well satisfied when the business came to hearing.

59.   He saith, that Mr. L. should say in the Pulpit, that *God hath an ugly face.*[93] Untrue; Had this Accuser challenged Mr. L. for saying, that God would shew a terrible or ugly countenance on wicked men at the last day,[94] he had spoken but the truth.

60.   He saith, that Mr. L. did say in the Pulpit, That *Christians must live above obedience.* Untrue; If he means hereby that Mr. L. hath discharged Christians from obedience, as we are jealous he would have the world to believe.

61.   He saith, *Our Pulpit hath great store of silly scraps.*[95] Answ. It was never so accounted by this Accuser till his devilish prejudice did blind his eyes, and pollute his ears.

62.   He saith (to add to his former untruths) That *this place was left unprovided for when Mr. L. went for* Ireland. Untrue; The place was cared for, as is before declared. [p. 22]

63.   He speaks of Mr. Ls. *dealing with such of his Church members as refused to hear those* Anabaptists *which preached in his house,* &c. Answ We know this to be altogether false.

64.   He saith, Mr. L. *is a vile person, and that he acted against his own conscience, in saying that Mr. Polwheele had no Call to preach when he was in* Ireland.[96] Answ. This is an hellish inference; for Mr. *L.* gave in this answer to this, and the other Articles in *Jan.* 1656. whereas the order was read by the Register of the Commissioners, at the time of this second prosecution, which was not until *October,* 1657. and therefore at this Oratory might well have been spared. And this slanderer and reproacher is more to be pittied then Mr. *L.* for his wicked abuses, though we cannot but pitty *Mr. Ls.* unhappiness to fall under the unbrideled pen of him that cares not what he sayes: besides, Mr. *L.* might falsely have said (without so many opprobrious words deserved at this Accusers hand) that Mr. *P.* did preach in *Tavistock* Pulpit, in the absence of Mr. L. into *Ireland*, on a Lords day in the After-noon, when he had no Call nor warrant thereunto; for besides that, he was not then Ordained, the Commissioners had not authorized him; but some time afterward.

65.   He saith, *Mr. P. was branded with a great reproach*, in that 'twas said, *he did curse Gods people,* &c.[97] Answ. If in the mouth of two or three witnesses every thing shall be established, *Mr. L.* then had ground enough for inserting that of *Mr. P.* for it was told him and many of us also, by more than three that heard it from his own mouth. If *Mr. P.* be desirous to know who they were, we shall on demand give him their names;[98] In the general we now tell him, they were some of them in communion with us.

66.   He saith again, That M[r].*P. had a Call from men to preach at the time.*[99] Answ. We say again, that he preached once when he had no Call from men (if you

---

93   Marginal note: 'Ibid.'
94   4 Ezra (2 Esdras) 13:3 (KJV): 'And I beheld, and, lo, that man waxed strong with the thousands of heaven: and when he turned his countenance to look, all the things trembled that were seen under him.'
95   Marginal note: 'Page 46.'
96   Marginal note: 'Page 47.'
97   Marginal note: 'Page 47.'
98   Marginal note: 'We could wish to find as fair dealing from *Mr P.*' (Polewhele).
99   Marginal note: 'Page 47.' Digory Polewhele, minister at Whitchurch.

mean the Commissioners) in the Pulpit of *Tavistock*, we are sure he had no Call from the Church with whom the care of the said place was left.

67.   He saith, *None will believe Mr. L. in saying* Mr. *D. P.*[100] *had no Call from God at that time of his preaching.* Answ. There are many scores in *Tavistock* that believe his running into the pulpit at that time, *viz.* that Lords day in the Afternoon, was before God sent him, and we know it was before the Commissioners did authorize him, though the contrary should be affirmed an hundred times over.

This false Accuser saith,[101] that Mr. L. *tells a strange story of the meeting of hundreds of choice Christians elsewhere, viz.* when Mr. *P.* preached in the Parish meeting-house, and thereupon accuseth Mr. L. *to have written a gross lye in his letter to* Mr. Stucley *and* Mr. Bartlet, which he saith he *would father upon the Church,* and that Mr. L. *should say he was not acquainted with it,* viz. the aforesaid letter, and he, *viz.* the Accuser of Mr. L. writes further that *one of the members that subscribed that letter told one of them so,* viz. one of them that are pretended to write his book, *That it was an untruth, viz.* that Mr. L. *wrote not the letter, and that upon his knowledge.* And in the close of this Paragraph this libeller writes of a flat contradiction between somewhat in Mr. Ls. answer, and the passage in the aforesaid [p. 23] letter. Now for answer unto all this long and tedious discourse, we say that herein we find no less than six untruths.

68.   First, That *Mr. L.* wrote that letter which is often impudently by him affirmed, but still by us denied.

69.   Secondly, this is another untruth, in that he saith (to use his rude phrase) *There is a gross lye in the letter.*

70.   Thirdly, he saith, that Mr. *L.* would father it upon the Church.

71.   Fourthly, that any one of the members which subscribed it, told him it was Mr. *Ls.* Letter must be with us an untruth; for all deny it (whom we are bound to believe, and shall) till the contrary be proved.

72.   Fifthly, that there is any contradiction betwixt this letter and Mr. *Ls.* answer is also an untruth. For besides, that there are above an hundred good Christians that are members of this Church, we mean comparatively (and if we seem to boast, we desire to be pardoned by the ingenuous Reader, being hereunto compel'd) there were above an hundred more (to speak within compass) of this Town and Parish and other places, at those meetings of the Church, and none of them at a *professed distance* with the Church.

73.   Sixthly, and lastly, it is another untruth, that it should be written in the aforesaid letter to *Mr. S.* and *Mr. B,*[102] *That there were not two in the place, that were at a professed distance from him, that ever had the face of Religion* (we have used his very words) but that *we {know not}* two in the place that are at a professed distance *from us.* All which untruths he might have saved us the labour to have taken notice of, had not his malice caused his pen to run faster then a good pace.

74.   His denial, That *godly men have liberty or leave from* Mr. *L. to preach in* Tavistock *Pulpit,* is another false accusation; for the very instances themselves will confute it. He saith himself, Mr. *L. could not deny him,* and brings in Mrs. *E. D.*[103] for a witness. If so many as have preached in *Tavistock* Pulpit, did preach without

---

100   Polewhele.
101   Marginal note: 'Ibid.'
102   Lewis Stucley of Exeter and William Bartlet of Bideford (*CR, ODNB*).
103   Emma Doidge? (A tenant of Larkham's, mentioned in the diary.)

the leave of *Mr. L.* (whose right it is) when he was at home (as this false Accuser writeth they did) let the godly Reader judge, who hath given the cause of difference they or *Mr. L.* but the truth is, that which *N. W.* saith is *notoriously false* in *Mr. Ls* answer, is notoriously true, *viz. That godly Ministers have liberty, if they please, with thanks to preach at* Tavistock *in the Name of the Lord.* As for his make bate[104] long tale of Ministers, with whose names he thinks to cover his lies and untruths, slanders and calumnies, they are (we hope) too wise and godly to be allured by his flatteries and hypocrisies, to approve of his unworthy carriage towards *Mr. L.* and the Church of God; his invidious Arithmetick and Geometry we pass by.

75.   He saith *Mr. L. might have done well to have taken truth along with him, which (*he saith*) he hath left behind him all along, as is manifest to the Reader:*[105] Two untruths; for 1. We have considered Mr. *Ls.* answers, and so have the 10 Commissioners who have long since acquitted him from scandal.

76.   2. To affirm *this to be manifest to the Reader,* is another impudent [p. 24] untruth, unless you mean your self, and such as you are. But we are weary to rake in this first dunghil any longer, because we resolve to look upon the rest.

77.   He saith, *A Narrative setting forth the grounds and reasons, upon which several late members of the Church in* Tavistock *have disowned, &c.*[106] Answ. We all know and do affirm, that these persons were first disowned by the Church, having been by us dealt with severally, for several miscarriages, and at last upon their contumacious deportment, in joyning with the common enemy, and for being familiar with such as we had formerly cast out of communion (whereupon their voices then concurred with ours) were judged by us worthy of excommunication.

78.   He implies, That Mr. *L.* would not *permit Gospel Ministers to have the scanning of the difference* (as he calls them) in agitation, &c.[107] Untrue, We refer the Reader to the Churches Letter, in answer to that motion made by *N.W. I.E. N.V. W.H. E.C.* which hereafter in due place you shall find.

79.   He saith, That Mr. L. *sent and carried abroad his book of Church Acts and censures, filled up with calumniating Articles, &c. thereby endeavouring to raise an Odium upon them,* &c.[108] Untrue, He never sent it, nor carried it abroad; neither did he ever shew it to any one, otherwise then to such as craved satisfaction in our proceedings, which we cannot deny to any Christian from the rising of the Sun, to the going down thereof.

80.   He saith, that M[r]. L. *hath an evil eye towards to the Ministry.*[109] Untrue, This is both a lye and a slander; He speaks not against the Office, although upon good grounds he hath spoken against some in that Office.

81.   He calls himself and others the *dismissed* and *deserting members* (to wa[i]ve the contradiction).[110] Both are untrue.

---

104   'Makebate': something that creates discord; incites quarrels, makes mischief (*OED*).
105   Marginal note: 'Page 51'.
106   Marginal note: 'Page 59'.
107   Marginal note: 'Ibid. '*N.W. I.E. N.V. W.H. E.C.*': Nicholas Watts, John Edgcombe, Nicholas Veale, William Hore, Edmond Condy.
108   Marginal note: [*Tavistock Naboth*] 'Page 60.'
109   Marginal note: [*Tavistock Naboth*] 'Page 63.'
110   Marginal note: [*Tavistock Naboth*] 'Page 64.'

They were not dismissed, nor did they desert us till they were (according to the Law of Christ) rejected.[111]

82.   He saith that *Mr. L.* said in *an exposition that he did not know for his part what he was himself, a very small matter could make him any thing.* We have great cause to Judge this an untruth.[112] For we who are constant attendents on the Ministry of *Mr. L.* never heard such expression as the rage of this Accuser would make the world believe. Indeed he [Larkham] hath oft manifested his Moderation as to that which by men about circumstantial matters to this day is so violently contended for, which the malice of this wretch doth most wickedly pervert. He calleth the disturbance which lately was in *Tavistock* about the opening of the Church doors *his Riot,* meaning *Mr. Ls.* Answ. Two lyes at a clap, for.

83.   It was not *A Riot.*[113] The Judge spoke it on the bench.

84.   Nor was it *his.* Witnesse his own hand and Arrest, &c.

85.   He insinuates that *Mr. L. must by the Church be paid all the money which he disbursed about* the Pretended Riot.[114] Untrue, Mr. *L.* gave five pounds out of his purse to that business although not bound over, about it. And this this Accuser swoare himself (upon a cross interrogatory) before the Commissioners, and that he himself with the Church consented that the other poor men should be holpen, they being not able to bear the charges. [p. 25]

86.   He saith, that *Mr. L.* was pleased to *call such as were professours* since his comming *Larkamites* &c. Untrue it was a nick-name put upon the whole Church by the prophane party, and one *J.P.* boasted that he was the first that gave them that name.[115]

87.   He saith, That there *was a New Church erected upon a new basis.*[116] Untrue. It was but a Reforming of the former, which was done by the renewing of our Covenant, This their captiousness would easily be at an end, did they but study that excellent book lately set out by *Mr Mall* of *Exon.*[117]

88.   He saith, *Mr. L. gave not satisfaction to* H.G. *for those charges he had against him.*[118] Untrue, Satisfaction in the presence of the said *H. G.* was given to the whole Church by Mr. L. And it was the wickedness of the said *H. G.* he had not received it too.

89.   He saith, Mr. L. uttered these words, *I dismisse you five.*[119] Untrue, He said that he would not be a Pastour to them more till they gave satisfaction for their miscariages. Nor indeed was this spoken to all five but only to four of them. This the Accuser himself once could not deny. And this nine more then present can bear

---

[111] Marginal note: 'Ideo Deus misit in terram bonam separationem, ut malam rumperet conjunctionem. Ad.' ('So God sent onto the earth a good separation, that he might break an evil joining together.' Author 'Ad.' not identified.)

[112] Marginal note: [*Tavistock Naboth*] 'Page 65.'

[113] Marginal note: [*Tavistock Naboth*] 'Page 66.'

[114] Marginal note: 'Ibid.'

[115] Marginal note: 'Page 67.' 'JP' is probably John Pointer.

[116] Marginal note: 'Ibidem.'

[117] [Thomas Mall], *A true account of what was done by a church of Christ in Exon (whereof Mr. Lewis Stucley is Pastor) the eighth day of March, 1657, when two members thereof were excommunicated* (London, 1658). The Exeter church also had a pamphlet debate sparked by excommunications. Mall's tract needs to be read alongside a tract by one of the two women cast out, Susanna Parr: *Susanna's apologie against the elders* (n.p., 1659).

[118] Marginal note: [*Tavistock Naboth*] 'Ib. pag. 68.'

[119] Marginal note: [*Tavistock Naboth*] 'page 68.'

witness to. Horrid therefore was the imprecation of one ——— the *act* was wicked; the person is in his grave, and therefore we can leave him to God.

90.   He saith that *Mr. L.* said *I lay nothing to your charge, you may joyne to what Church you will.*[120] Untrue; for at that very time he charged them with miscariages all round save one. But incredible were the reproaches and abuses they gave him, And were in their behaviour under Admonitions more like Heathens than Christians. If any Saint hereupon will think that either Mr. L. or the members which were present could be so absurd as to Judge them meet for other Churches, we have lost our aim.

91.   He affirmes that the *members which met at* John Sheeres *declared themselves satisfied with their answers, &c. and that there was a sweet composure, &c.*[121] Untrue; All the members were not satisfied in them. True it is, one of them seemed to give satisfaction (*viz. N.W.*) to some of them that were appointed to talke with them, but not to others then present, and the consequent of things argued his pretended satisfaction faigned, and in few dayes after he returned with the dog to his vomit.[122]

92.   He saith that *Mr. L. did very easily vouch safe that the members pretended to be dismissed might be joined with in Religious duties.*[123] Untrue; No such tolleration was there given to any member, but were charged to withdraw from them as from men infected with the plague.

93.   He saith, *Mr. L. told a Church-member that there would be no peace in the Church, unless his wife would give his daughter the place.* All that we shall say to this is, We have no reason to believe it. We have it only on the credit of this Accuser who hath told too many ——— already to be believed in this. We have Mr. Ls. word to the contrary, whom we cannot but believe, for he hath said, he remembers not any thing to that import. [p. 26]

94.   As for that tale about Mr. Ls *son in Law rising up to give him* (the Accuser means himself) *the place, and the great sin of* Mr. L. *in taking notice of it, &c.* Is most wretchedly handled.[124] True indeed, he was offended at the straining of courtesies, and using of Complements at that time when they were communicating in the ordinance, which cannot (as we conceive) be confirmed by any to arise from a principle of pride in the said Mr. L. as this Accuser doth suggest, but only to prevent ridiculous behaviour and impertinent Ceremonies in such a season as that was. The malice of this man never wanteth matter to asperse his Neighbour, who is more excellent than himself.

95.   As to that *motion* (he saith) Mr. L. *made of a day to be set apart to pray for the confusion of such as opposed the Church and him,* Is a most damnable untruth.[125]

96.   He saith, Mr. L. *solicited the Cornet of Capt.* Foxes *Troop, and one more to become members of the Church.* We have examined one of them that he means therein, and he saith it is (to use his own expression) a lye, for Mr. L. did only acquaint them of some members in the society which did exercise their gifts which

---

120   Marginal note: 'Ibidem.'
121   Marginal note: 'Ibid. 'Note, that this was after the pretended dismission from the Church.'
122   Proverbs 26:11 (KJV): 'As a dog returneth to his vomit, so a fool returneth to his folly.'
123   Marginal note: [*Tavistock Naboth*] 'page 70.'
124   Marginal note: [*Tavistock Naboth*] 'page 70.'
125   Marginal note: [*Tavistock Naboth*] 'page 71.'

they (if they pleased) might be partakers of. But not a word of joining with the Church.

97. *He made* (saith he) *a bargain with* Will Hore, *&c. for an horse and when he came to pay for it, said, His price was five shillings lesse.*[126] Untrue; The mony was paid (*viz.* five pounds, five shillings) in hand and the Acquittance which under the said *Hores* hand was given may be yet seen. True, indeed, Mr. *L.* did promise to give five shillings more in case the bargain proved according to his expectation, which the said *Hore* had after his journey which indeed was gotten by a lye of the said *Hores* out of the hand of his Son in Law, telling him that Mr. *L.* sent him for the same, which was no such matter.

98. The tale about the *Tenths*, &c hath 2. Lyes. There was no *ten pound* gathered, but much less.[127]

99. Nor is the *mony unpaid*, as acquittances will determine.

Having now ended a very unpleasing rasque[128] in the enumerating of and swearing to so many horrid lyes and untruths (though no doubt several have escaped our view) which this Accuser (without the fear of God or reverence to man) hath suffered to fall from his pen, that he might satisfie his lust of revenge against Mr. *L.* for being the mouth of the Church in all those Admonitions under which they have passed: We cannot but a little further proceed to give the World account of that hellish[129] language which is found almost in every page of his book. And we shall leave it to the Reader to judge how far such an one degenerates from a Christian, yea from civility, that hath suffered his tongue thus to run at *Random*, but indeed *he must needs go that the Devil drives.* It is sad to think into what cells of wickedness men are hurried when the Lord and his people do withdraw and separate from them. It was not many yeares ago that *N.W.* had as lofty words in commendations of Mr. *L.* as possibly a man could have concerning a Minister. *See his Letters and Certificates*; many souls (his conscience knows) have been converted in this place under his Ministry: yet now, as if no man alive were company [p. 27] bad enough for him, he sends him (if words would do it) as low as Hell; nor age nor office must have the least respect, but equally fall under the lash of his unbridled tongue. We shall not any longer insist here, but give the Reader an account of the mans breed, in these following phrases.

Solomons mad man, besotted with unruly passions, barbarous disrespect to Christian admonitions, machivilian, shameless papers, malice over-shot his wit, wolfe in sheeps clothing, turbulent and revengeful spirit, hells of wickedness, he bends his bow against God himself, boysterous & foaming passions, unbridled

---

[126] Marginal note: [*Tavistock Naboth*] 'page 74', and also the initials 'DC' (Daniel Condy, son-in-law) and 'AD' (Arthur Dew: *Strange metamorphosis*, p. 24), cited as witnesses to the transaction. In February 1653/4 Larkham noted £5-5s 'Paid for a horse to W. Hore' (Diary, fo. 14r). *Tavistock Naboth* (p. 74) added detail: when others asked how good the horse was, Larkham spoke warmly – it covered forty miles a day – but when the former owner Hore asked, Larkham 'said it failed him, and that he was fain keep company with the Wood carriers'.

[127] Marginal note: [*Tavistock Naboth*] 'Page 75.'

[128] 'Rasque': the word is not in the *OED* but could be related to the old Norman French 'rasque' (mud, filth).

[129] Marginal note: 'The Divel is not more black mouth'd, than a slanderer, nor a slanderer lesse malicious than the Divel, *War.*' The source of this quotation has not been identified.

tongue, lavish pen, slanderous pamphleter, he hath shaken hands with civility, a conscience eaten out, regardless of his oaths, rashness and folly, he hath an unwashed mouth, a common rayler in the Pulpit, notorious lyar, a scandal to the Gospel, a disgrace to his calling, wrath of pride, scandalous conversation, black teeth of malicious calumniation, black Oratory, venomous discourse, a bird that loves not his own nest,[130] cursing men in publique, horrible wickedness, supercilious, one of g[h]astly looks, rancorous spirit, plundering coward, malicious forged calumniations against the checks of his own conscience, basely, horrible, monstrous overgrown indomitable passions. Billings-gate names, fool, mad-man, vile person, proud, Bragadoceo,[131] notorious gross, ignorance, abominable practices, *Shimei, Rabshake*,[132] one of no good name at all, hypocritical, lying and slandering, two or three lyes at a clap, ill acquainted with what praying means, devourer of good names, made his dinner on the reputation of an whole Town and Parish, picking their bones, venemous teeth, he hath the whetstone, the Country cryes shame on him, scandalous pen, an abuser of his wife, compared to *Biddle, Cop, Nayler*,[133] proud arrogant disdainful spirit, wanton, roving, luxuriant fancy, came off blewly,[134] invectives bred in his bones, profanely derides, a vile person, guilty of many lies and falshoods, cursing the excellent ones, hypocritical, slanderous, lend him an handkerchief, let him wipe his mouth, malicious unquiet spirit, base, prophane, he useth lascivious words, rotten communication.

So much for some of his language.

Having now made good the title of our Book, we shall now come to speak a little in reply to his answers to two objections which he heath made and answered himself in his 60. Page.

His first objection is, *if he be such as your papers make him, why have you let him alone all this while, and never declared against him, until your own interest was concerned?*

To which he answers (having acknowleged, it may be justly raised upon the view of his Papers.)

It may be [that] as God knew us unworthy, so also he thought us unfit for that honour in the Church of God, which would have attended such plain and faithful dealing with him, when nothing of their own particular concernment had been moving thereunto.[135] [p. 28]

Before we come to handle this answer,[136] we shall first take notice of what is laid down by way of concession (as may be seen by glancing partly on the Objection, and partly on the Answer.)

---

130 An allusion to Larkham's relations with Mrs Larkham, or to the accusation that Larkham had fathered children outside marriage.
131 'Bragadoccio': an empty, idle boaster (*OED*).
132 'Shimei' cursed David, the Lord's anointed (2 Samuel 16:7,13; 19:21). 'Rabshake' is perhaps Rabshakeh, the agent of the king of Assyria (Isaiah 36:1–22).
133 John Biddle (1615/16–62), anti-trinitarian exegete; Abiezer Coppe (1619–72), Baptist preacher and Ranter; James Nayler (1618–60), Quaker preacher and writer. *ODNB*.
134 Perhaps miserable, melancholy; 'blue devils' was a contemporary term for depression. 'Blue in the face' – livid with emotion – captures the sense better (but the *OED*'s earliest citation of that phrase is from Anthony Trollope in 1864).
135 Marginal note: 'First Answ.
136 Marginal note: '*Reply.*'

1.   The first is, That *they left him* (*viz.* Mr. *L.*) *alone a long time.*

2.   That *their own interest and concernment* first moved them *to declare against him.*

But to the first,[137] How unanswerable this was to their relation, while members of the same body with him, and that solemn Covenant which in the presence of God and man (with lifted up eyes, and spreading of hands)[138] was by them entered into, let their own consciences (if not doubly feared) be their impartial judges: doubtless such unfaithful members were not worth the keeping, that for a *long time* can be gazers on the wounds of their Pastor, and not endeavour to lay a plaister to them. And as men unwilling to bestow the crums of their charity on him, could be contented to *let him alone,* as the Priest and Levite did the wounded Travellor, who *looked on him* onely, but *passed by on the other side.* Certainly, were your invidious papers cloathed in a far more candid garbe then as yet they do appear in, their unseasonable issuing into the world, cannot in all rational eyes, but to discover them suspitious; If the Reader desires to be informed when this monstrous birth came first to light, take them to their word in a

Second concession,[139] *viz. when their own interest was concerned.* These men (it seems) could contentedly see the soul of their Pastor bleeding; The divine injunctions of Christ touching adomonitions neglected, and consequently the *interest* of Christ go down the wind, with this *proviso, that their own interest be not concerned.* Might these men have slept in their Rebellion, might their honours have been preserved, though themselves had rotten in their sins. Had we hearkened to their termes, in putting the Pastors pretended wronging them into the balance with their obstinacy (a thing indispensable by us and abominable) no doubt, they would not thus have barked nor bitten so shrewdly as they have done, nor had we made ourselves so liable to their unparalleled calumnies. But though they are so shameless to acknowledge that their own *interest and concernment*, puts them on their Rebellion, yet we can appeal to Christ in this thing, that his interest onely moved us to lay them under censure. But to weigh their answer.

We have them ingeniously acknowledging two things.

1.   That *their plain and faithful dealing* (if any Reader can be so charity-blind as to interpret it so) comes not forth without the shrowd of *interest.* We shall believe them in this, seeing they speak truth but seldom.

2.   That they have over-slipt a fair opportunity for *honour in the Church of God, which had not the Lord thought them unworthy of and unfit for, they might have attained unto.* To which we shall onely say this, That they needed not to enforce us to the credit of these affirmations, for whoever hath the charity to believe them in these ingenous concessions will ever judge such as these are, *both unworthy and unfit for honour in the Church of God*, that have been so faithful in it. 'Twere indeed a wonder to find these men so (seemingly) ingenuous, were it not that [p. 29] we found a serpent under this herb. It can ever stand with malice, to dispense sometimes with abatements of her own *honour*, if by such a loss she may gain upon her

---

137   Marginal note: '*First.*'

138   A small window onto the worship of Tavistock's gathered church: they made their covenant with eyes raised and hands spread in prayer. Solomon 'spread forth his hands towards heaven' as he prayed before the Ark of the Covenant (1 Kings 8:22). Jesus 'lifted up his eyes to heaven' in prayer (John 17:1).

139   Marginal note: '*Secondly.*'

intended object. And these forlorn wretches can be contented together with former damages in estate, to hazard also the little honour they have left themselves; if by their revengeful calumnies they can but fasten *dishonour* upon their once *honoured* Pastor. But how prevalent this argument of Gods judging them unworthy and unfit for honour in the Church of God, will be to plead for their being defective in duties; and what an useless Apology this will appear to be at the last day, when Jesus Christ shall call men to account for their faithless deportment in Church-relation, we leave to the spiritual Reader to determine, and so we came to their second answer.

You may take in this too, the neglect of a duty in a time that was more fit, doth not altogether take us off from our doing it at all.[140]

Your ne[g]lecting of a duty must needs be a sin, especially when ye had an opportunity to do it.[141] Had there been no differences betwixt the Pastor and yourselves, your deferred admonitions must at best, have argued your sinful modesty, but now it discovers your undeniable malice. We cannot but observe how these men are put to their shifts, and *Adam*-like, the sence of their nakedness drives them to use fig-leaves rather then be discovered. But this so late arrival of their inveterate rancour into the world against our reverend Pastor (we conceive) will by understanding and impartial Readers be attributed rather to their satisfying of their lust of revenge, then to their discharge of duty. But as men suspitious of the validity of their former answer, they resolve now to strike the nail on the head, and therefore this they say in a

Third answer,[142] *Most of us have dealt with him many moneths before any of those differences about his disorderly preaching, and can yet (if need be) produce what hath been written to him about it,* &c.

He must needs pass for a blind man, that in this plea of their seeth not an evident antilogy or contradiction.[143] Let the reader but compare this defence with the two former pleas, and he shall find it as evident as the noon day; wherein they do imply, if not affirm, that they never dealt with him until *their own particular interest or concernments* induced them thereunto: yet now would they make the world believe that they dealt with him *many moneths before these differences* did arise. Had this only answer stood by itself, and the other two been quite expung'd, we confesse, their craft had more covertly been conceald which now their contradiction makes evidently to appear; But will the Reader know where about *they dealt with him*? you have them acquainting us. *About his disorderly preaching*, But grant that this were true, And that an Admonition had been given for this one defect: How can this their Admonition for one particular fault Apologize for their many scores of accusations wherewith their book is stuffed? Had their (almost) innumerable calumnies centred in this only charge, this answer had been far more plausible, and the truth of things been more obscured[.] But their charging with scores of crimes which (they say) were committed even while they were yet Church members, And they admonishing [p. 30] him only but for one cannot but argue them then to be very unfaithful, but since it argues their Notorious malice. And so much for the first objection.

How could ye joyne with him all this while?[144]

---

[140] Marginal note: '*Ans[wer]. Second.*'
[141] Marginal note: '*Reply.* [to second answer].'
[142] Marginal note: '*3. Answ.*'
[143] Marginal note: '*Reply* [to third answer].' 'Antilogy': 'a contradiction in terms of ideas' (*OED*).
[144] Marginal note: '*2. Ob.[jection]*'

That God may have the glory,[145] *we here ingeniously confesse it was our great fault. Those fair and flattering speeches of us in publique and to us in private made us unmindful of his unchristian expressions towards others. *Haberis confitentis non reos.*[146]

It is almost high time for *N.W.* and his consorts to think upon Confession of faults that have made such work for repentance in the former part of their book.[147] But least the world should misjudge them they desire to be accounted *ingenious*, altho (the Lord knows) far enough from being ingenuous penitents. The ingenuity of their repentance, (It seems) consisteth altogether in this. That they can willingly be accounted great offenders, provided alwayes Mr. L. escape not the Arrowes of their venomous slaunders.[148] *Those fair and flattering speeches of us in publique, &c.* When nothing else can serve the turne of these offenders to free them from that Guilt they have attracted on them-selves and which they cannot possibly avoide, they will endeavour to cast their dirt in the face of another, if thereby they can extenuate their offences, and get them partners in their shame. And this must passe (among fools) for *ingenious penitence* that God may be glorified. But we shall refer it to the impartial Reader whether by this *ingenious* Confession the Accuser aimed at Gods, or rather his own glory, and come to the

Second evasion.[149] *We might add which God*[150] *knows to be true that there were many in this place who are looking towards* Zion, *and comming on the profession of the Gospel, that perhaps might not take such notice of his digressions as others did, and so possibly have profited by those discourses, which have sadned other[s]: and these too looking (it may be) upon some of us more than they ought, upon our comming off from him, might have been ready to lay aside all.*

Ere we speak to this,[151] we shall observe again a double concession that falls from their pen. (1.) *That many looking towards* Zion *might not take such notice of his digressions as others*[152] *did.* (2.) *That many looking towards* Zion *might profit by such discourses.* Had this Accuser looked the same way, no doubt he had profited too. The reason of one observing this, is, that the Reader, while he passes through the dirty Jakes[153] of this slanderous book, may carry with him these two concessions as a preservative against the unwholesome vapours which the unlimitted malice of

---

[145] Marginal note: '1. A[nswer].'
[146] Marginal note: '*Such a Confession is not a blotting out your sin, but rather an Aggravating thereof.'
[147] Marginal note: 'Reply'
[148] Marginal note: 'The woman gave it to me (said *Adam*) and I did eat.' (Genesis 3:12.)
[149] In the original, a misprint, 'evision'.
[150] Marginal note: '*The Accuser useth the name of God to as good purpose as some of whom *Luther* said. *In nomine Domini incipit omne malum.*' ('All mischief begins in the name of the Lord'.) Luther, writing against religious fanatics, argued that 'in his ministers the devil does not want to be deformed and black but beautiful and white ... he presents and adorns everything ... with the color of truth and with the name of God. This is the source of that familiar German proverb: "All misfortune begins in the name of God."' *Commentary on Galatians* (1535), *Luther's works*, ed. Jaroslav Pelikan and Helmut T. Lehmann, 55 vols. (St Louis and Philadelphia, 1955–76), XXVII, p. 50.
[151] Marginal note: 'Reply.'
[152] Marginal note: 'Who had the Spiders nature.' Probably an allusion to the biblical text which named spiders as one of 'four things which are little upon the earth, but ... are exceeding wise ... The spider taketh hold with her hands, and is in kings' palaces': Proverbs 30:24, 28 (KJV).
[153] 'Jakes': literally a privy, but in Devon the word was used for excrement or any kind of filth (*OED*).

these persecutors have raised against the preaching of this our Reverend Pastour, almost in every page.

We shall say the lesse to this second Evasion, because it is confessed,[154] above, that their joining with Mr. *L.* was their great sin. Yet we cannot but take notice how many stones they tumble, and how many tricks they have to extenuate those offences which their own tongues cannot but for shame acknowledge, and their pens but publish. Sometime they labour to[155] shift off their undeniable wickedness on the *flatteries* of the Pastour, and sometime *on the lookers towards* Zion. Let their sin be as [p. 31] abominable as it will, It is their comfort they have a shift at last. Can any man alive (that reads the Epithets they have given our Pastour, and their savage deportment all along their book, the injury they have done his person, and the scandal they have brought up against his ministry) have so much charity as to believe the good of souls lay so much upon their hearts to restrain their impetuous progresse? Can any judge these men friends to such as are lookers towards *Zion*, which have done their utmost to pluck out their eyes, by robbing them of that Ministry which their own Consciences know hath been instrumental for the conversion of so many souls in this place? Certainly he must be a very dark-sighted man that cannot discerne the horrid Hypocrisie of this defence, and conclude, that though they have reard a bubble from the shel of their inventions, and blown it up into the aire; By the Diabolical subtilty Hypocritical flourishes whereof they thought to have ravished such as should gaze thereon: Yet at last it proves a drop only of watery matter which hath been stuffed out with the wind of their unfathomed malice and vain glory.

Having therefore scanned the validity of their answers to those (as they confess) just objections: We cannot but write TEKEL on them, for *they are weighed, and found too light.*[156]

The Reader (we hope,) by this time cleerly sees how far the malice of this Accuser hath sadly transported himselfe. And how manifestly his sundry contradictions, lyes, slanders, unbred language, and hypocritical shifts have witnessed to his unheard of malice, trechery and unchristian demeanure, we need not (we believe) informe the world. It yet remains that we say somewhat in reference to the letters which were sent by *J. E.* to the Pastour, especially sith they are looked on by the Accuser of such excellent use to wipe off the aspersion of *Apostates* and *Revolters.* But how short they come in fulfilling that end, these following circumstances will declare.

1.   These letters came to the Pastour long after their suspension.

2.   That the things laid to the Pastours charge (to omit the great vanity and froth therein contained for it is nought else to such as know that matter alright) were acted and done long since the Pastours dealing with them in the name of the Church.

3.   That it was never known by any of us that the said *J. E.* did give any the least Admonition to our Pastour, or manifested the least dislike of his preaching or conversation till they were under suspension. And for these very causes it was

---

[154] Marginal note: 'The Devil himself will be a Confessor on the same termes; for he will readily confesse what every one doth know, may he but be believed in those assertions which deserve no credit.'

[155] The original has a misprint, 'so'.

[156] Daniel 5:27 (KJV): 'TEKEL; Thou art weighed in the balances, and art found wanting.'

judged both by the Pastour and the Church not convenient to answer his admoni-
tory Letters (as they would have them be) in any other form than the Pastour did.[157]
Being all of us verily persuaded that all this scribling, tended to nothing else (be
the pretences what they will[)] than to selfe-justification, and by casting of dirt in
the Pastour, were in hope to wipe off their own. As for that letter which was sent
by *J. E.* and *E. C.* &c.[158] to the Pastour, we will give an account of it in an answer
thereto immediately, which indeed the craft of the Accuser hath altogether judged it
disadvantageous to his cause, and therefore hath omitted it in his pamphlet. But in
the interim, let us make our appeal to the judicious and unbyassed Reader whether
these letters of *J. E.*,[159] are of such singular use as the Accuser would have them
be, or whether on the consideration of the aforementioned circumstances (for the
truth of which the credit of the Church must lye at [p. 32] stake) they can import
any thing less then the product of malice and revenge, Or (to make the best of it)
the issue of a galled Conscience. Indeed, if for men to justife themselves in sin, If
to cast dirt in the face of their Admonishers, and if (palpably) to play the Hypocrite by[160] the taking off that aspersion (which they say is cast upon them) Then
hath *J. E.* in his letter and *N. W.* in the presse very nobly acted their parts. But if
this be no other (as indeed it is none other) than the very badge and character of
revenge and rebellion, let then the apostasy lye not at the Pastours but their own
door. Neither let this Accuser so far blind-fold the Reader as to make him Imagine
that they had any other than Christian dealing from the Pastour and the Church.
For whatever be pretended to the contrary we must needs professe, that we never
knew so much Indulgence shewed, nor so much patience and long suffering used
by the Church and Pastour thereof to any offenders as to these: We (at their request)
have given them meetings both in publique and in private, & though before we
were conven'd, they promised nothing lesse than satisfaction for their miscarriages,
yet the Lord knowes most uncivilly did they fly in the face of the pastour and the
whole Church. Sometimes telling us of *their Gentility,*[161] sometimes of their *Deserts
of better usage a the Churches hands than to be dealt with for so small a fault,*[162]
&c. So that indeed our expectations of repentance from them were exchanged into
tears for and into mourning over them. One among the rest, a woman, related to the
Accuser pretended humiliation and no sooner had acknowledged her offence, but
presently with a loud voice[163] calls out to the pastour in words to this effect. *Sir,
Seeing I have given satisfaction for my fault, pray do you the like, for I am sure your
fault is no lesse than mine.* But how answerable this expression is to her pretended
modesty and bashfulnesse, and how little to evidence the truth of that humiliation
she pretended to, let the unbyassed Reader judge. Again, we cannot but acquaint
the Reader, that when it was but thought that the pastour was too severe against

---

[157] Marginal note: 'The Accuser himself did once say to *D.S.* a member in communio[n] with us, That
the letters of *J.E.* sent to the Pastour did discover much folly and wickedness.' ('The Accuser',
Watts; Daniel Sowton, John Edgcombe.)

[158] One of various letters to Larkham, and to the church, from John Edgcombe, Edmond Condy and
others: *Tavistock Naboth*, pp. 51–81.

[159] Marginal note: 'Which compared with what was sent, the Accuser is found by his additions and
alterations as abusive to *J.E.*' (John Edgcombe).

[160] Printed as 'be'.

[161] Marginal note: '*J.E.*' (John Edgcombe).

[162] Marginal note: '*N.W.*' (Nicholas Watts).

[163] Marginal note: 'Her countenance spiteful, and her gesture very irreverent.'

them, He asked of them in these words, *To which of the Saints will ye turne?* and withal desired them to chuse out from among the brethren any 4. 5. or 6. to whom they would refer their causes and could they be satisfied, he should quickly be satisfied also. And indeed, so they did; but alas! they found these offenders as stout as ever, and as hard-hearted as the neather milestone,[164] and with sad hearts did they acquaint both the whole Church and the pastour that they had spent their labour in vaine. One of the brethren[165] among the rest gave in this return to the Church of that affair, *that if to justifie themselves in sin be repentance, then indeed he was satisfied in them, not else.* One among these offenders[166] seemed once to relent, but a few dayes experience of him discovered him and his repentance very faigned, for he was very intimate with such as were formerly cast out of communion, contrary to that of the rule in 2. *Thes. 3. 6.*[167] Goes up and down the Countrey with lyes and slanders, tending to the repreach of the Ministry, of the pastour, &c. At length, having tyred the Churches patience, we resolved on an irksome tasque, *viz.* to lay them under excommunication. Since which time, as men inspired by Satan (in whose clutches they are) they have let their tongues and pens run at random [p. 33.] even against the light of their own Consciences, without either fear of God or reverence to man.

Here followed an answer sent by diverse brethren of the Church in *Tavistock*, to a letter directed to the Pastour of the said Church, from *Nicholas Wats, William Hore, J. E.* (since dead) *Nicholas Veale,* and *Edmond Condy* (persons censured for their obstinacy, &c) which we have thought meet to be published to accompany their letter, which hath formerly been printed without it.

Sirs. We lately found a paper straggling out of its way, in the nature of a letter, with your names subscribed to it, and therefore we judge it yours. Which letter (though misdirected, because it did more properly appertain unto us then to the party superscribed) for your sakes we took it up, from whom you have this following answer.

2.   Its errand was (as it pretended) to inquire for peace, but because it came with a sword in its hand, rather purporting War, we could not believe it, and therefore no wonder if it return ashamed.

But because we cannot spent time (nor is it our work at present) to complement, we come to your letter; and at the first view you tell us of a *little cloud like a mans hand,*[168] which cloud we thought would have distilled sweet (at least humble) dews from your convinced hearts, but ah alas, how did your boysterous spirits blow that black cloud over all our heaven, pouring down such worm-wood drops on Gods heritage here, as could not possibly (we conceive) stand consistent with those sad groans, for the preventing of that (which in yours) you pretend you feared: for had there been such yieldingness of spirit in some, as we found elsewhere, the cloud had been as soon dissolved as gathered, as that God whom you confidently call to witness knows.

---

164 'Nether millstone': 'the lower of the two millstones, which remains stationary, and is exceptionally hard', usually used figuratively (*OED*). Job 41:24 (KJV), of Leviathan: 'His heart is as firm as a stone; yea, as hard as a piece of the nether millstone.'

165 Marginal note: '*E.F.*' (Emmanuel Frost).

166 Marginal note: '*N.W.*' (Watts).

167 2 Thessalonians 3:6 (KJV): 'Now we command you, brethren, in the name of our Lord Jesus Christ, that ye withdraw yourselves from every brother that walketh disorderly, and not after the tradition which he received of us.'

168 1 Kings 18:44.

And whereas as you say you prosecuted your indeavours, till all was ended, and that our Pastor approved and confirmed with a protestation, *that he should not look upon him as a friend that shou'd endeavour to make a rupture again, and yet (you say) the next day, you know whose hand drew up Articles to give to the Church,* thereby *occasioned the subversion of all that had been done.*

Before we answer this, we would ask you one question; and we pray you ingenuously answer yourselves; which is,

Whether or no all you the subscribers were concerned in that business(which you say) was ended? If all were, we would fain know how you[169] all came to be concerned in it, if not, why are you now as one man confederated to justifie and plead one for another, as if the cause of one has been the cause of all, whereas in truth we have wherewith to charge every one of your distinctly, and a part for an Unsaint-like walking in several and distinct miscarriages; therefore we would have you to know, and (oh) that the Lord would make you see it, that this shouldering of your selves together as one body against Christ and his Scepter, will prove pernitious to you (which the Lord forbid) for while you justifie and plead one for another, you incourage and harden one another, and so wrap your selves each in others sins. Wherefore we pray you, as you love your souls, and that peace you pretend to seek, let your agreement be disannulled, and smite on the thigh each one for himself before the Lord,[170] which when we see, we shall have good cause to grant that which you say you pursue. But if you will not (as God forbid you should not) give us leave to rent [p. 34] you assunder, as we must in our answer to your affirmed pretended ends.

For know you not (at least the pen man,[171] as we conceive, of your letter) that that which was confirmed with a protestation (if it were so) was in that personal difference one of your wifes and another; now suppose that all was ended between them two, as it might, for ought we (or the most of us) know, yet tell us plainly, had these made satisfaction to the Church of God (for their miscarriages, which occasioned the way of God to be blasphemed) as it was meet they should, or was the business ended between Christ and them, in whose names, and on whose behalf as his Church we acted. If you say and believe it was, we answer, how comes the Church to know that without outward testimonies of humiliation, under the sence of sin? Which the Church (as on your part and behalf, or those related to you) as yet never had. And the subversion you speak of, made by Articles, is untrue, as some of you know; for one of us in the name of many, upon point of conscience, at a general meeting, desired, for as much as the sin was publique, the Church might have answerable satisfaction, least [lest] like unjust judges we should respect persons in judgement, which God abhors. And therefore it was not the Articles (you speak of) not any members, not the Churches craving satisfaction, made the subversion, but we fear (we are loath to anger you) but to speak plainly, it was highth[172] of spirit made the subversion, as if you had been above the reach of Christ in his Ordinances, which appeared for that you refused to stoop unto. Besides, was there any more required

---

[169] Marginal note: 'It is the pievish industrie of wickedness to find or make a fellow. *Warwick.*'

[170] Ezekiel 21:12 (KJV): 'Cry and howl, son of man: for it shall be upon my people, it shall be upon all the princes of Israel: terrors by reason of the sword shall be upon my people: smite therefore upon thy thigh.'

[171] Marginal note: '*N.W.*' (Watts).

[172] 'Highth' (height) of spirit: haughtiness, pride.

of one party then of the other? contradict us if you can; and if there were not, why might not the other party have stood upon their termes as well as those which did? which if that party, or those that were related, did stand upon termes of refusal of giving the Church satisfaction (as hitherto they do) how dare all of you, one for another, give it under your hands that all was ended? whereas the principal part to make the sweet composure, to wit, a sight and sence of sin, as to the Churches eye, hath hitherto been refused and omitted. And whereas still you urge again and again, that it was ended at Mrs *Sitwels*;[173] we say it was no otherwise ended then above you have written, which was as good as no end: for still the Church could have no satisfaction, which was the main thing we stood upon. And because you put us in mind of it, when many of us met after that end, you speak of in a way to receive satisfaction, that so there might be an end in Gods way (we will not lash you with it) but pray remember how you behaved yourselves in affronting of us. And further, you dare affirm under your hands, that at a general meeting, *our Pastor made a dissolution of the fabrick of this Church, and that every one had his liberty to joyn where he pleased.* We must tell you, instead of writing plainer English, it is untrue, for neither did he, and as (we conceive) neither could he nor any man dissolve the fabrick of that which we believe Christ hath erected; therefore pray be advised next how you dare to write or speak such things, for we know neither was nor could there be any such liberty granted. But this is not all the untruths you write, for your further say, That *our Pastor sent for you at his house, and gave you a clear dismission to the Catholick Church, and that he did nothing to your charge, and that you might joyn where you would.* Alas friend, (and oh that we could (as once we did) call you brethren) how are you fallen, or what words shall we use to answer, that we might not inrage you, nor fire your Gun-powder spirits, as you confess you have, and for the sight of it, we do commend you, but how (we say) shall we speak the truth and not prove you? Well, we will use the best language we can. Have you forgotten your carriage there? Or can you not remember how [p. 35] the Pastor in most of our presence charged you all distinctly (except as we conceive the pen-man of your Letter) with several miscarriages, and have you forgotten what boysterousness of spirit and inhumane carriage appeared amongst you, in as much that our Pastor said, That forasmuch as he could not rule you, *he gave you up to the Catholick Church*; what think you to be cherished in rebellion against Christ and his Ordinances? or rather, was it not to be censured by them all? (for those that are censured by one Church (if regularly) are censured by all which we apprehended to be regularly done by us, or by him for us) and if this be a clear dismission. oh how are we (or rather are you) deceived! besides, were you all so dismissed? or did not the pen-man (as we conceive) of your better object, whether or no he were meant? and was not the answer made by the Pastor, that he had nothing to say to him for that time? and yet he went away with the rest of you, and you all affirm you were dismissed.[174] Oh gross mistakes! which under our hands, as many as were there present, we give it to be manifestly untrue. But again (it seems your minds run much upon liberty) you say that our Pastor publickly told the Church, those *that would not*

---

173   Margaret Sitwell.
174   Against all this, in the margin: 'The Accuser did once acknowledge to *I.S.* that to his knowledge the Pastor dismissed onely 4. yet sith they would swear all 5. were dismissed, to the Devil they should go for him. Yet this *Watts* was present, and pleads admission, but heard no such thing himself. Horrible wickedness!' 'I.S.': John Sheere.

subscribe the renewing of our Covenant should trouble him no more, but take their liberty. Were any of your there pray, to hear this? if not, how can you give that for truth under your hands, which you have by hear-say, especially to those who were present, who know no such liberty given? and if hereupon, as you say, you *had a clear and manifest dismission,* and so you do *judge it, and every man else to whom you have related it.* We say your judgements are darkened in this particular through prejudice and self-conceitedness, and if others judge it so too, no wonder they do as you tell your tales, for it so many untruths you dare affirm with confidence to be true unto us, which we know to be false; what stuff do you tell to others think we which know nothing of the business: and therefore if they judge with you, it is as we conceive, because you have blinded their eyes, and would, we perceive if you could, put out ours also.

As to that *dust* which you say was *raised against you at every meeting* more especially you intimate *the two pots.*[175] Tell that reporter from us who ever he, or she be, that it did not become them (as some do) to catch pieces of sentences, such as may make for their prejudiced purposes, for they might have observed how that was not laid to your charge as a sin, but the Pastour speaking of your being at such a place, and at such a time, and named that by such a token, ask the repenter, and see if he or she can deny it. *As to the biting of your nailes, gestures, &c.* In the place of meeting, and in time of worship, was and yet is such as is grivious to the spirits of such of us which can see and observe (especially) the Bearing[176] of one of you in time of publique worship, since we received your letter, which argueth you but mock both at God and us, and will not take up that which you pretend to seek, though you find it.

What our *booking down of things is,* you are not ignorant, we have sure the pen-man of your letters hand to our book, to book down the miscarriages of others (which you know we do) onely for remembrance, that all the Church might know why such are censured that are censured.[177] And why not your miscarriages as well as others that some of you have acted and consented to give us a reason: But to book what we know, and sheet it out as some of you have done, catching, perverting and reporting in that manner and nature you do, we abhor the practice.

What you meane by your blind quotation out of 2. *Sam.* we know [p. 36] not, could we light upon the Chapter, we would labour to give you an answer to it, but perhaps alleaged to so good a purpose as your following scripture, *Jude* 1.7. but more proper if you had quoted, 2. *Sam.*16. 8. spirits we fear like unto like.[178]

You proceed on to shew your earnest prosecution to *get out of the fire of contention to your meeting the Church* (as you say) we cannot chuse but note it to you *where some* (of you) *were referred to certain members,* we remember one of you was. Well, what then? *To whome* (you say) *such Christian satisfaction was given unto every particular that they had to object, as that they declared themselves to be*

---

[175] Perhaps an event, or a Biblical allusion: it has not been possible to trace the reference.

[176] The initial letter in print, 'n', has been corrected in ink to 'B'.

[177] A reference to the 'church book' of the gathered church, which contained a record of discipline.

[178] Jude 1:7 (KJV): 'Even as Sodom and Gomorrha, and the cities about them in like manner, giving themselves over to fornication, and going after strange flesh, are set forth for an example, suffering the vengeance of eternal fire.' 2 Samuel 16:8 (KJV) conveyed the curse of Shimei against the 'man of Belial': 'The Lord hath returned upon thee all the blood of the house of Saul, in whose stead thou hast reigned; and the Lord hath delivered the kingdom into the hand of Absalom thy son: and, behold, thou art taken in thy mischief, because thou art a bloody man.'

fully satisfied, & went away rejoycing; and one was desired by the rest to give thanks for this friendly composure. What, you will be still in a body, was this composure (if so) made with you all, if not, why do not each answer and speak for himself, do you think this shouldering will stand before Christ? shall not every one stand naked & bare by himself alone? if they shall, why then do you gather yourselves together, and unite against those that act in his name? And hence is it that we find fault with your prayers, not as they are prayers, nor as each of your may pray, but as you set yourselves together, give us leave to say schismatically to rent your self from the Church, thinking to bear all before you, and to terrifie us with your noise, making yourselves herein a receptacle and City of refuge for all those disorderly walkers, be they of what kind or nature soever to fly unto and so as you oppose Christ and his Scepter by your prayers, so far we oppose you in them, and do believe (ah we fear to write it) God hath answered you according to the lusts of your own hearts.

But to answer your plea, were they all satisfied? Here they are, they answer for themselves in this particular by the subscribing of their names in the end hereof, and say thus much, that what was received in way of satisfaction was only by one of you, to wit, the pen-man (as we conceive) of your letter, and with him only, with this exception, that he would withdraw from the rest, which he did not, but brak himself the conditions, which was so far from satisfaction, that he made himself the more uncapable of it: And whereas you say that *one desired to give thanks to God for so friendly a composure,* what was it but a rejoicing that they should find him such as he pretended to be; but being frustrated of their expectations, they now again with us, turn their praying for you to mourning over you; you see how you have made work for us, your letter was long, we cannot touch every word, but that which you most object we have here laboured to answer; and did we know where your strongest fortification was, we doubt not but by help of God we should break it to ground.

Towards the close, you come to pitch upon your main design, which is as you say, *to seek peace, and pursue it;* But friends, can we believe you? what do you think to lash it out of us? do we think you seek peace, when you throw fire-brands, arrows and death to us, how many times do you lash at our Pastour, fetching him over with that secret whip of *grave divines, &c.* then again fetching him about with a secret nip of your *two-pot-tale in the face of the County.* And yet again trebling your lash, with your story of your *appeal to King Philip,*[179] with other privy nips which we could not chuse but take notice of; and this is not all, but some of us, must have a jerke[180] too, which you struck out with your pen, as if you did note it in Capital Letters. Thus you keep lashing of us, & yet would bear us in hand you *seek peace and pursue it,* surely if this be your way of seeking peace, we must needs tell you that the way of peace you have not known. [p. 37]

But what would you have us do? why, that we with you should *send for two,*

---

[179] 'Should we do as that man in the story, that appealed from King Philip to King Philip; and appeal no farther, than from Mr Larkham in a passion to Mr. Larkham in his more serious consideration[?]' (*Tavistock Naboth*, p. 78). Ralph Waldo Emerson deployed this ancient tale in 1844: 'You remember the story of the poor woman who importuned King Philip of Macedon to grant her justice, which Philip refused: the woman exclaimed, "I appeal": the king, astonished, asked to whom she appealed: the woman replied, "From Philip drunk to Philip sober."' *Collected works*, ed. R. E. Spiller and A. R. Ferguson (Cambridge, MA, 1983), III, p. 159.

[180] 'A lash of sarcasm' (*OED*).

three or four Ministers to end the difference (as you call it) we know not what you mean by it, but if you will send for two, three or four, nay a hundred, nay not only Ministers, but Churches to come & view our preceedings, we are ready to be accountable unto them. We are in our place, here we stand come all Ministers, nay all Christians from the rising of the Sun to the sitting of the same to crave satisfaction in the name of the Lord, and we professe ourselves to be ready to give it. And therefore if you will write to *Plymouth*, or elsewhere, write onely write not this, that the difference is between Mr. *Larkham* and you, as in your paper you have written, but that it is between the Church on Christs behalf and you, and then you will write the truth; we know no difference; For, as we are men, between *Mr. Larkham,* and ourselves, and you (though you have given cause) but between Christ and you, and so by consequence, as we act in Christ his stead between not only us and you, but every Christian and beleever else, and you, if they walk by rule as we indeavour to do.

In the close of your letter you say, you *look upon this as the last stone, and therefore shall not leave it unturn'd, if it be the will of God you may find peace under it.* Now we think it not, there is one stone, you have not (we fear) turn'd, yet for your sakes, because we wish you well, we will tell you where it lieth, even within your bosomes, which if God give you grace to turn up, or rather to turn out, a *Thousand* to one but you find peace under it, else what are we to grant peace where we apprehend Christ grants none, were the cause ours, we knew what to say. *If one man sin against another, the Judge shall judge him; but if a man sin against the Lord, who shall intreat for him?*[181] The cause is yours, we would if we could, the cause is not ours but the Lords: get peace from Christ, and you have it from us, for who are we to deny peace one hour to such as Christ hath granted peace unto? Wherefore friends, we pray you, nay, we intreat you for your own sakes suspect your selves; let each think thus with himself, may I not be deceived? the heart is deceitful, who knows it? and why not yours? why will you bear it out thus against Christ & his people? Hath not the Lord said, *the Law shall go forth out of* Zion, *and the word of the Lord from Jerusalem.*[182] Oh, that we could perswade you to return with humble spirits, and seek peace in the way of peace. We envy you not, we pitty you much; we mourn over you, we pray for you, and now again have written to you, and what you find irksome to the flesh, remember your compulsory lines[183] have drawn it from us; we are careful over you, we might have written much more, but we will not anger you, we know your spirits, you cannot bear that balm which we would pour upon you; yet while there is hope, we will not cease to pray for you. So your grieved (once we could say brethren for you, yet still we say lamenting) friends over you, and well-wishers unto you.

---

181 Marginal note: '1 Samuel 2: 25', Eli's warning to his sons about God's impending judgment of their evil.

182 Micah 4:2–3 (KJV): 'And many nations shall come, and say, Come, and let us go up to the mountain of the Lord, and to the house of the God of Jacob; and he will teach us of his ways, and we will walk in his paths: for the law shall go forth of Zion, and the word of the Lord from Jerusalem. And he shall judge among many people, and rebuke strong nations afar off; and they shall beat their swords into plowshares, and their spears into pruninghooks: nation shall not lift up a sword against nation, neither shall they learn war any more.'

183 'Compulsory letters': 'letters issued to compel the production of documents or the appearance of witnesses' (*OED*).

Reader, we know such particular things as these papers treat of, will not be read by many. But we hope yea desire, that such as have read the book set out by Nicholas Watts, *will be pleased to read this discourse, lest they be poisoned to their own hurt. 'Tis also humbly desired by us the publishers hereof that it might not be so much as suggested that this Rejoinder owns any other for its Author than the Church at* Tavistock, *the Pastour (upon serious thoughts) altogether exempted herefrom. And moreover, that there might not be the least occasion administered to any of Imagining a disjuncture of spirit among the brethren in the publication hereof (which heretofore without any ground at all hath very impudently been aserted) We do farther acquaint the Reader that on a day of fasting and prayer (set a part to seek the face of God for* [p. 38] *counsel in this thing) It was unanimously by the Church agreed on, that somewhat in the vindication of our much abused Pastour, and for the unvailing the wickedness and hypocrisie of this Apostatized member (the Accuser) be immediatly composed; which when effected by some certaine members, it was again and again at several general meetings of the Church read over, and then assented to & owned (without the least contradiction) by each particular member. And now have we presented it unto publique view, These considerations among many others strongly inducing us hereto.*

1.   *The first thing that sits on our hearts is, that which should be the chiefest end of all endeavours {viz.} the glory of God. We cannot but judge it then high time to vindicate his glory, when by so many lyes, untruthes, Notorious slanders and hypocritical shifts, there is such an earnest endeavour to rob him thereof, and when the credulousnesse of some innocent Readers is likely to betray them to the same abomination.*

2.   *In the next place we thought it meet to salve our own reputation which this Accuser* implicitly at least *hath exceedingly wounded, for if the Pastour be so notoriously scandalous as his pamp[h]let makes him, what are the people that do joyne with him?*[184]

3.   *It is meet the glory of the Gospel should be kept up, which from his mouth hath so exceedingly shined forth in the conversation of a multitude of souls in this place. Which as the pen of this Accuser in former times hath sufficiently borne witnesse to, so, we hope his malice will never be able to hinder.*

4.   *Another thing is the love we bear to the soul of this Accuser which can be no better manifested than by discovering what* he is, & *unto who he hath been* delivered up, *that all such as fear the Lord may* note him, *and have no fellowship with him, that he may be ashamed. And were it not that we did think the ingenuity of some confederated with him in this pamphlet prevented us, we could caution them,* though they love the treason, how they hugge the traitour.

5.   *Lastly, (If we mistake not) the reputation of such as were of the Committee for plundred Ministers in* London, *besides such as are the Commissioners for ejecting scandalous Ministers in* Devon, *and those that have lately approved him, is very much questioned by this Accuser, which in conscience we cannot but vindicate. For if those many accusations mentioned in articles from time to time exhibited to these honourable courts should be true (which to make so, a multitude of rash Oaths have not been wanting) these Commissioners must of necessity be concluded*

---

[184] Marginal note: 'Meam injuriam patienter tuli, injuriam contra sponsam Christi ferre non potui. Jerom. ad vigil.' ('My own injury I have taken patiently, but injury against the Bride of Christ I was not able to bear.' Jerome, *Adversus vigilantium*.)

faithlesse in their trust. But so far have the out-cryes of this Accuser hitherto proved ineffectual to his ends, that not only the testimony of this Church now, but a double quorum *of Commissioners (before whom the Pastour was convented to answer the cavils of this adversaries) did (not many moneths ago) acquit him from any thing laid to his charge which might come within compasse of scandal. And were there nothing else, we humbly conceive this might be enough to satisfie any Impartial or unbyassed Reader touching the scandalous matters asserted against our Pastour by the malitious Accuser. 'Tis strange to us that this Accuser who lately had been both a prosecutour and a witness also against Mr. L. (and so had a fit opportunity for the accomplishing his purpose of outing him) had not borne his testimony against one of the many scandals he hath put in print against him, especially sith it was his sole business at* Exon *in attending on the Commissioners for ejection, &c. and was sworne to that end. Tho he would have us believe him to be cautious of his oathes, we see him very prodigal of his words; But we verily think the time is not far off that will discover him to be a man hardly to be believed in either. The less we say in the unvailing this backslider and in vindicating our much wronged Pastour, the more (we have cause to believe the Lord as a returns to the dayly prayers of a despised handful in* Tavistock*) will work, either in some ordinary or extraordinary providence. In the meane space* we shall stand on our watch and set us upon the Tower, and will watch to see what he will say unto us, and what we shall answer when we are reproved.

FINIS.

Appendix 1

Gifts and sales of *The wedding-supper* (1652)

Larkham worked from the back of the manuscript to make lists of various kinds. The first list, on the last folio, dates from 1652: 'the Names of such as I gave bookes unto Called The Wedding Supper'. He worked untidily across three columns of unequal size, headed 'how the 300 bound are disposed of'; 'given in the quire'; 'delivered in the assise weeke'. Instead of replicating the original complexity, each column is here listed separately.[1]

The wedding-supper, Larkham's first publication, came from the press of Giles Calvert 'at his shop at the black spread Eagle, neer the West end of Pauls'.[2] It contained fourteen sermons on Matthew 22, prefixed with a portrait of Larkham by the engraver Thomas Cross.[3] In 1656, Francis Eglesfield published a second edition (without the portrait) as *The parable of the wedding-supper explained*.[4]

[*H*]er[*ewith*] the Names of such as I gave bookes unto Called The Wedding Supper.[5] and how the 300 bound are disposed of

To Mr Sheriffe Ireton[6]	1	
[To] Collonell Blount [7]	1	this was none of the 300 but bound of purpose
To Mr John Adrian	1	
^To Mr Eveleigh^	1	
To my Cosen Catnes	1	

1   To add to the complexity, Larkham later crossed through some of his entries. Also, George Larkham wrote fragmentary phrases in spaces his father had left: these are not included. The left edge of the folio is worn and ragged.

2   Ariel Hessayon, 'Calvert, Giles' (*bap.* 1612, *d.* 1663)', *ODNB*.

3   Antony Griffiths, 'Cross, Thomas (*fl.* 1644–1682)', *ODNB*. Larkham's portrait (Plate 1) was dated 4 May 1652.

4   Eglesfield added to this edition a new tract, Larkham's *A discourse of paying tithes*. Later in 1656, Eglesfield also brought out Larkham's *The attributes of God*, in three parts (see Appendix 2), and re-issued *A discourse* separately.

5   This heading stands at the top of the left column.

6   John Ireton, sheriff of London and Middlesex, 1651–2: Gary S. De Krey, 'Ireton, John (1615–1690)', *ODNB*.

7   Thomas Blount, a local politician and landowner in north Kent, and colonel of a Kentish regiment in the 1640s: Anita McConnell and Tim Wales, 'Blount, Thomas (1605/6–1678)', *ODNB*. Larkham moved in Blount's circles as minister at East Greenwich, 1645–7, and acquired George Lane's paper book there. His first entry in the manuscript (June 1647) referred to £2 owed to him for books by 'Mr Obed Wills Schoolmaster at Collonell Blounts' (fo. 'W'r).

To Cosen Covert[1] & His Mother & Sister   3

To Mr Moore of threadnedle streete
    to send to Cumberland to my Sonne   6

I[s]sued for himselfe   1

To Mr Raddon[2]   1

To Mr Budleigh   1

To be disposed of by My Brother &
    Systers at Lyme[3]   20

To Henry Greene[4]   1

To Emmanuell frost   1

To Mary Sheere   1

To William Baker   1

To Dinah Woodman   1

To Mrs Thomasin Dodge   1

[To] My Wife & daughter   2   46 this summe[5]

[To] Li[e]ut Coll Barnes[6]   1

Mr *Elmiston* of honniton   1

[Se]nt to John Middleton [at K]irton   6

[Delivere]d at Exeter to J Mon[gw]ell 12.
    Yong Mungewell 1 [&] others   17   Rec 00-17-00

[Lef]t with Mr Raddon 6 [*where*]of I had
    one *returned* as above to [*illegible*]   5
    and [*was paid*] for two.   Received 00-2-8
    and 3 [*remaineth*] in his hand   Of which one I sent to Mr Leigh
    by Mr *Pern* Minister of
    Littleham[7] & I gave him another
    for himselfe the other I gave to
    Mrs *Fold* of *Broadnives*[8]
    for 6 bound received 5s-3d[9]

[D]elivered to Mr Drewe [of]
    Okehampton   12   received 4s for 3 gave 5
    brought backe 4

---

1 Richard Covert, a London merchant. Larkham's eldest son Thomas married Mary Covert, Richard's sister.

2 Edward Raddon acted for Larkham in his dealings with various London committees such as the Trustees for the Maintenance of Ministers.

3 Michael, Elizabeth and Jane Larkham at Lyme Regis.

4 From Greene to 'wife and daughter', Larkham listed recipients in Tavistock.

5 The number of books accounted for to this point.

6 Larkham referred later to Lieut. Col. Barnes of Honiton (March 1654/5, fo. 17r).

7 Likely to be Alexander Ley, Curate of Frithelstock 1638–41 (by the 1650s at Monkleigh, Devon Record Office B156/L/B/10/4) and 'Samueles Peryn', Rector of Littleham; both near Larkham's old parish of Northam. See the Clergy of the Church of England Database (http://www.theclergydatabase.org.uk) Person IDs 98949, 100415.

8 Illegible: the surname and placename are conjectures.

9 He accounted for the whereabouts of all six copies lodged with Raddon and wrote this last line alongside, in the right margin.

[So]ld at Tavistocke [all] of them
　for 1[s]. 4d　　　　　　　　35　Received 02-06-8[1]

[Delivere]d to Martin Holman [of]
　Biddeford　　　　　　　　4

[At] Exeter in a boxe　　　130　　　　　　　　　　out of　130
　　　　　　　　　　　　　　　　　　　　　　　deduct　　40
　　　　　　　　　　　　　　　　　　　August 31　　　090
　　　　　　　　　　　remaining
　　　　　　　　　　　　　　　　　which were brought to
　　　　　　　　　　　　　　　　　Tavistocke August 20th 1652

　　　　　　　　　　　　　　　6 to Plimouth Bookseller delivered
　　　　　　　　　　　　　　　8 I laid aside eight red forrells[2]
　　　　　　　　　　　　　　　5 delivered to Wil: Martin to sell 12s
　　　　　　　　　　　　　　　1 I gave him one for his owne use
　　　　　　　　　　　　　　　1 Sold one to a Maide for 1s
　　　　　　　　　　　　　　　3 sold by Daniel Condy 03s-3d
　　　　　　　　　　　　　　　2 sent to Peter Glubb & Ed. Condy.
　　　　　　　　　　　　　　　　each one Oxford

[*In*] house I have　　　　　4　Elizabeth Penniwell had one. one
　　　　　　　　　　　　　　　　I gave to send to young Bloy at
　　　　　　　　　　　　　　　　ˆOxfordˆ[.] one I gave to
　　　　　　　　　　　　　　　　Willia[m] Hores son July 26. one
　　　　　　　　　　　　　　　　to Mr John Edgcombe ˇat
　　　　　　　　　　　　　　　　Oxfordˇ.[3]

Left in London bound　　　26

here are with Ed Condy　　4　of which I have received for two.
　　　　　　　　　　　　　　　　2s-8d & one booke received: one
　　　　　　　　　　　　　　　　ˇgiven to himˇ

[&] with Daniell Condy　　11　Received 0-6-8 for 5. July 23 for
　　　　　　　　　　　　　　　　the other 6 Sept 6th. 8s.

[*illegible words*]　　　　300　they cost carriage [*illegible*] 30 in
　　　　　　　　　　　　　　　　quire *now* came *into* Devon
　　　　　　　　　　　　　　　　14s-10d at Exon 12s [?]d
[*illegible*] [4]

---

[1]　£2-6s-8d: thirty-five copies sold at 1s-4d each.
[2]　*OED* 'forel, forrel': 'a case or covering in which a book or manuscript is kept, or … sewn'.
[3]　Larkham sent copies to four Oxford students from Tavistock: Peter Glubb and Edmond Condy (Corpus Christi), Stephen Bloy and John Edgcombe (Exeter). J. Foster, *Alumni Oxonienses 1500–1714* (Oxford, 1891). Hore's son has not been traced.
[4]　After accounting for the 300 copies, Larkham seems to have summed up receipts and costs. Unfortunately, the lower edge of the folio is badly worn: the amount is illegible.

Given in the quire[1]
+ to Mr Leere	1
+ to W Hore	1
+ to John Sheere	1
+to Da:[ughter] Condy	1
+to Ellis Bray	1
+ to Tho:[mas] Thorne	1
+to Mr Stone at Exeter my landlord	1
+to Mr Clapp	1
+ to Mr Slade of Exeter	1
+Augustine Bond	1
+To Mr Brownsdon which I paid for the binding up	1
	11

Those 95 bookes remaininge of the 130 that came last &c
To Mrs Wallplatt*es* one	1
to John Bishop one[2]	1
to Richard Arnold one	1
to William Webb one	1
to Mr Mayor of *Okingha*[m] viz Shilbeer[3] 2 sisters to	
Mr drew & one sent to Mr *Fines*	5
to John Heyward one	1
to Walter Burges one	1
to Mary Charls	1
to William Saxfen	1
to Ane Hele [*illegible*] *to her fath*[er]	1
to one Mr *Phenre*	1
to Mr *Weston* of Drayton	1
to Mary Edgcumbe	1

August 9th 1652 Delivered in the assise weeke[4]

To Mr John Mongwell in the quire[5]	20: paid in Diodate[6]
To Mr Hunt of Exeter in the quire	20 rec*eived* in bookes for 10 of them

---

[1]   Unbound copies, which went to people in Tavistock and Exeter. This is the middle column.
[2]   Larkham knew Bishop from his Northam days: Devon Record Office, Exeter, CC23/301, 320.
[3]   Probably Shebbear, Beaworthy, Devon.
[4]   Right column. After the first entries about deliveries to Exeter booksellers, he made notes (not a formal list).
[5]   On John Mungwell and Thomas Hunt, Exeter booksellers, see Ian Maxted, 'A history of the book in Devon: 38: The structure of the 17th century book trade in Exeter', *Exeter working papers in British book trade history*, http://bookhistory.blogspot.com/2007/01/devon-book-38.html, accessed 8 April 2011.
[6]   John (Giovanni) Diodati, *Pious and learned annotations upon the Holy Bible* (1643). Perhaps Larkham received the third edition (1651). He valued it elsewhere at 11s (fo. 10r).

I gave a note to Mr Ratliffe bookseller
    of Plimouth to send to Exeter for 2   16s received Dec.2.
    dozen in the quire

Sold 13 bookes Jan: 4 for 13s
Sold to Rich Peeke one for 1s

$$
\begin{array}{r}
3\text{-}\ 1\text{-}4 \\
2\text{-}\ 0\text{-}0 \\
1\text{-}\ 3\text{-}6 \\
\text{-}19\text{-}6 \\
\text{-}\ 2\text{-}0 \\
\underline{8\text{-}15\text{-}0} \\
16\text{-}01\text{-}4 \\
\underline{14\text{-}15\text{-}0} \\
1\text{-}\ 6\text{-}4^{1}
\end{array}
$$

Sent by my son George to Cumberland
    whereof 2 were tokens to T. Blathwith
    & Jen: Bews[2]   22

Sent to Ireland   10

---

[1]   The figures are accurate here but it is not clear how they relate to the book sales.

[2]   In February 1652/3 Larkham recorded 2s, 'sent out of Cumberland' as tokens from 'T. Blethwaite and Jennet Bews' (fo. 11r). Blethwaite, a reasonably affluent shoemaker, was one of the seven 'foundation stones' of the church at Cockermouth, and later a deacon. Jennet Bowes had five children baptized by George Larkham, 1652–60, and members of the Bowes family were firm supporters from the start. Cumbria Record Office and Local Studies Library, Whitehaven, MS YDFCCL 3/1: the register of Cockermouth congregational church, 1651–1771. I am indebted to Robert Wordsworth, who will shortly publish an edition of the Cockermouth church book, for his help on this.

Appendix 2

Gifts and sales of *The attributes of God* (London, 1656)

The London bookseller George Thomason marked the title-page of Larkham's *The attributes of God* with the date he received it, 10 February 1655/6.[1] Larkham received his copies from London five days later. This time he worked with the publisher Francis Eglesfield, whose shop stood 'at the Marigold in Paul's Churchyard'. Eglesfield had strong links with West Country authors.[2]

Larkham's list relates only to the First Part of *The attributes of God*. In 1656, he published on 'the eighteen Attributes of God' in three instalments (six Attributes apiece – first, Life, Perfection, Holiness, Benignitie, Mercy and Truth). The Second and Third Parts came out later.[3] Eglesfield's publicity described Larkham's work as 'the substance of Sundry Lectures', presumably preached at the Tavistock lecture on Wednesdays.[4] Larkham's agreement with Eglesfield meant he received fifty-six copies of *The attributes* (First Part) to sell on, which is what he accounted for here. His list has recently been used to show how a provincial minister could finance the publication of sermons and provide copies for local supporters.[5] Almost all the people named lived in Tavistock.[6]

Working from the back of his book, Larkham made entries on the reverse of the folio used to list sales of *Wedding-supper*, in the right column.[7]

Rec[eived] from London, Feb. 15th 165[5][8]
48 bookes bound & 8 unbound of
the attributes of God, printed by F. Ege[lsfield]

	£ s d
I paid for their carriage to ex[e]ter & from exeter heere in all	00-14-00

1   Thomas Larkham, *The attributes of God unfolded and applied* (1656), Thomason Collection, British Library, E.867(1). David Stoker, 'Thomason, George (c.1602–1666)', *ODNB*.
2   Ian Maxted, 'A history of the book in Devon: 38: the structure of the 17th century book trade in Exeter', *Exeter working papers in British book trade history*, http://bookhistory.blogspot. com/2007/01/devon-book-38.html, accessed 8 April 2011.
3   E.867(2) and E.867(3) in the Thomason Collection. Larkham's prefatory epistles mentioned that time had elapsed between the instalments, but it is not clear how long.
4   This information about *Attributes* comes from Eglesfield's advertisement on the last page of Larkham's *A discourse of paying tithes* (1656).
5   Arnold Hunt, *The art of hearing* (Cambridge: Cambridge University Press, 2009), pp. 164–5.
6   This is in contrast to *Wedding-supper*, which he sent far afield and to prominent people (see Appendix 1).
7   Later, he used the left column of this folio to account for expenses incurred for a 'French boy' James Cottonlieu, 1659–61: see the entry about Cottonlieu, November 1659, fo. 35v.
8   1655/6. The edge is worn.

And paid him in London in money & books		10-00-00
	In all	10-14-00

Disposed of as followeth

Inprimis sold to Aug: Bond one of them that are bound	00+04-00
To Bevile Wivell one of the same	00+04-00
To Brother Condy one	00+04-00
To Cozen David Condy one	00+04-00
To John Sheere one	00+04-00
To John Tolman 3 in the quire	00+09-00
To Richard Hitchins one	00+04-00
To Richard Peeke one	00+04-0[0]
To John Trowt one	00+04-00
To one of Mary Tavy[1] a book sold for	00+04-0[0]
To Peter Tricks one	00+04-0[0]
To Mrs Sitwell one	00+04-0[0]
To Daniell Sowton one	00+04-0[0]
To my Da:[ughter] for James Holland one	00+04-0[0]
To William Webb one	00+04-0[0]
Delivered to John Sheere two bookes	00+08-0[0]
ˆIt[em] received of one bookeˆ	00+04-0[0]
To Thomas fleshman one	00+04-[00]
To Edward Bound one	00+04-[00]
~~To Peter Grills one~~	~~00+------~~
Received of John Sheere for one booke	00+04-[00]
to one of Holsworthy[2] sold one for	00+04-0[0]
To Mr Leere one	00+04-[00]
To Joan Serjeant one	00+04-[00]
To Mr Brownsdon one	00+04-[00]
John Sheere sold one more for me	00+04-[00]

Sold to Ellis Bray one in quire for	00+[3-00]
Sent to Plimouth to John Radcliffe 2[3]	00+08[-00]
~~Delivered to~~ [*illegible*]	
Delivered to Augus[tine] Bond to sell 5 ˇ& received for themˇ	£1+00s[-00]
Deli:[vered] to Ellis Bray 2 in quire	00+06[-00]
Given to John Lapthorne one bound	00+04[-00]

---

[1] Mary Tavy: four miles north-east of Tavistock.
[2] Holsworthy, Devon: twenty-five miles from Tavistock, on the road to Bideford.
[3] 'Mr Ratliffe bookseller of Plimouth' (see p. 381).

Appendix 3

Apothecary shop accounts, 1664–1666

Larkham kept an 'Apothecary Shop' in Tavistock from late November 1664 to January 1665/6, initially in partnership with a local doctor, John County. His accounts cover this enterprise from the start to a final debt recovered in July 1666. The material complement entries he wrote in the main body of the manuscript. Working from the back, he began in the first available space, after his record of book sales and expenses for James Cottonlieu, and set out his record in parallel columns. When the Five Mile Act (1665) prevented Larkham from staying in Tavistock, he resolved to 'give over shopkeeping' but put some of his equipment into store.[1]

Received out of the Apothecary-shop weekly from the time of my buying the Moyety or halfendeale of all shelves chests boxes utensills & medicins therein as by a particular Note besids what is weekly bought in out of receipts[2]

1664
weekes ended

		s	d	
[1] is Broken November 26th weeke end[ed][3]		04	09	
2	Decemb. 3	16	06	Hitherto all is paid for wages
3	Decemb. 10th	11	00	unto the Boy &c
4	Decemb. 17th	11	00	untill Xtide paid wholy by me[4]
5	Decemb. 24th	10	00	
	Rec[eived].	53	03	

Now beginneth my quarter ~ ~ ~

---

[1] The afterlife of the venture can be seen in scattered references later on. He referred in March 1668 to 'apothecaries bills yet unpaid' and sold off some apothecary utensils in April 1667 and July 1668 (fos. 47v and 48r). He specified in his will that 'My apothecary ware & utensils shall remain to the use of Patience my undone daughter yet so as it be managed … for her use that her husband may not have the wasting of it as he hath the rest of her estate': A. G. Matthews's Notes of Nonconformist Ministers' Wills, Dr Williams's Library, London, MS 38.59, fos. 607–11 (the original at the Devon Record Office perished in the Blitz).

[2] Unfortunately the folios are not numbered. He wrote untidily on three sides of folio, in rough columns. The earliest entries are closest to the end of the manuscript. A 'moiety'or 'halfendeal': a legal agreement to take a half share (*OED*).

[3] This matches his entry in November 1664 (fo. 44v), of 4s-9d 'Received out of the shop this first broken weeke besides 13d laid out in sugar & paper'.

[4] Larkham's grandson Thomas Miller. 'Xtide': 'Christ-tide' (25 December), the start of a new quarter.

At first my Paiment for the half of the shopp was	43-08- 9
˅charges about the division˅	00-02-00
afterward for oyle of bayes & hony my p[ar]t[1]	00-11-11
Item paid for my part in the Iron presse and in half an oz of muske	
& in 6 pound of middle aloes & in a quart of Cynamon water[2]	
& in the carriage of these things from Salisbury & Exon	02-10-00
Feb. 27. for my part in 18 p[oun]d ½ of Hogsgrease	00-05-04
	46-18-00
paid ^Aprill 3ʳᵈ^ for my part of the greate Morter & Pestell	04-08-00
Item for the carriage from exeter for my p[ar]t	00-01-08
Item for pretious stones for my p[ar]t[3]	00-02-04
	51-10-00[4]
Laid out for my part in sugar for use for the shopp. which was	
bought at Plimouth	01-11-00
	53-01-00
Aprill 25ᵗʰ I tooke the other Moiety or halfendeale into my hands	
paying	54-10-00
and *ten[d]eringe* to Mr Contes [for] sugar.	01-11-00
And also I am to pay my part of Mr Dennys Bills to Mr Contee he	13-00-00
discharging me from the whole £26 & from all accounts	13-00-00
whatsoever of Moneyes due unto the said Mr Henry Denny	
^to be added to my p[ar]t ut supra £53-1s^[5]	
	135-02-00

---

[1] Here and below, 'pt' is likely to be 'part' (his share of the costs) but could also be 'payment'.
[2] Cinnamon water: a popular compound water, in Latin, *aqua cinamonis* (*DTGC*).
[3] In the body of the manuscript he made a similar entry about the mortar and precious stones (12 April 1665, fo. 46r). Stones like lapis lazuli were used in small quantities in medicine.
[4] Below this he scored out an entire line.
[5] In other words, these expenses should be added to the previous total of £53-01s-0d.

to pay rent for shop & garden 40s
 which being valued in £14 Jo. County is to pay halfe which is £7 per annum
& £4 per anum to the Boy viz T. Miller besides his diet ˆ£8 per annumˆ in
Janu[a]r[y]/.

weekes		s d
1	Ended Dec. 31	05-00
2	Jan. 7th	04-06
3	Jan. 14th	04-06
4	Jan. 21st	06-00
5	Jan. 28th	10-00
6	Feb. 4th	7-06
7	Feb. 11th	6-06
In all received this farre[2]		44-00

paid for one weeke to the boy T.M.	1s+06
paid for Barbers boxe[1] to Son Condy for him	~~10-00~~ I am paid
Feb. 27th paid more	01+00
March 25th paid more	06+00
Item to satis[fy] wages for the quarter	01+06
for the boyes diet one ¼ for my p[ar]t	20+00[3] 30-00[4]
rent for shop & garden	5-00

Feb 18th beginneth
the third quarter of mine age

Upon the paying in of 53s to Mr Symdry,[5]
I allowed 10s & 37s & 4s-6d & paid the
boy 1s- 6d more[.] So the whole is
accounted for & I have of his in my hand
in new Money 17s having changed an old
for a new[.] all accounted for Aprill 19th
& he oweth me 3s and the Dr £1 & to him
the Dr oweth 10s.
                   All even to Aprill 25th 1665[6]

R[eceived] this first weeke 08-00d
Febr. 25. R this weeke *out*
    of the second of third
    quarter of 63 ætatis I
    say rec: 10-00
[Ma]rch 3rd I had   04-00
[Mar]ch 4th I had   05-00
[M]arch 11th   10-04
[Mar]ch 18th   01-14-00
[Mar]ch 25   01-00-00
              Received 04-11-04

The end of the first compleate quarter of

---

1   A 'barber's box' might contain equipment for 'trimming' (Larkham frequently paid 6d to a barber) but perhaps, in connexion with the apothecary shop, for dentistry or minor surgery.
2   He deleted a line of text below this.
3   At first he entered 40s but changed this to 20s. (his half share of the quarterly payment of £2 for Thomas Miller's wages).
4   This total for expenses excludes the 10s for the barber's box (which Miller had repaid).
5   'Mr Syndry' of London.
6   Once the debt had been paid he scored out the entry except for the last sentence, which he added sideways running up the margin. 'The Dr': John County.

So my p[ar]t in all was £66-1s allowinge Mrs Denies Bill £13-0
& Mr Conties which I have bought is £3 more which is 69-01s

66-01-0   So the whole shopp is valued ut supra
69-01-0   I gave £3 *It*[1] than my p[ar]t came unto to Mr Contie to yeild up all
135-02-0 & paid all his p[ar]t in Denys Bills & for sugar

I have paid £33-10s to Mr Contie Aprill 25[th] 1665. I have his receipt
I owe to be paid at all Demands unto Mr John Contes this day   21+00-00[2]
I owe for Dennys last Bills there being some deductions
   to be paid June 24[th] next   13-00-00[3]
It[4] to be paid at Xtide next com[m]ing   13-00-00
It to be paid to Stephen Rundle for Mr Contees p[ar]t in sugar   01+11-00
           laid out since I had the whole shoppe   48-11-00

May the 9[th] paid Mr Watts for 4 Dozen of Potts[5]   00-03-00
May 11[th] laid out for measures for the shop and a lattin[6] Candlestick 00-02-06
May 12[th] for 2 Dozen ½ of little potts   00-01-03
for juggs paid to Lego[7]   00-00-10
these things & other small commodities were paid for
   above the summe in the other columne   00-11-07
         & that to the balance of in all   00-19-02

all this was paid out of the shop above what I had weekely

Item Paid for unguent pest[8] 6s-8d to Mr Contie which was out of the
   stores that Henry Denny left with him
& for £10 of course sugar to Mr Hernaman 5s
& for rent & boyes wages & diet untill midsommer next £4
So the shop & charges Hitherto stands me in

                  £140-3s-8d July 27th 1665

---

[1]   Perhaps 'iterato' (again).
[2]   Written below this: 'paid in part May 25th & £7- 10s June 3rd'.
[3]   Written below this: 'paid £2-10s'.
[4]   'It' could be 'item' (enumerating the next entry) or 'iterato' (again, likewise).
[5]   Here and below, it could be 'potts' or 'polts' ('pestle' *OED*): perhaps the former, given the number.
    Larkham often failed to cross double 't's completely.
[6]   'Lattin': 'latten', brass or something resembling brass (tin-plate, iron tinned over; brass-plated). *OED*.
[7]   Probably James Lego, who appears in the town's 1662 Hearth Tax return (Devon Record Office,
    Exeter, QS79/1/32) and other documents.
[8]   Probably 'unguent paste' (ointment).

my enjoying the shopp ~~T. Miller oweth~~
~~Hac:[tenus] 4-6~~ I am paid[1]

[M]arch. 31	01-05-00	
Aprill 7th	00-16-06	
Aprill 14th	01-12-00	
Aprill 22	00-16-00	
Aprill 25th	05-00-00	Received being allowed in paiment of money to Mr Contee which was for the Moyety of the debts due upon the shop booke
[9-]9-6	09-09-06	

In all sold out of the shopp
hacte[n]us   18-19-1[2]   18-18-1   The shop is wholy mine.
paid Thom Miller beforehand 10s for his
quarter due June 24 ˇnext.ˇ[3]

[A]prill 26th	00-11-00	
April 29th	00-14-06	1
[May] the 6th	01-12-09	2
[May] the 9th	00-10-00	
May the 12th	00-08-10	3
May 19th & 20th	01-06-06	4
May 26th & 27th	02-09-00	5
June 3rd	01-02-06	
	01-10-03	6
June 10th in shopp taken	01-15-00	7
June 17th	00-13-00	8
[June] 24th	01-15-05	9
[Ju]ly the first	01-12-07	10
[July] *the 8th*	00-16-11	11
[July 15th]	01-01-05	12
[*July 22nd*]	[*illegible*]	13[4]

July 27th 1665 the whole of the shopp with the boyes wages[5]	£140- 3-8
Since the boyes wages & Diet until Xtide 1665	06- 0-0
a Bill & goods from London	06- 9-4
To drake[6] for carriage ~~& what he paid~~ &c	00-12-6

---

1   'Hactenus': hitherto. He crossed out the note when Miller repaid the debt.
2   Earlier, he corrected an entry from £4-12s-4d to £4-11s-4d: he carried over the mistake here, but the total to the right has been altered.
3   Larkham noted below this, in the same column, his next quarterly payment to Thomas Miller and what Thomas owed him: see opposite.
4   He numbered the weeks of the quarter. The lower edge of folio is worn, so the final week's takings and the total cannot be read. On 12 August Larkham referred back to a previous total of £18-6s-6d.
5   Larkham squeezed this column of figures onto the right-hand folio facing the earlier entries.
6   A carrier who plied the route to and from Exeter.

Item June 19th paid him 5s
Item June 24th 5s in full for
midsommer quarter

T.M. sold a *Carret*[1] for	1s
& which he owed me	6d
paid for him to Cosen Rundle	2s-10d
Item delivered to his mother for him	0- 02
Item paid for making his coate to Bennet Serjeant	3s-0
Item paid my wife for him	3- 0
Paid Son Condy	16-10
Paid Cos[en] Rundle	1- 2- 6
[*illegible*]	2- 9-10

[1] Carat or 'carret': the seed or bean of the carob-tree (OED).

for sugar 25s & potts 4-6. & hogsgrease 5s-6d   <u>01-15-0</u>
Item for rent of shop house & garden one yeare   <u>05-00-0</u>
                                                                 ~~159-19-0~~
summe of the whole shop   <u>160- 0-6</u>

All the Receipts of the shopp went for some weekes   before   18-6-6
to pay the debts of the shop[,] for roses[,]and necessaries last week   <u>19-0</u>
owing to W. Webb & St:[ephen] Rundle & others[1]   <u>19-5-6</u>

And yet the shop is indebted for druggs &c £26 this 12th day of August 1665

                                                        £   s   d
I received in all this weeke   00-19-00[2]

1   Rec[eived] the weeke ended August 19th   00-10-06
2   Rec the weeke ended August 26th   00-16-06
3   Rec the weeke ended September 2nd   00-13-06
4   Rec the weeke ended September the 9th   00-05-06
5 }
6 }   Rec for these 2 weekes at my returne   00-16-00
7 }   Rec at my returne for these weekes   <u>05-17-09</u>
8 }   ^unto^ November the 18th. 1665   08-19-09
9 }
10 }   Received since unto the departure
11 }   of my daughter[3] & givinge over
12 }   shopkeeping Jan 12th   05-19-0
13 }   & allowed which Mr Contie hath
          acknowledged to have had in medicines <u>03-10-0</u>
                                                         09- 9-0

Unto that summe in the other column   56-13-4
is to be added (whereof £40 is from Mr Contie   <u>68-09-6</u>
    owed June 15th & as yet unpaid)
June 15th 1666   Summa Hactenus   <u>125-02-10</u>

July 2nd I had a debt received by my Cosen
    Elizabeth[4] of one Bennett   00-02-0

---

1   From this point the entries are roughly written, on the next folio (working backwards in the notebook)
     after the initial entries. His references here parallel notes in August 1665 on fo. 46v. He seems to
     have liked roses – 'I pluckt in my Garden at Tavistocke the first Rose' (3 June 1653, fo. 12r).
2   These takings (for the week ending 12 August) belong to the previous quarter and are not included
     in the total of £8-19-09 below.
3   Patience Miller, who probably returned to Ireland.
4   Elizabeth Rundle.

Received out of the shop   19- 5-[06]
in all untill August18th 1665   18-19-[01]
                                 38- 4 - 7 [1]

Put this to the end of the 63
yeare of mine age

So I received since the shop
was wholy mine untill
August 18th 1665 £19-5s-6d
& £18-19-1d before time

So I have had in all out of the shop at
the end of the 63 yeare of mine age   38- 4- 7

Item Received the first quarter of
the 64th yeare of mine age   08-19-9
                                              47-04-4
Summa Hactenus. Novemb 17th 1665

Item adde as on the other Columne   09-09-0
                                             56-13-4

I have entrusted diverse to make the best of my shop & for salvs[2] & medicaments
    & to be accountable to me or my son George (whose the shop is)
                        witnesse my hand Jan. 18th 1665[3] Thom Larkham

The shop rent & boyes wages stood me.   £160-00-06d

---

[1]   He jotted rough figures alongside this.
[2]   'Salve': ointment.
[3]   18 January 1665/6.

Index

As many individuals appear fleetingly in Larkham's manuscript and the printed pamphlets, and are otherwise unknown, where possible a brief identification is given here. Contemporary sources from the Devon Record Office have helped to fill out the picture: the Tavistock parish register, 1614–1793 (482A/add 2/PR1); estate papers of the Dukes of Bedford, with tithe and rental lists from the 1640s and 1650s (W1258 – B117/39, B117/40, Add/12/2, LP9/14); the Quarter Sessions Order Book, 1652–61 (QS1/9) and associated bundles; commissions for Justices of the Peace (QS28/4–12); the Tavistock Hearth Tax Return of 1662 (QS79/1/32). The Devon Protestation Returns list adult males in Tavistock, 1641/2 (Parliamentary Archives, London, Protestation Returns Devon E, HL/PO/JO/10/1/87, transcribed and edited in two volumes by A.J. Howard and T.L. Stoate, 1973). A search of wills in the National Archives (http://www.nationalarchives.gov.uk) has suggested the identity of some of Larkham's London contacts. The Clergy of the Church of England Database (http://www.theclergydatabase.org.uk) has helped to pinpoint various clerics. People who are likely to have been members of Larkham's gathered church are identified, but because the church book has not survived the evidence is inevitably fragmentary. All individuals are from Tavistock unless otherwise stated (apart from national figures such as John Milton). Variant spellings of names are in square brackets. Numbers in bold type, at end of entries, refer to illustrations and their captions.

PUBLICATIONS

1. VISITATION ARTICLES AND INJUNCTIONS OF THE EARLY STUART CHURCH. VOLUME I. Ed. Kenneth Fincham (1994)

2. THE SPECULUM OF ARCHBISHOP THOMAS SECKER: THE DIOCESE OF CANTERBURY 1758–1768. Ed. Jeremy Gregory (1995)

3. THE EARLY LETTERS OF BISHOP RICHARD HURD 1739–1762. Ed. Sarah Brewer (1995)

4. BRETHREN IN ADVERSITY: BISHOP GEORGE BELL, THE CHURCH OF ENGLAND AND THE CRISIS OF GERMAN PROTESTANTISM 1933–1939. Ed. Andrew Chandler (1997)

5. VISITATION ARTICLES AND INJUNCTIONS OF THE EARLY STUART CHURCH. VOLUME II. Ed. Kenneth Fincham (1998)

6. THE ANGLICAN CANONS 1529–1947. Ed. Gerald Bray (1998)

7. FROM CRANMER TO DAVIDSON. A CHURCH OF ENGLAND MISCELLANY. Ed. Stephen Taylor (1999)

8. TUDOR CHURCH REFORM. THE HENRICIAN CANONS OF 1534 AND THE *REFORMATIO LEGUM ECCLESIASTICARUM*. Ed. Gerald Bray (2000)

9. ALL SAINTS SISTERS OF THE POOR. AN ANGLICAN SISTERHOOD IN THE NINETEENTH CENTURY. Ed. Susan Mumm (2001)

10. CONFERENCES AND COMBINATION LECTURES IN THE ELIZABETHAN CHURCH: DEDHAM AND BURY ST EDMUNDS, 1582–1590. Ed. Patrick Collinson, John Craig and Brett Usher (2003)

11. THE DIARY OF SAMUEL ROGERS, 1634–1638. Ed. Tom Webster and Kenneth Shipps (2004)

12. EVANGELICALISM IN THE CHURCH OF ENGLAND c.1790–c.1890. Ed. Mark Smith and Stephen Taylor (2004)

13. THE BRITISH DELEGATION AND THE SYNOD OF DORT 1618–1619. Ed. Anthony Milton (2005)

14. THE BEGINNINGS OF WOMEN'S MINISTRY. THE REVIVAL OF THE DEACONESS IN THE NINETEENTH-CENTURY CHURCH OF ENGLAND. Ed. Henrietta Blackmore (2007)

15. THE LETTERS OF THEOPHILUS LINDSEY. VOLUME I. Ed. G. M. Ditchfield (2007)

16. THE BACK PARTS OF WAR: THE YMCA MEMOIRS AND LETTERS OF BARCLAY BARON, 1915–1919. Ed. Michael Snape (2009)

17. THE DIARY OF THOMAS LARKHAM 1647–1669. Ed. Susan Hardman Moore (2011)

18. FROM THE REFORMATION TO THE PERMISSIVE SOCIETY. A MISCELLANY IN CELEBRATION OF THE 400TH ANNIVERSARY OF LAMBETH PALACE LIBRARY. Ed. Melanie Barber and Stephen Taylor with Gabriel Sewell (2010)

Forthcoming Publications

BRITISH STATE PRAYERS, FASTS, THANKSGIVINGS AND DAYS OF PRAYER 1540s–2002. Ed. Alasdair Raffe, Philip Williamson, Natalie Mears and Stephen Taylor

LETTERS OF THE MARIAN MARTYRS. Ed. Tom Freeman

THE PARKER CERTIFICATES. Ed. Ralph Houlbrooke, Helen Parish and Felicity Heal

THE CORRESPONDENCE AND PAPERS OF ARCHBISHOP RICHARD NEILE, Ed. Andrew Foster

THE CORRESPONDENCE OF ARCHBISHOP LAUD. Ed. Kenneth Fincham and Nicholas Cranfield

THE DIARY OF JOHN BARGRAVE, 1644–1645. Ed. Michael Brennan, Jas' Elsner and Judith Maltby

Suggestions for publications should be addressed to Professor Stephen Taylor, General Editor, Church of England Record Society, Department of History, University of Reading, Whiteknights, Reading RG6 6AH, or at s.j.c.taylor@reading.ac.uk.

Membership of the Church of England Record Society is open to all who are interested in the history of the Church of England. Enquiries should be addressed to the Honorary Treasurer, Professor Alec Ryrie, Department of Theology and Religion, Durham University, Abbey House, Palace Green, Durham DH1 3RS.